Recent Developments in
RUMINANT NUTRITION

Recent Developments in
Ruminant Nutrition

Editors

W HARESIGN
D J A COLE

University of Nottingham School of Agriculture

BUTTERWORTHS
London Boston Sydney Wellington Durban Toronto

First published 1981

© The several contributors named in the list of contents, 1981

ISBN 0 408 10804 5

British Library Cataloguing in Publication Data

Recent developments in ruminant nutrition
1. Ruminants — Feeding and feeds
I. *Haresign*, W.   II. *Cole*, D.J.A.
636.2'08'4   SF203

ISBN 0-408-10804-5

Typeset by Gatehouse Wood Limited, Sevenoaks, Kent
Printed by Robert Hartnoll Ltd., Bodmin Cornwall

CONTENTS

INTRODUCTION

There is a continued need for agricultural research to seek to improve efficiency of production, and within the livestock sector much of the research effort is directed towards nutrition, since feed is a major cost of production. In the case of the ruminant such feeds include forages, whether provided as fresh grass over the summer months or conserved forages in winter, as well as compound feeds. Because of the high costs of feeds any increase in the efficiency with which an animal converts these into meat or milk can have a substantial effect on the overall economic efficiency of the production system.

Within the context of ruminant nutrition it is not sufficient to consider nutrient requirements in isolation from other aspects of the production cycle. In the case of the dairy cow, for example, it has been shown that the calving interval has a large effect on economic efficiency. It is therefore necessary to understand the factors that influence the ability of the cow to conceive again in early lactation as well as those factors which determine both the yield and quality of the milk that it produces. Moreover, it has been demonstrated that the nutritional status of a dairy cow in one lactation can have a substantial carry-over effect in the next. In attempting to understand the nutrient requirements for production it is therefore important to consider not only present production but future production as well.

The ruminant poses a particularly interesting challenge to anyone involved in livestock nutrition. The microbial population of its rumen allows the animal to utilize large quantities of forages which are unsuitable for inclusion in rations for non-ruminant species. In addition these microbes can synthesize substantial quantities of protein from non-protein nitrogen. As such the ruminant does not compete directly with man and non-ruminant species of farm livestock for much of its feed requirements. However, these special features of the ruminant necessitate an understanding not only of the requirements of the host animal for growth and/or lactation but also an understanding of the detailed biology and biochemistry within the rumen itself, and the implications that these may have on animal performance. The end-point of meeting the animal's nutrient requirements is the matching of this information with the specifications of available feedstuffs in an attempt to design the most economically efficient feeding systems.

The recent introduction of the metabolizable energy system, replacing the old starch equivalent system, to describe energy requirements of the ruminant owes a lot to many years of research by Sir Kenneth Blaxter and colleagues initially at the Hannah Research Institute and latterly at the Rowett Research Institute. Under the guidance of various ARC working parties, together with the interpretation of Geoffrey Alderman and his colleagues, this research effort has culminated in a new workable system for calculating and meeting energy requirements in practical production systems. Bulletin 33, 'Energy Allowances and Feeding Systems for Ruminants' is now used by teachers, research workers and advisory staff. In spite of the fact that ME values of individual forage samples are as yet difficult to determine quickly and cheaply from chemical analysis, this new ME system still provides a much better understanding of how to estimate and meet the energy requirements of ruminants.

By way of contrast protein requirements are still based on crude protein or digestible crude protein estimates. The microbial population within the rumen is able to degrade some sources of dietary protein, and the ammonia from this degradation together with that from non-protein nitrogen sources is used for the synthesis of microbial protein. In order to maximize the rate of microbial protein synthesis it is necessary to match the available supplies of energy and ammonia within the rumen at any one time with the requirements of the microbial population. Lack of synchrony in the release of energy and ammonia within the rumen will result in a much reduced rate of microbial protein synthesis. This has led to interest in alternative types of non-protein nitrogen in an attempt to match the supplies of ammonia and energy.

The degradability of individual proteins within the rumen varies according to source and processing treatment. Some proteins pass through it relatively unchanged and this can alter both the total amount of protein and the amino acid supplies available to the host animal. Such changes can have a marked effect on animal productivity particularly in high-yielding dairy cows, and contribute to the concept of protein quality. One of the major problems in utilizing such information for estimating the animals' protein requirements at this stage is the paucity of data on degradability and retention times for the whole range of protein sources used in ruminant rations. There is also a difficulty in estimating the rate of microbial protein synthesis under different feeding situations. Nonetheless, the next decade is likely to witness major changes in the way in which protein requirements are estimated for practical feeding situations, and these should result in marked improvements in both the biological and economic efficiencies of the different production systems.

Having established the requirements for both protein and energy at a given level of production it is necessary to determine how to attempt to meet these requirements as economically as possible within the appetite limits of the animal and from the range of available feedstuffs. The nature and quantities of these will vary according to the systems of production adopted, and will therefore determine the feeding strategy to be used. Since the bulk of the ration in many systems of ruminant production is forages a knowledge of their nutritional values and the factors which influence them are clearly required. Even within the concentrate component of the diet the processing of the various ingredients can affect their nutritional value. All of these factors must be borne in mind when designing the overall ration.

In the case of dairy cows the concentrate:forage ratio in the overall diet will have a marked effect on both the quantity and quality of the milk produced. This poses a particular problem to the dairy producer since on the one hand the cow in early lactation has a very high requirement for energy and on the other a low appetite. Too much recourse to the feeding of energy dense feeds may more closely meet the animal's energy requirements and prevent the mobilization of body tissue, but this is achieved only at the expense of milk quality. The overall rationing of dairy cows must therefore seek a compromise between feeding sufficient good quality forage at this time to maintain milk quality while feeding sufficient concentrates to avoid the mobilization of too much body tissue.

In addition, the sudden change from a non-lactational to a lactational state at parturition results in a dramatic increase in the dairy cow's requirements for calcium and phosphorus. Unfortunately intestinal absorption of these two minerals cannot adapt sufficiently quickly to meet these increased demands, with the result that the animal may well suffer from milk fever. Careful attention to the mineral content of the ration immediately prior to and at the time of parturition can, however, go a long way to offsetting the occurrence of this problem.

The use of anabolic agents to improve the efficiency with which growing ruminants convert the feed into edible tissue has recently attracted much attention. This is particularly important in the UK where the majority of fattening units do not lend themselves readily to the use of entire males with their superior growth rates and feed conversion efficiencies. The use of such materials has been and still is a very emotive issue because of the possible hazards to human health. However, the proper use of these materials can have a significant impact on both the biological and economic efficiencies of beef production systems.

It is hoped that the chapters contained in this book will provide useful information on recent developments in these many important facets of ruminant nutrition and feeding. All of them were originally published in the proceedings of the University of Nottingham Nutrition Conferences for Feed Manufacturers over the past four to five years. The decision to publish this particular book is an attempt to draw together under one title all of these very important topics. As such the book is likely to be of value to advisory staff, research workers and students of animal agriculture alike.

1

BODY CONDITION, MILK YIELD AND REPRODUCTION IN CATTLE

W. HARESIGN
University of Nottingham School of Agriculture

Introduction

Since the initiation of lactation in the dairy cow requires that a calf be carried to term, milk production is dependent on the reproductive efficiency of the herd. Recent estimates of the overall economic importance of reproductive efficiency indicate a reduced margin per cow of £2.08/d when the mean calving interval for the herd increases from 365 to 385 days (MMB, 1978). This is composed of a reduced annual milk production per cow, reduced calf sales per cow and increased herd depreciation costs.

The average calving interval of the United Kingdom national dairy herd is 395 days, representing a reduced margin per cow of £62.40 compared with that achieved with a calving interval of 365 days. Since there are 3.2m dairy cows in the United Kingdom this means a loss to the industry of nearly £200m.

Esslemont (1978) suggests a more conservative reduced margin per cow of £1.20 for every day the calving to conception interval exceeds 45–50 days, although beyond an open period of 120 days this estimate shows a marked increase. However, one must remember that maximum calculated economic efficiency may not always be compatible with management systems: a calving to conception interval of 50 days is equivalent to a calving interval of only approximately 336 days compared to the more readily acceptable target figure for many herds of 365 days.

Much of the discrepancy between these two estimates of the costs of an extended open period is explained by the estimates of the required culling rates which may or may not be applicable, and are dependent on whether the farmer is trying to maintain a tight calving pattern for the herd. Nonetheless, no matter which value is used these estimates illustrate the impact that poor fertility can have on the economics of milk production. The purpose of this chapter, therefore, is to discuss the various forms of infertility that may exist in dairy cattle and their relationship to such factors as energy status, body condition, and milk yield. It must be recognised at the outset that this is a rapidly expanding field of research, and as such many of the problems have yet to be solved. Nonetheless, it is hoped that a study of the basic principles involved in these relationships, supplemented by the limited data available, may provide some guidelines for improving reproductive performance in dairy cows.

1

One commonly held belief among dairy farmers and advisory staff is that the 'infertile' or 'problem' cow is often the high yielding cow. Taken at its face value this statement would imply that, as genetic selection for increased yield in dairy cows continues to push up herd averages, the problem of infertility or subfertility is likely to increase. A critical appraisal of the problems of fertility in dairy cows is therefore justified at this stage of development in modern dairy farming.

A further point to remember is that, when using records to assess the reproductive status of an individual herd, the calculation of the herd mean calving interval usually only includes records for those cows which remain in the herd. Often the 'problem' or 'infertile' cows will have been culled, either because they failed to conceive or alternatively because their open period was too long to maintain the desired calving pattern for the herd.

Recent estimates for the culling rate in MMB recorded herds give a figure of 22% with up to a half of this being for infertility reasons. When examining individual herd records it is therefore important to determine both the replacement rate and the reasons for culling to ensure than an apparently acceptable mean calving interval for the herd is not masking a herd infertility problem.

The lactation cycle

Any consideration of the influence of nutrition, body condition, and milk yield on reproductive activity in the lactating dairy cow must take into account the relationships between food or energy intake, energy exchanges within the body, and milk production. The evolutionary purpose of lactation is to provide nourishment for the calf during its early life, and this is fundamental to the survival of the species. In many range conditions, especially where the level of nutrition is marginal, cows do not usually conceive while still lactating. Their calving interval is therefore much nearer to 2 years than one. In modern dairy farming systems lactation has been exploited by both genetic selection and improved nutrition, and the objective of good management is to maximise yield while striving to obtain a calving interval for the herd of as close to 365 days as possible. Such an aim requires that the cow conceives in early lactation while still producing large quantities of milk, and is probably also in negative or marginal energy balance. For this reason the present discussion will concentrate on the early lactation period.

Figure 1.1 shows the general relationships between dry matter (DM) intake capacity (appetite), bodyweight changes, and milk yield throughout the lactation cycle. After parturition the daily milk yield increases rapidly to a maximum between days 35 and 50 of lactation; thereafter there is a steady decline at the rate of about 2.5% per week until the cow is dried off in preparation for the next lactation. In contrast, the voluntary food intake of the cow rises much more slowly after parturition and the maximum may not be reached until many weeks after maximum milk yield. The level of DM intake, the rate of increase in intake, and the time of peak intake is determined by the composition of the ration as well as by a variety of other physical and physiological factors (Bines, Napper and Johnson, 1977; Broster, Sutton and Bines, 1979). During early lactation the intake of energy from conventional rations is generally lower than the animal's total capacity to utilise energy for maintenance

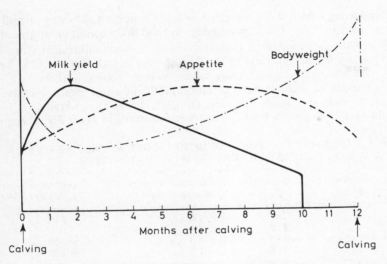

Figure 1.1 Changes in milk yield, bodyweight and appetite of dairy cows throughout the lactation cycle

and milk production. Consequently, it is necessary to feed large quantities of high energy feeds, but even so recourse to the withdrawal of body reserves is inevitable if milk production is to attain its genetically determined limits. As a result the cow is often seen to lose an appreciable amount of bodyweight over this critical period (Broster, Sutton and Bines, 1979). As lactation proceeds the voluntary food intake of the cow continues to increase and the partition of nutrients between milk and body tissues moves towards the latter. The net result of this is that milk yield declines and bodyweight, due to repletion of body stores, increases. It has been postulated that such changes in the partition of nutrients are under the control of the endocrine system with the result that lactation and reproduction are co-ordinated with tissue energy balance (Swan, 1976).

EFFECTS OF BODY CONDITION AND LEVEL OF FEEDING ON MILK YIELD

When summarising the literature on the effects of supplementary feeding in late lactation and the dry period on milk yield in the subsequent lactation, Broster (1969) suggested that the responses obtained depended on the level of feeding at that time. There was no response when supplements were added to generous rations, small responses when they were added to moderate rations, and large responses when added to poor rations. Since the energy requirements for maintenance and pregnancy in the dry period are relatively low (van Es, 1968; MAFF, DAFFS and DANI, 1975), these responses may well reflect the build up of body stores which can be mobilised to meet the energy deficit in the subsequent early lactation period.

Supporting evidence for the effect of body condition at calving on milk yield is presented in *Table 1.1*. Cows calving in good body condition produced more milk in early lactation than those calving in poor condition (Croxton, 1976). The greatest increase in yield in the first 84 days of lactation was +182 kg more milk and was obtained with cows calving in body condition score 3.5. Since a given increase in yield in early lactation results in a still greater increase when measured over the whole lactation (Broster, 1969) the overall gain in yield would have been greater than the responses measured in *Table 1.1*. The apparent

Table 1.1 THE EFFECT OF BODY CONDITION SCORE AT CALVING ON MILK YIELD IN EARLY LACTATION (DAYS 0–84) (CROXTON, 1976)

Body condition score at calving	Number of cows	Difference in daily milk yield (kg/d)	Difference in total yield days 0–84 (kg)
0.5 to 1.5	283	− 1.8	− 150
2.0	159	0	0
2.5 to 3.5	213	+ 1.1	+ 95
4.0	8	− 1.8	− 150

depression in yield of cows calving in condition score 4.0 is questionable. First, there were only eight cows in this group compared to more than 150 in the other groups, and secondly, these individuals may well have been genetically low yielders with a tendency to partition nutrients towards body tissue rather than milk production in this early critical stage of lactation. One noteworthy feature of concern from this survey is the large number of cows which were in poor condition at calving: 442 out of a total of 663 cows (67%) were in body condition 2.0 or less at calving. The implications of this on reproductive activity in the early *post-partum* period will be considered in a later section.

The response to the level of feeding in late pregnancy, when measured as milk yield in the subsequent lactation, is not independent of the feeding rate in early lactation. Cows calving in poor body condition will have a higher feed energy requirement in early lactation than cows of similar genetic potential which calved down in good body condition if their genetic potential for milk yield is to be realised. However, there is evidence that cows which are in poor condition at calving not only have smaller amounts of stored energy to meet the energy deficit of early lactation but also have a changed partition of nutrients to the extent that less of those stores which are potentially available are actually mobilised (Broster, 1969). The consequence of this is that higher levels of feeding in early lactation cannot compensate fully for low levels of feeding in late pregnancy, with the result that milk yield will suffer.

It is important to remember that the dry period in the dairy cow represents the time when the tissues of the mammary gland are regenerated to provide for the next lactation. Both lactogenesis and galactopoiesis are controlled by the endocrine system, as also is energy balance within the body. Therefore, it is quite conceivable that during the dry period and at the time of parturition the cow will monitor its energy balance and regulate accordingly the endocrine determinants of lactation and/or their effects at the target tissue (i.e. mammary gland). In this way the cow would or would not, according to its level of body reserves during this critical period, allow its full genetic potential for milk yield to be expressed independently of level of nutrition during the ensuring lactation.

During mid and late lactation the energy status of the cow moves from negative to positive. This is achieved not only by an increased DM intake capacity, but also by a gradual change in the partition of nutrients away from milk production and towards body tissue deposition. This change in partition of nutrients is exemplified by the data of Broster, Broster and Smith (1969) in *Figure 1.2.* The response to an increase in energy intake, when measured in terms of extra milk production, becomes progressively less as lactation advances. The overall effect of these changes is that the cow gains weight and therefore body condition during mid and late lactation.

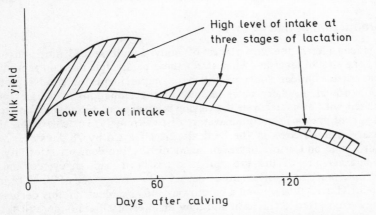

Figure 1.2 The response to extra food at three stages of lactation (Broster, Broster and Smith, 1969)

Modern feeding practices attempt to maximise milk output with least cost inputs of feed. As lactation advances the proportion of expensive high energy concentrates in the diet is reduced at the expense of an increased roughage component in accordance with the changing appetite limits of the cow. *Technical Bulletin 33* (MAFF, DAFFS and DANI, 1975) provides guidelines on how this can be achieved. During mid lactation through to calving it is possible to meet the animal's energy requirements with a diet based predominantly on good quality roughages; the difficulty arises in early lactation when the cow is in negative energy balance.

Broster, Sutton and Bines (1979) have considered in detail the forage: concentrate ratio requirements of the high yielding cow. Suffice it to say that similar increases in milk yield can be obtained by both an increase in the proportion of concentrates in the diet and a greater total amount of food. However, a diet based on 90:10 concentrates:roughages favoured body reserves at the expense of milk fat. Even when fed this diet *ad libitum,* the cows still lost weight in early lactation, albeit to a lesser extent and for a shorter period of time than their counterparts on diets containing a higher proportion of roughages. Clearly, therefore, some degree of weight loss is inevitable in early lactation, even with high levels of concentrates fed *ad libitum.* From the standpoint of milk production the objectives of feeding the cow throughout lactation must be to increase the cow's energy intake in early lactation, but the farmer should remember that there is no advantage in overfeeding. Ensuring an adequate proportion of roughages in the diet, together with frequent feeding, are likely to prove more beneficial than feeding vast amounts of concentrates in early lactation. During mid and late lactation concentrate supplementation should be sufficient to allow the cow to recoup lost body stores in preparation for the next lactation. Leaving this to the dry period is not only too late to allow sufficient gain to be made, but is also energetically less efficient. In the lactating cow the efficiency of utilisation of ME for bodyweight gain (kg) has a value of 0.62 while during the dry period it varies with the energy density (M/D) of the ration (van Es, 1976; MAFF, DAFFS and DANI, 1975). As M/D varies from 7 (poor quality roughage) to 14 (cereals) kg varies from 0.30 to 0.61.

Reproduction in dairy cows

Having considered the importance of body condition and nutrition on milk yield, one should ascertain what affect these parameters have on reproduction. Let us first consider some of the basic requirements of good reproductive performance in the dairy cow. In spite of the reductions in margins per cow associated with an increase in the calving interval from 336 to 365 days, current management systems aim for an average of 1 calf/cow/y. To achieve this aim it is necessary that all cows in the herd are in calf again by 78 days *post partum.*

Much time and effort has been spent on the problems of infertility in the cow, but in spite of this little progress has been made in overcoming them. Embryonic mortality, for example, occurs with a frequency of 20—50% in most mammals (David, Bishop and Cembrowicz, 1971). Much of this occurs in the first few days after fertilisation and may manifest itself as no more than returns to service. If on the other hand it occurs later than this the problem may be more serious because it may cause a delay in the return to service interval. Much of this unexplained embryo mortality may represent natural variation in the ability of gametes to form an embryo of suitable genetic makeup and thus be unavoidable. Such variation in the competency of one or other of the gametes will automatically impose a maximum limit on conception rates to a single mating.

The national average conception rate to a single insemination in cattle is 63% (David, Bishop and Cembrowicz, 1971), but even so it should still theoretically be possible to achieve a mean calving interval for the herd of 365 days. A 63% conception rate to a single mating requires a mean of only 1.67 services/cow to obtain a 99% conception rate for the herd, equivalent to mean increase of 14 days (0.67 × 21 days) in the length of the mean service period over that which is required for a single insemination. If the mean time of first service for the herd was 60 days *post partum* the mean calving interval for the whole herd would then be 361 days. The fact that the majority of herds fail to achieve this target illustrates the need for an appraisal of the factors which may lead to an increased calving interval.

OESTRUS DETECTION RATE AND CONCEPTION RATE

Both conception rate and oestrus detection rate are of paramount importance in maintaining herd fertility irrespective of any other factors which may influence reproductive activity. The fact that they are not independent of each other is demonstrated by the data in *Table 1.2*. An increase in both parameters will

Table 1.2 THE EFFECT OF OESTRUS DETECTION AND CONCEPTION RATES ON THE CALVING TO CONCEPTION INTERVAL WHEN FIRST SERVICE OCCURS AT 70 DAYS POST PARTUM

Oestrus detection	*Average conception rate (%)*				
rate (%)	40	45	50	55	60
	Mean calving to conception interval (days)				
40	143	134	122	112	105
50	133	121	112	104	97
60	122	112	104	98	93
70	115	106	100	94	89
80	109	102	96	91	87
100	101	95	91	87	84

shorten the calving to conception interval, but to achieve a short open period it is essential to have both a good conception rate and a high oestrus detection rate. These figures were calculated assuming a mean interval from calving to first service of 70 days, which, according to MMB statistics, should be commensurate with a conception rate to a single insemination of 60%. Even when inseminations are carried out between 32 and 52 days after calving the probability of conception is still 0.55 (MMB, 1969).

Accurate determination of oestrus is important to ensure that inseminations are given at the correct time in relation to oestrus. Inseminations conducted at stages of the cycle other than oestrus not only fail to result in a pregnancy being established but may, by causing damage to the reproductive tract, even cause cows to stop cycling. Moreover, mistimed inseminations carried out during early pregnancy may well result in abortion (Bulman, 1977; Bulman and Lamming, 1978).

POST PARTUM OVARIAN ACTIVITY

Immediately after parturition the ovaries of the cow are relatively inactive and fail to show ovulation. In addition the uterus requires to go through a phase of regression and repair before it is capable of accepting another pregnancy. This involution takes approximately 35 to 40 days and appears to be independent of any nutritional influence (*Table 1.3;* Wiltbank *et al.*, 1962). Therefore, it is necessary that the cow commences regular recurrent oestrus cycle activity before a pregnancy can be re-established.

Past methods to assess ovarian activity of the dairy cow in the early *post-partum* period involved rectal palpation techniques. While it is relatively easy to distinguish between ovarian activity and inactivity it is far less easy to differentiate between normal and abnormal ovarian structures, especially with a single examination. Nonetheless, this technique has established that the first ovulation normally occurs between 13 and 40 days after calving (Marion and Gier, 1968; Menge *et al.*, 1962; Oxenreider and Wagner, 1971), and it was assumed that cows continued to ovulate regularly thereafter.

More recently the ability to measure progesterone concentrations in milk has provided a very useful means of rapidly monitoring ovarian activity in a large number of animals (Lamming and Bulman, 1976). In a survey involving 535 cows in four well managed dairy herds it was established that ovarian cycles started at a mean time interval of 24.1 ± 0.6 days after calving. While this figure varied significantly with season (see *Table 1.5*) there was no relationship between this interval and milk yield (Bulman, 1977).

From these figures it would appear that neither ovarian activity nor uterine involution should influence the ability to re-establish a pregnancy by 78 days *post partum*. However, there are problems when using mean figures of this type. First, it masks those 'problem' cows with much longer *post partum* intervals to first ovulation, secondly, it assumes that animals continue to cycle normally after their first ovulation, and thirdly, it assumes that all ovulations are accompanied by oestrus. As will be discussed in a later section these assumptions are not necessarily valid.

NUTRITION AND REPRODUCTION

There is much experimental evidence to indicate that reproductive efficiency in sheep is determined by the energy balance of the ewe in the period just prior to mating, and these data form the basis of the well established practice of flushing (Allen and Lamming, 1961; Coop, 1966; Lamming, 1971). It is also evident from this information that not only is energy balance *per se* important, but that there exists an interaction between energy balance and body condition.

It is perhaps pertinent, therefore, to consider whether similar relationships between energy status and reproduction occur in the dairy cow, especially since many dairy cows are in negative or marginal energy balance at the very time that it is important to re-establish pregnancy. One must, however, remember at the outset that there is a basic difference between the ewe and the dairy cow at the time of mating. The ewe has only to provide energy for maintenance and reproductive function while the dairy cow has the added burden of a very large energy requirement for milk production.

Table 1.3 THE EFFECT OF PRE- AND POST-PARTUM LEVEL OF FEEDING ON REPRODUCTIVE ACTIVITY IN CATTLE

Level of feeding		Condition score at calving*	% Showing oestrus by 90 days post partum	Interval calving to 1st oestrus (days)**	Calving to uterine involution (days)
Pre-partum	Post-partum				
High	High	6.8	95	48	35
High	Low	6.5	86	43	38
Low	High	4.4	85	65	40
Low	Low	4.5	22	52	42

* Based on scale 1 = thin to 9 = fat
** Applies only to cows showing oestrus by 90 days pp
(After Wiltbank *et al.*, 1962)

In the suckled beef cow it has been established that both *pre-* and *post-partum* levels of nutrition have a marked effect on reproductive function (*Table 1.3*). Animals fed on a high plane of nutrition prior to calving had a shorter interval to first oestrus than cows fed on a low level of nutrition *pre-partum*, irrespective of the post-calving level of nutrition. The *post-partum* level of

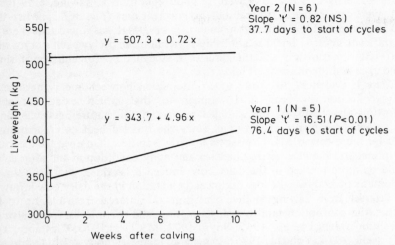

Year 2 (N = 6)
Slope 't' = 0.82 (NS)
37.7 days to start of cycles

y = 507.3 + 0.72 x

y = 343.7 + 4.96 x

Year 1 (N = 5)
Slope 't' = 16.51 (P< 0.01)
76.4 days to start of cycles

Figure 1.3 Weight changes in suckled cows following two successive parturitions and their effects on the interval to the start of ovarian cycles (Bulman, Hewitt and Webb, 1977)

nutrition had little effect on the reproductive activity of cows in good body condition at calving, but had a marked influence on the percentage of cows that were poorly fed prior to calving showing oestrus by 90 days *post partum.* Bulman, Hewitt and Webb (1977) have also noted that body condition or body weight of cows at calving is relatively more important than the *post-partum* level of nutrition. Cows in poor condition at calving, but fed to gain weight thereafter, had a mean interval to first ovulation of approximately 76 days. This

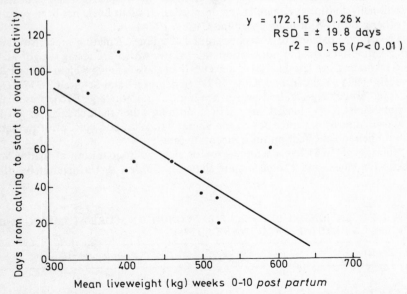

y = 172.15 + 0.26 x
RSD = ± 19.8 days
r^2 = 0.55 (P< 0.01)

Figure 1.4 Effects of liveweight on the interval from calving to initiation of ovarian activity in suckled cows (Bulman, Hewitt and Webb, 1977)

figure was halved when cows were in good condition at calving, even though they were fed thereafter to maintain bodyweight only (*Figure 1.3*). When these data are expressed in a different manner (*Figure 1.4*) it was found that there was a significant negative linear relationship between mean bodyweight during weeks 0–10 after parturition and the time to first ovulation for animals of similar breed type and therefore adult body size.

There is evidence, therefore, of an interaction between energy balance and body condition in beef cattle similar to that which exists for sheep. Unfortunately, there are few detailed reports of this nature available for the dairy cow. One might expect that, since the suckled beef cow partitions its food far more towards body reserves in early lactation than does the dairy cow, the interaction between energy balance and body condition at and after calving would be more marked in the dairy cow. Indeed it is evident that both the rate and extent of bodyweight loss during early lactation in the dairy cow influences the interval from calving to first ovulation, the interval from calving to first oestrus, the conception rate to a single mating, and the interval from calving to conception (Menge *et al.*, 1962; Boyd, 1972; McClure, 1970; Whitmore, Tyler and Casida, 1974; Youdan, 1975). In general, increased bodyweight loss in early lactation is associated with a reduction in reproductive efficiency primarily due to both a delay in remating and a lowered conception rate.

Haresign, Peddle and Swan (1978) noted that Friesian cows which lost less than 35 kg bodyweight during early lactation had a mean interval to first service of 72 days while those losing more than 35 kg had a mean interval to first service of 104 days, even though the breeding policy of the herd was to inseminate at the first observed oestrus after 50 days *post partum*. Ovarian activity of these cows was monitored by milk progesterone analysis and indicated that one of the major factors responsible for extending the interval to first service was an increase in the number of missed or 'silent' heats. A nutritionally induced increase in the proportion of silent heats has been reported by other groups (Whitmore, Tyler and Casida, 1974).

The energy balance of the cow around the time of mating may also have a significant effect on the conception rate. Cows which are losing weight at the time of mating are less likely to conceive than those gaining weight (King 1968; Youdan, 1975; Youdan and King, 1977; Sonderegger and Schurch, 1977). Only the long-term changes in bodyweight are important (Youdan, 1975), presumably because short-term changes may reflect nothing other than changes in gut fill. Moreover, short-term increases in the energy intake of cows just prior to mating have no beneficial effect on the conception rate.

Mulvaney (1978) has attempted to correlate body condition at mating with conception rates, and the results are shown in *Table 1.4*. Unfortunately, other

Table 1.4 RELATIONSHIP BETWEEN BODY CONDITION SCORE AT MATING AND CONCEPTION RATE (AFTER MULVANEY, 1978)

Score at mating	Conception rate (%)
≲1	45
1½–2	64
≲2½	72

groups have been unable to identify such a relationship (Broster, 1973; Parker and Blowey, 1976; Somerville, 1977). Perhaps this discrepancy can be explained by a critical weight concept or critical body condition concept below which reproduction may be impaired, but only if the cow is still in negative energy balance. Above this critical condition bodyweight change and energy balance have little or no effect on reproductive efficiency. Certainly the higher conception rates achieved for cows gaining weight at the time of service would support such a concept. In addition, the better the body condition of the cow at calving the greater the degree of bodyweight loss that can be allowed before this critical condition is reached, and therefore nutrition is less likely to be of importance with regard to reproductive activity.

Infertility problems

Excessive bodyweight loss in early lactation is likely to be detrimental to cow fertility, and such losses should therefore be avoided. An increase in the severity of undernutrition in sheep is associated with an increased incidence of silent heats and a lowered conception rate. In extreme cases ovulation may well be inhibited altogether. Do similar situations occur in cows? As discussed earlier, poor nutrition or high bodyweight losses do result in an increase in the proportion of missed or silent heats, although no figures were given.

Tables 1.5 and *1.6* present the results obtained from a survey which investigated the *post-partum* reproductive activity of cows in four well managed dairy herds (Bulman, 1977; Bulman and Lamming, 1978). Milk samples were collected twice weekly from all cows commencing shortly after parturition and

Table 1.5 EFFECT OF MONTH OF CALVING ON THE INTERVAL FROM PARTURITION TO THE ONSET OF OVARIAN CYCLES (BULMAN, 1977)

Month of calving	Number of cows	Days to start of cycles
January	25	31.3 ± 5.6
February	9	20.3 ± 1.6
March	16	38.6 ± 6.9
April	5	52.4 ± 15.1
May	12	38.2 ± 6.1
June	10	23.1 ± 2.6
July	28	20.4 ± 1.7
August	69	25.0 ± 1.7
September	74	22.7 ± 1.6
October	120	19.8 ± 1.0
November	82	24.8 ± 1.5
December	55	22.8 ± 0.9
Overall	506	24.1 ± 0.6

continuing until each animal was diagnosed pregnant. The overall mean interval from calving to the onset of ovarian cycles was 24.1 ± 0.6 days although there was a significant ($P < 0.01$) effect of month of calving on this interval (*Table 1.5*). The interval was considerably longer for cows calving in March, April and May than in any of the other months.

Table 1.6 REPRODUCTIVE ACTIVITY OF DAIRY COWS BY MONTH OF CALVING (BULMAN, 1977)

Month of calving	A Normal	B Delayed start to cycles	C Cessation of cycles	D Persistent luteal activity	E Silent heat	Total
			Category of reproductive activity			
January	18	2	1	1	3	25
February	7	0	0	0	2	9
March	10	4	1	0	1	16
April	4	1	0	1	0	6
May	6	3	0	0	3	12
June	13	0	0	0	2	15
July	36	1	4	0	5	46
August	57	2	4	2	9	74
September	58	6	0	2	8	74
October	92	3	9	2	14	120
November	70	6	4	1	2	83
December	45	0	3	1	6	55
Total	416	28	26	10	55	535

Using the milk progesterone profiles, cows were split into the five categories of reproductive activity as shown in *Table 1.6*. Delayed start to ovarian cyclical activity (category B) represents animals which were not cycling by 50 days *post partum*, and cessation of cycles (category C) represents animals in which ovarian cycles commenced prior to day 50 *post partum* but then ceased for a period of not less than 14 days. The silent heat group (category E) represents cows in which normal ovarian cycles were monitored by milk progesterone analysis but which were not observed to come into oestrus. Of the 535 cows studied only 416 (77.6%) were classified as normal; the remaining 119 all showed some form of aberrant reproductive activity, the largest single problem being silent heats.

One criticism of including cows showing silent heats within the abnormal groups is that it may be a failure on the part of the stockman to determine oestrus rather than failure of the cow to exhibit oestrus. In this particular survey it was possible from the milk progesterone profiles to forewarn the stockman of which individual cows within his herd should be coming into oestrus. In spite of this information oestrus was still not detected in these cows. Whether the cows underwent a silent heat or whether oestrus was of a low intensity or short duration is really unimportant. What is clear is that there was a problem of either suboestrus or no oestrus in this group.

Although this survey was not designed to investigate the causes of reproductive abnormality, it was clear that there was no relationship between milk yield and the incidence of reproductive abnormality. While other groups have reported a relationship between yield and fertility in dairy cows (Horvarth, 1967; Marion and Gier, 1968; Francis and Rattner, 1975; Matsoukas and Fairchild, 1975) many have found none (Touchberry, Rottensen and Andersen, 1959; Smith and Legates, 1962; Everett, Armstrong and Boyd, 1966; Slama *et al.*, 1976). Since most of these reports do not provide data on the level of nutrition, body condition at calving, or bodyweight loss in early lactation, it is impossible to separate the effects of milk yield from these other factors. Sound evidence for an effect of yield *per se* on reproductive activity is lacking. In view of the many and variable interactions of level of nutrition and bodyweight loss in early lactation with body condition at calving on both milk yield and reproduction this is not altogether surprising.

It is interesting to speculate whether the categories of reproductive inactivity E, C and B respectively in *Table 1.6* represent a response to the increased levels of undernutrition. From the discussions in earlier sections this is highly probable. In fact the effect of month of calving on the interval to first ovulation noted in *Table 1.5* may well also be nutritional in origin. The spring calving cows in many herds with a protracted calving season tend to receive either low quantities of or the poorer quality winter roughages since they are not lactating. Consequently, they tend to be in poorer condition at calving than their herd mates which calve at other times of the year.

The mechanisation by which nutrition influences reproductive function is poorly understood. One feature of nutritionally induced herd infertility is hypoglycaemia (McClure, 1968; Anon, 1970; McClure, 1972), and McClure (1972) has suggested that this results in an inhibition or reduction of GnRH secretion from the hypothalamus. This in turn would reduce gonadotrophin secretion from the pituitary and thus reduce gonadal activity. However, it is important to remember that hypoglycaemia may also have direct effects on the ovary and other parts of the reproductive system.

Homeostasis is essential for survival, and during early lactation the rate and extent of bodyweight loss is determined and limited endocrinologically. It is quite possible that the endocrine co-ordinates of lactation and energy balance are closely associated with those controlling reproduction in such a way that pregnancy may be inhibited in situations of energy insufficiency. The degree of inhibition may in this way be determined by the degree of energy insufficiency, the differing forms of reproductive inactivity noted in *Table 1.6* representing different degrees of inhibition.

Practical recommendations

It is evident that the requirements for milk production are not incompatible with those for ensuring a high level of reproductive performance: adequate nutrition both before and after calving is required to allow the cow to attain its true genetic potential for milk production and to ensure that reproduction is not impaired. MAFF, DAFFS and DANI (1975) suggest weight change patterns for cows in early lactation, and recommend that a weight loss of 35 kg during the first 70 days is desirable. In reality this system of rationing dairy cows entails feeding them to lose weight in early lactation. Such a system is fraught with danger since there exists considerable between-cow variation in the way in which food is partitioned between milk and body tissues. Evidence from Nottingham (Haresign, Peddle and Swan, 1978) indicates that when feeding for a bodyweight loss of 0.5 kg/d during the first 70 days of lactation, some cows will lose considerably more weight than this and it is these individuals which have reproductive problems. It may well be inevitable that some degree of bodyweight loss occurs at this time to meet the energy deficit of lactation. However, limiting a cows energy intake by feeding for bodyweight loss at this time may mean recourse to additional bodyweight loss to meet the requirements for milk production. If this loss reaches the maximum that the cows can sustain then milk yield and reproduction may well suffer. Therefore, it is more advisable to ensure that the cow is able to eat as much energy dense feed as possible to minimise this weight loss while still ensuring an intake of sufficient good quality roughage to maintain milk quality. This practice should allow high levels of milk production while still maintaining herd fertility. The time for limiting food intake, particularly of concentrates, is after peak yield when the cow's appetite limit is in excess of requirement. Such a system does not necessarily imply the feeding of more concentrates per lactation, rather re-allocation to early lactation.

Regular body condition scoring of dairy cows is to be recommended to allow appropriate management decisions to be made on an individual cow and a whole herd basis. Croxton (1976) has suggested appropriate target scores for the different stages of lactation (*Figure 1.5*). Reference to these figures will enable

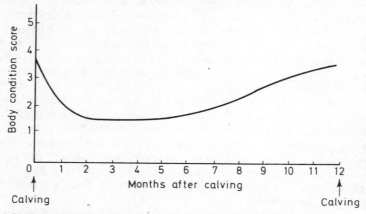

Figure 1.5   Target body condition scores of Friesian dairy cows throughout the lactation cycle (Croxton, 1976)

the farmer to identify any individual cows which are losing too much weight in early lactation and to facilitate the appropriate action to be taken. In addition, if the whole herd falls below this line, due for example to overestimation of either roughage quality or roughage intake, then management can immediately be changed.

The most important score is that at calving; if this is correct then it should be relatively easy to ensure that the others will be. It is not sufficient to feed heavily during the dry period in an attempt to establish the correct condition at calving. First, the efficiency of bodyweight gain in the dry period, as mentioned earlier, is lower than during lactation, and secondly, there may well be insufficient time to achieve the gains required. Therefore, by scoring at regular intervals the farmer is able not only to ensure adequate levels of nutrition for the present lactation but also to prepare the cow properly for the next.

The genetic potential of cows is unlikely to be a major factor in limiting the milk yields of many cows in the United Kingdom dairy herd. Significant increases in yield can be achieved by both better nutrition of the cow during lactation and by better preparation of the animal for the following lactation. Body condition scoring of cows provides a relatively easy method of attaining these objectives. Since the requirements for high levels of milk production are compatible with those for good herd fertility then such an aid to management should also provide a means of improving the reproductive performance.

References

ALLEN, D.M. and LAMMING, G.E. (1961). *J. agric. Sci., Camb.*, **56**, 67
ANON (1970). *I.R.A.D. Annual Report*
BINES, J.A., NAPPER, D.J. and JOHNSON, V.W. (1977). *Proc. Nutr. Soc.*, **36**, 146A
BROSTER, W.H. (1969). *Technology in Agriculture* (May), p. 105
BROSTER, W.H. (1973). *Vet. Rec.*, **93**, 417
BROSTER, W.H., BROSTER, V.J. and SMITH, T. (1969). *J. agric. Sci., Camb.*, **72**, 179
BROSTER, W.H., SUTTON, J.D. and BINES, J.A. (1979). In *Recent Advances in Animal Nutrition – 1978*, p. 99. Eds W. Haresign and D. Lewis. London; Butterworths
BOYD, H. (1972). *Vet. Rec.*, **91**, 193
BULMAN, D.C. (1977). PhD Thesis, University of Nottingham
BULMAN, D.C. and LAMMING, G.E. (1978). *J. Reprod. Fert.*, **54**, 447
BULMAN, D.C., HEWITT, D. and WEBB, R. (1977). Personal Communication
COOP, I.E. (1966). *J. agric. Sci., Camb.*, **67**, 305
CROXTON, D. (1976). In *Making the Most of your Dairy Cows. Proceedings of the Conference at the Welsh Agricultural College*, p. 39
DAVID, S.E., BISHOP, M.W.H. and CEMBROWICZ, H.J. (1971). *Vet. Rec.*, **89**, 181
ESSLEMONT, R.J. (1978). Personal Communication
ESSLEMONT, R.J. and ELLIS, P.R. (1975). *The Melbreed Dairy Herd Health Researching Scheme*. University of Reading, Dept. Ag and Hort, Study No. 21
EVERETT, R.W., ARMSTRONG, D.V. and BOYD, L.J. (1966). *J. Dairy Sci.*, **49**, 879
FRANCIS, G. and RATTNER, D. (1975). *J. agric. Sci., Camb.*, **85**, 527
HARESIGN, W., PEDDLE, B. and SWAN, H. (1978). Unpublished data
HORVARTH, M. (1967). *Anim. Br. Abstr.*, **35**, No. 1330
KING, J.O.L. (1968). *Vet. Rec.*, **83**, 492
LAMMING, G.E. (1971). In *Proceedings of the 5th Nutrition Conference of Feed Manufacturers*, p. 2. Eds H. Swan and D. Lewis. Edinburgh; Churchill Livingstone
LAMMING, G.E. and BULMAN, D.C.(1976). *Br. Vet. J.*, **132**, 507
McCLURE, T.J. (1968). *Aust. Vet. J.*, **44**, 134
McCLURE, T.J. (1970). *Res. Vet. Sci.*, **11**, 247
McCLURE, T.J. (1972). *Vet. Record*, **91**, 193
MAFF, DAFFS and DANI (1975). *Technical Bulletin 33*. London; HMSO
MARION, G.B. and GIER, H.T. (1968). *J. Anim. Sci.*, **27**, 1621
MATSOUKAS, J. and FAIRCHILD, T.P. (1975). *J. Dairy Sci.*, **58**, 540
MENGE, A.C., MARES, S.E., TYLER, W.J. and CASIDA, L.E. (1962). *J. Dairy Sci.*, **45**, 233
MMB (1969). *Report of the Breeding and Production Organisation*, No. 19, p. 120
MMB (1978). Personal Communication
MULVANEY, P. (1978). Personal Communication

OXENREIDER, S.L. and WAGNER, W.G. (1971). *J. Anim. Sci.,* **33**, 1026
PARKER, N.J. and BLOWEY, R.W. (1976). *Vet. Rec.,* **98**, 394
SLAMA, H., WELLS, M.E., ADAMS, G.D. and MORRISON, R.D. (1976). *J. Dairy Sci.,* **59**, 1334
SMITH, J.W. and LEGATES, J.E. (1962). *J. Dairy Sci.,* **45**, 1192
SOMERVILLE, S.H. (1977). PhD Thesis, University of Edinburgh
SONDEREGGER, H. and SCHURCH, A. (1977). *Livestock Prod. Sci.,* **4**, 327
SWAN, H. (1976). In *Principles of Cattle Production,* p. 85. Eds H. Swan and W.H. Broster. London; Butterworths
TOUCHBERRY, R.W., ROTTENSEN, K. and ANDERSEN, H. (1959). *J. Dairy Sci.,* **42**, 1157
WHITMORE, H.L., TYLER, W.J. and CASIDA, L.E. (1974). *J. Anim. Sci.,* **38**, 339
VAN ES, A.J.H. (1976). In *Principles of Cattle Production*, p. 237. Eds H. Swan and W.H. Broster. London; Butterworths
YOUDAN, P.G. (1975). PhD Thesis, University of Liverpool
YOUDAN, P.G. and KING, J.O.L. (1977). *Br. Vet. J.,* **133**, 635

2

DEGRADABILITY OF PROTEIN SUPPLEMENTS AND UTILIZATION OF UNDEGRADED PROTEIN BY HIGH-PRODUCING DAIRY COWS

E.R. ØRSKOV, M. HUGHES-JONES and I. McDONALD
Rowett Research Institute, Aberdeen

The editors of this book have asked that this chapter should deal with the factors affecting protein degradability in the rumen, the techniques for assessing protein degradability and the importance of this to the high-yielding dairy cow. These topics relate essentially to two subjects, one concerned with microbial and physical factors affecting protein metabolism in the rumen, and the other with the needs of host animals for amino acids. It is most convenient and logical to deal with each as separate topics.

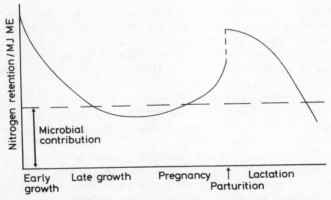

Figure 2.1 The effect of age and production on potential nitrogen retention in relation to ME intake

Ten years ago it was proposed that it was most logical to consider host animal and rumen microbial requirement separately (Ørskov, 1970). The net amino-acid needs of host animals were described during early and late growth, and during pregnancy and lactation. The potential outflow of rumen microbial amino acid, also expressed as a net contribution relative to energy, was then superimposed on the graph describing the host animal need. The suggestions are shown in *Figure 2.1* derived from Ørskov (1970). The technique which made this suggestion a logical direction to move in to estimate the protein requirement of ruminants was the ability to bypass the rumen by manipulating the oesophageal groove reflex in functioning ruminants.

Much work has been carried out since then, to elaborate the concept and to provide quantitative data. The consideration of outflow of protein from the rumen and the nitrogen requirement of rumen microbes, separately from the protein needs of the host animal, is the basis of the new ARC proposals for estimating protein requirements of ruminants (Roy *et al.*, 1977). The degradability of the dietary protein plays a central part in the proposals, because it determines not only the contribution which dietary protein makes to the rumen microbial need, but also the amount of protein which passes through the rumen undegraded and which subsequently becomes available for digestion by the host animal.

The determination of protein degradation in the rumen

The measurement of protein degradability can be made in several ways and these will be considered individually. The three basic approaches are:

(1)   sampling of contents from the abomasum or duodenum;
(2)   incubation of feedstuffs in synthetic fibre bags suspended in the rumen;
(3)   laboratory procedures.

ABOMASAL OR DUODENAL SAMPLING

Total collection or sampling of gut contents distal to the rumen, combined with the use of various markers, allows an estimate to be made of the total protein entering the abomasum. Having estimated or determined the total protein, the proportion of microbial protein can be estimated by the use of endogenous markers such as diamino-pimelic acid (DAPA), which is a component of bacterial cell walls, or exogenous markers such as ^{35}S which is taken up by the microbes from a soluble inorganic salt infused into the rumen. Such techniques rely on the estimation of undegraded dietary nitrogen by subtraction of the microbial contribution from the nitrogen present in the sample, once a correction has been made for the endogenous nitrogen.

The resultant estimates of the microbial protein have varied considerably between different marker techniques. For example, Siddons *et al.* (1979) have found a four-fold variation in the estimates for the microbial contribution by considering different microbial markers. The use of DAPA takes no account of the protozoal contribution in a sample, because no DAPA is found in their cell walls. Differences between bacterial cell contents, and cell wall digestion within the rumen, could also affect the accuracy of the method. The techniques of employing microbial markers suffer from the disadvantage that the error present in the determination of the microbial contribution is, by subtraction, transferred to the generally much smaller undegraded dietary protein fraction. For instance, if the microbial nitrogen content in duodenal digesta could be determined as 70 ± 10 per cent, and the endogenous contribution was 10 per cent, then the estimated dietary protein content would be 20 ± 10 per cent, and this would therefore have a coefficient of variation of 50 per cent.

Recent work by Wenham (1979) suggested that the use of re-entrant, and to a lesser extent, T-piece, cannulae in the duodenum produced substantial abnormalities in the flow of gut contents. An alteration in flow cast a doubt on the normality of estimates of the passage of feedstuffs from the rumen and hence also on estimates of effective degradability.

The values for the degradation of protein obtained by postruminal determination of flow are applicable only to the particular feeding conditions under which they were determined. A change in the level of feeding or type of diet will alter the outflow rate from the rumen and hence the effective degradation of the protein.

INCUBATION OF FEEDSTUFFS IN SYNTHETIC FIBRE BAGS

The technique of using a nylon bag incubated in the rumen was originally developed as a means of assessing the digestion of roughage samples (Balch, 1950). Much of the early work produced poorly reproducible results. Mehrez and Ørskov (1977) have used the technique in recent years for the estimation of the disappearance of nitrogen (N) from protein sources, and consistent results have been obtained by attention to the following points:

(1) > 50 cm^2 of bag area/g dry matter of sample;
(2) adequately long string attaching bag to the cannula cap (25 cm in sheep, 50 cm in cattle);
(3) pore size of synthetic fibre material within the range 30—100 μm, which is large enough to prevent accumulation of gas in the bags which would cause them to float on the rumen liquor and inhibit degradation (Uden, Parra and Van Soest, 1974), but small enough to keep particulate losses to a minimum;
(4) rumen conditions such that substrates for maximal microbial degradation are not limiting the degradation of the sample.

The nylon bag technique provides values for the percentage N disappearance (p) at each of a series of incubation times (t). The relationship between p and t has been found to be exponential and can be described by equations of the form

$$p = a + b(1 - e^{-ct})$$

where a, b and c are constants particular to each protein and type of diet (Ørskov and McDonald, 1979). In many instances, a may be interpreted as a measure of the rapidly soluble protein fraction and b of the fraction which is subject to degradation.

Before the results of incubation measurements can be applied in practice, it is necessary to allow for the progressive outflow of particles of protein from the rumen. Measurements of the outflow rate are therefore required and involve the use of a marker within the protein, or of a marked material which behaves in the same way as the protein. Subsequent analysis of the marked material would be much simplified if it could be rendered undegradable, as there would then be no problem of contamination of the marker material with microbial or gut contents.

Recently, a technique based on the labelling of protein supplements with chromium according to the method of Ganev, Ørskov and Smart (1979), using techniques developed by Uden, Calucci and Van Soest (1979) has been used in which the protein is rendered completely undegradable in the rumen. The disappearance of the labelled material from the rumen, with differing levels of feeding and different diets, enables fractional outflow rates to be obtained. The method assumes that the marked proteins disappear at the same rate as untreated material, and therefore assumes that the small differences in specific gravity of the materials do not alter outflow rates.

Having obtained fractional outflow rates and the constants a, b and c derived from incubation measurements, the effective nitrogen degradability (P) can be calculated from the relationship:

$$P = a + \frac{bc}{c + k}$$

where k is the fractional outflow rate per hour (Ørskov and McDonald, 1979). In some instances the constant a is negative and it has been concluded that this indicates an initial delay before the start of protein disappearance. Under these circumstances the relationship is modified to:

$$P = \frac{bc}{c + k} \left(\frac{a + b}{b} \right)^{\frac{c + k}{k}}$$

but on the whole there appears to be little alteration in the calculated effective degradability by using the simple formula:

$$P = a + \frac{bc}{c + k}$$

even if a is negative.

The different rates of N disappearance between animals fed dried grass or barley is best illustrated by the results in *Table 2.1*, obtained by Ganev, Ørskov and Smart (1979) which corroborated work by earlier workers (Mehrez, 1976; Mohammed and Smith 1977). It can be seen that, for the protein supplements of vegetable origin, the rate of disappearance was greater in the animal given a roughage-based diet while the degradation of fish meal was similar on both diets. The differences are most likely to be the result of quantities of cellulosic material, albeit small, present in the vegetable protein and which could act as a protective factor.

In *Table 2.2* a number of effective N degradability values (P) have been calculated over a range of rumen outflow rates from incubation measurements

Table 2.1 EFFECTS OF INCUBATION ON DISAPPEARANCE OF N (g/100 g) FROM ARTIFICIAL FIBRE BAGS INCUBATED IN THE RUMENS OF SHEEP RECEIVING BARLEY (B) OR DRIED GRASS (G) DIETS (Ganev, Ørskov and Smart, 1979)

| Incubation times (h) | Nitrogen disappearance (g/100 g) | | | | | | | |
| | Soya bean | | Groundnut | | Sunflower | | Fish meal | |
	B	G	B	G	B	G	B	G
3	22.9	38.4	27.5	36.1	32.6	52.1	42.8	41.3
6	30.6	50.6	40.9	60.8	43.7	64.0	47.2	47.8
9	39.7	59.2	49.8	65.2	53.4	77.5	55.7	50.3
15	47.4	78.7	65.9	89.7	65.7	84.5	62.0	55.6
24	61.7	89.0	89.0	92.0	79.9	91.9	71.5	68.0

Table 2.2 NITROGEN DEGRADABILITY ESTIMATED OVER A RANGE OF OUTFLOW RATES FROM THE RUMEN OF SHEEP FED A DRIED GRASS DIET

Protein	Reference	a	b	c	Nitrogen degradability (%) Fractional outflow rate/h (k)							
					0.01	0.02	0.03	0.04	0.05	0.06	0.08	0.10
Fish meal	(1)	30.4	69.6	.019	76.0	64.3	57.4	52.8	49.6	47.1	43.7	41.5
Meat and bone	(1)	23.7	35.8	.077	55.4	52.1	49.4	47.2	45.4	43.8	41.2	39.3
Cotton seed	(1)	32.2	60.2	.082	85.8	80.6	76.3	72.6	69.6	67.0	62.7	59.3
Linseed	(1)	−31.6	128.6	.111	86.8	78.1	70.8	64.4	58.9	54.1	46.0	39.6
Soya bean	(1)	−12.4	111.5	.101	89.1	80.8	73.8	67.7	62.5	58.0	50.4	44.3
Groundnut	(1)	−45.2	140.8	.2138	89.7	84.3	79.4	74.9	70.8	67.0	60.2	54.3
Soya bean	(2)	9.9	80.1	.082	91.2	84.2	78.5	73.7	69.6	66.1	60.4	55.9
Groundnut	(2)	7.2	92.8	.128	93.2	87.4	82.3	77.8	74.1	70.3	64.3	59.3
Sunflower	(2)	30.5	63.6	.135	89.7	85.9	82.5	79.6	76.9	74.5	70.4	67.0
Fish meal	(2)	36.9	63.1	.026	82.5	72.6	66.2	61.8	58.5	56.0	52.4	49.9
Sunflower	(3)	56.4	43.6	.201	97.9	96.1	94.3	92.8	91.3	90.0	87.6	85.5
Rapeseed	(3)	−35.3	120.2	.467	82.5	80.2	78.0	75.9	73.9	71.9	68.3	64.9
Guar meal	(3)	9.6	90.4	.0856	90.5	82.9	76.5	71.2	66.7	62.7	56.3	51.3
Sugar beet pulp	(3)	34.4	65.6	.016	74.7	63.5	57.2	53.1	50.3	48.2	45.3	43.4
Ground pea	(3)	51.1	48.9	.073	94.0	89.4	85.7	82.6	80.0	77.9	74.4	71.7
Fava bean	(3)	8.6	91.4	.087	90.6	82.9	76.6	71.2	66.6	62.7	56.2	51.1
Caustic treated barley	(3)	18.5	81.5	.034	81.5	69.8	61.8	55.9	51.5	48.0	42.8	39.2
Fish meal, fresh, preserved	(4)	6.2	16.9	.076	22.9	22.7	22.4	22.2	22.0	21.9	21.5	21.1
Fish meal, stale, untreated	(4)	39.0	48.7	.017	70.0	61.7	56.9	53.8	51.6	50.0	47.7	46.2
Pressed fish meal	(5)	1.2	21.4	.013	19.9	18.0	16.4	15.0	13.9	12.9	11.3	10.2

(1) Hughes-Jones (1979); (2) Ganev, Ørskov and Smart (1979); (3) Hancock, M. and Ørskov, E.R. (Unpublished data); (4) Mehrez, Ørskov and Obstvedt (1979); (5) Norwegian Herring Oil and Meal Inudstry.

Table 2.3 NITROGEN DEGRADABILITY ESTIMATED OVER A RANGE OF OUTFLOW RATES FROM THE RUMEN OF SHEEP FED A WHOLE BARLEY DIET

Protein	Reference	a	b	c	Nitrogen degradability (%) Fractional outflow rate/h (k)							
					0.01	0.02	0.03	0.04	0.05	0.06	0.08	0.10
Fish meal	(1)	30.6	31.2	.036	55.0	50.6	47.6	45.4	43.7	42.3	40.3	38.8
Meat and bone	(1)	27.6	22.9	.094	48.3	46.5	44.9	42.5	41.6	40.7	39.3	38.1
Cotton seed	(1)	22.1	60.0	.078	75.3	69.8	65.4	61.8	58.7	56.0	53.7	50.0
Linseed	(1)	−9.8	104.0	.097	84.5	76.5	69.8	64.0	59.1	54.7	47.6	41.9
Soya bean	(1)	5.2	94.8	.055	85.3	74.7	66.5	60.0	54.8	50.5	43.8	38.8
Groundnut	(1)	6.0	90.4	.064	84.2	74.9	67.6	61.7	56.8	52.7	46.2	41.3
Soya bean	(2)	14.4	72.4	.043	73.0	63.8	57.0	51.9	47.8	44.6	39.7	36.1
Groundnut	(2)	12.1	87.9	.064	88.0	79.0	71.9	66.1	61.4	57.4	51.1	46.4
Sunflower	(2)	19.8	77.8	.061	86.7	78.4	72.0	66.8	62.6	59.0	53.5	49.3
Fish meal	(2)	35.0	51.0	.051	77.6	71.6	67.1	63.6	60.7	58.4	54.8	52.2

(1) Hughes-Jones (1979); (2) Ganev, Ørskov and Smart (1979).

with sheep given diets of dried grass, i.e. with a very active cellulose digestion. *Table 2.3* gives effective N degradability values obtained with sheep given a diet consisting mainly of whole barley in which the rumen environment is less conducive to cellulolysis. The fractional outflow rates on the two types of diets have been shown to differ (Ganev, Ørskov and Smart, 1979), outflow being reduced with the barley diet where the particle size was small, and where the liquid and solid phases in the rumen are not so distinct. *Tables 2.2* and *2.3* illustrate the influence of outflow rate on the effective degradability and demonstrate that there cannot be a single constant value for the degradability of a protein supplement. It can also be seen that the effects of outflow rates vary between proteins. Although effective degradability always increases as outflow rate becomes less, the total possible cumulative increase is greatest when the constant *b* is large, and the increase continues to be substantial over a wider range of outflow rates when the constant *c* is small. Roughly speaking, a small *c* and a large *b* indicate a protein source which degrades relatively slowly, but which, given time, will be degraded to a high extent. *Figure 2.2* shows the degradation pattern of three typical protein supplements. The pattern for the

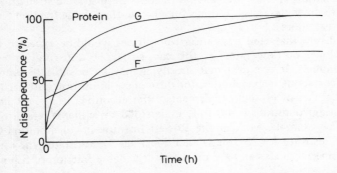

Figure 2.2 Typical nitrogen disappearance curves of protein incubated in the rumen

protein source F, which represents animal protein, is influenced relatively little by outflow rate because *b* is small, although *c* is also small. The pattern representing groundnut, cotton seed meal, etc. and labelled G, will be affected more, because the *b* value is greater. The greatest influence of passage rate will be for a protein of the L type such as linseed, in which *b* is large and *c* relatively small, and effective degradation can vary from less than 40 per cent to more than 80 per cent.

THE DEVELOPMENT OF LABORATORY PROCEDURES

Although the use of rumen-cannulated sheep is convenient in a research institute, for the determination of the rate of protein degradation, it is quite clear that a method which can be used routinely in laboratories concerned with feed evaluation must be developed. There are several possibilities, including the use of neutral proteases or an *in vitro* incubation procedure (*see* Chamberlain and Thomas, 1979). It is important, however, that the relationship of degradation to time is described and not just the amount degraded during a single time interval, as this would be of very limited value. The description of the degradation process obtained should then be compared with disappearance rates determined by synthetic fibre bag incubations.

One of the problems for laboratory procedures is that the degradation rate varies with the type of feed given and, in particular, on whether it is a mainly starch or a mainly cellulose type diet. This can be seen clearly in *Table 2.1*. The rate of protein disappearance was much lower in the concentrate-fed animal, particularly for protein sources of vegetable origin. It will follow that the rumen fluid used for *in vitro* fermentations would ideally have to originate from diets similar to that for which the information is required.

The technique of being able to maintain rumen conditions in a laboratory vessel (Czerkawski and Breckenridge, 1979), would seem to hold possibilities where the degradation curves could be determined by nylon bag incubations.

The development of a technique to estimate the rapidly soluble fraction of the nitrogen in proteins has received attention recently. Autoclaved rumen fluid has been compared with inorganic salt solutions and *in vivo* incubations (Crawford *et al.*, 1978; Crooker *et al.*, 1978). The factors which need to be considered for determination of the water-soluble fraction are pH, ionic strength and ionic species in the medium, but it is doubtful whether the soluble fraction on its own is of any great interest.

It is unlikely that feed evaluation laboratories would be expected to determine fractional outflow rates, as this can, so far, be done only in surgically prepared animals. It is hoped that shortly it may be possible to supply some tables for correcting degradabilities for differences in outflow rates. The extent to which batches of protein supplements differ according to variety, harvesting and processing conditions is not fully understood for either vegetable or animal proteins. For example, work at the Rowett Institute in collaboration with the Norwegian Institute for Herring Oil and Meal has demonstrated the effect that the processing methods can have on the undegradable fraction of fish meal (*see Table 2.2*).

It is quite possible that, when more information on rate of protein degradation becomes available and is related back to the harvesting and processing conditions, it will be possible to predict degradability with such accuracy that routine determinations will become unnecessary.

DEGRADATION OF BASAL FEEDS

The discussion so far has been concerned with the rate and extent of degradation of protein supplements and not with basal feeds. It is correct, however, to consider the protein supplements separately because, in general, they are given as a separate entity, with a particle size distribution that is different from the basal feed. The particle size of the supplement is usually such that it can pass the reticulo-omasal orifice without further size reduction.

Space does not permit a lengthy discussion on protein degradation of basal feeds. Ørskov and Mehrez (1977) have suggested, and used the assumption, that the undegraded N is that which is left when 90 per cent of the digestible organic matter (DOM) has disappeared. The determination therefore requires a knowledge of the DOM content and makes the assumption that 90 per cent of DOM is fermented in the rumen. This assumption is obviously not correct in all cases, but of greater importance is the description of rate of DOM and N disappearance. If the N and DOM disappearances are very dissimilar, as for instance with silages, where 70–80 per cent of the N can disappear during the first hour, then these feeds can be combined with other feeds in such a manner that the deficiency in one can be matched by the excess in another.

Protein utilization by the high-producing dairy cow

DAIRY COWS IN POSITIVE ENERGY BALANCE

It can be seen in *Figure 2.1* that one of the features of lactation is the very rapid increase in protein requirement when lactation starts, and that, at least in as far as the hypothesis in *Figure 2.1* was originally formulated, the protein requirement could not be met by microbial protein alone. In *Table 2.4* some

Table 2.4 EFFECT OF LEVEL OF MILK PRODUCTION AND EXTENT OF NEGATIVE ENERGY BALANCE ON THE NET AAN NEED IN COWS WEIGHING 600 kg (Ørskov, 1980)

Level of production (kg FCM/d)	ME requirement (MJ/d)	ME intake (MJ/d)	Net AAN requirement (g/d)	Net microbial contribution (g/d)	Net AAN requirement (g/MJ of ME)	Net AAN deficit (%)
0	61.9	61.9	9.7	32.8	0.16	–
10	110.5	110.5	65.7	58.6	0.59	11
20	159.1	159.1	121.7	84.3	0.76	31
40	256.3	256.3	232.7	135.8	0.91	42
40	256.3	207.8	232.7	110.1	1.12	53
50	353.5	353.5	346.7	187.4	0.98	46
50	353.5	256.3	346.7	135.8	1.35	61

calculations based on microbial outflow illustrate that, at least theoretically, the need for protein additional to the microbial N outflow increases with increasing milk yield. This is simply because the yield of net amino acid N (AAN) from microbial protein synthesis is insufficient for the net AA requirement for incorporation into milk protein. On the other hand, the deficiency is reduced if it is assumed that the ME requirement is met and the cows are not in negative energy balance. In a review of literature, Clark (1975) summarized work in which casein was infused into the abomasum of lactating cows. Animals which gave a positive response in milk yield to casein infusion were calculated from the feed data given to be in negative energy balance (Clark, Spires and Derrig, 1973; Derrig, Clark and Davis, 1974). Regrettably there are insufficient feed data in other work cited (Tyrrell *et al.*, 1972; Spires, Clark and Derrig, 1973).

Although there are very few data in which increases in milk yield have been obtained from feeding a source of protein with a low degradability to cows in energy balance, or in marginally positive energy balance, the basic concept, if it is true, implies that protein requirement increases with yield. Because the microbial protein produced is considered to be relatively constant per unit of ME, there is, theoretically, a requirement for a less degradable protein as milk yield increases. Experiments conducted to test this hypothesis, using practical milk production trials, have often failed to reveal any detectable change in milk yield when proteins expected to have different degradability have been used (Clay *et al.*, 1978; Clay and Satter, 1979; Foldager and Huber, 1979; Kaufmann and Lüpping, 1979), although milk protein yield has been increased (Kaufmann and Lüpping, 1979). It must, of course, be remembered that, if the cows are consuming ME in excess of their requirement, then more microbial protein will be available and this may occasionally mask responses to dietary protein; however, what is probably more important is that the rate of outflow of protein from the rumen increases as the food intake increases. If it is assumed that the cows eat to meet their ME requirement, then intake increases with increasing milk yield. In this respect it can be seen from *Tables 2.2* and *2.3* that a change in fractional outflow rate from, say 0.03 to 0.06, can make a substantial difference to the effective degradability of the protein, and, as a result, there is something of a self-compensating mechanism whereby an increase in intake leads to a lower degradability. This is probably the reason why the expected responses to changes in degradability for high-yielding cows are not always forthcoming. There is also some evidence that the effective yield of microbial protein increases with outflow rate (Harrison *et al.*, 1975).

For the high-yielding dairy cow, in positive energy balance, the importance of supplying more of an undegraded source of protein with increasing yield may have received too much emphasis.

COWS IN NEGATIVE ENERGY BALANCE

The situation is rather different for cows in negative energy balance, where the need for dietary protein increases. The examples given in *Table 2.4* show the deficit in microbial N for cows giving 40 or 60 kg milk when in energy balance and also when in negative energy balance. The calculations in *Table 2.4* make the assumption that no protein is available from body tissues, which is not correct: however, it seems doubtful whether labile body protein reserves can make any substantial contribution to the nitrogen economy of the animal, except perhaps during the first week or two of lactation.

There is good evidence that cows in early lactation respond by increasing their yield of milk when they are given protein supplements which largely escape rumen degradation. This was dramatically illustrated in an experiment in which potentially high-yielding cows were offered ME to support only 10 kg of fat-corrected milk (FCM) (Ørskov, Grubb and Kay, 1977). The cows were then given either casein or glucose, abomasally. The cows increased their yield of milk, milk fat and milk protein, and it may be calculated that they doubled their negative energy balance in response to casein influence (*Table 5.5*). Unpublished work, with fish meal as the source of undegraded protein, tends to support this observation. Only when the cows were restricted in intake during early lactation, or given a diet which did not enable them to meet their protein need, did the animals respond to supplements of protected protein. Similar observations have been reported by Cressman *et al.* (1977), Verite and Journet (1977) and Roffler *et al.* (1978).

Ewes have been shown to respond in the same way when the animals were also in negative energy balance (Gonzales *et al.*, 1979). In fact, these workers

Table 2.5 EFFECT OF GLUCOSE OR PROTEIN INFUSION INTO THE ABOMASUM ON MILK YIELD AND COMPOSITION IN DAIRY COWS (Ørskov, Grubb and Kay, 1977)

Dry matter intake (kg/d)	Casein infused (g/d)	Glucose infused (g/d)	Milk yield (kg/d)	FSM yield (kg/d)	Protein yield (g/d)	Calculated energy balance (MJ/d)
8.7	0	750	16.8	18.9	423	−20.5
8.6	250	500	19.8	22.7	566	−30.5
8.8	500	250	21.6	25.2	644	−38.6
8.9	750	0	21.4	26.1	676	−41.0

established a close relationship between effective protein degradability, determined by the dacron bag technique, and the milk yield of ewes in early lactation. It would appear that protein stimulates milk yield and thereby increases weight loss in early lactation, but a similar response is not seen in mid and late lactation.

The fact that a protein passes through the rumen and is available in the lower gut for digestion does not necessarily mean that it is digested efficiently by the animal nor, once digested, that the amino acid profile is such that the protein can be used efficiently for milk production. Some unpublished results from this laboratory, in which protein supplements were digested with pepsin HCl solutions *in vitro* after 18 hours' incubation in the rumen, indicate that, for example, meat and bone meal residues may be rather poorly digested, whereas fish meal residues are almost completely digested. Enhanced milk yields have been obtained in early lactation from high-yielding dairy cows close to energy balance, by the administration of encapsulated methionine (Broderick, Kowalczyk and Satter, 1970), which indicates that shortcomings in the amino acid balance of the absorbed protein can occur.

While responses in milk yield to feeding protein supplements in a form which is poorly degraded in the rumen have sometimes been disappointing, the importance of establishing a high peak of lactation is probably such that the inclusion of a supplement with a very low degradability at least helps to ensure that animals will reach their potential milk yields. This is more important, however, for the breeder who wishes to ensure that the expression of genetic potential for milk yield is not constrained by protein limitations. For the commercial herd with peak milk yields of 25–35 kg milk, the importance of feeding a protein source of low degradability in early lactation has probably received unjustified emphasis, particularly in situations where the management of feeding is such that high intakes of total feed are achieved in early lactation.

It could be argued that a large amount of fat deposition in late lactation is not desirable if the cost of feed is the same in late and early lactation and if the animal, by good feeding management, can achieve high intakes in early lactation. However, in many circumstances the fat deposited in late lactation has been derived from a less expensive diet, and so the process of fat deposition and subsequent mobilization may be economical. The feeding of proteins with a low degradability can thus be used as a method of mobilizing body fat tissue in early lactation in order to maintain a reasonable production with a low input of the expensive energy source. This circumstance could arise with cows calving indoors in early spring, which would be let out to consume lush pastures, *ad libitum.* The feeding of protein in early lactation can therefore be used as a too to manipulate body tissue mobilization when it is economical and desirable so to do.

Conclusion

At present, the only practical way of obtaining measurements of rumen de gradability of protein supplements appears to be from determinations of th disappearance of protein from nylon bags incubated in the rumen, and from estimates of fractional outflow rates of protein from the rumen. The incorpora tion of outflow rate into the calculation is very important, its effect on th degradability depending on the shape of the curve describing protein disappear ance against incubation time. The greater the fractional outflow rate, the lowe will be the effective degradability.

From experiments carried out so far, the outflow rate increases with increas ing level of feeding and with increasing structural roughage in the diet. Unti more information becomes available, an outflow rate of 0.09 may be considered to be appropriate when the diet is given to high-yielding cows and where rough ages, such as silage or hay, form a substantial part of the diet.

The use of analytical values from digesta collected postruminally and frac tionation of the proteins is too slow, involves large errors and is applicable only to the feeding level examined. Research must be directed towards developing laboratory methods.

The requirement for protein by dairy cows per unit of energy consumed increases with increasing yield. However, if the cows are meeting their energy requirement for milk yield, then feed intake increases with milk yield. The effect of level of feeding on increasing the outflow rate may act as a self-compensating mechanism, so that more dietary protein is made available with increasing milk yield. As a result, the importance of the degradability of protein supplement may have been overestimated for cows able to meet their energy requirement

If the cows are in negative energy balance, the need for protein increases because the dietary protein must essentially support two sources of energy namely the energy from the diet and the energy mobilized from body tissue The degradability of the protein is therefore very important and can be used effectively to manipulate body tissue mobilization.

References

BALCH, C.C. (1950). Factors affecting the utilization of food by dairy cows. *Br. J* *Nutr.,* 4, 361–388
BRODERICK, G.A., KOWALCZYK, J. and SATTER, L.D. (1970). Milk production response to supplementation with encapsulated methionine per os or casein per abomasum. *J. Dairy Sci.,* 53, 1714–1721
CAMPLING, R.C. and FREER, M. (1962). The effect of specific gravity and size on the mean time of retention of inert particles in the alimentary tract of the cow. *Br. J. Nutr.,* 16, 507–518

CHAMBERLAIN, D.G. and THOMAS, P.C. (1979). Prospective laboratory methods for estimating the susceptibility of feed and proteins to microbial breakdown in the rumen. In *Proc. Nutr. Soc.*, 38, 138A

CLAY, A.B. and SATTER, L.D. (1979). Milk production response to dietary protein and methionine hydroxy analog. *J. Dairy Sci.*, 62 (supplement 1), 75–76 (abstract)

CLAY, A.B., BUCKLEY, B.A., HASBALLAH, M. and SATTER, L.D. (1978). Milk production response to either plant protein or NPN. *J. Dairy Sci.*, 61, (supplement 1), 170–171 (abstract)

CLARK, J.M. (1975). Lactational responses to postruminal administration of proteins and amino acids. *J. Dairy Sci.*, 58, 1178–1197

CLARK, J.M., SPIRES, H.R. and DERRIG, R.G. (1973). Postruminal administration of glucose and sodium caseinate in lactating cows. *J. Anim. Sci.*, 37, 441 (abstract)

CRAWFORD, R.J., HOOVER, W.H., SNIFFEN, C.J. and CROOKER, B.A. (1978). Degradation of feedstuff nitrogen in the rumen vs nitrogen solubility in three solvents. *J. Anim. Sci.*, 46, 1768–1775

CRESSMANN, S.G., GRIEVE, D.G., MacLEOD, G.K. and YOUNG, L.G. (1977). Influence of dietary protein concentration on milk production by dairy cattle during early lactation. *J. Dairy Sci.*, 60 (supplement 1), 68 (abstract)

CROOKER, B.A., SNIFFEN, C.J., HOOVER, W.H. and JOHNSON, L.L. (1978). Solvents for soluble nitrogen measurements of feedstuffs. *J. Dairy Sci.*, 61, 437–447

CZERKAWSKI, J.W. and BRECKENRIDGE, GRACE (1979). Experiments with long-term rumen simulation technique. *Br. J. Nutr.*, 42, 217–228; 229–245

DERRIG, R.G., CLARK, J.H. and DAVIS, C.L. (1974). Effect of abomasal infusion of sodium caseinate on milk yield, N utilization and amino acid nutrition of the dairy cow. *J. Nutr.*, 104, 151–159

FOLDAGER, J. and HUBER, J.T. (1978). Protein and non protein nitrogen for cows in early lactation. I. Feed intake and milk production. *J. Dairy Sci.*, 61 (supplement 1), 173 (abstract)

GANEV, G., ØRSKOV, E.R. and SMART, R. (1979). The effect of roughage or concentrate feeding and retention time on total degradation of protein in the rumen. *J. agric. Sci., Camb.* 93, 651–656

GONZALEZ, J.S., ROBINSON, J.J., McHATTIE, I. and MEHREZ, A.Z. (1979). The use of lactating ewes in evaluating protein sources in ruminants. In *Proc. Nutr. Soc. (355th meeting).*, 38, 145A

HARRISON, D.G., BEEVER, D.E., THOMSON, D.T. and OSBOURN, D.F. (1975). Manipulation of rumen fermentation in sheep by increasing the rate of flow of water from the rumen. *J. agric. Sci., Camb.*, 85, 93–101

HUGHES-JONES, M. (1979). The influence of rate of passage, diet composition and species on the degradation of protein in the rumen. PhD Thesis, University of Aberdeen

KAUFMANN, W. and LÜPPING, W. (1979). Zum Einfluss van protected protein und -Ca auf die Leistung von Milchkuhen. *Z. Tierphysiol. Tierernähr. Futtermittelk.* 41, 202–217

MEHREZ, A.Z. (1976). Assessment of the nitrogen requirement for rumen fermentation in sheep. PhD Thesis, University of Aberdeen

MEHREZ, A.Z. and ØRSKOV, E.R. (1977). A study of the artificial fibre bag technique for determining the digestibility of feeds in the rumen. *J. agric. Sci., Camb.*, 88, 645–650

MEHREZ, A.Z., ØRSKOV, E.R. and OBSTVEDT, J. (1979). Processing factors affecting the degradability of fish meal in the rumen. *J. Anim. Sci.,* **50**, 737–744

MOHAMMED, O.E. and SMITH, R.M. (1977). Measurement of protein degradation in the rumen. *Proc. Nutr. Soc.,* **36**, 152A

ØRSKOV, E.R. (1970). Nitrogen utilization in young ruminants. In *Proceedings of the 4th Nutrition Conference for Feed Manufacturers,* Eds H. Swan and D. Lowe. London; J.A. Churchill

ØRSKOV, E.R. (1980). How to meet energy and amino acid requirements in the highly productive ruminant. In *Digestive Physiology and Metabolism in Ruminants, V*, p. 309, Ed. P. Thivend. Lancaster; MTP Press

ØRSKOV, E.R. and McDONALD, I. (1979). The estimation of protein degradability in the rumen from incubation measurements weighted according to rate of passage. *J. agric. Sci., Camb.,* **92**, 499–503

ØRSKOV, E.R. and MEHREZ, A.Z. (1977). Estimation of extent of protein degradation from basal feeds in the rumen of sheep. *Proc. Nutr. Soc.,* **36**, 78A

ØRSKOV, E.R., GRUBB, D.A. and KAY, R.N.B. (1977). The effect of postruminal glucose or protein supplementation on milk yield and composition in Friesian cows in early lactation and negative energy balance. *Br. J. Nutr.,* **38**, 397–405

ROFFLER, R.E., SATTER, L.D., HARDIE, A.R. and TYLER, W.J. (1978). Influence of dietary protein concentration on milk production by dairy cattle during early lactation. *J. Dairy Sci.,* **61**, 1422–1428

ROY, J.H.B., BALCH, C.C., MILLER, E.L., ØRSKOV, E.R. and SMITH, R.H. (1977). Calculations of the N requirement for ruminants from nitrogen metabolism studies. In *EAAP Publication 22*, pp. 126–129. Ed. S. Tamminga. Wageningen, Holland; Centre for Agricultural Publishing and Documentation

SIDDONS, R.C., BEEVER, D.E., NOLAN, J.V., McALLAN, A.B. and MacRAE, J.C. (1979). Estimation of microbial protein in duodenal digesta. *Ann. Rech. Vet.,* **10**, 286–287

SPIRES, H.R., CLARK, J.H. and DERRIG, R.G. (1973). Postruminal administration of sodium caseinate in lactating cows. *J. Dairy Sci.,* **56**, 664 (abstract)

TYRRELL, H.F., BOLT, D.J., MOE, P.W. and SWAN, H. (1972). Abomasal infusion of casein or glucose in Holstein cows. *J. Anim. Sci.,* **35**, 277 (abstract)

UDEN, P., CALUCCI, P.E. and VAN SOEST, P.J. (1979). Investigation of chromium, cerium and cobalt as markers in digestion rate of passage studies. *J. Sci. Food Agric.* **31**, 625–632

UDEN, P., PARRA, R. and VAN SOEST, P.J. (1974). Factors influencing the reliability of the nylon bag technique. *J. Dairy Sci.,* **57**, 622 (abstract)

VERITE, R. and JOURNET, M. (1977). Utilization des fourteaux traites au formol par les vaches laitières. II. Effets sur la production laitière du treatment des fourteaux et du viveau d'apport azote au debut de la lactation. *Ann. Zootech.,* **26**, 183–205

WENHAM, G. (1979). Effects of cannulation on intestinal motility. *Ann. Rech. Vet.,* **10**, 157–159

3

MICROBIAL PROTEIN SYNTHESIS AND DIGESTION IN THE HIGH-YIELDING DAIRY COW

H. HAGEMEISTER, W. LÜPPING and W. KAUFMANN
Institut für Physiologie und Biochemie der Ernährung der Bundesanstalt für Milchforschung, Kiel, Germany

In recent years a number of comprehensive papers on microbial protein synthesis in the ruminant stomach have been published (Buttery, 1976, 1977; Satter and Roffler, 1977; Thomas and Rook, 1977; Czerkawski, 1978; Tamminga, 1978, 1979). Because, in most of the trials summarized in these papers, either sheep or low-yielding cows were used, the present Chapter deals only with those factors which are likely to show differences between high-yielding cows and the above-mentioned animals, and which should be considered for calculating their requirements. The nutritional requirements of the rumen microorganisms are extremely complex (Hungate, 1966; Giesecke and Henderickx, 1973). It is well recognized, however, that the microbial energy supply expressed in terms of fermentable organic matter is the dominant factor for the synthesis of microbial protein. It is, of course, also possible to express fermentable organic matter in terms of microbial ATP production, which can be demonstrated experimentally *in vitro*.

Energy availability for microbial protein synthesis in the rumen

The energy source for microbial protein synthesis in the rumen is derived mainly from dietary carbohydrates. Neither lipids nor proteins play any major part in the energy supply for protein synthesis. In the case of lipids, although hydrolysis of fatty acids does take place, the significance of the energy released is unknown but probably of little or no importance. In addition, our own experiments have shown that there is no measurable degradation of fatty acids in the rumen (Hagemeister, Kaufmann and Weichen, 1979). The same applies for degraded protein, as shown by Tamminga (1979) in his stoichiometric calculations. *In vitro* studies using casein (Demeyer and Van Nevel, 1979) demonstrated that, relative to the amount of fermentable organic matter, the energy made available by the metabolized protein was only about half that provided by metabolized carbohydrates.

Further, in dairy cow rations, a relatively constant amount of organic matter is provided by the protein fraction which accounts for 14—20 per cent of the ration. Because as much as 30 per cent of this will escape degradation, it can be estimated that dietary protein contributes less than 10 per cent of the microbial energy supply and is, therefore, of relatively minor importance only. Hence, it may be concluded that the supply of energy available to the rumen microflora is mainly dependent on the proportion of digestible carbohydrates degraded in the rumen.

Energy availability for microbial protein synthesis in rumen of high-yielding cows

The high-yielding cow is characterized by a high level of feed intake. Concomitant with this is the necessity for the inclusion of concentrates in the ration. A high level of feeding will result in a high rate of passage through the rumen, although this is associated with an increasing proportion of more readily fermentable carbohydrates in the ration. The possible decline in the rate of fermentation due to the high rate of passage is, therefore, almost compensated by the more rapid fermentation of these carbohydrates. The results of our own experiments are given in *Figure 3.1.* The regression equation indicates that

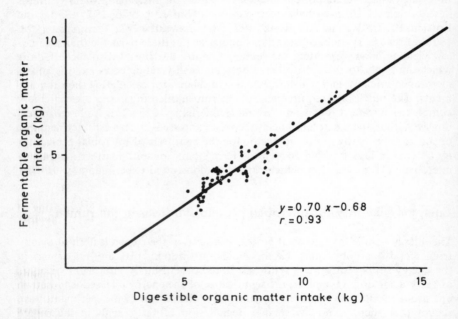

$$y = 0.70\ x - 0.68$$
$$r = 0.93$$

Figure 3.1 The relationship between the intakes of digestible organic matter and fermentable organic matter in cows fitted with duodenal re-entrant cannulae (N = 62)

within the range 6–12 kg of digestible organic matter ingested, 60–65 per cent of this is apparently fermented in the rumen (as calculated from organic matter intake minus organic matter at the duodenum). No influence of feed intake on the extent of ruminal digestion has been observed. This is in agreement with the findings of Tamminga, Van Der Koelen and Van Vuuren (1979) who concluded, from studies with diets containing up to 12 kg/day of organic matter, that the extent of rumen digestion was not markedly influenced by dry matter intake.

When different results are reported for ground and pelleted hay and straw (Kaufmann and Hagemeister, 1974; Voigt *et al.*, 1977), this may be due to the fact that these values were obtained under non-physiological conditions, in that the efficiency of ruminal fermentation was limited by the mechanical processing of the feed.

Utilization of available energy for microbial protein synthesis in the rumen

If it is assumed that the amounts of available energy produced per kg digestible organic matter intake are equal for high-yielding cows, low-yielding cows and sheep, the question arises as to whether the utilization of energy for microbial protein synthesis is also constant. The relationship between microbial protein synthesis and fermentable organic matter in the rumen is illustrated in *Figure 3.2*. The measurements involved 75 trials using cows with duodenal re-entrant cannulae and different levels of intake. Regression analysis of the data showed an increase of 22.1 g of microbial protein per 100 g increase in fermentable organic matter. No marked influence of feed intake or rate of passage on energy utilization for microbial protein synthesis was observed. However, Rohr *et al.* (1979), using high-yielding cows with intakes of either 140 or 170 MJ metabolizable energy (ME)/day from a diet of constant composition, found a

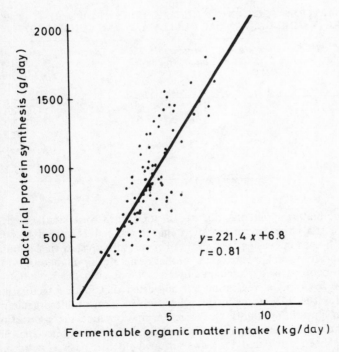

Figure 3.2 The relationship between fermentable organic matter intake and bacterial protein synthesis in dairy cows (N = 75)

Table 3.1 BACTERIAL PROTEIN SYNTHESIS IN COWS AT DIFFERENT LEVELS OF ENERGY INTAKE (ROHR *ET AL.*, 1979)

ME intake (MJ/day)	Fermentable OM[†] intake (kg/day)	Bacterial protein synthesis (g/day)	Bacterial protein synthesis (g/100 g fermentable OM)	(g/MJ ME)
141	5.22	1288	24.7	9.13
141	4.98	1325	26.6	9.40
138	4.11	1262	30.7	9.14
170	6.32	1719	27.2	10.11
170	6.22	1856	29.8	10.92
167	5.36	1681	31.3	10.07

† Calculated as ($OM_{intake} - OM_{duodenum}$), where OM = organic matter

tendency towards slightly higher rates of microbial protein synthesis relative to the amount of fermentable organic matter in the cows with the higher energy intakes (*Table 3.1*). However, these studies were carried out using animals with 'T' cannulae in the duodenum. The cows with ME intakes of 170 MJ ME/day synthesized approximately 10 per cent more microbial protein than the cows with intakes of 140 MJ ME/day.

Corresponding trials by Tamminga, Van Der Koelen and Van Vuuren, (1979) did not confirm this influence of increased amounts of fermentable organic matter on energy utilization (*Table 3.2*). On average, 22 g microbial protein per

Table 3.2 BACTERIAL PROTEIN SYNTHESIS IN COWS AT DIFFERENT LEVELS OF FEED INTAKE (TAMMINGA, VAN DER KOELEN AND VAN VUUREN, 1979)

OM intake (kg/day)	Crude protein content of ration (% in DM)	Fermentable OM[†] intake (kg/day)	Bacterial protein synthesis (g/day)	Bacterial protein synthesis (g/100 g fermentable OM)
7.7	13.4	3.71	842	22.7
7.9	19.1	3.76	838	22.3
7.1	24.3	3.41	759	22.3
11.6	13.4	5.23	1206	23.1
11.5	19.1	5.17	1032	20.0
12.2	24.3	5.06	1201	23.7

† Calculated as in *Table 3.1*

100 g organic matter apparently digested in the rumen were synthesized. However, in these trials the proportion of roughage was reduced from 40 per cent to 32 per cent with increasing feed intake. These results suggest that two factors, namely composition and intake, were probably acting simultaneously. In addition, in our own trials depicted in *Figures 3.1* and *3.2*, the deviation of individual values from the regression line suggested that further factors may be responsible for the differences in the utilization of fermentable organic matter for microbial protein synthesis. Such factors may include the proportions of concentrates:roughage in the ration. Accordingly, the rate of microbial protein synthesis has been calculated for cows grouped on this basis (*Figure 3.3*). It appears that (1) an extremely low energy supply (i.e. a high proportion of roughage in the ration) will yield only 15—20 g microbial protein per 100 g

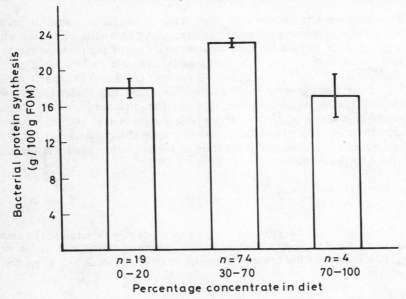

Figure 3.3 The influence of the proportion of concentrates in the diet of dairy cows on the rate of bacterial protein synthesis (expressed in g/100 g fermentable organic matter (FOM))

Table 3.3 BACTERIAL PROTEIN SYNTHESIS IN COWS FED DIFFERENT LEVELS AND KINDS OF CONCENTRATES (OLDHAM, SUTTON AND McALLAN, 1979)

| *Intake and synthesis* | *Concentrate : hay ratio* | | | |
| | *6:4* | | *9:1* | |
	Barley	*Maize*	*Barley*	*Maize*
ME intake (MJ/day)	129	128	132	122
Protein intake (g/day)	1787	1818	1681	1756
Bacterial protein synthesized (g/day)	1350	850	1212	438
Bacterial protein synthesized (g/100 g fermentable OM†)	21.2	13.7	19.2	8.3

† Calculated as in *Table 3.1.*

organic matter apparently digested in the rumen; (2) with extremely high levels of concentrates in the ration (which result in low pH, narrow acetic/propionic acid ratios and lactic acid formation in the rumen (rumen acidosis)), synthesis of only about 14–18 g microbial protein per 100 g organic matter apparently digested in the rumen can be expected. This tendency towards decreased microbial protein synthesis in the rumen, with rations offered to cows under non-physiological conditions, has been confirmed by Mathers and Miller (1977) and also by Chamberlain and Thomas (1979) in recent trials with sheep.

The composition of the concentrates (especially using maize) may have an additional effect on bacterial protein synthesis. This was shown in the studies of Oldham, Sutton and McAllan (1979) (*Table 3.3*). With rations containing maize, the extent of protein synthesis was very low, i.e. 13.7 and 8.3 g/100 g fermentable organic matter compared with 21.2 and 19.2 g/100 g respectively for barley.

Sucrose-containing rations may also cause variations in microbial protein synthesis per unit fermentable organic matter intake. In studies with sheep which were given diets containing more than 50 per cent of their energy intake as sucrose, utilization of the fermented energy available for microbial protein synthesis was reduced by more than 50 per cent (Al Attar, Evans and Axford, 1976). These findings were confirmed by Hvelplund and Möller (1978), who conducted studies with cows and reported that microbial protein synthesis decreased from 21 to 15 g/100 g fermentable organic matter. Such high amounts of sucrose are not normal and lead to the formation of lactic acid.

In Germany, therefore, the proportion of soluble carbohydrates in the ration is defined by the quotient:

$$\frac{\text{Nitrogen-free extract (NFE)}}{\text{Crude fibre (CF)}}$$

and this is used for the practical assessment of dairy cow rations. The results given in *Figure 3.4* confirm that microbial protein synthesis will be low only when rations outside the optimal composition (NFE/CF of 2.3–3.3) are fed to

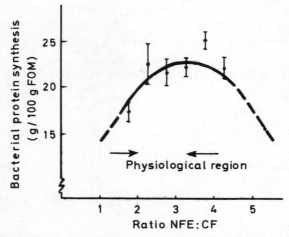

Figure 3.4 The effect of the ratio of nitrogen-free extract (NFE) to crude fibre (CF) in the diet on the rate of bacterial protein synthesis in dairy cows. (The physiological region represents the range over which NFE:CF has no effect on milk fat percentage and does not induce lactic acid production in the rumen)

dairy cows. Hence, it can be concluded that statistically significant differences in the efficiency of energy utilization for microbial protein synthesis are found only under extreme feeding conditions which are unlikely to be encountered in practice.

Finally, a particular effect which was described by Broome (1968) demonstrated by Baldwin, Koong and Ulyatt (1977) in simulation models and measured by Tamminga (1979) using dairy cows, should be mentioned. According to their results, energy availability for microbial protein synthesis is improved by increased feeding frequency. Tamminga (1979), for example, reported an increase of about 20–30 per cent of protein at the intestine with increased frequency of feeding. With sheep, however, increased feeding frequency of high-roughage rations did not result in increased amounts of protein at the duodenum (MacRae *et al.*, 1972).

Reasons for reduced energy utilization when feeding extreme rations

The results shown in *Figures 3.3* and *3.4* indicate clearly that the effect of the type of organic matter (NFE/CF; proportion of concentrate) on the rate of microbial protein synthesis can be measured only when rations of extreme composition are fed. This may be related to the influence of organic matter composition and pH in the rumen on both the number and the composition of the microbial population (Kirstner *et al.*, 1979). However, because the microbial numbers are also dependent on other factors (e.g. rate of passage through the rumen, saliva production and rumen fluid volumes) the type of bacteria involved and their adaptation to organic matter composition appear to be of greater importance in this context.

With rations containing large amounts of crude fibre, the utilization of fermented energy for microbial protein synthesis is lower, due to the relatively slow rate of fermentation by the microbial population. This leads to slow microbial growth rates, so that the maintenance requirements of these bacteria are relatively high. With mixed rations, bacteria with high growth rates over varying periods of time are present in the rumen. The high growth rate is then associated with a lower requirement for maintenance.

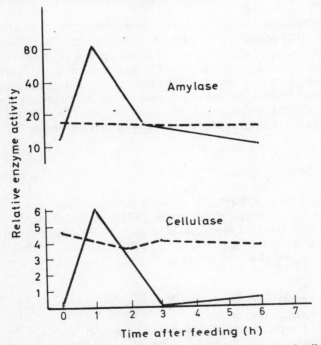

Figure 3.5 The influence of type of feed on the activity of amylases and cellulases in the cell-free rumen liquor of dairy cows (------ hay; ——— concentrate)

Figure 3.5 illustrates the differences in microbial growth rate measured by enzymatic activity in cell-free rumen liquor for two types of diet. With high crude fibre rations the energy (ATP) gain per 100 g of fermentable organic matter remains unchanged, as can be calculated from the production of volatile fatty acids. With rations rich in concentrates, however, the gain of energy (ATP) per 100 g of fermentable organic matter is reduced because of the production, in the rumen, of lactic acid. This leads to a reduced microbial protein synthesis (Van Nevel and Demeyer, 1977; Russel and Baldwin, 1979 a, b; Tamminga, 1979). In addition, the following possible additional effects must be considered.

RATE OF PASSAGE

Harmeyer, Martens and Vogelsang (1974), Cole *et al.* (1976) and Harrison, Beever and Osbourn (1976) reported an effect of the rate of passage of digesta on microbial protein synthesis. This effect cannot be considered separately from other factors in *in vivo* experiments, because the rate of passage is closely related to the kind of fermentable organic matter fed, and in particular to the proportion of roughage in the ration. In rations with high proportions of ground roughage, a reduced quantity of microbial protein is found at the duodenum (Kaufmann and Hagemeister, 1974).

RATIO OF VOLATILE FATTY ACIDS IN THE RUMEN

From stoichiometric calculations the energy gain per mole of acetic (C_2) or propionic (C_3) acids can be considered to be constant. Therefore, no particular effect of the C_2/C_3 acid ratio on microbial protein synthesis can be expected. Influences reported in the literature (Thomas and Rook, 1977) are more related to the composition of fermentable organic matter and its influence on the kind of microbes. Only in extreme concentrate rations can a reduced rate of microbial protein synthesis be expected, i.e. when propionic acid is produced via the acrylate pathway because of reduced energy gains (Tamminga, 1979).

NUMBER OF PROTOZOA

On average, protozoal protein accounts for 20–25 per cent of the microbial protein at the duodenum (Hagemeister, 1975; Ling and Buttery, 1978; John and Ulyatt, 1979; Harrison, Beever and Osbourn, 1979). Although experiments with defaunated sheep show an increase of about 20 per cent in the rate of bacterial protein synthesis (Lindsay and Hogan, 1972), this effect is of minor importance, because

(1)   the variation of the protozoal count of cattle on normal rations is only of a very small magnitude;

(2)   only the proportion of protozoal to bacterial protein at the duodenum is altered, and not the total supply of microbial protein (John and Ulyatt, 1979).

Summing up, it may be emphasized that under physiological conditions (35–70 per cent concentrate in the ration; NFE:CF ratio of 2.3–3.3) there will be a constant rate of microbial protein synthesis of around 22 g bacterial protein per 100 g fermentable organic matter.

Digestibility of microbial protein in the intestine of the dairy cow

To measure the digestibility of microbial protein a technique has been developed in sheep, based on continuous intra-abomasal infusions of microbial protein. A comparison between the digestibility of microbial protein measured by this technique (Schwarting and Kaufmann, 1978; Hagemeister and Kaufmann, 1979) and of other proteins related to the respective protein concentration in the infused substrate, is given in *Table 3.4*.

Table 3.4 'TRUE' DIGESTIBILITY OF DIFFERENT PROTEIN SUPPLEMENTS AND RUMINAL PROTOZOAL/BACTERIAL PROTEIN, DETERMINED BY THE ABOMASAL INFUSION TECHNIQUE

Protein supplement	Protein content (%)	Digestibility (%)
Soya bean meal	52	84 ± 3
Ground nut meal	49	90 ± 1
Cotton seed meal	42	93 ± 2
Rape seed meal	42	88 ± 5
Sunflower meal	37	75 ± 10
Linseed meal	36	80 ± 6
Palm kernel meal	15	54 ± 11
'Pruteen'	82	91 ± 4
'Toprina'	60	90 ± 2
Fish meal	75	90 ± 3
Codfish meal	70	89 ± 5
Skimmed milk powder	37	92 ± 4
Bacteria	53	83 ± 5
Protozoa/bacteria	47	81 ± 6

Both the amount and the fermentability of the carbohydrates in the food are responsible for the varying degrees of fermentation found in the hind gut. As a result, varying amounts of bacterial protein are present in the faeces, influencing the digestibility value of the infused protein. These relationships are given in *Figure 3.6*. Extrapolation to 100 per cent protein content, as shown in this Figure gives a digestibility of 90–95 per cent for both the microbial protein and the other sources of protein involved in these studies. Similar high values of protein digestibility were obtained in experiments using other measurement techniques, such as labelled bacteria. Measurements of the labelled substance in the faeces (Hoogenraad *et al.*, 1970; Salter and Smith, 1977; Tas, Axford and Evans, 1977; Verma and Singh, 1977) showed a mean digestibility between 79 and 95 per cent.

Significance of microbial protein synthesis for high-yielding cows

The significance of microbial protein synthesis in the rumen of the dairy cow

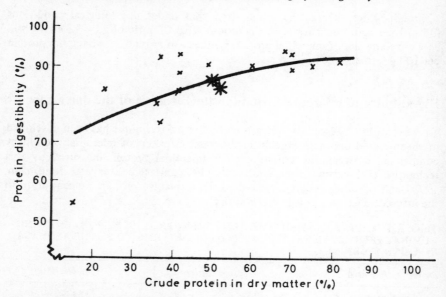

Figure 3.6 Protein digestibility in the monogastric part of the gut of ruminants in relation to the estimated crude protein content of the different protein sources used, as determined by abomasal infusion of feedstuffs and microbial protein (*microbial protein)

relates, on the one hand, to the extent to which the microbial protein can meet the total protein requirements of the dairy cow, and on the other to its amino acid profile, that is the 'biological value' of the microbial protein compared with the dietary protein. In cows, 50—100 per cent of the protein supply, relative to the amount needed for maintenance and milk production, is of microbial origin. The biological value of microbial protein for milk production, which can be derived by comparison of arteriovenous differences in amino acid profiles across the mammary gland with the amino acid profile of milk protein, or by experiments with infusions of amino acids, appears to be very high (Hagemeister and Kaufmann, 1978).

Virtanen, Ettala and Mäkinen (1972) conducted trials to determine whether microbial protein synthesized in the rumen was sufficient to meet the requirements of the high-yielding cow. In this work, the dietary protein was substituted by non-protein nitrogen, but lactation yields of only 3000 ℓ/year were obtained. The lactation curve showed high yields in early lactation (two weeks) and a rapid decline, thereafter to as little at 10—12 ℓ/day. These results clearly demonstrate that, despite increased energy supply, the microbial protein does not meet the total requirements for protein of the high-yielding cow. These results were confirmed in feeding trials, using varying proportions of urea in the ration, by Kaufmann and Hagemeister (1975).

The optimum level of milk production, resulting from optimal utilization of dietary protein, is much more interesting and of practical importance. In this context, the proportion of dietary protein entering the duodenum undigested has to be considered. This proportion varies between 20—40 per cent. A mean value of 30 per cent has been established and adopted, because the levels measured in mixed rations have not been found to differ greatly from this.

Optimum utilization of dietary protein is reached when the 70 per cent degradable proportion of the dietary protein is utilized to the full by the bacteria, so that neither deficiency nor excess of NH_3 occurs in the rumen (Roy *et al.*, 1977).

Our own measurements (*Figure 3.7*), using cows with duodenal re-entrant cannulae, have shown that optimum utilization of dietary protein is reached when rations with a mean concentration of 600 starch equivalent (SE) units/kg

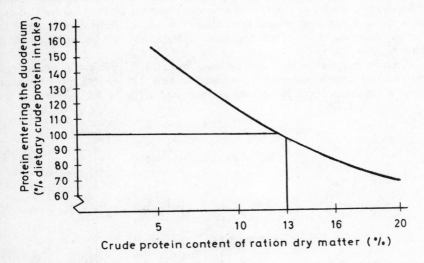

Figure 3.7 Relationship between the amount of protein entering the duodenum (expressed as % of dietary crude protein intake) and the crude protein content of the ration dry matter of cows fed a ration containing 600 SE/kg DM (11.0 MJ ME/kg DM)

DM (or 11.0 MJ ME/kg DM) contain 13 per cent crude protein on a dry matter basis. This optimum protein concentration in the ration of 13 per cent is, of course, determined by the energy content of the ration as the following model calculation will show. If it is assumed that on average 60–65 per cent of the digestible organic matter is fermented in the rumen (*see Figure 3.1*), that 100 g of digestible organic matter is equivalent to 90 SE units, and that bacterial protein is synthesized at the rate of 22 g/100 g fermentable organic matter (*see Figure 3.2*) then 100 SE units (or 1.84 MJ ME) would produce $\sim$ 15 g bacterial protein (Kaufmann, 1977). The 600 SE units/kg DM (11.0 MJ ME/kg DM) cited for the above ration would therefore facilitate the production of 90 g (i.e. 6 × 15 g) bacterial protein/kg feed, and this would be synthesized from the ammonia produced in the rumen from degradation of feed protein. However, because feed protein, as mentioned earlier, has an average degradability in the rumen of 70 per cent, the feed would need to contain 129 g/kg (i.e. $90 \times \dfrac{100}{70}$ g/kg), or approximately 13 per cent crude protein on a dry matter basis for optimal utilization of dietary protein. If, on the other hand, the feed contained only 500 SE units/kg DM (or 9.2 MJ ME/kg DM), then bacterial protein synthesis would be reduced to only 75 g (i.e. 5 × 15 g)/kg feed, which would therefore need to contain only 107 g/kg or approximately 11 per cent crude protein on a dry matter basis to ensure optimum utilization of dietary protein.

Similar results were obtained by Satter and Roffler (1975, 1977) and Slyter, Satter and Dinius (1979), who carried out measurements of HN_3–concentrations.

Energy concentrations above 600 SE/kg DM or 11.0 MJ ME/kg DM cannot be fed within normal physiological limits to dairy cattle because they result in acidosis and a decline in milk fat content.

On the basis of the feeding standards proposed by Kaufmann (1979b), maintenance plus approximately 20 kg milk/d can be produced with optimal utilization of dietary protein. Production in excess of 20 kg milk/d will induce differences in the protein requirements of the animal relative to those of the rumen microorganisms, in that the needs of the animal will become increasingly higher.

Such an increase in milk production above 20 kg/day is accompanied by an increasing excess of rumen NH_3, associated with the need to meet the tissue protein requirements of the animal as illustrated in *Figure 3.8.* Seventy per cent

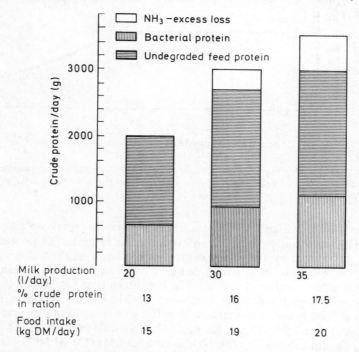

Figure 3.8 The efficiency of utilization of dietary protein in the rumen of dairy cows with different levels of milk production, determined by the proportions of dietary crude protein intake represented by undegraded feed protein and bacterial protein leaving the rumen, and ammonia excesses in the rumen

of the dietary protein (i.e. the rumen degradable fraction) above 13 per cent crude protein suffers this fate. The consequences of this in terms of crude protein requirement for the milk produced, are demonstrated in *Figure 3.9* (Kaufmann, 1979b).

The increase in excess rumen NH_3 production due to increasing milk production is particularly striking in view of the frequently observed energy deficiency which occurs at high levels of milk production. As shown in *Figure 3.10,* energy

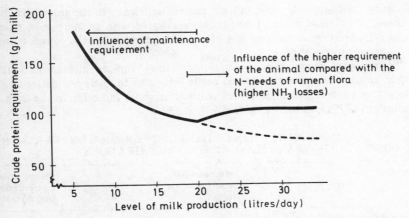

Figure 3.9 Relationship between milk yield and crude protein requirements (including maintenance requirement) in diary cows (expressed as g crude protein/ℓ milk produced)

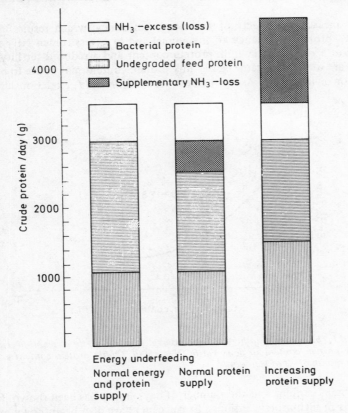

Figure 3.10 The effect of energy underfeeding, with either a normal or an increased dietary protein supply, on the efficiency of protein utilization in high-yielding dairy cows (35 ℓ milk/day), determined by the proportions of dietary crude protein intake represented by undegraded feed protein and bacterial protein leaving the rumen, and ammonia excesses in the rumen

deficiency does not only result in a net protein deficiency to the animal (i.e. less synthesis of bacterial protein), but is also associated with an increase in excess rumen NH_3 production because less of the NH_3 produced in the rumen is used for bacterial protein synthesis.

The increased rumen NH_3 production resulting from an increase in dietary protein content of the ration fed to cattle subjected to energy underfeeding is reflected in an increased plasma urea concentration, as indicated in the data of Kaufmann (1979a), shown in *Table 3.5*.

Table 3.5 INFLUENCE OF PROTEIN CONTENT OF THE RATION ON THE RUMEN NH_3 CONCENTRATIONS AND PLASMA UREA CONCENTRATIONS

Treatment	Ruminal NH_3 concentration (mg %)	Plasma urea concentration (mg %)
16% crude protein	8.8	7.9
19% crude protein	16.8	16.8

The measurable effects of an energy deficiency, which results in both an effective protein deficiency to the animal and in excess rumen NH_3 concentrations, are a reduction in milk protein content and a reduced fertility. As both effects are due to the same cause, milk protein content may prove to be a useful indicator of infertility. As can be seen from *Figure 3.11*, a relationship between

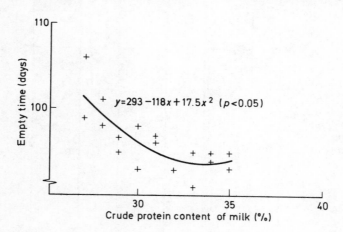

*Figure 3.11 The relationship between the interval from calving to conception (empty time) and milk protein content in dairy cattle (N = 3500). (*Milk protein content expressed as mean for months 1–3 of lactation)*

milk protein content and the number of days empty has been shown. Infertility problems in high-protein rations (19 per cent) have also been shown by Sonderegger (1976), Jordan and Swanson (1979) and Treacher, Stark and Collis (1979). It may be concluded that the protein metabolism of the dairy cow is not well adapted to high levels of production, and therefore a decrease in reproductive rate can be expected with increasing levels of production.

Table 3.6 INFLUENCE OF PROTEIN CONTENT OF THE RATION AND PROTECTED PROTEIN ON THE FERTILITY OF DAIRY COWS

Treatment	16% crude protein	16% crude protein (30% protected)†	19% crude protein
Number of cows	19	20	20
Conception rate (%)	56	69[a]	44[b]
Services per conception	1.79	1.45[a]	2.25[b]
Days empty	97.5	83.7	102.1

† 30% of the crude protein was fed as protected soya bean meal
a vs b: $P < 0.05$

There is neither a decrease in the rate of ruminal degradation of the food protein nor an increase in the rate of microbial protein synthesis with higher yields. Further, it has not yet been possible to provide evidence for better utilization of the available protein at higher levels of milk production. In order to improve tissue protein supply in high-yielding dairy cows, efforts have been made to reduce the rate of dietary protein degradation in the rumen, either by formaldehyde treatment or by heat treatment. During the last five years a

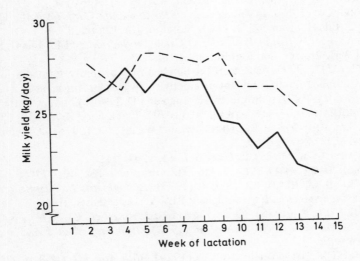

Figure 3.12 The influence of protected protein on the milk yield of dairy cows in early lactation (N = 42)

method of formalin treatment has been developed in Germany (Kaufmann and Hagemeister, 1976) and, as a result, it has been possible to reduce the rate of degradation of dietary protein in the rumen from 70 to 30 per cent without affecting its digestibility in the intestine. Using this protected protein, it has been possible to demonstrate a beneficial effect on fertility (*Table 3.6*), in spite of the higher levels of milk production which can be obtained by using such a protected protein (*Figure 3.12*).

Conclusion

Within the normal range of energy concentrations of rations fed to dairy cows, constant rate of microbial protein synthesis of 22 g/100 g fermentable organic matter (15 g/100 SE units or 15 g/1.84 MJ ME) can be expected. It follows that the increased intake of dietary protein necessary to meet the tissue protein requirements of the high-yielding cow are associated with increasing excesses of NH_3.

An energy supply below the requirement gives rise, not only to a protein deficiency to the animal, but also to a major excess of NH_3. For this reason, not only reduced milk protein contents but also disturbances in fertility are to be expected. It is possible to extend the point at which this occurs by using protected protein.

References

AL ATTAR, A., EVANS, R.A. and AXFORD, R.F.E. (1976). *Proc. Nutr. Soc.*, **35**, 108A

BALDWIN, R.L., KOONG, C.J. and ULYATT, M.J. (1977). *Agr. Syst.*, **2**, 225

BROOME, A.W. (1968). In *Proceedings of the 2nd Nutr. Conf. Feed Manufacturers*, p. 92. Eds H. Swan and D. Lewis. London; J.A. Churchill

BUTTERY, P.J. (1976). In *Principles of Cattle Production*, p. 145. Eds H. Swan and W.H. Broster. London; Butterworths

BUTTERY, P.J. (1977). Aspects of the biochemistry of rumen fermentation and their implication in ruminant productivity. In *Recent Advances in Animal Nutrition – 1977*, p. 8. Eds W. Haresign and D. Lewis. London; Butterworths

CHAMBERLAIN, D.G. and THOMAS, P.C. (1979). *J. Sci. Food Agric.*, **30**, 677

COLE, N.A., JOHNSON, R.R., OWENS, F.N. and MALES, J.R. (1976). *J. Anim. Sci.*, **43**, 497

CZERKAWSKI, J.W. (1978). *J. Dairy Sci.*, **61**, 1261

DEMEYER, D. and VAN NEVEL, C. (1979). *Ann. Rech. Vet.*, **10**, 277

GIESECKE, D. and HENDERICKX, H.K. (1973). *Biologie und Biochemie der mikrobiellen Verdauung.* München; BLV-Verlagsgesellschaft

HAGEMEISTER, H. (1975). *Kieler Milchw. Forschungsber.*, **27**, 347

HAGEMEISTER, H. and KAUFMANN, W. (1978). *29th Ann. Meet. EAAP, Stockholm*

HAGEMEISTER, H. and KAUFMANN, W. (1979). *30th Ann. Meet. EAAP, CN 2.5, Harrogate, England*

HAGEMEISTER, H., KAUFMANN, W. and WIECHEN, A. (1979). *Kieler Milchw. Forschungsber.*, **31**, 5

HARMEYER, J., MARTENS, H. and VOGELSANG, G. (1974). *Z. Tierphysiol. Tierernähr. Futtermittelk.*, **33**, 188

HARRISON, D.G., BEEVER, D.E. and OSBOURN, D.F. (1976). *J. Sci. Fd. Agric.*, **27**, 617

HARRISON, D.G., BEEVER, D.E. and OSBOURN, D.F. (1979). *Br. J. Nutr.*, **41**, 521

HOOGENRAAD, N.J., HIRD, F.J.R., WHITE, R.G. and LENG, R.A. (1970). *Br. J. Nutr.*, **24**, 129

HUNGATE, R.E. (1966). *The Rumen and its Microbes.* New York and London; Academic Press

HVELPLUND, T. and MÖLLER, P.D. (1978). In *Proceedings of 3rd World Congress on Animal Feeding, Madrid 8*. p. 26

JOHN, A. and ULYATT, M.J. (1979). *Proc. Nutr. Soc.*, **38**, 144A

JORDAN, E.R. and SWANSON, L.V. (1979). Effect of crude protein on reproductive efficiency, serum total protein and albumin in the high-producing dairy cow, *J. Dairy Sci.*, **62**, 58

KAUFMANN, W. (1977). In *Protein Metabolism and Nutrition*, p. 130. Ed. S. Tamminga. Wageningen; Cent. Agric. Publ. Doc.

KAUFMANN, W. (1979a). *'Geschütztes' Eiweiß in der Rinderfütterung*. DLG-Mitteilungen, H. 7. 430

KAUFMANN, W. (1979b). *Z. Tierphysiol. Tierernähr. Futtermittelk.*, **42**, 326

KAUFMANN, W. and HAGEMEISTER, H. (1974). In *Energy Metabolism of Farm Animals, EAAP Publ. No. 14*, p. 107. Eds K.H. Menke, H.-J. Lantzsch and J.R. Reichl. Stuttgart; EAAP

KAUFMANN, W. and HAGEMEISTER, H. (1975). *Übers. Tierernähr.*, **3**, 33

KAUFMANN, W. and HAGEMEISTER, H. (1976). *Kieler Milchw. Forschungsber.*, **28**, 335

KIRSTNER, A., THERION, J., KORNELIUS, J.H. and HUGO, A. (1979). *Ann. Rech. Vet.*, **10**, 268

LINDSAY, J.R. and HOGAN, J.P. (1972). *Austr. J. agric. Res.*, **23**, 321

LING, J.R. and BUTTERY, P.J. (1978). *Br. J. Nutr.*, **39**, 165

MacRAE, J.C., ULYATT, M.J., PEARCE, P.D. and HENDTLASS, J. (1972). *Br. J. Nutr.*, **27**, 39

MATHERS, J.C. and MILLER, E.L. (1977). *Proc. Nutr. Soc.*, **36**, 78A

OLDHAM, J.D., SUTTON, J.D. and McALLAN, A.B. (1979). *Ann. Rech. Vet.*, **10**, 290

ROHR, K., BRANDT, M., CASTRILLO, O., LEBZIEN, P. and ASSMUS, G. (1979). *Landbauforschung Völkenrode*, **29**, 32

ROY, J.H.A., BALCH, C.C., MILLER, E.L., ØRSKOV, E.R. and SMITH, R.H. (1977). In *Proceedings of the 2nd Symposium on Protein Metabolism and Nutrition*, p. 126. Ed. S. Tamminga. Wageningen; Centre Agric. Pub. Doc.

RUSSEL, J.B. and BALDWIN, R.L. (1979a). *Appl. Environ. Microbiol.*, **37**, 531

RUSSEL, J.B. and BALDWIN, R.L. (1979b). *Appl. Environ. Microbiol.*, **37**, 537

SALTER, D.N. and SMITH, R.H. (1977). *Br. J. Nutr.*, **38**, 207

SATTER, L.D. and ROFFLER, R.E. (1975). *J. Dairy Sci.*, **58**, 1219

SATTER, L.D. and ROFFLER, R.E. (1977). In *Recent Advances in Animal Nutrition*, p. 25. Eds W. Haresign and D. Lewis. London; Butterworths

SCHWARTING, G. and KAUFMANN, W. (1978). *Z. Tierphysiol. Tierernähr. Futter-mittelk.*, **40**, 6

SLYTER, L.L., SATTER, L.D. and DINIUS, D.A. (1979). *J. Amin. Sci.*, **48**, 906

SONDEREGGER, H. (1976). *Die Fruchtbarkeit des Rindes und ihre Beziehungen zu einigen Ernährungsfaktoren*, Diss. ETH5764, Zurich

TAMMINGA, S. (1978). In *Ruminant Digestion and Feed Evaluation*, p. 5. Eds D.F. Osbourn, D.E. Beever and D.J. Thomson. London; ARC

TAMMINGA, S. (1979). *Relation Between Different Carbohydrates and Microbial Synthesis of Protein, Kiel Group Seminar, Rep. No. 130*, Uppsala

TAMMINGA, S., VAN DER KOELEN, C.J. and VAN VUUREN, A.M. (1979). *Livestock Prod. Sci.*, **6**, 255

TAS, M.V., AXFORD, R.F.E. and EVANS, R.A. (1977). *Proc. Nutr. Soc.*, **36**, 76A

THOMAS, P.C. and ROOK, J.A.F. (1977). In *Recent Advances in Animal Nutrition*, p. 83. Eds W. Haresign and D. Lewis. London; Butterworths

TREACHER, R.J., STARK, A.J. and COLLIS, K.A. (1979). The health and performance of cows fed large amounts of urea. *J. Dairy Res.*, **46**, 1

VAN NEVEL, C.J. and DEMEYER, D.I. (1977). *Br. J. Nutr.*, **38**, 101

VERMA, D.N. and SINGH, U.B. (1977). *J. agric. Sci., Camb.*, **88**, 237

VIRTANEN, A.I., ETTALA, T. and MÄKINEN, S. (1972). In *Festskrift til Knut Breiren*, Oslo

VOIGT, J., PIATKOWSKI, B., KRAWIELITZKI, R. and TRAUTMANN, O.-K. (1977). *Arch. Tierernähr.*, **27**, 393

4

AMINO ACID REQUIREMENTS FOR LACTATION IN HIGH-YIELDING DAIRY COWS

J.D. OLDHAM
National Institute for Research in Dairying, Reading

The new systems for assessing protein feeding standards for ruminants (Burroughs, Nelson and Mertens, 1975; Kaufmann and Hagemeister, 1975; Satter and Roffler, 1975, 1977; Roy *et al.*, 1977; Verite, Journet and Jarrige, 1979) have, in theory at least, put this aspect of ruminant feeding on a more rigorous fundamental basis than ever before. The present proposals are by no means perfect and will need further development in both technical and conceptual aspects. Ørskov, and Wilson and Strachan, have discussed technical aspects elsewhere in this book.

Two conceptual developments stand out as likely possibilities. First, it would be desirable on theoretical grounds to move towards a dynamic description of the variables affecting nitrogen utilization. Baldwin, Koong and Ulyatt (1977) and Beever (1978) have already proposed dynamic models of ruminant metabolism which might form the basis of such development. The practical application of these apparently complex systems would not necessarily present particular difficulties. The pig growth model developed by Whittemore (1977) can be cited as a precedent.

The other likely conceptual development is that attention will turn to the possibility of feeding ruminants to meet particular amino acid requirements. It is this aspect which will be covered in detail here in relation to the high-yielding dairy cow.

The subject of amino acid requirements for ruminants has attracted attention repeatedly in the last decade. Sheep and growing cattle have been the most common targets (Hutton and Annison, 1972; Armstrong and Annison, 1973; Chalupa and Scott, 1976; Lewis and Mitchell, 1976; Hatfield, 1977), but recently the dairy cow has come under close scrutiny (Oldham, 1979; Smith, 1980; Tamminga and Oldham, 1980). The main conclusion has been that there is insufficient reliable information to allow a proper description of requirements for, or production responses to, individual amino acids. This is especially true for cows.

The reasons for considering the subject again here are three-fold. First, to examine the concept of amino acid requirements as it might apply to the high-yielding dairy cow; second, to consider methods for measuring requirements, and third, to assess the likelihood that requirements for individual amino acids might be met if they were known.

Because of the general lack of information of direct relevance to the high-yielding cow, much of what follows is speculative. Wherever possible, results are quoted from experiments with cows rather than 'model' ruminants and, in general, topics have been chosen to highlight issues which are germane to the future development of protein feeding systems (e.g. Roy *et al.*, 1977) as they might apply in practice to the high-yielding cow.

The concept of amino acid requirements for dairy cows

It is important in the first instance to clarify our objectives in considering amino acid requirements. For what purpose might we wish to manipulate amino acid status of the cow? The important alternatives are:

(1)   to minimize wastage of dietary nitrogen, protein or amino acid in relation to protein production, or
(2)   to maximize/optimize lactation performance.

The two are not the same, as it may be necessary to waste some dietary nitrogen or protein to achieve the objective of maximizing/optimizing lactation performance. The extent to which maximal differs from optimal performance will depend on economic considerations and is outside the scope of this review. It is, however, implied in the description of these two objectives that amino acids may have important parts to play in affecting production, which are separate from the obvious one of supplying substrates for protein synthesis. These deserve some consideration in moving towards a practically useful concept of amino acid requirements for dairy cows.

CONSIDERATIONS OF THE ROLES OF AMINO ACIDS

Specific amino acid requirements in the rumen

The only well-documented responses of rumen microbes to specific amino acids refer to methionine. *In vitro* methionine has been found to stimulate microbial growth (Gil *et al.*, 1973), to increase cellulose digestion (Gil, Shirley and Moore, 1973) and to increase microbial fatty acid synthesis (Patton, McCarthy and Griel, 1968, 1970). The effects on fatty acid synthesis appear to be specific to polar lipids (Patton, McCarthy and Griel, 1970).

Methionine hydroxy analogue (MHA; DL-α-hydroxy-γ-methyl mercapto-butyrate) produces the same effects (Gil *et al.*, 1973; Patton, McCarthy and Griel, 1968) but inorganic sulphur sources do not. Methionine and MHA therefore appear to act in the rumen by a specific mechanism which is not simply a reflection of their sulphur content.

The consequences of feeding 'free' DL methionine or MHA to milking cows are similar (*Table 4.1*). In general, milk fat output has been found to increase by about 10 per cent, with little or no change in milk protein output. It seems likely that responses in milk fat output are related to the effects of methionine and MHA on rumen microbial fatty acid synthesis, already mentioned.

Table 4.1 THE EFFECTS OF INCLUSION OF DL-METHIONINE (DL-Met) OR METHIONINE-HYDROXY ANALOGUE (MHA) IN THE DIET ON MILK PROTEIN AND FAT PRODUCTION BY COWS.

Treatment	Milk yield (kg/day)	Percentage increase with DL- Met or MHA treatment in milk: Protein (g/day)	Fat (g/day)	Reference
DL-Met	20	NM	16	Stoikov *et al.*, 1976
DL-Met	24	2	10	Remond *et al.*, 1971
MHA	23	NM	3	Chandler *et al.*, 1976
MHA	32	1	4	Clay and Satter, 1979
MHA	28	6	15	Bhargava *et al.*, 1977
MHA	32	NM	13	Polan, Chandler and Miller, 1970
MHA	30	NM	7	Griel *et al.*, 1968

NM = not measured.

Thus methionine and MHA can be used to manipulate milk fat production with equal effect. This is a desirable aim where payment for milk is related to its fat content and, in this context, it is appropriate to include in the concept of amino acid requirements, production responses which can be generated via amino acid effects at the rumen level.

Rumen microbial growth and digestion

Although amino acids are rapidly deaminated in the rumen (Chalupa, 1976; Scheifinger, Russell and Chalupa, 1976), under practical conditions the rumen

Table 4.2 THE PROPORTION OF RUMEN BACTERIAL OR PROTOZOAL NITROGEN (N) DERIVED FROM SOURCES OTHER THAN RUMEN AMMONIA-N. IN ALL EXPERIMENTS A ^{15}N-LABELLED AMMONIUM SALT WAS USED TO LABEL RUMEN NH_3-N. THE PROPORTION OF BACTERIAL OR PROTOZOAL N DERIVED FROM RUMEN NH_3-N (x) WAS CALCULATED AS THE TRANSFER COEFFICIENT OF ^{15}N LABELLING BETWEEN NH_3-N AND BACTERIAL OR PROTOZOAL N. THE VALUES IN THE TABLE WERE CALCULATED BY DIFFERENCE (i.e. $(1 - x) \times 100\%$).

Ration	Animal	Proportion of N derived from sources other than NH_3-N Bacteria	Protozoa	Reference
Hay	Sheep	50	63	Mathison and Milligan, 1971
Barley	Sheep	43	47	
Oat hulls + Solkafloc + N supplements	Lambs	34	48	Kempton, Nolan and Leng, 1979
Wheaten chaff + lucerne hay	Sheep	38	–	Nolan and Stachiw, 1979
Brome grass	Sheep	37–50	–	Kennedy and Milligan, 1978
Concentrates + hay (75:25)	Lactating cows	25	–	Oldham, Bruckental and Nissenbaum, 1980

microbial population derive 25—50 per cent of their nitrogen from sources other than ammonia *(Table 4.2)*. These are presumably intact amino acids or peptides which originate either directly from food proteins, from protein recycled to the rumen (largely salivary mucoproteins) or from turnover of bacterial and protozoal protein within the rumen. As the turnover time of bacterial and protozoal protein within the rumen is relatively short (Nolan, 1975; Singh *et al.*, 1977) compared with the duration of $^{15}NH_4^+$ labelling in at least some experiments quoted in *Table 4.2* (especially Mathison and Milligan, 1971; Kennedy and Milligan, 1978) it seems reasonable to suggest that the values quoted make partial allowance for microbial recycling. A substantial part of the microbial nitrogen (N) derived from sources other than rumen NH_3-N can therefore be attributed to food amino acids or peptides. Thus food amino acids supplied to rumen microbes can be used as such. But are they required for optimal microbial digestion?

A series of *in vitro* studies (Maeng *et al.*, 1976; Maeng and Baldwin, 1976a,b; *Figure 4.1*) suggests that microbial growth, both in absolute terms (microbial N/time) and in energetic efficiency (microbial N/mole VFA produced), is improved when the N substrate contains preformed amino acids. Hume (1970) made a similar suggestion from *in vivo* studies with sheep fed semipurified rations.

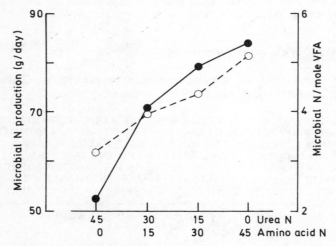

Figure 4.1 The effect of N substrate on rumen microbial growth in vitro. *Rumen liquor containing a mixed microbial population was incubated* in vitro *with isonitrogenous substrates containing different ratios of urea and a mixture of amino acids. Microbial N production (g/day; ●) and the energetic efficiency of microbial growth (g microbial N/mole VFA produced; ○) were calculated. Data of Maeng* et al. *(1976)*

Oldham *et al.* (1979a) found that ration digestibility increased when fish meal-N replaced urea-N in isonitrogenous rations. The differences in ration digestibility were too large to be explained by the difference in digestibility between fish meal and the barley it replaced and were sufficient to explain production responses (milk yield + liveweight change) to fish meal inclusion, entirely in terms of a change in energy status *(Table 4.3)*. It is therefore possible

Table 4.3 PERFORMANCE OF COWS FED ISONITROGENOUS RATIONS CONTAINING UREA (U), FISH MEAL (F) OR TWO INTERMEDIATE RATIOS OF UREA-N:FISH MEAL-N (2:1 UREA:FISH MEAL = UF; 1:2 UREA:FISH MEAL = FU). VALUES FOR MILK YIELD, LIVEWEIGHT CHANGE AND MILK COMPONENT YIELD ARE MEANS FOR WEEKS 2–12 OF LACTATION. ORGANIC MATTER (OM) DIGESTIBILITY WAS MEASURED IN DRY HEIFERS AT MAINTENANCE. PRODUCTIVE PROTEIN (MILK PROTEIN + PROTEIN CONTENT OF LIVEWEIGHT CHANGE) PER kg DOM INTAKE WAS CALCULATED FROM MEASURED OM INTAKES BY THE COWS AND DIGESTIBILITY OF OM IN THE HEIFERS. DATA OF OLDHAM ET AL., 1979a

Treatment	Milk yield (kg/d)	Yield (g/d) of: Fat	Protein	Liveweight change (g/d)	OM digestibility	Productive protein per kg digestible organic matter (DOM) intake	Mean rumen[a] NH_3 conc. (mM)
U	26.1	669	785	+370	0.73	77	18.0
UF	29.4	642	894	+530	0.78	83	15.8
FU	28.4	664	888	+180	0.80	74	17.0
F	28.1	797	848	+130	0.83	76	14.1
SE of difference between means	1.95	44.3	31.4	165	0.011		

a Mean of samples taken at 0600, 0900, 1200, 1500, 1800 and 2200 hrs from three rumen-fistulated cows fed rations at half level of intake of cows on production experiment.

that part of this effect was related to amino acid status of the rumen, because degradable N, in the form of ammonia, was unlikely to be limiting when urea was fed.

Van Horn *et al.* (1979) have similarly reported differences in digestibility of isonitrogenous rations containing soya bean meal or cotton seed meal. The higher digestibility of soya rations was again sufficient to account for milk yield differences between the two protein sources in terms of differences in energy status (*Figure 4.2*).

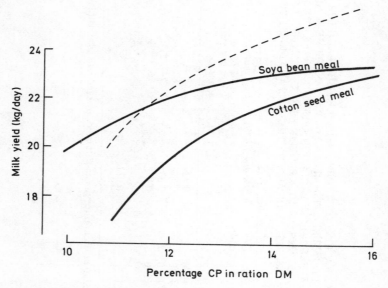

Figure 4.2 The effect of ration crude protein content (percentage CP in ration DM) on milk production by cows fed rations containing soya bean meal or cotton seed meal as the major protein supplement. The response relationships were derived by Van Horn et al. (1979) from a survey of published experiments. Note the diminishing return curve for both protein supplements – perhaps suggesting energy limitations. Van Horn et al. (1979) found cotton seed rations to be three percentage units lower in DM digestibility than soya bean rations. The broken line (– – –) is a revised response curve for cotton seed calculated on the assumption of equal DM digestibilities. The yield difference between the solid cotton seed line and the broken line therefore represents the reduction in milk yield due to the difference in ration DM digestibility between soya and cotton seed meal

These are important observations. Although they do not necessarily show that amino acids *per se* are needed in practice to optimize digestion in the rumen, they do show the potential importance of source of dietary protein in determining ration digestibility and hence M/D.

In the same vein one can point to the importance of level of crude protein (CP percentage) in affecting ration digestibility in cows. From a survey of experiments conducted in cows, Oldham (1980) concluded that, as a rough guide, an increase in ration digestibility of 0.01 units might be expected per unit increase in ration CP percentage for rations containing up to, and possibly more than, 16 per cent CP in dry matter. Thus, protein effects on digestibility might be expected in cows over the full range of ration CP percentage to be found in practice, whereas in sheep or growing cattle, protein effects on digestion might be maximal for rations containing no more than 12 per cent CP in DM (Balch and Campling, 1962). This difference may be due to the high level of food intake achieved by cows.

Increasing food intake has been found to decrease the proportion of dietary N degraded in the rumen and to decrease organic matter digestibility in the rumen of lactating cows (Tamminga, Van der Koelan and Van Vuuren, 1979). In other work (*Table 4.4*) it has been found that feeding rations containing a large

Table 4.4 RUMEN MICROBIAL SYNTHESIS, ENERGY DIGESTION IN THE RUMEN AND RUMEN AMMONIA CONCENTRATIONS IN LACTATING COWS FED RATIONS CONTAINING ROLLED BARLEY OR GROUND MAIZE AS THE MAJOR CEREAL OF THE CONCENTRATES. CONCENTRATES AND HAY WERE FED IN THE RATIOS (CONCENTRATES:HAY) 90:10 OR 60:40. DATA OF OLDHAM *ET AL.*, 1979b; SUTTON, OLDHAM AND HART, 1980, AND UNPUBLISHED

| *Digestion factors* | Concentrates:hay ratio and major cereal | | | |
| | 60:40 | | 90:10 | |
	Barley	*Maize*	*Barley*	*Maize*
N intake (g/d)	286	291	269	281
DE (digestible energy) intake (MJ/d)	157	155	161	149
Microbial N synthesis (g/d) (RNA as marker)	237	173	226	104
Microbial N synthesis (g/kg OM apparently digested in the rumen)	37.1	27.9	35.8	19.7
Proportion of DE intake apparently digested in the rumen	0.74	0.70	0.72	0.63
Rumen NH_3 (mM/ℓ) (mean of 12 determinations at 2-hourly intervals)	5.6	6.2	5.2	7.4

proportion of maize substantially reduces energy digestion in the rumen and the energetic efficiency of microbial growth (microbial N/kg organic matter (OM) apparently fermented in the rumen). According to current hypotheses (Roffler and Satter, 1975; Okorie, Buttery and Lewis, 1977) rumen ammonia concentration would not have been a limiting factor; some other factor therefore appears to have been limiting, possibly a limited supply of preformed amino acids or peptides.

An hypothesis to be considered is that, at high levels of food intake, the proportion of dietary N fermented in the rumen is relatively low and that the supply of degraded N can be insufficient, or in the wrong form, or produced at a rate inappropriately matched to the rate of energy release (Johnson, 1976; Oldham *et al.*, 1977), to maintain optimal rumen digestion at ration CP percentage levels which might otherwise be considered adequate. There are insufficient data to evaluate this hypothesis properly at present.

Food intake

In non-ruminant species amino acid status, especially amino acid balance, can have substantial effects on food intake (Rogers, 1976). Such effects on intake of amino acid supply to the tissues are not well documented in ruminants, but Egan (1980) has shown they may exist. In addition protein, or amino acid, effects on digestibility (above) may have consequent effects on intake (Bines, 1979).

In a recent experiment, Clay and Satter (1979) increased protein intake of cows by replacing maize grain with soya bean meal. The effect was to increase milk production almost linearly (*Figure 4.3*) but, at the same time, food intake increased so that the milk production response could be accounted for completely by a change in energy status.

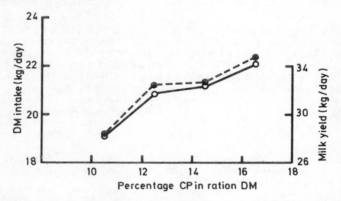

Figure 4.3 The effect of increasing ration crude protein conent on milk yield (●) and food intake (○) in cows. Data from Clay and Satter (1979)

Through effects on digestion, or by mechanisms at tissue level, it may therefore be possible to manipulate food intake and energy status. In view of the effects of plane of nutrition, especially during early lactation, on lactation performance (Broster, 1974) this aspect of protein or amino acid feeding could have a dominant role.

Endocrine effects

Amino acid supply to the intestines or to the tissues can affect endocrine status. In non-ruminants insulin, glucagon, growth hormone (GH) and various gut hormone secretions are all responsive to amino acids (Colwell, Zuckerman and Berger, 1970; Blackard and Andrews, 1974; Gerich, Charles and Grodsky, 1976; Ungar, 1977; Bloom, 1978)

There is less extensive information for ruminants. However, it has been shown (*Table 4.5*) that abomasal infusion of casein into goats, or feeding formaldehyde-treated casein to cows (it is assumed that formaldehyde treatment increases protein supply to the intestines) can increase circulating levels of GH. This effect has not always been found (Gow *et al.*, 1979), but it would appear from *Table 4.5* that increased protein supply to the intestines of lactating goats or cows may at least sometimes be associated with changes in blood GH concentrations.

It is not clear whether these changes are involved in causing milk yield responses to extra protein (Clark, 1975) or whether they occur as a consequence of a change in performance. However, in view of the relationship between blood GH concentration and milk yield (Hart, Bines and Morant, 1979) and the effects

Table 4.5 EFFECT OF INCREASING PROTEIN SUPPLY TO THE INTESTINES ON CONCENTRATION OF GROWTH HORMONE IN JUGULAR VENOUS PLASMA

Animal and treatment	Growth hormone concentration (ng/ml)	Source
Goats: Infusion into abomasum		
saline	9.1	Oldham, Hart and Bines, 1978
casein	14.0	
Infusion into abomasum		
saline	8.2	Gow *et al.*, 1979
casein	5.3	
Cows: Feeding isonitrogenous diets containing		
casein	3.0	Oldham, Hart and Bines (unpublished)
formaldehyde-treated casein	5.9	

of injection of GH on milk yield (Machlin, 1973; Bines, Hart and Morant, 1980), nitrogen retention (GH decreases urinary N and increases milk protein N output; Bines, Hart and Morant, 1980) and urea production (GH decreases urea production, presumably by decreasing amino acid oxidation; Hart, Bines and Morant, 1979) in cows, these effects may be important in determining production responses to change in amino acid supply to the tissues.

It is interesting that GH can respond not only to a change in amino acid status (*Table 4.5*), but that it may also play a part in directing amino acid metabolism towards milk protein output or oxidation (Bines, Hart and Morant, 1980; Hart, Bines and Morant, 1980).

Liver effects

Some time ago, McCarthy, Porter and Griel (1968) put forward the hypothesis that methionine may have specific effects on lipoprotein metabolism in the liver. Methionine supply may limit either apoprotein synthesis or phospholipid synthesis – the latter through its role as methyl donor in phosphatidylcholine synthesis. In either case, methionine supply may limit lipoprotein synthesis in the liver and hence lipid transport from the liver. This could, therefore, be a factor relevant to partition of fat between body tissue and milk.

It has been argued (*Chapter 2*) that protein supply to the tissues can affect the extent to which cows go into negative energy balance early in lactation. Amino acid effects on endocrine status or liver lipid metabolism may be important in this regard. The practical evidence is, however, confusing. In some experiments, low protein rations have been found to increase body weight loss early in lactation (Remond and Journet, 1978; Oldham *et al.*, 1979b), while in others, high protein rations have had this effect (Gordon and Forbes, 1970; Robinson *et al.*, 1974). The issue is complicated even further as there appears to be an interaction between energy density of the ration (forage:concentrate ratio) and protein feeding which influences the magnitude of this protein or amino acid effect (*see Chapter 2*).

The main point to note is that yet another consideration in assessing amino acid requirements is that it may be possible at some time in the future to use protein or amino acids to manipulate energy partition in cows.

In the mammary gland

Excellent reviews of amino acid metabolism in the mammary gland have been published by Mepham (1976, 1979) and Clark *et al.* (1977). *Figure 4.4* is an attempt to summarize the major points with regard to essential amino acid metabolism within the gland.

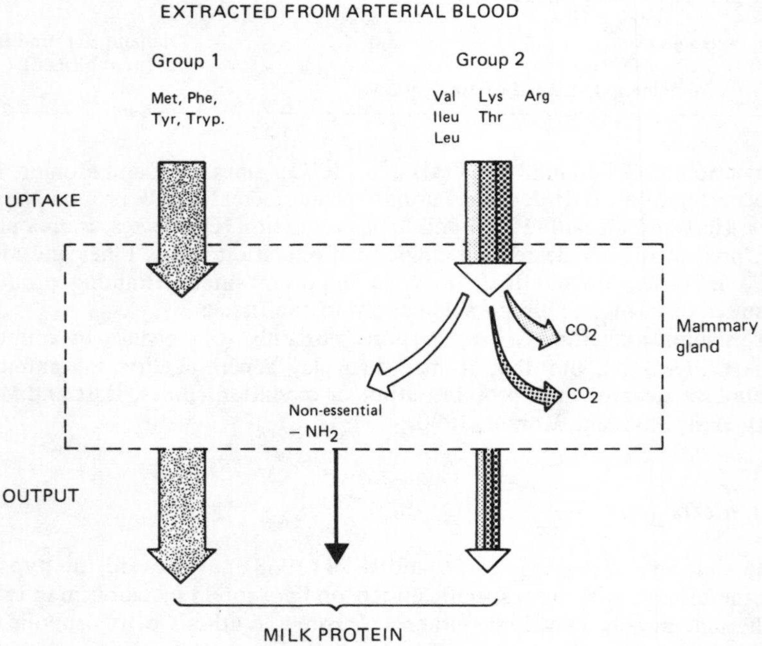

EXTRACTED FROM ARTERIAL BLOOD

Group 1

Met, Phe,
Tyr, Tryp.

Group 2

Val   Lys   Arg
Ileu   Thr
Leu

UPTAKE

CO_2

Mammary
gland

Non-essential
– NH_2

CO_2

OUTPUT

MILK PROTEIN

Figure 4.4 A simplified representation of essential amino acid (EAA) metabolism within the mammary gland. The EAA shown are all extracted from arterial blood with different efficiencies. See text and Mepham (1976; 1979) for more details

Amino acids which pass to the mammary gland in arterial blood are extracted into the gland with varying efficiencies. One criterion which has been applied to identify potentially limiting amino acids at the mammary gland is to say that those amino acids which are in shortest supply relative to demand (and hence potentially limiting) will be extracted most efficiently from arterial blood supply to the gland. On this basis, methionine, phenylalanine, leucine and threonine are the most limiting amino acids.

A second and similar criterion is that those amino acids in shortest supply relative to demand (and hence potentially limiting) will undergo minimal metabolism within the gland. On this basis methionine, phenylalanine, tyrosine and tryptophan would be potentially limiting. These four amino acids appear to undergo no net metabolism within the gland – the amounts extracted from blood appear quantitatively in protein secreted in milk.

Of the other essential amino acids, valine, leucine and isoleucine are partly oxidized, with lysine and threonine being oxidized to a lesser extent. Much of the carbon of arginine appears in proline in secreted milk protein. The amino groups from this set of amino acids can be used for non-essential amino acid synthesis in the gland.

At the level of the mammary gland it would appear that methionine and phenylalanine are used most efficiently for milk protein synthesis. This suggests that they are potentially limiting for production, but does not prove it.

The concept

From the foregoing it is clear that if we are to move towards a rigorous and practically useful concept of amino acid requirements for the high-yielding dairy cow a number of complex issues must be integrated. These embrace possible protein, or amino acid, effects on digestion, food intake and energy partition. There is, therefore, scope for development from the present proposals on protein requirements (which allow, in theory, prediction of protein responses in animals of *defined energy status* (*see* Roy *et al.*, 1977)) to use protein feeding to *manipulate energy status.*

In addition, there is justification for investigating the specific role of methionine as it affects milk fat, and there is also the question of how best to meet requirements for protein synthesis within the mammary gland.

The requirement for amino acid(s) is therefore best defined as the minimum amount needed to establish a particular level of lactation performance. To be rigorous, the level of performance must be defined in terms of food (metabolizable energy; ME) intake, energy partition between tissue and milk, milk composition and time. It is important to include time, because lactation is a cyclical process in which performance at any one time can exert substantial effects on subsequent events.

Application of this concept in practice is limited by lack of quantitative data to describe relationships between amino acid/protein status and intake or energy partition. The approaches which might be taken to quantify requirements can, however, be described.

Measurement of amino acid requirements

There are, classically, two ways of measuring amino acid requirements:

(1)   the empirical, 'dose-response' method or
(2)   the causal or 'factorial' method.

THE DOSE-RESPONSE APPROACH

In theory, the 'dose' could be given either in an appropriate form in the food to identify an intake requirement, or into the intestines to identify a duodenal requirement.

Responses might be measured in terms of production (milk yield, milk protein yield, N retention) or a change in a metabolic parameter (production or concentration of urea or amino acids in blood, amino acid oxidation) but a series of doses is needed to identify a requirement. It has been more usual, in experiments with cows, to use only one or two dose levels: no clear identification of requirements by this method is possible, therefore. The magnitude of responses which have been found should, however, give an indication of the potential for manipulating lactation yields by varying protein inputs.

Protein.   Numerous studies have reported milk yield responses to abomasal infusions of casein. Clark (1975) reviewed many of these and *Table 4.6* provides an updated summary of the results. Apart from the results of Ørskov, Grubb and Kay (1977), the conclusion to be drawn is that the average response to be expected from abomasal infusion of casein is of the order of 10–15 per cent in milk protein yield and rather less in milk yield (5–10 per cent). No clear dose response is apparent and the level of CP in the basal rations varied from 11 to

Table 4.6 THE RESPONSE OF DAIRY COWS TO INFUSION OF CASEIN INTO THE ABOMASUM. RESPONSE IS GIVEN AS A PERCENTAGE INCREASE OVER CONTROL VALUES

Stage of lactation	Milk yield	Casein dose (g/day)	Percentage response in: Milk output	Milk protein output	Source
Mid	22 (Range 13–33)	170– 1200	Mean 7 (Range −6 to +22)	Mean 12 (Range −3 to +31)	Clark, 1975
Mid	30	450	9	13	Clark *et al.*, 1977
Early	20	250–750	18–27	34–60	Ørskov, Grubb and Kay, 1977
Early	23	240–460	5	15	König, Oldham and Parker (unpublished)

17 per cent with apparently little effect. This is misleading, however, as the most relevant parameter to measure would have been amino acid supply to the intestines on the basal ration. This has never been measured in any experiment where abomasal casein infusions have been given to cows, so no estimate of total protein, or amino acid supply, is available against which to compare measured response. No estimate of dose response is therefore possible.

The experiment of Ørskov, Grubb and Kay (1977) stands out in terms of the magnitude of the response achieved. The cows in that experiment were deliberately underfed in order to be in negative energy balance before the infusions started. Casein infusion then increased calculated negative energy balance. It seems likely that this experiment points to an important underlying mechanism, although the nature of that mechanism has yet to be identified. In simple terms, it is reasonable to expect that, in the animal mobilizing energy-yielding nutrients but little protein, more protein must be absorbed from the intestines to maintain the right ratio of protein:energy-yielding nutrient for production. This would not, however, explain why extra absorbed protein apparently increased negative energy balance. This effect could be related to the casein effects on GH secretion with consequent effects on lipolysis (Jagannadha and Ramachandran, 1977), or methionine effects on liver lipid transport, previously mentioned. Because the responses in energy balance were calculated and not measured, it is possible that part of the increase in milk nutrient output resulted from increased efficiency of ME utilization (k_ϱ) when casein was infused. This is contentious (Schneider, 1980) although Moe and Tyrell (1977) have provided some supporting evidence.

The major point to note from all the casein infusion experiments is that production responses have usually been achieved, but they cannot be quantified in dose-response terms.

Amino acids. Some attention has been focused on methionine as being, potentially, a first-limiting amino acid at the mammary gland (*see above*). However, on the few occasions when methionine has been infused intravenously into cows, production responses have been small or non-existent (Teichman, Caruolo and Mochrie, 1969; Fisher, 1969, 1972; Erfle and Fisher, 1977).

Abomasal infusion of methionine has produced either no response (Schwab, Satter and Clay, 1976; Oldham, unpublished data) or only a small response (Rogers and McLeay, 1977). The latter was, however, in cows yielding only 5–6 kg/day.

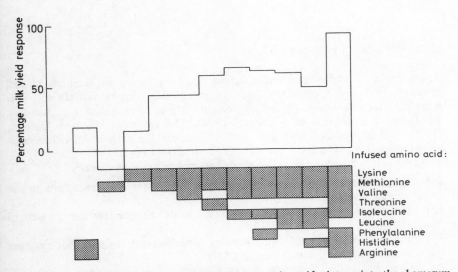

Figure 4.5 Milk yield response to infusion of various amino acid mixtures into the abomasum of cows. The lower half of the diagram shows the amino acid infused (hatched areas). Milk yield response is shown in the top half as a percentage of the response achieved in the same cows with an infusion of casein or a mixture of all essential amino acids in the same amounts as found in casein. Data of Schwab, Satter and Clay (1976)

Schwab, Satter and Clay, 1976 (*Figure 4.5*) have provided the most comprehensive description of production responses to abomasal supplements of amino acids. They concluded that lysine was perhaps first-limiting under their conditions but that it was probably most appropriate to consider a group of amino acids as being closely co-limiting. As can be seen from *Figure 4.5*, responses to amino acids were always much smaller than responses to casein (*see also Table 4.6*). Only one dose level of each amino acid was used and basal supply of amino acids to the abomasum was not measured. Thus no estimate of requirement can be calculated. It was perhaps not surprising that lysine was probably first-limiting as the ration used was largely based on maize products, which is likely to reduce abomasal lysine proportions (*see p. 73 and Table 4.13*).

The abomasal infusion approach has therefore given few clues regarding the absolute requirements for individual amino acids. Rather, it has demonstrated that, under certain circumstances, milk protein output can be increased by giving extra protein per abomasum. Such experiments have never been linked directly with measurements of amino acid flow into the abomasum, so that milk production responses could be compared with total supply of various essential amino acids (EAA) to the intestines. This is a fundamental flaw in all such experimental work conducted so far with dairy cows and is undoubtedly a contributory factor to the problems which still surround interpretation of the data.

The type of experiment necessary to clarify the issues would entail measurements of duodenal amino acid flow and milk nutrient output in cows of defined energy status and supplemented with graded levels of proteins, amino acid mixtures or individual EAA. Numerous such estimates would be needed to allow comprehensive interpretation of responses to amino acid supplementation. As the current lack of data is at least partly due to the great difficulty and cost of achieving even one estimate, it is unlikely that very many will appear in the future.

FACTORIAL CALCULATIONS

An estimate of amino acid requirements can be achieved by factorial means, provided that the appropriate steps in metabolism can be quantified. This approach has been used previously for growing cattle (Hutton and Annison, 1972) and for dairy cows (Oldham, 1979). The approach taken by Oldham (1979) will be outlined here and used to calculate the daily duodenal requirements for individual amino acids throughout a lactation cycle.

Three pieces of information are needed to make the calculations:

(1) net daily deposition or secretion of protein, plus maintenance (productive protein + maintenance; P + M);
(2) the efficiency of absorption of amino acids which enter the duodenum (DAA);
(3) the net efficiency of utilization of absorbed amino acids for product formation plus maintenance (EAAU).

Daily requirement is then calculated as:

$$\frac{P + M}{DAA \times EAAU}$$

The units to be used will be mM amino acid required per MJ ME intake per day to provide a link with energy status.

Productive protein output

Some definition of the 'high-yielding' dairy cow is needed at this point. A reasonable definition of the high-yielder is a cow capable of yielding more than 6000 ℓ milk per lactation, or more than 30 ℓ/day at 'peak' production. This definition would apply to the top third of cows in National Milk Records (Milk Marketing Board, 1978).

For the calculations which follow, a composite picture has been constructed for a cow yielding 35 kg milk/day at peak production (*Figure 4.6*). (Sources of data for *Figure 4.6* were Agricultural Research Council, 1965; Broster, Broster and Smith, 1969; Broster *et al.*, 1975; Johnson, 1977; Broster, Sutton and Bines, 1979; Oldham *et al.*, 1979b).

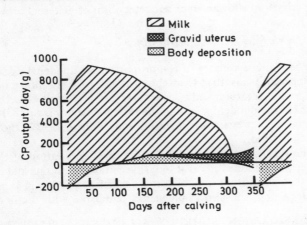

Figure 4.6 Net protein synthesis (g/day) throughout a lactation cycle by a 550 kg Friesian cow with a peak daily milk yield of 35 kg. Lactation length and calving interval were assumed to be 300 and 365 days respectively. Components of net daily synthesis appearing in milk, maternal tissue and gravid uterus are shown separately. See text for sources of data

There are a number of points to note. First, it is important to look on lactation as a cyclical process. Within the cycle, protein deposition in milk, the gravid uterus and in maternal tissue must all be accounted for at different times.

Second, it may be necessary to allow for net catabolism ('mobilization') of maternal protein in late pregnancy to support the fetus (Naismith and Morgan, 1976) or in early lactation to support milk production. This latter point is an unresolved hypothesis. It is interesting to speculate on the possibility that mechanisms established in late pregnancy to allow net catabolism of maternal protein to occur could predispose the cow to 'lose' more body protein early in lactation when demands for protein are high. While there is no doubt that, under conditions of dire protein stress, cows will go into negative nitrogen balance (Paquay, De Baere and Lousse, 1972; Botts, Hemken and Bull, 1978), direct evidence that this happens early in lactation is meagre. Indirect techniques have suggested that maternal protein mass can fall after parturition (Belyea *et al.*, 1978). Body composition data from ewes, on the other hand, has shown that maternal protein mass can be maintained even when liveweight loss is substantial (Cowan *et al.*, 1979).

For the purpose of constructing *Figure 4.6,* it was assumed that protein accounted for 150 g/kg liveweight change (gain or loss).

The third point is also relevant to the 'mobilization' discussion. It concerns the changes in productive output which occur around parturition. In the example (*Figure 4.6*) the calculated daily rate of protein output increases from 160 g/day immediately before parturition, to 800 and 1050 g protein/day at days 10 and 30 *post partum* respectively. The way in which the cow might adapt to this major increase in protein demand when her capacity to eat is limited (Bines, 1979) will be assessed below.

Lastly, note the dominance of milk protein output in *Figure 4.6*. In early lactation, when there is the greatest possibility that protein could limit performance, the main considerations are milk protein output and maintenance requirements, with perhaps an allowance for net catabolism of maternal protein.

Absorption of amino acids from the intestines

Some of the available estimates of the proportion of duodenal essential amino acid supply apparently absorbed from the small intestine are shown in *Table 4.7*. In all instances the measurements were made using animals fitted with permanent cannulas in the duodenum and in the terminal ileum. Despite the potential errors of using such preparations (Sutton and Oldham, 1977) the agreement between values is good.

There is, however, reason to doubt the universal application of these values, none of which was obtained in early lactation. Studies with rats and ewes (*Table 4.8*) suggest that absorption may be a more efficient process in lactation compared with pregnancy, and also in pregnancy compared with the non-pregnant,

Table 4.8 NET ABSORPTION FROM THE SMALL INTESTINE OF LEUCINE (RAT), NITROGEN (EWE) OR NON-AMMONIA N (NAN; EWE) IN NON-PREGNANT NON-LACTATING (NPNL), PREGNANT OR LACTATING FEMALES. VALUES RELATE TO NPNL AS 100

Compound	Animal	NPNL	Pregnant	Lactating	Source
Leucine	Rat	100	107–111	122–142	Cripps and Williams, 1975
Abomasal N	Ewe	100	118	131	Thompson, Robinson and McHattie, 1978
Abomasal NAN	Ewe	100	106	103	Weston, 1979

non-lactating state (Cripps and Williams, 1975; Thompson, Robinson and McHattie, 1978; Weston, 1979). There are no comparable data for cows, but it will be important to get this information in the near future. In particular, it will be necessary to find out whether absorption in early lactation is higher than in mid or late lactation. Taking account of the differences in lactation length (per reproductive cycle) in rats and ewes compared with cows, the results in *Table 4.8* perhaps suggest that a higher value for DAA in early lactation might be expected.

Table 4.7 THE PROPORTION OF AMINO ACIDS ENTERING THE SMALL INTESTINE WHICH ARE ABSORBED BETWEEN THE DUODENUM AND THE TERMINAL ILEUM (D_{AA})

Methionine	Lysine	Threonine	Amino acid Isoleucine	Leucine	Valine	Phenyl-alanine	Animal	Source
0.80	0.74	0.70	0.76	0.76	0.72	0.67	Sheep	Coelho da Silva et al. (1972a)
0.84	0.72	0.73	0.76	0.76	0.76	0.60	Sheep	Coelho da Silva et al. (1972b)
0.76	0.70	0.71	0.66	0.69	0.68	0.71	Sheep	Tagari and Bergman (1978)
0.65	0.75	0.67	0.67	0.70	0.67	0.68	Cow	Tamminga, 1973
0.80	0.80	0.82	0.83	0.86	0.83	0.85	Cow	Tamminga, 1975

Efficiency of utilization of absorbed amino acids

Values for this efficiency are valid only when determined under protein-limiting conditions. Unfortunately this condition did not always hold for the few available estimates. The methods which have been used to measure it are, however, of interest as these are likely to be the ones used in future to refine current values.

By definition, this efficiency is the proportion of the daily amount of amino acid absorbed from the intestines, which appears as net daily productive protein

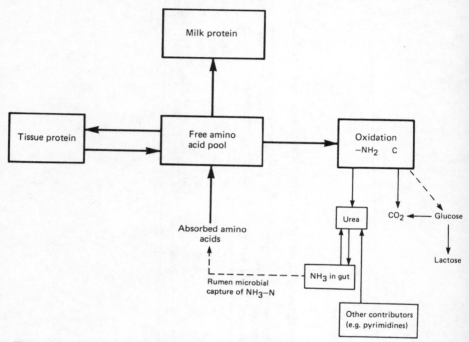

Figure 4.7 A simplified diagram of the major pathways of amino acid metabolism in lactating cows. See text for details. For a comprehensive picture of N transactions in ruminants see Nolan (1975). See Picou and Taylor-Roberts (1967) for an interesting analogous description of net amino acid metabolism in the non-ruminant. Although the diagram is not to scale as a quantitative picture of the fate of absorbed amino acids, nevertheless net glucose synthesis from amino acid −C is likely to be very small (see Lindsay, 1976; Bruckental, Oldham and Sutton, 1980) and recent evidence suggests that the recapture of 'recycled' N into rumen microbial N may be relatively small (Norton, Moran and Nolan, 1979; Kennedy, 1980). These routes are shown by dotted lines

output. Its derivation can be readily seen by reference to *Figure 4.7* which is a grossly simplified picture of the main routes of amino acid use by cows. On a net daily basis, amino acid input to the tissues (free amino acid pool) is used either productively (net tissue protein accretion or milk protein secretion) or it is oxidized. The end-products of amino acid oxidation are largely CO_2 or urea. Thus, with reference to *Figure 4.7*:

> absorbed protein + catabolized tissue protein =
> milk protein + synthesis of tissue protein + oxidation product;

but net tissue protein accretion =
    synthesis of tissue protein − catabolized tissue protein;
so absorbed protein =
    milk protein + net tissue protein accretion + oxidation product.

Reference to *Figure 4.6* will show (1) that net tissue protein accretion is zero or negative in early lactation − which is probably the period of greatest interest, and (2) that milk protein output is large compared with possible contributions from labile reserves (if these are used, *see p. 63*). In practice it is therefore reasonably justified to simplify the calculation to:

absorbed protein = milk protein + oxidation product.

The efficiency of utilization of amino acid (EAAU) or of protein (EPU, Oldham, 1978) is then calculated as:

$$\frac{\text{milk amino acid or protein}}{\text{milk amino acid or protein + oxidation product}}$$

The two techniques which have been used to measure EAAU and EPU therefore involve measurements of ^{14}C-amino acid oxidation to $^{14}CO_2$ or urea-N production from amino acid N catabolism.

Oxidation of ^{14}C-amino acids. In practice, the flux of amino acid through venous or arterial blood is measured. Transfer of ^{14}C (^{13}C could also be used) into $^{14}CO_2$ gives the proportion of flux which is oxidized (O). Amino acid output in milk (P) is also calculated as a proportion of flux. So,

$$EAAU = \frac{P}{P + O}$$

In experimental terms, the largest source of error is contained in the measurement of transfer of amino acid ^{14}C into $^{14}CO_2$. This error is reduced to some extent in the final calculation, as P is likely to be large relative to O. A greater source of error lies in the difficulty of making such measurements for conditions in which particular amino acids are known to limit production. EAAU for a particular amino acid will be maximal, and O minimal, when that amino acid is limiting for production. Because of this, ^{14}C-amino acid oxidation can be used to identify requirements in dose-response experiments (*see* Lewis and Mitchell, 1976). Low (1981) has suggested that EAAU can approach 100 per cent for lysine when lysine limits growth in pigs. In growing calves, EAAU values for methionine (($1-^{14}$C) methionine oxidation) have been found to be very high (82 per cent) when methionine appeared to limit growth (Mathers and Miller, 1979).

Under such limiting conditions, oxidation represents the inevitable oxidation of a particular amino acid under the prevailing nutritional and physiological conditions and represents the minimal non-productive metabolism of that amino acid − in other words, the maintenance requirement.

If a situation could be achieved in which the balance and amount of amino acids absorbed from the gut was ideal (*see* Cole, 1979) for a particular level of production, i.e. in relation to energy status, amino acid oxidation would be a

Table 4.9 EFFICIENCY OF TRANSFER OF AMINO ACIDS INTO PRODUCT. TWO EFFICIENCIES ARE RECORDED – THE NET CONVERSION INTO PRODUCTIVE N[a] OF AMINO ACIDS ENTERING THE INTESTINES OF COWS, OR THE EFFICIENCY OF UTILIZATION OF ABSORBED AMINO ACIDS FOR PRODUCTIVE N FORMATION (EFFICIENCY OF PROTEIN UTILIZATION, EPU)

Source	Milk yield (kg/day)	Weeks after calving	Net conversion of duodenal amino acids to product[a]	EPU†	Diet	Technique
Oldham, Sutton and McAllan, 1979	15	>14	0.42	0.6+	40% hay + barley concentrates	Duodenal flow and feeding trial.
	16	>14	0.47	0.67+	40% hay + maize concentrates	
	19	>14	0.49	0.7+	10% hay + barley concentrates	
	16	>14	0.56	0.8+	10% hay + maize concentrates	
Bruckental, Oldham and Sutton, 1980	27	2	—	0.71	25% hay + 75% barley concentrates	Amino acid oxidation (urea production)
	31	4	—	0.72		
	28	9	—	0.61		
Calculated by Oldham (1980) from various reports by Black and Colleagues	<15	>20	—	Leucine 0.84	Alfalfa hay plus concentrates (approx. 50:50)	^{14}C amino acid oxidation
	<15	>20	—	Phenylalanine 0.64		
	<15	>20	—	Threonine 0.64		
	<15	>20	—	Isoleucine 0.61		
Ørskov, Grubb and Kay, 1977	17–20	2–9	0.57	0.82+	Mixed diet (~65% concentrates)	Incremental response to abomasal protein
Robinson et al., 1979	(Ewes)	1–4	0.51	0.73+	50:50 hay:rolled barley concentrates	Incremental response to abomasal protein

a Productive N = milk N + N content of liveweight change.
+ Calculated from net conversion assuming 0.7 of duodenal amino acids are absorbed from the intestines.
† Efficiency of protein utilization.

true reflection of maintenance needs. Outside such ideal conditions, oxidation reflects maintenance needs combined with extra oxidation caused by an excess and/or an imbalance in the supply of amino acids for product formation. Because clear statements on limiting amino acids for milk production by cows are difficult to make at present, any values for EAAU obtained by this method should be considered as minimum estimates.

Values for EAAU can be calculated from the published data of Black, 1968; Black *et al.*, 1970 and Egan and Black, 1968 (*see* Oldham, 1979 for more detail). These values are included in *Table 4.9*. They are the only ones available for individual amino acids in cows, but milk yields were low (<15 ℓ/day) and it is unlikely that production was protein-limited.

Urea production as a measure of amino acid oxidation. This method has been used and discussed by Bruckental, Oldham and Sutton (1980). In addition to the problems already mentioned there are some additional considerations. The main one is to identify urea production from amino acid catabolism, because a substantial proportion of urea production is from other nitrogen sources, largely ammonia produced in the gut (Nolan, 1975). This is a major drawback but, as with estimates of amino acid -C transfer to CO_2, the error associated with values for the proportion of urea production derived from amino acid-N are reduced somewhat in the final calculation because of the relative magnitude of amino acid N in produce or oxidized form. The calculation in this case is:

$$\frac{\text{amino acid N in milk}}{\text{amino acid N in milk } + \text{ Urea-N from amino acid N}} = \text{EPU}$$

The efficiency term in this case (EPU) refers to the net efficiency of utilization of amino acid N as a whole. It is consequently more relevant to current systems of protein evaluation (e.g. Roy *et al.*, 1977) than is EAAU, as all current systems describe total N transfers, not individual amino acids.

Other methods. Values for the transfer of amino acids entering the intestines into 'productive' protein have been obtained by three other methods. Such values are, of course, combinations of DAA and EPU (EAAU). The methods used were: (1) measurement of duodenal amino acid supply in intestinally cannulated cows and estimation of amino acid output in milk or retention in tissue in intact cows fed the same rations (Oldham, Sutton and McAllan, 1979); (2) measurement of incremental response in milk protein output to controlled addition of protein (casein) into the abomasum in cows (Ørskov, Grubb and Kay, 1977); (3) measurement of incremental responses in milk protein output to dietary induced increments of abomasal amino acid supply in ewes (Robinson *et al.*, (1979).

The results of all these studies are not constant and they appear to be a little higher for measurements in early, rather than in mid lactation (*Table 4.9*). This may simply reflect a closer approximation to protein-limiting conditions in the early lactation studies than the others. The observation is, however, relevant to the choice of value to be used in the calculation of requirements.

GLUCONEOGENESIS FROM AMINO ACIDS IN HIGH-YIELDING COWS

An interesting consequence of knowing values for EPU is that the probable contribution of amino acid carbon to net glucose synthesis (gluconeogenesis) can be assessed. This has been done by Oldham (1978) and Bruckental, Oldham and Sutton (1980) with the conclusion that, in the high-yielding cow, where both glucose and amino acids are in short supply relative to demand, the net contribution of amino acids to glucose requirements is very small indeed (perhaps 1–2 per cent of glucose need). Thus one aspect of amino acid requirements which has little quantitative importance in the high-yielder is a requirement for net glucose synthesis. This does not, however, mean that non-essential amino acids may not have an important part to play in sparing glucose (*see* Lindsay, 1979).

SPECULATIVE WORKING VALUES FOR DAA AND EAAU

On the basis of available evidence, *Table 4.10* has been produced to suggest reasonable working values for DAA and EAAU for three stages of lactation.

Table 4.10 FACTORS DESCRIBING THE APPARENT ABSORPTION OF EAA FROM THE SMALL INTESTINE (DAA) AND THE EFFICIENCY OF USE OF ABSORBED AMINO ACIDS (EAAU) IN COWS IN DIFFERENT PHYSIOLOGICAL STATES

Amino acid	DAA			EAAU		
	Dry	Late pregnancy and mid to late lactation	Very early lactation	Dry	Late pregnancy and mid to late lactation	Very early lactation
Threonine	0.66	0.73	0.80	0.59	0.64	0.74
Valine	0.67	0.74	0.81	0.60	0.65	0.75
Methionine	0.69	0.78	0.86	0.60	0.65	0.75
Isoleucine	0.67	0.74	0.81	0.56	0.61	0.70
Leucine	0.68	0.75	0.82	0.78	0.84	0.95
Phenylalanine	0.63	0.70	0.77	0.59	0.64	0.74
Lysine	0.68	0.75	0.82	0.60	0.65	0.75

These values can be used to calculate duodenal amino acid requirements (mM/day/MJ ME intake) provided that the net rate of amino acid secretion in milk or deposition in tissue is known. This is readily calculated from net rate of protein output (*Figure 4.5*) and the amino acid content of milk protein (Lindqvist, 1968; Witney *et al.*, 1976) or of bovine carcase (Williams, 1978).

CALCULATED REQUIREMENTS IN RELATION TO POTENTIAL
AMINO ACID SUPPLY

Figure 4.8 shows the results of such calculations for the first 160 days of lactation. The requirements have been calculated using either mid lactation or

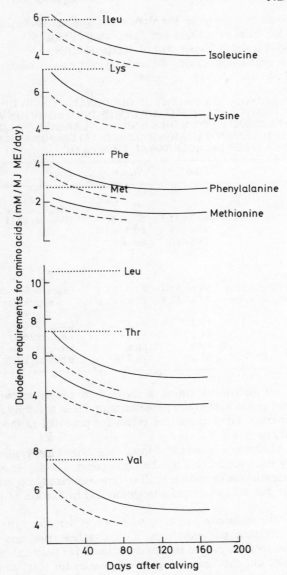

Figure 4.8 Duodenal requirement (mM/MJ ME intake/day) for isoleucine, lysine, phenylalanine, methionine, leucine, valine and threonine during the first 160 d of lactation, calculated by a factorial method (see text and Oldham, 1979 for details). · · · · · , *an estimate of duodenal supply of each amino acid, calculated as described in the text.* ————, *the calculated requirements assuming increased efficiencies of intestinal absorption and utilization during early lactation*

early lactation values for DAA and EAAU to show the effect of the (probable) higher efficiencies early in lactation.

The numerical values have little meaning unless they can be compared with potential amino acid supply. This can be estimated taking account of the following:

(1) non-ammonia N supply to the duodenum appears to be limited at 3 g NAN/MJ ME intake (Oldham and Tamminga, 1980);
(2) amino acid N is about 70 per cent of duodenal NAN;
(3) the amino acid composition of duodenal contents is relatively constant (*see p. 73* and *Table 4.11*).

Table 4.11 THE AMINO ACID CONTENT OF DUODENAL DIGESTA OF MATURE WETHER SHEEP AND OF LACTATING DAIRY COWS IN COMPARISON WITH RUMEN BACTERIA AND PROTOZOA, COW'S MILK AND CALF CARCASE. VALUES ARE EXPRESSED AS MOLE ESSENTIAL AMINO ACIDS (EAA) OR NON-ESSENTIAL AMINO ACIDS (NEAA) PER 100 MOLE TOTAL AMINO ACID

Analysate	*EAA*	*NEAA*	*Source*
Sheep digesta			
Rations containing			
soya bean meal	40.3–42.5	57.5–59.7	Oldham, 1973
urea	38.6–39.7	60.3–61.4	
fish meal	38.8–40	60–61.2	
Cow digesta			
Rations containing			
60% concentrates + hay	38.6–38.7	61.3–61.4	Oldham, Sutton and McAllan
90% concentrates + hay	37.4–37.9	62.1–62.6	(unpublished)
Rumen bacteria	39.2	60.8	Ling, 1976
Rumen protozoa	44.1	55.9	Ling, 1976
Cow's milk	41.9	58.1	Lindqvist, 1968
Calf carcase	29.9	70.1	Williams, 1978

Daily supply of individual amino acids is then simply calculated as the proportion of that amino acid in the potential amino acid N supply (2.1 g amino acid N/MJ ME intake). These calculated values for potential amino acid supply are also shown in *Figure 4.8*.

From these calculations it would appear that isoleucine, lysine and valine might potentially limit production by the high-yielder. The degree of limitation, or indeed the potential for limitation at all is, however, clearly dependent on the values chosen for the efficiencies of absorption and utilization of these amino acids.

Consequently, the main conclusion to be drawn is that this type of exercise will become of practical relevance only if these efficiencies, and the factors which cause them to vary, can be rigorously defined for practical situations. It is relevant to point out that the analogous efficiencies for total amino acid, or protein, absorption and utilization used in the new protein requirements systems must be equally rigorously defined to make them quantitatively reliable. In the future we can expect advances towards these goals to be made. Some comment on the likelihood that it will be possible to act on this information when available, is therefore warranted.

Control of amino acid supply to the intestines

It may be desirable to control either the amount or the composition of amino acids passing to the intestine — or both.

QUANTITY

Methods to vary amounts of amino acids passing to the intestine have recently been reviewed (Oldham and Tamminga, 1980) with the conclusion that there is substantial scope for varying amino acid supply to the intestines within a limit fixed by ME intake. The limit is about 3 g non-ammonia-N (about 2.1 g amino acid N) per MJ ME intake per day. Within this limit, chemical (formaldehyde, tannins etc.) or physical (heat etc.) treatment of proteins can be used to increase supply, with some degree of reliability (Beever and Thomson, 1977).

QUALITY

To vary the composition of amino acids entering the intestines two options are open. The first is to select proteins which are resistant to rumen breakdown and which have a suitable amino acid profile which will complement the profile in rumen microbial fragments and endogenous secretions, giving a desirable amino acid pattern in mixed duodenal digesta.

Examination of the amino acid composition of duodenal digesta from ruminants fed a very wide range of diets and protein supplements suggests that the scope for achieving this objective is limited (*Tables 4.11, 4.12*). With the exception of values from Hagemeister, Kaufmann and Pfeffer (1976) the variability in composition is very low, with good agreement between sources of data. Hagemeister, Kaufmann and Pfeffer (1976) fed a wide range of protein supplements to their cows and achieved a greater degree of variation in digesta amino acid composition. The changes in digesta amino acid composition did not, however, accord with the amino acid profiles of the supplementary proteins (Food and Agriculture Organization, 1970). This is not perhaps, surprising as the amino acid composition of the protein, or parts of protein, which escape rumen breakdown may not necessarily be the same as the amino acid composition of the original food proteins. The magnitude of such changes is uncertain and probably depends on the protein in question. For some dietary ingredients the amino acid composition of undegraded protein may be substantially different from the ingredient as fed (MacGregor, Sniffen and Hoover, 1978) whereas for others the changes may be small (Ganev, Ørskov and Smart, 1979). An associated problem is the availability of amino acids in the 'undegraded' protein. Mathers *et al.* (1979) have observed that, not only is the nutritional quality of food protein escaping degradation in the rumen likely to differ for different feeds, but that the quality of the original feed protein may be an unreliable guide to that of the protein reaching the small intestine. Smith and Mohamed (1977) reached a similar conclusion.

In general it would, therefore, appear unlikely that reliable and precise changes in the amino acid pattern of the duodenal digesta will be achieved by judicious choice of dietary protein supplement. An important exception is for diets containing a large proportion of maize products, when the molar content of lysine in duodenal digesta is substantially lower than 'normal' (*Table 4.13*). Such a reduction in duodenal lysine with maize rations is probably the reason why milk production responses to abomasal lysine supplementation have been found in studies in the USA (Schwab, Satter and Clay, 1976). It seems unlikely that such a situation would apply to the UK, as maize products would rarely be

Table 4.12 THE MOLAR CONTENT OF ESSENTIAL AMINO ACIDS (EAA) PASSING TO THE DUODENUM OF SHEEP AND COWS. MEAN VALUES ARE GIVEN AS MOLE AA/100 MOLE OF TOTAL EAA, WITH RANGES IN PARENTHESES, FOR COMPARISON, THE MOLAR COMPOSITION OF EAA IN RUMEN BACTERIA AND PROTOZOA, IN MILK PROTEIN AND IN CALF CARCASE PROTEIN ARE ALSO GIVEN

Essential amino acids	Animals and number of rations				Rumen flora + other protein sources		Milk protein[f]	Tissue protein[g]
	Sheep[a] 9	Cows[b] 4	Cows[c] 4	Cows[d] 11	Bacteria[e]	Protozoa[e]		
Leucine	20.8 (19.4–22.0)	22.4 (20.1–25.7)	21.3 (20.4–22.9)	21.4 (18.6–23.8)	18.3	17.7	22.3	22.7
Isoleucine	13.9 (13.1–14.7)	12.3 (11.6–12.9)	11.7 (11.1–12.5)	15.2 (14.2–16.1)	13.3	14.3	13.5	9.2
Valine	18.2 (17.0–19.6)	15.5 (14.8–16.1)	17.2 (16.8–17.7)	20.4 (18.6–24.3)	17.4	14.5	16.9	14.3
Methionine	3.6 (1.9–5.4)	4.5† –	5.8 (5.2–6.4)	4.3 (3.7–5.2)	4.4	3.6	5.3	4.9
Phenylalanine	9.8 (9.5–10.3)	9.7 (9.6–9.8)	9.8 (9.6–10.0)	11.2 (9.1–13.0)	8.9	10.4	8.9	9.4
Threonine	14.3 (13.5–15.0)	15.4 (14.8–15.8)	14.1 (13.3–14.9)	15.7 (14.1–19.9)	16.7	13.8	11.6	14.5
Lysine	16.4 (15.6–16.9)	15.2 (13.8–16.6)	16.1 (16.1)	9.8 (8.2–12.3)	17.7	22.5	16.7	18.9
Histidine	3.1 (1.4–4.0)	5. (4.8–5.1)	4.2 (4.0–4.3)	2.1 (1.4–3.0)	3.2	3.3	4.8	6.2

[a] Duodenal cannulas immediately distal to pylorus (Oldham, 1973). Rations contained straw, barley or molasses with urea, soya bean meal or fish meal.
[b] Duodenal cannulas immediately distal to pylorus (Oldham, Sutton and McAllan, unpublished). Rations contained barley or maize concentrates fed with hay in the ratio 60:40 or 90:10.
[c] Duodenal cannulas after bile and pancreatic duct (Tamminga, 1975). Rations contained concentrates plus grass silages or dried grass plus hay in ratio approx. 50:50.
[d] Duodenal cannulas after bile and pancreatic duct (Hagemeister, Kaufmann and Pfeffer, 1976). Rations were forage or mixed forage and concentrates (ratio 40:60) with a variety of protein supplements.
[e] Data of Ling, 1976.
[f] Data of Lindqvist, 1968.
[g] Data of Williams, 1978.
† Assumed value.

Table 4.13 THE MOLAR CONTENT OF LYSINE IN DUODENAL ESSENTIAL AMINO ACIDS (mM LYSINE/100 mM EAA)

Ration	*mM lysine/100 mM EAA in*		*Source*
	Food	*Duodenal digesta*	
60% barley concs., 40% hay	12.2	16.6	Oldham, Sutton and
90% barley concs., 10% hay	12.4	15.6	McAllan
60% maize concs., 40% hay	11.9	14.8	(unpublished)
90% maize concs., 10% hay	11.9	13.8	
Maize concentrates: Normal	8.6	13.4	Redd *et al.*, 1975
Opaque 2	10.3	15.8	
Average value for digesta	–	15	*Table 3.12*

predominant in rations. Even where substantial amounts of maize silage are fed, the lysine content of UK silage is much greater than that from the USA (Phipps and Oldham, 1980) because the crop is harvested at a much earlier stage of maturity in the UK.

The second possibility for manipulating the supply of specific amino acids to the intestines is to use amino acids protected by chemical or physical treatment from breakdown within the rumen. Several compounds have been suggested, but few have undergone rigorous practical tests. Up to 54 per cent of supplemental N-stearoyl-DL-methionine has been found to pass from the rumen into duodenal digesta in sheep (Langer, Buttery and Lewis, 1978). Hydroxymethyl-DL-methionine (HMM) also appears to be resistant to breakdown within the rumen (Buttery, Manomai-Udom and Lewis, 1977). Strong practical support for this comes from a recent trial with high-yielding cows which has shown substantial production responses to inclusion of HMM in the diet (Kaufmann and Lüpping, 1979). Earlier reports of feeding trials with fat-coated methionine showed no difference in milk yield between cows which were or were not supplemented with the 'protected' methionine (Broderick, Kowalczyck and Satter, 1970; Williams, Martz and Hildebrand, 1970). This may have been because maize products made up a large part of the basal ration, so that lysine was perhaps the first-limiting amino acid (Schwab, Satter and Clay, 1976; *see also Table 4.13*). A more recent report suggests that increases in milk fat output with coated methionine can be achieved under some conditions (Daugaard, 1978).

Although still at an early stage of development, it seems more likely that protected amino acids, rather than selection of particular food proteins, could be used to manipulate duodenal amino acid composition with an acceptable degree of reliability.

The extent to which it is desirable to manipulate specific amino acid supply to the intestines will depend on the magnitude of response which can be achieved and the cost of achieving it.

Conclusion

Discussion of the amino acid requirements for lactation in the high-yielding dairy cow is of academic interest only until we can answer most, if not all, of the following questions:

(1)   Which amino acids limit production?
(2)   When does this happen and what is the site of action?
(3)   Can amino acid supply to that site of action be manipulated with precision?

We must then ask what are the benefits to be reaped by meeting amino acid requirements and what is the cost.

The evidence presented here was selected to draw attention to a number of points which have particular relevance to the high-yielding dairy cow and which might not be apparent with other classes of ruminant livestock.

First are the effects which protein or amino acids can have on energy status. These include effects on ration digestibility, food intake and partition of energy between body tissue and milk. Present proposals (e.g. Roy *et al.*, 1977) have provided a means for assessing protein requirements in animals of defined energy status. In cows, protein input can influence energy status as well as being influenced by it. Application of new principles (Roy *et al.*, 1977) to cows must take this into account. In general we are likely to get protein feeding right only when energy input can be properly defined. How accurately can ME intakes be assessed on the farm? It may be that protein feeding can be used to manipulate, or even to maximize, energy intake with consequent effects on production. Many experiments with cows have failed to distinguish between protein effects on production brought about through a change in amino acid status and those induced by a change in energy status. This situation must change if we are to move towards feeding systems which allow precise matching of nutrient input to productive output. In many experiments with dairy cows, inclusion of a simple digestibility trial (on the cows) could make a huge difference to interpretation of results.

Secondly, we must begin to allow for metabolic adaptation in the high-yielding cow, which would conserve amino acids for product formation. This could be brought about by improvements in the absorptive capacity of the gut and by reduction in oxidation of absorbed amino acids. The net effects on calculation of requirements, and on the need for net tissue protein catabolism to occur, can be considerable.

Thirdly, the problems of identifying amino acids which are clearly limiting for milk production have not been overcome. No one amino acid stands out as limiting for conventional feeding systems and even where mixtures of supplemental amino acids have been used to prompt production, responses have generally been small.

What, then, is the future for feeding to meet particular amino acid requirements? In sheep, wool growth can be doubled by abomasal supplements of sulphur-containing amino acids. In growing cattle, methionine appears to be clearly limiting for a number of dietary circumstances. But in neither case is it economic to feed to meet estimated requirements.

In dairy cows, where no clear case can be made for any one amino acid as being limiting, the chance of an economic return from amino acid supplementation would not, at present, seem to be very strong from the point of view of meeting an amino acid deficiency in conventional terms. But there is a case for looking afresh at the role of dietary protein for manipulating intake in the high-yielder, and particular amino acids may have a part to play in this. In addition, methionine or MHA can be used to manipulate milk fat in some circumstances.

There can be no doubt that the recent proposals on protein feeding (Roy *et al.*, 1977) represent a great advance over previous systems. It is doubtful whether they will ever be refined to the level of sophistication which allows description of requirements for particular amino acids. Rather, we might expect to see progress towards assessment of needs for total essential amino acids.

Buttery (1977) suggested that 'The time is approaching when it will be possible to feed the ruminant with the precision normally associated with the broiler chicken'. In terms of application of principles on the farm, this is almost certainly going too far. In striving for unattainable perfection we are, however, likely to clarify at least some of the obscurities which at present still surround the subject of amino acid utilization by the high-yielding dairy cow.

References

AGRICULTURAL RESEARCH COUNCIL (1965). *Nutrient Requirements of Farm Live stock. No. 3, Ruminants.* London; HMSO

ARMSTRONG, D.G. and ANNISON, E.F. (1973). *Proc. Nutr. Soc.,* 32, 107–113

BALCH, C.C. and CAMPLING, R.C. (1962). *Nutr. Abstr. Rev.,* 32, 669–686

BALDWIN, R.L., KOONG, L.J. and ULYATT, M.J. (1977). *Agric. Syst.,* 2, 255–288

BEEVER, D.E. (1978). In *Ruminant Digestion and Feed Evaluation*, pp. 9.1–13. Eds D.F. Osbourn, D.E. Beever and D.J. Thomson. London; Agricultural Research Council

BEEVER, D.E. and THOMSON, D.J. (1977). In *Recent Advances in Animal Nutrition*, pp. 66–82. Eds W. Haresign and D. Lewis. London; Butterworths

BELYEA, R.L., FROST, G.R., MARTZ, F.A., CLARK, J.L. and FORKNER, L.G. (1978). *J. Dairy Sci.,* 61, 206–211

BHARGAVA, P.K., OTTERBY, D.E., MURPHY, J.M. and DANKER, J.D. (1977). *J. Dairy Sci.,* 60, 1194–1604

BINES, J.A. (1979). In *Feeding Strategy for the High-Yielding Dairy Cow*, pp. 23–48. Eds W.H. Broster and H. Swan. London; Granada

BINES, J.A., HART, I.C. and MORANT, S.V. (1980). *Br. J. Nutr.,* 43, 179–188

BLACK, A.L. (1968). In *Isotope Studies on the Nitrogen Chain*, pp. 287–307. Vienna; IAEA

BLACK, A.L., EGAN, A.R., ANAND, R.S. and CHAPMAN, T.W. (1968). In *Isotope Studies on the Nitrogen Chain*, pp. 247–261. Vienna; IAEA

BLACK, A.L., THOMPSON, J.R., ANAND, R.S. and CHAPMAN, T.W. (1970). In *Energy Metabolism of Farm Animals*, pp. 73–76. Eds A. Schurch and C. Wenk. Zurich; Jaris Druck & Verlag

BLACKARD, W.G. and ANDREWS, S.S. (1974). In *Current Topics in Experimental Endocrinology*, pp. 129–153. Eds V.H.T. James and L. Martini. New York; Academic Press

BLOOM, S.R. (1978). *Proc. Nutr. Soc.,* 37, 259–271

BOTTS, R.L., HEMKEN, R.W. and BULL, L.S. (1978). *J. Dairy Sci.,* 62, 433–440

BRODERICK, G.A., KOWALCZYCK, T. and SATTER, L.D. (1970). *J. Dairy Sci.,* 53, 1714–1721

BROSTER, W.H. (1974). *Bienn. Rev. Nat. Inst. Res. Dairying*, pp. 14–34

BROSTER, W.H., BROSTER, VALERIE J. and SMITH, T. (1969). *J. agric. Sci., Camb.,* 72, 229–245

BROSTER, W.H., SUTTON, J.D. and BINES, J.A. (1979). In *Recent Advances in Animal Nutrition – 1978*, pp. 99–126. Eds W. Haresign and D. Lewis, London; Butterworths

BROSTER, W.H., BROSTER, VALERIE J., SMITH, T. and SIVITER, J. (1975). *J. agric. Sci., Camb.*, **84**, 173–186

BRUCKENTAL, I., OLDHAM, J.D. and SUTTON, J.D. (1980). *Br. J. Nutr.*, **44**, 33–45

BURROUGHS, W., NELSON, D.K. and MERTENS, D.R. (1975). *J. Dairy Sci.*, **58**, 611–619

BUTTERY, P.J. (1977). In *Recent Advances in Animal Nutrition – 1977*, pp. 8–24. Eds W. Haresign and D. Lewis. London; Butterworths

BUTTERY, P.J., MANOMAI-UDOM, S. and LEWIS, D. (1977). *J. Sci. Fd. Agric.*, **28**, 481–485

CHALUPA, W. (1976). *J. Anim. Sci.*, **43**, 828–834

CHALUPA, W. and SCOTT, G.C. (1976). In *Tracer Studies on Non-protein Nitrogen for Ruminants, III*, pp. 13–25. Vienna; IAEA

CHANDLER, P.T., BROWN, C.A., JOHNSON, R.P., MacLEOD, G.K., McCARTHY, R.D., MOSS, B.R., RAKES, A.H. and SATTER, L.D. (1976). *J. Dairy Sci.*, **59**, 1897–1909

CLARK, J.H. (1975). *J. Dairy Sci.*, **58**, 1178–1197

CLARK, J.H., SPIRES, H.R. and DAVIS, C.L. (1978). *Fed. Proc.*, **37**, 1233–1238

CLARK, J.H., SPIRES, H.R., DERRIG, R.G. and BENNINK, M.R. (1977). *J. Nutr.*, **107**, 631–644

CLAY, A.B., and SATTER, L.D. (1979). *J. Dairy Sci.*, **62** (Suppl. 1), 75–76

COELHO DA SILVA, J.F., SEELEY, R.C., BEEVER, D.E., PRESCOTT, J.H.D. and ARMSTRONG, D.G. (1972a). *Br. J. Nutr.*, **28**, 357–371

COELHO DA SILVA, J.F., SEELEY, R.C., THOMSON, D.J., BEEVER, D.E. and ARMSTRONG, D.G. (1972b). *Br. J. Nutr.*, **28**, 43–61

COLE, D.J.A. (1979). In *Recent Advances in Animal Nutrition – 1978*, pp. 59–72. Eds W. Haresign and D. Lewis. London; Butterworths

COLWELL, A.R., ZUCKERMAN, L. and BERGER, S. (1970). *Diabetes*, **19**, 217–227

COWAN, R.T., ROBINSON, J.J., GREENHALGH, J.F.S. and McHATTIE, I. (1979). *Anim. Prod.*, **29**, 81–90

CRIPPS, A.W. and WILLIAMS, V.J. (1975). *Br. J. Nutr.*, **33**, 17–32

DAUGAARD, J. (1978). Diss. Kopenhagen

EGAN, A.R. (1980). *Proc. Nutr. Soc.*, **39**, 79–87

ERFLE, J.D. and FISHER, L.J. (1977). *Can. J. Anim. Sci.*, **57**, 101–109

FISHER, L.J. (1969). *J. Dairy Sci.*, **52**, 943

FISHER, L.J. (1972). *Can. J. Anim. Sci.*, **52**, 497–504

FOOD AND AGRICULTURE ORGANIZATION (1970). *Amino Acid Content of Foods*. Rome; FAO

GANEV, G., ØRSKOV, E.R. and SMART, R. (1979). *J. agric. Sci., Camb.*, **93**, 651–656

GERICH, J.E., CHARLES, M.A. and GRODSKY, G.M. (1976). *Ann. Rev. Physiol.*, **38**, 353–388

GIL, L.A., SHIRLEY, R.L. and MOORE, J.E. (1973). *J. Anim. Sci.*, **37**, 159–163

GIL, L.A., SHIRLEY, R.L., MOORE, J.E. and EASLEY, J.F. (1973). *Proc. Soc. Exp. Biol. Med.*, **142**, 670–674

GORDON, F.J. and FORBES, T.J. (1970). *J. Dairy Res.*, **37**, 481–491

GOW, C.B., RANAWANA, S.S.E., KELLAWAY, R.C. and McDOWELL, G.H. (1979). *Br. J. Nutr.*, **41**, 371–382

GRIEL, L.C., PATTON, R.A., McCARTHY, R.D. and CHANDLER, P.T. (1968). *J. Dairy Sci.*, **51**, 1866–1868

HAGEMEISTER, H., KAUFMANN, W. and PFEFFER, E. (1976). In *Protein Metabolism and Nutrition*, pp. 425–439. Eds D.J.A. Cole, K.N. Boorman, P.J. Buttery, D. Lewis, R.J. Neale and H. Swan. London; Butterworths

HART, I.C., BINES, J.A. and MORANT, S.V. (1979). *J. Dairy Sci.*, **62**, 270–277
HART, I.C., BINES, J.A., NAPPER, D.J. and MORANT, S.V. (1980). Annual report
    Nat. Inst. Res. Dairying, 1979, p. 64
HATFIELD, E.E. (1977). *Proc. Dist. Feed Res. Council*, **32**, 53–62
HUME, I.D. (1970). *Aust. J. agric. Res.*, **21**, 305–314
HUTTON, K. and ANNISON, E.F. (1972). *Proc. Nutr. Soc.*, **31**, 151–158
JAGANNADHA, A. and RAMACHANDRAN, J. (1977). In *Hormonal Proteins and
    Peptides*, pp. 43–60. Ed. C.H. Li. New York; Academic Press
JOHNSON, C.L. (1977). *J. agric. Sci., Camb.*, **88**, 79–94
JOHNSON, R.R. (1976). *J. Anim. Sci.*, **43**, 184–191
KAUFMANN, W. and HAGEMEISTER, H. (1975). *Übers. Tiernähr.*, **3**, 33–65
KAUFMANN, W. and LÜPPING, W. (1979). *Z. Tierphysiol. Tierernähr.*, **41**, 202–217
KEMPTON, T.J., NOLAN, J.V. and LENG, R.A. (1979). *Br. J. Nutr.*, **42**, 303–315
KENNEDY, P.M. (1980). *Br. J. Nutr.*, **43**, 125–140
KENNEDY, P.M. and MILLIGAN, L.P. (1978). *Br. J. Nutr.*, **39**, 105–117
LANGER, P.N., BUTTERY, P.J. and LEWIS, D. (1978). *J. Sci. Fd. Agric.*, **29**, 808–814
LEWIS, D. and MITCHELL, R. (1976). In *Protein Metabolism and Nutrition*,
    pp. 417–424. Eds D.J.A. Cole, K.N. Boorman, P.J. Buttery, D. Lewis, R.J.
    Neale and H. Swan. London; Butterworths
LINDQVIST, B. (1968). PhD Thesis, The Royal Veterinary College, Stockholm
LINDSAY, D.B. (1976). In *Protein Metabolism and Nutrition*, pp. 183–197.
    Eds D.J.A. Cole, K.N. Boorman, P.J. Buttery, D. Lewis, R.J. Neale and
    H. Swan. London; Butterworths
LINDSAY, D.B. (1979). In *Protein Metabolism in the Ruminant*, pp. 7.1–9.
    Ed. P.J. Buttery. London; Agricultural Research Council
LING, J.R. (1976). PhD Thesis, University of Nottingham
LOW, A.G. (1981). In *Recent Advances in Animal Nutrition – 1980*, pp. 141–
    156. Ed. W. Haresign. London; Butterworths
MacGREGOR, C.A., SNIFFEN, C.J. and HOOVER, W.H. (1978). *J. Dairy Sci.*, **61**,
    566–573
McCARTHY, R.D., PORTER, G.A. and GRIEL, L.C. (1968). *J. Dairy Sci.*, **51**, 459–462
MACHLIN, L.J. (1973). *J. Dairy Sci.*, **56**, 575–580
MAENG, W.J. and BALDWIN, R.L. (1976a). *J. Dairy Sci.*, **59**, 643–647
MAENG, W.J. and BALDWIN, R.L. (1976b). *J. Dairy Sci.*, **59**, 648–655
MEANG, W.J., VAN NEVEL, C.J., BALDWIN, R.L. and MORRIS, J.G. (1976). *J. Dairy
    Sci.*, **59**, 68–79
MATHERS, J.C. and MILLER, E.L. (1979). In *Protein Metabolism in the Ruminant*,
    pp. 3.1–11. Ed. P.J. Buttery. London; Agricultural Research Council
MATHERS, J.C., THOMAS, R.J., GRAY, N.A.M. and JOHNSON, I.L. (1979). *Proc. Nutr.
    Soc.*, **38**, 122A
MATHISON, G.W. and MILLIGAN, L.P. (1971). *Br. J. Nutr.*, **25**, 351–366
MEPHAM, T.B. (1976). In *Principles of Cattle Production*, pp. 201–220. Eds H.
    Swan and W.H. Broster. London; Butterworths
MEPHAM, T.B. (1979). In *Protein Metabolism in the Ruminant*, pp. 4.1–12,
    Ed. P.J. Buttery. London; Agricultural Research Council
MILK MARKETING BOARD (1978). *Breeding and Production 1977/78. No. 28.*
    Thames Ditton; Milk Marketing Board
MOE, P.W. and TYRRELL, H.F. (1977). *J. Dairy Sci.*, **60**, (Suppl. 1) 69–70
NAISMITH, D.J. and MORGAN, B.L.G. (1976). *Br. J. Nutr.*, **36**, 563–566

NOLAN, J.V. (1975). In *Digestion and Metabolism in the Ruminant*, pp. 416–431. Eds I.W. McDonald and A.C.I. Warner. University of New England, Armidale

NOLAN, J.V. and STACHIW, S. (1979). *Br. J. Nutr.*, **42**, 63–80

NORTON, B.W., MORAN, J.B. and NOLAN, J.V. (1979). *Aust. J. agric. Res.*, **30**, 341–351

OKORIE, A.E., BUTTERY, P.J. and LEWIS, D. (1977). *Proc. Nutr. Soc.*, **36**, 38A

OLDHAM, J.D. (1973). Dietary nitrogen and carbohydrate interactions in the rumen. PhD Thesis, University of Nottingham

OLDHAM, J.D. (1978). In *Ruminant Digestion and Feed Evaluation*, pp. 13.1–13.14. Eds D.F. Osbourn, D.E. Beever and D.J. Thomson. London; Agricultural Research Council

OLDHAM, J.D. (1979). In *Protein Metabolism in Ruminants*, pp. 5.1–16. Ed. P.J. Buttery. London; Agricultural Research Council

OLDHAM, J.D. (1980). In *Feeding Strategies for Dairy Cows*, pp. 114–147 Ed. W.H. Broster. London; Agricultural Research Council

OLDHAM, J.D. and TAMMINGA, S. (1980). *Livest. Prod. Sci.*, **7**, 437–452

OLDHAM, J.D., BRUCKENTAL, I. and NISSENBAUM, A. (1980). *J. agric. Sci., Camb.*, **95**, 235–238

OLDHAM, J.D., BROSTER, W.H., NAPPER, D.J. and SMITH, T. (1979a). *Proc. Nutr. Soc.*, **38**, 128A

OLDHAM, J.D., BROSTER, W.H., NAPPER, D.J. and SIVITER, J. (1979b). *Br. J. Nutr.*, **42**, 149–162

OLDHAM, J.D., HART, I.C. and BINES, J.A. (1978). *Proc. Nutr. Soc.*, **37**, 9A

OLDHAM, J.D., SUTTON, J.D. and McALLAN, A.B. (1979). *Ann. Rech. Vet.*, **10**, 290–293

OLDHAM, J.D., BUTTERY, P.J., SWAN, H. and LEWIS, D. (1977). *J. agric. Sci., Camb.*, **89**, 467–479

ØRSKOV, E.R., GRUBB, D.A. and KAY, R.N.B. (1977). *Br. J. Nutr.*, **38**, 397–405

PAQUAY, R., DE BAERE, R. and LOUSSE, A. (1972). *Br. J. Nutr.*, **27**, 27–37

PATTON, R.A., McCARTHY, R.D. and GRIEL, L.C. (1968). *J. Dairy Sci.*, **51**, 1310–1311

PATTON, R.A., McCARTHY, R.D. and GRIEL, L.C. (1970). *J. Dairy Sci.*, **53**, 460–465

PHIPPS, R.H. and OLDHAM, J.D. (1980). *Anim. Feed. Sci. Technol.*, **4**, 163–168

PICOU, D. and TAYLOR-ROBERTS, T. (1969). *Clin. Sci.*, **36**, 283–296

POLAN, C.E., CHANDLER, P.T. and MILLER, C.N. (1970). *J. Dairy Sci.*, **53**, 607–610

REDD, T.L., BOLING, J.A., BRADLEY, N.W. and ELY, D.G. (1975). *J. Anim. Sci.*, **40**, 567–572

REMOND, B. and JOURNET, M. (1978). *Ann. Zootech.*, **27**, 139–158

REMOND, B., CHAMPREDON, C., DECOEN, C., PION, R. and JOURNET, M. (1971). *Ann. Biol. anim. Bioch. Biophys.*, **11**, 455–469

ROBINSON, J.J., FRASER, C., GILL, J.C. and McHATTIE, I. (1974). *Anim. Prod.*, **19**, 331–339

ROBINSON, J.J., McHATTIE, I., CORTES, J.F.C. and THOMPSON, J.L. (1979). *Anim. Prod.*, **29**, 257–269

ROFFLER, R.E. and SATTER, L.D. (1975). *J. Dairy Sci.*, **58**, 1889–1898

ROGERS, G.L. and McLEAY, L.M. (1977). *Proc. N.Z. Soc. Anim. Prod.*, **37**, 46–49

ROGERS, Q.R. (1976). In *Protein Metabolism and Nutrition*, pp. 279–301. Eds D.J.A. Cole, K.N. Boorman, P.J. Buttery, D. Lewis, R.J. Neale and H. Swan. London; Butterworths

ROY, J.H.B., BALCH, C.C., MILLER, E.L., ØRSKOV, E.R. and SMITH, R.H. (1977). In *Protein Metabolism and Nutrition*, pp. 126–129. Wageningen; Pudoc.

SATTER, L.D. and ROFFLER, R.E. (1975). *J. Dairy Sci.*, **58**, 1219–1237

SATTER, L.D. and ROFFLER, R.E. (1977). In *Protein Metabolism and Nutrition*, pp. 133–136. Wageningen; Pudoc.

SCHEIFINGER, C., RUSSELL, N. and CHALUPA, W. (1976). *J. Anim. Sci.*, **43**, 821–827

SCHNEIDER, W., FRITZ, D., REICHL, J.R. and MENKE, K.H. (1980). In *Energy Metabolism*, Proc. 8th EAAP Symp. on Energy Metabolism, 1979, pp. 341–344 Ed. L.E. Mount. London; Butterworths

SCHWAB, C.G., SATTER, L.D. and CLAY, A.B. (1976). *J. Dairy Sci.*, **59**, 1254–1270

SINGH, A.B., VERMA, D.N., VARMA, A. and RANJHAN, S.K. (1977). *Br. J. Nutr.*, **38**, 335–340

SMITH, R.H. (1980). *Proc. Nutr. Soc.*, **39**, 71–78

SMITH, R.H. and MOHAMED, O.E. (1977). *Proc. Nutr. Soc.*, **36**, 153A

STOIKOV, D., GANOVSKI, Hr., KARABASHEV, G., SHISHKOV, Iu. and APOSTOLOV, K. (1976). *Vet. Science, Sofia*, **13**, 79–84

SUTTON, J.D. and OLDHAM, J.D. (1977). *Proc. Nutr. Soc.*, **36**, 203–209

SUTTON, J.D., OLDHAM, J.D. and HART, I.C. (1980). In Proc. 8th EAAP *Energy Metabolism* Symp. on Energy Metabolism, 1979, pp. 303–306 Ed. L.E. Mount. London; Butterworths

TAGARI, H. and BERGMAN, E.N. (1978). *J. Nutr.*, **108**, 790–803

TAMMINGA, S. (1973). *Z. Tierphysiol. Tierernährg.*, **32**, 185–193

TAMMINGA, S. (1975). *Neth. J. agric. Sci.*, **23**, 89–103

TAMMINGA, S. and OLDHAM, J.D. (1980). *Livest. Prod. Sci.*, **7**, 453–463

TAMMINGA, S., VAN DER KOELAN, C.J. and VAN VUUREN, A.M. (1979). *Livest. Prod. Sci.*, **6**, 255–262

TEICHMAN, R., CARUOLO, E.V. and MOCHRIE, R.D. (1969). *J. Dairy Sci.*, **52**, 942

THOMPSON, J.L., ROBINSON, J.J. and McHATTIE, I. (1978). *Proc. Nutr. Soc.*, **37**, 71A

UNGER, R.H. (1977). In *The Year in Metabolism 1975/76*, pp. 73–111. Ed. N. Frienkel. New York; Plenum Medical Book Co.

VAN HORN, H.H., ZOMETH, C.A., WILCOX, C.J., MARSHALL, S.P. and HARRIS, B. (1979). *J. Dairy Sci.*, **62**, 1086–1093

VERITE, R., JOURNET, M. and JARRIGE, R. (1979). *Livestock Prod. Sci.*, **6**, 349–367

WESTON, R.H. (1979). *Ann. Rech. Vet.*, **10**, 442–444

WHITNEY, R. McL., BRUNNER, J.R., EBNER, K.E., FARRELL, H.M., JOSEPHSON, R.V., MORR, C.V. and SWAISGOOD, H.E. (1976). *J. Dairy Sci.*, **59**, 785–815

WHITTEMORE, C.T. (1977). In *Recent Advances in Animal Nutrition – 1977*, pp. 158–166. Eds W. Haresign and D. Lewis. London; Butterworths

WILLIAMS, A.P. (1978). *J. agric. Sci., Camb.*, **90**, 617–624

WILLIAMS, L.R., MARTZ, F.A. and HILDEBRAND, E.S. (1970). *J. Dairy Sci.*, **53**, 1709–1713

5

THE POTENTIAL OF PROTECTED PROTEINS IN RUMINANT NUTRITION

D.E. BEEVER
D.J. THOMSON
The Grassland Research Institute, Berkshire

The ruminant animal derives its protein from digestion in the abomasum and small intestine of both microbial protein, synthesized in the rumen, and dietary protein which has escaped degradation in the rumen. The combination of amino acids derived from these two sources constitutes the total supply to the animal. The requirements for protein may be derived by a factorial approach (ARC, 1965), which can be extended to a specification of amino acid requirements (Hutton and Annison, 1972; Armstrong and Annison, 1973), or requirements can be assessed by alternative metabolic techniques (Armstrong and Annison, 1973; Lewis and Mitchell, 1976). The potential of protected proteins for ruminants is in essence an assessment of the supply of amino acids to the animal and a knowledge of the extent to which this supply meets, or is deficient in meeting, the requirement for a prescribed rate of animal production. A nutritional requirement is a single point on a response curve relating output to input (Fisher, 1976), so that for the productive ruminant the potential for protected proteins must be assessed in the context of supply from the food and requirement by the animal.

Recent reviews of nitrogen digestion in the ruminant (Armstrong, 1976; Armstrong and Hutton, 1975; Buttery and Annison, 1973; Clark, 1975; Hogan and Weston, 1970; Hogan, 1975; McMeniman, Ben-Ghadalia and Armstrong, 1976; Mercer and Annison, 1976; Satter and Roffler, 1975; Smith, 1975) have covered most aspects of digestion and synthesis in the rumen, and digestion and absorption from the small intestine; and several reviews have specifically considered the protection of proteins or amino acids from degradation in the rumen (Annison, 1973; Barry, 1976; Chalupa, 1975; Ferguson, 1975).

The principal objective of protecting proteins from ruminal degradation is to enhance the supply of essential amino acids to the productive animal. This chapter will deal with the protein sources available to the ruminant animal, the extent to which proteins escape rumen fermentation, the methods and techniques which may be used to protect plant and animal protein from degradation in the rumen and some of the consequences for protein utilisation, and lastly some of the circumstances under which protection of proteins or supplementation of diets with protected proteins may be beneficial.

Proteins consumed by ruminants

Ruminants consume a wide variety of proteins and non-protein nitrogen sources. The dietary protein habits of ruminants in the UK are given in *Table 5.1*. Imported and home-produced sources of crude protein have been combined under the

Table 5.1 PROTEIN SOURCES FOR RUMINANTS 1973–74 (KILOTONNES (kt) OF CRUDE PROTEIN) (JCO, 1976)

Energy feeds	
Barley	375
Wheat	35
Oats	75
Maize and sorghum	41
Other cereals	18
Cereal offals	99
Other energy feeds	21
Total	664
Protein feeds	
Oil cakes and meals	363
Animal protein	26
Maize gluten	41
Distillers by-products	28
Field beans	24
Dried grass	15
Dried poultry waste	30
Urea	40
Other protein feeds	1
Total	568
Grassland	
Forage plus root and green crops	3422

three broad categories of high energy feeds, high protein feeds, and bulk feeds. Grassland feeds provide 73.5 per cent of the crude protein consumed by ruminants. The two most important sources in the energy and protein feed categories, barley and oil cakes and meals, together contribute 20 per cent of the crude protein consumed.

The majority of feed ingredients are processed prior to incorporation in a compound food. Forage crops, other than when grazed, can be subjected to a wide variety of treatments when they are conserved. The concentration as well as the nature of the protein in these protein sources can influence the treatment and whether protection of the proteins enhances the supply of amino acids to the ruminant animal.

McDonald (1952) and McDonald and Hall (1957) demonstrated that proteins of different solubility, zein and casein, were digested in the rumen to different degrees. Approximately 95 per cent of the highly soluble protein casein was digested in the rumen, compared with 50 per cent of the relatively insoluble zein. Chalmers, Cuthbertson and Synge (1954) heat treated casein. This reduced its solubility in the rumen and enhanced the supply of protein to the animal. They supported their conclusion of more efficient post-ruminal digestion of protein by measuring a higher nitrogen retention compared with untreated casein. These early studies provided the basis on which formaldehyde (Ferguson,

Hemsley and Reis, 1967) was used as a method of reducing the solubility of protein in the rumen and thereby conferring some measure of protection.

Problems of technique and development of satisfactory methods of measuring protein degradation in the rumen and the accompanying synthesis of microbial protein delayed progress. Several techniques are now in current use which permit *in vivo* estimates of protein breakdown and microbial synthesis to be made (Smith, 1975).

In *Table 5.2* values for the percentage of dietary protein which escapes ruminal digestion are given for various forage diets fed fresh or as untreated silage, seed meals normally produced with minimal heat, and casein.

Table 5.2 THE PROPORTIONS OF DIETARY PROTEINS ESCAPING DEGRADATION IN THE RUMEN – FORAGE AND PROTEIN MEALS

Feed	% Protection	Reference
Animal origin		
Casein	9	Hume (1974)
Plant origin		
Seed meals:		
Sunflower seed meal (high intake)	19	Miller (1973)
Groundnut meal	22	Miller (1973)
Field beans (unheated)	22	McMeniman, Ben-Ghedalia and Armstrong (1976)
Sunflower seed meal (low intake)	28	Miller (1973)
Lupin seed meal	35	Hume (1974)
Groundnut meal	37	Hume (1974)
Forage:		
Grass silage (unwilted)	15	Beever *et al.* (1977)
Subterranean clover (green)	26	Hume and Purser (1974)
Perennial ryegrass (fresh)	26	Walker *et al.* (1975)
Short rotation ryegrass (fresh)	30	Ulyatt *et al.* (1975)
Perennial ryegrass (fresh)	31	Ulyatt *et al.* (1975)
Short rotation ryegrass (fresh)	41	Walker *et al.* (1975)
Perennial ryegrass (fresh)	48	Beever, Cammell and Wallace (1974)
Perennial ryegrass (frozen)	52	Beever, Cammell and Wallace (1974)
White clover (fresh)	53	Walker *et al.* (1975)
Subterranean clover (mature)	55	Hume and Purser (1974)
Sainfoin	70	Beever, Harrison and Thomson (1972)

Hume (1974) confirmed the earlier observations of McDonald (1952) and showed that casein is a highly soluble protein; only 9 per cent escaped ruminal digestion (*Table 5.2*). For protein seed meals, the values for percentage protection ranged from 19, for sunflower meal fed at a high level of intake (Miller, 1973), to 37 for groundnut meal (Hume, 1974). Hume's value of 37 per cent for groundnut meal contrasts with the value of 22 per cent obtained by Miller (1973).

The effect of level of feeding on the proportion of protein escaping degradation in the rumen is shown by the results of Miller (1973) for sunflower seed. This effect of level of feeding may be expected to apply with proteins of low solubility, resistant to attack in the rumen, but may not apply to highly soluble proteins. For forage diets, fed as silage or fresh, the percentage protection ranged from 15 to 55, with the legume sainfoin, which has naturally occurring tannins,

outside this range at 70 per cent (*Table 5.2*). Unwilted silage, with a high proportion of NPN and readily soluble protein, had a low (15 per cent) proportion
of the protein escaping degradation in the rumen. However, the values for fresh
grass, 26–52 per cent, are somewhat higher than might previously have been
anticipated. Values for the degree of protection in 'natural' proteins (*Table 5.2*)
indicate that for the categories examined, 50 per cent or less of the protein is
protected. On the basis of present evidence, initial approximate values of 15, 25
and 35 per cent could be used for unwilted silage (without additive), untreated
seed meals and fresh grass respectively.

The protection of plant and animal protein from degradation in the rumen

The stimulus provided by the earlier work with formaldehyde treatment of
casein (Ferguson, Hemsley and Reis, 1967) and the subsequent responses in
wool growth which have been measured (Ferguson, 1975), have led to the
examination of other aldehydes, such as acetaldehyde and glutaraldehyde (West
and Mangan, 1972), tannins (Leroy, Zelter and François, 1964; McLeod, 1974)
and heat (Tagari, Ascarelli and Bondi, 1962; Beever, Thomson and Cammell,
1976), and the extension of the use of formaldehyde to a variety of protein
sources, including forage. In *Table 5.3*, values for the proportion of protein

Table 5.3 THE PROPORTION OF DIETARY PROTEINS ESCAPING
DEGRADATION IN THE RUMEN – HEAT DRIED AND FORMALDEHYDE
TREATED PROTEINS

Feed	% Protection	Reference
Animal origin		
Fish meal	69	Miller (1973)
Fish meal	71	Hume (1974)
Plant origin		
Heat treated:		
Clover hay	58	Walker *et al.* (1975)
Soya bean meal	61	Hume (1974)
Perennial ryegrass	71	Beever, Cammell and Wallace (1974)
Formaldehyde treated:		
Silage	78	Beever *et al.* (1977)
Formaldehyde + heat:		
Silage	84	Beever *et al.* (1977)

protected from ruminal digestion for a variety of processed, heat treated and
formaldehyde treated diets are presented. In contrast to the values in *Table 5.2*
for untreated diets, those in *Table 5.3* range from 58 to 84 per cent and show
clearly that the imposed treatments have increased the proportion of the dietary
protein escaping fermentation in the rumen, i.e. additional protection has been
conferred.

Heat treatment

Heat is often used in the extraction and preparation of feedstuffs for ruminants and this may have some nutritional advantage. Earlier work with forage demonstrated an increased flow of nitrogen into the duodenum with drying (Beever, Thomson and Harrison, 1971). This observation was extended in a more comprehensive examination of the effects of drying using perennial ryegrass. Different drying treatments were imposed, and the solubility of the protein in the forage was reduced from 72 per cent in the fresh (frozen) herbage to 42 per cent with drying, and further to 36 per cent with formaldehyde treatment of high temperature dried forage (Beever, Thomson and Cammell, 1976). The flow of nitrogen at the duodenum and the disappearance of nitrogen within the small intestine was elevated for sheep consuming the dried diets compared with the original herbage in the frozen form. Solubility of the protein in heat treated diets was related both to flow of nitrogen entering the small intestine (per 100 g of total nitrogen consumed) (*Figure 5.1*), and the uptake of nitrogen in the total intestine (per 100 g of digestible organic matter consumed) (*Figure 5.2*). These two relationships show quite clearly the enhanced supply from the rumen, and uptake from the intestines, when forage is heat treated and the proteins are denatured and the solubility reduced.

In a further study of the effects of heat treatment of forage, Beever, Cammell and Wallace (1974), also using ryegrass, showed that oven drying led to a 51 per cent increase in the quantity of amino acids entering the small intestine compared with fresh ryegrass. Two-thirds of this increase in amino acid flow could

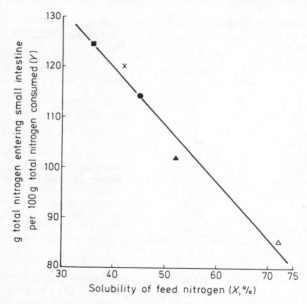

Figure 5.1 Relationship of solubility of feed nitrogen of perennial ryegrass and the amount of nitrogen flowing into the small intestine per 100 g nitrogen consumed. △, *Frozen;* ▲ *High temperature dried;* ×, *Oven dried;* •, *Low temperature dried;* ■, *High temperature dried plus HCHO.*

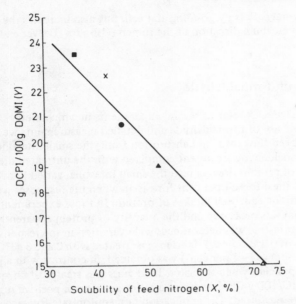

Figure 5.2 Relationship of solubility of feed nitrogen and the amount of crude protein digested in the total intestines (DCPI) per 100 g digestible organic matter intake (DOMI). For explanation of symbols see Figure 5.1

be attributed to an increase from 48 to 71 per cent in the proportion of dietary protein escaping rumen fermentation with heat treatment of the forage, the remainder of the increase to an enhanced synthesis of microbial protein in the rumen.

Adverse effects of excessive heat treatment, either during initial drying or subsequent processing, can reduce the absorption of amino acids in the small intestine, despite an enhanced flow from the rumen compared with control untreated forage. This is demonstrated in results for red clover given in *Table 5.4*. The availability of protein within the small intestine was reduced from 72 per cent to 54 per cent with heat treatment and processing (Beever, Thomson and Harrison, 1971).

Table 5.4 EFFECT OF HEAT TREATMENT ON THE FLOW OF PROTEIN INTO, AND ABSORPTION FROM, THE SMALL INTESTINE OF SHEEP AND ON THE DIGESTIBILITY OF PROTEIN WITHIN THE SMALL INTESTINE (BEEVER, THOMSON AND HARRISON, 1971)

	Red clover	
Diet treatment	*Frozen*	*Dried and wafered*
g protein/24 h		
(*a*) Consumed	127	124
(*b*) Entering small intestine	134	145
(*c*) Leaving small intestine	37	67
(*d*) Absorbed	97	78
Digestibility (d/b) (%)	72	54

Processing forage diets by grinding and pelleting also increases the amount of dietary protein escaping digestion in the rumen (Osbourn, Beever and Thomson, 1976).

Treatment with formaldehyde

The results in *Table 5.5* refer to several experiments in which dietary protein was protected by the use of formaldehyde and detailed measurements were made of protein or nitrogen flow into, and absorption from, the small intestine. The response to formaldehyde treatment compared with the untreated diet, in terms of the amount of protein flowing into the small intestine, varied between −3 per cent for peanut meal to +64 per cent for casein when the responses were calculated on the basis of equalised intakes of protein. In those experiments in which flow at the ileum was measured and the quantity of protein apparently absorbed from the small intestine was determined, wide variation in the response to formaldehyde (HCHO) was noted. For dried grass treated with 2 and 3 g HCHO/100 g CP a negative response (−5 per cent) was obtained, in contrast with a positive response of 33 per cent when the same dried grass was treated at an application rate of 1 g HCHO/100 g CP. For casein and for grass silage positive responses of 20 per cent were measured. The application rate appropriate for each feed requires more precise delineation. Ferguson (1975) considered the effect of increasing formaldehyde application on crude protein and non-protein organic matter digestibility for lucerne, linseed meal and rapeseed meal and concluded that below 1 g HCHO/100 g crude protein there was no effect. Above this level, there was a progressive decline in apparent crude protein digestibility, but of a lesser magnitude than previously reported for casein (Hemsley, Reis and Downes, 1973). Ferguson (1975) reported that the digestibility of non-protein organic matter was not affected at levels of HCHO up to 6 g/100 g crude protein. Barry (1976) reviewed results from a range of four diets on which optimal levels of application had been determined (Ferguson, 1975; Wilkinson, Wilson and Barry, 1976; Thomson and Beever, unpublished data), and calculated HCHO application rate in relation to the true protein content of the diet which, from data presented in *Table 5.2*, could be classed as unprotected. Barry (1976) then derived application rates, on the basis of degradable true protein, of 4.6−7.8 for grass products and 7.8−10.7 for legume crops, expressed as g HCHO/100 g degradable true protein.

The effect of protein protection on rumen function

Rapid and extensive degradation of valuable protein in the rumen helped lead research to the concept of protection, but the maintenance of an active and efficient rumen fermentation is essential. Structural carbohydrates are digested and volatile fatty acids (VFA) formed (Leng, 1970) by bacteria and protozoa in the rumen in a symbiotic relationship with the animal (Hungate, 1966; Allison, 1970). Degradation of energy-rich substrates to VFA yields adenosine triphosphate (ATP) which is essential for microbial cell maintenance (Stouthamer, 1973) and growth (Bauchop and Elsden, 1960). In addition, microbial growth

Table 5.5 EFFECT OF FORMALDEHYDE ON THE FLOW OF PROTEIN INTO, AND THE ABSORPTION FROM, THE SMALL INTESTINE, AND THE DIGESTIBILITY OF PROTEIN WITHIN THE SMALL INTESTINE

Diet component treated	Casein		Casein		Peanut meal		Peanut meal		Grass (ensiled)		Soya bean meal		Clover hay		Grass (dried)			
Diet component*(%) Total diet	40		30		33		50		100		55		100		100		100	100
HCHO application rate (g/100 g CP diet component)	1.2		3.0		0.9		0.9		6.0		0.6		4.0		1.0		2.0	3.0
Species	Sheep U**	T**	Sheep U	T	Sheep U	T	Sheep U	T	Sheep U	T	Cattle U	T	Sheep U††	T††	Sheep U††	T	Sheep T	Sheep T
g protein/24 h:																		
(a) consumed	231	234	170	170	102	110	187	194	161	153	–	–	179	180	136	142	138	133
(b) entering small intestine	136	226	135	159	132	138	154	197	133	169	751†	897†	126	187	182	229	187	178
(c) leaving small intestine	ND	ND	42	47	ND	ND	ND	ND	33	56	ND	ND	ND	ND	52	49	61	57
(d) absorbed	ND	ND	93	112	ND	ND	ND	ND	100	113	ND	ND	90†	144†	130	180	126	121
Digestibility (d/b) %	ND	ND	69	70	ND	ND	ND	ND	75	67	ND	ND	ND	ND	71	78	68	68
Reference	1		2		1		1		3		4		5		6		6	6

Footnotes:

* With respect to nitrogen in the diet and in the treated component

** U = Untreated; T = Treated

† Absorption from small and large intestine

†† Nitrogen or non-ammonia nitrogen × 6.25

ND Not determined

References:

1. Faichney, 1974
2. MacRae et al., 1972
3. Beever et al., 1977
4. Verite and Journet, 1977
5. Hemsley, Hogan and Weston, 1970
6. Thomson and Beever, unpublished data

requires a source of sulphur (Bray and Till, 1975), branched chain fatty acids (Hemsley and Moir, 1963) and amino acids and/or ammonia (Allison, 1970; Bryant and Robinson, 1962). Doubt still remains as to the preferred nitrogenous substrate, and growth requirements could be related to microbial species. Pilgrim, Gray, Weller and Belling (1970) found that 63 and 77 per cent of bacterial N and 38 and 53 per cent of protozoal N were derived directly from NH_3 in sheep fed lucerne chaff or wheaten hay respectively; whilst Mathison and Milligan (1971) derived values of 50 and 57 per cent for bacterial N and 40 and 55 per cent for protozoal N on a hay or barley diet respectively. Nolan and Leng (1972) obtained a value of 80 per cent for the proportion of bacterial N derived from the ammonia pool on a diet of lucerne chaff, and more recently, Nolan (1975) reported a value of 31 per cent for another lucerne diet. Gawthorne and Nader (1976) calculated that approximately 45 per cent of the sulphur amino acids in microbial protein could be derived by the direct incorporation of amino acids of dietary or salivary origin. More research is required in this area, but nonetheless Satter and Slyter (1974), Miller (1973) and Buttery and Annison (1973) among others have suggested optimum concentrations of rumen ammonia at which microbial growth rate would be maximal. Satter and Slyter's value of 5 mM is considerably less than the value of 20 mM obtained by Miller (1973) using lambs fed diets containing urea, but the lower value is supported by recent *in vivo* evidence (Okorie, Buttery and Lewis, 1977). To date no quantitative requirements of amino acids for maximal microbial growth are available. A balanced supply of amino acids to the rumen micro-organisms, in addition to a non-protein nitrogen (NPN) source, may be essential, and the substitution of NPN for protected protein in the nutrition of rumen micro-organisms may lead to a depression in microbial growth and structural carbohydrate degradation when a major part of the dietary protein has been protected. Supporting evidence for this is afforded by the digestion data for a high temperature dried grass which was subsequently treated with 1 g HCHO/100 g crude protein prior to feeding (Beever, Thomson and Cammell, 1976). Estimates of microbial and feed protein at the duodenum were not made, but the quantity of cellulose digested in the rumen was 21 per cent less than that observed on the high temperature dried grass without HCHO, indicating a reduced extent of microbial cellulolytic activity. With formalin silage, where 78 per cent of the dietary protein escaped rumen degradation, Beever *et al.* (1977) observed only a 7 per cent decline in the extent of cellulose digestion within the rumen compared with the untreated silage and postulated the occurrence of an uncoupled fermentation (Hobson and Summers, 1967).

Effect of protein protection on total nutrient supply

There is some indirect evidence (Ekern, Blaxter and Sawers, 1965; Corbett *et al.*, 1966; Blaxter *et al.*, 1971) that excessive proteolysis within the rumen may be energetically inefficient both in terms of rumen fermentation and supply of energy to the host animal following digestion. The fermentative equations proposed by Baldwin, Lucas and Cabrera (1970) support this general contention; from these Beever *et al.* (1977) calculated that the production of heat and methane within the rumen of sheep fed unwilted silage could be at least four times higher than those values predicted for HCHO silage fed fresh or dried. In addition, Beever *et al.* (Beever, Cammell and Wallace, 1974; Beever, Thomson and Cammell, 1976; Beever *et al.*, 1977) have shown the efficiency of conversion of ruminally digested energy to VFA energy on untreated diets to have a mean value of 59 per cent, but for the same diets treated with HCHO or dried, a mean value of 78 per cent was obtained. Several observations from this laboratory indicate that a reduction in protein degradation within the rumen can lead to an increase in the total energy absorbed from the alimentary tract (Beever, Thomson and Cammell, 1976; Beever *et al.*, 1977). With the limited data available, it is not possible to predict the magnitude of increases, but it is a further aspect to be considered when determining the value of protected proteins.

Protein supply and demand

Burroughs, Trenkle and Vetter (1974) proposed the system of protein evaluation for cattle and sheep involving metabolizable protein, defined as 'the quantity of protein digested in the post-ruminal portion of the digestive tract of ruminants', or as used in this chapter, and strictly more correct, 'in the small intestine'. Whilst the concept of Burroughs, Trenkle and Vetter is accepted, the manner in which they derived estimates of metabolizable protein must be viewed circumspectly.

Diets are known to vary widely in the quantity and digestibility of microbial and dietary protein which enter the small intestine. Microbial protein generally comprises the largest part of the metabolizable protein supply, and Miller (1973) calculated a theoretical maximum for microbial protein N synthesis of 27 g/kg organic matter digested in the rumen. Subsequently, McMeniman, Ben-Ghadalia and Armstrong (1976) summarised a series of measured growth rates and derived values of 33 g/kg organic matter for forage diets and 22 g/kg organic matter for cereal diets. Making similar calculations to those employed by Egan and Walker (1975), with the exception of a value of 4.81, not 4.10 kJ energy/g organic matter digested (based on studies in this laboratory), the data of McMeniman, Ben-Ghadalia and Armstrong (1976) were found to be equivalent to 6.21 and 4.16 g digestible microbial protein per MJ metabolizable energy for forages and cereals respectively. Comparison of these estimates, with measured values in *Table 5.6*, indicates the contribution of protected protein to total metabolizable protein supply, and the artifacts which may be introduced by accepting generalisations similar to those proposed by Burroughs, Trenkle and Vetter (1974). However, to examine the potential of protected protein in any practical situation, it is essential to estimate metabolizable protein supply and demand on the basic diet, identify any deficiencies, and consider how best these may be overcome.

Metabolizable protein demand will clearly depend on the body size of the animal, its productive potential, its metabolizable energy intake and the composition of the absorbed amino acids.

Lactation requirements

An example has been taken based on a 640 kg cow, losing 1 kg of bodyweight day^{-1} for the first 6 weeks of lactation and thereafter showing varying rates of

Table 5.6 MEASURED YIELDS OF METABOLIZABLE PROTEIN (MP) PER MJ OF METABOLIZABLE ENERGY (ME) FOR A RANGE OF DIETS FED TO RUMINANTS

Diet	Dry matter intake (g/24h)	Protein absorbed (g/24h)	Digestible energy (DE) (%)	ME intake (MJ/24 h)	g MP/MJ ME/24 h	Reference
Wheaten straw					6.3	
Clover hay					7.5	
Wheaten hay					7.6	Walker et al., 1975
Lucerne hay					7.6	
Perennial ryegrass (fresh)					7.9	
Unwilted silage	1042	100	80	12.13[1]	8.2	Beever et al., 1977
White clover (fresh)					8.5	Walker et al., 1975
Tama ryegrass (fresh)					8.7	
Formalin silage	1022	113	75	12.09[2]	9.3	Beever et al., 1977
Red clover wafers	880	78	65	8.37[2]	9.3	Beever, Thomson and Harrison, 1971
Dried grass pellets	1058	130	78	12.59[2]	10.3	Thomson and Beever (unpublished)
Red clover pellets	900	96	66	8.70[2]	11.0	Beever, Thomson and Harrison, 1971
Red clover (fresh)	878	97	68	8.24[1]	11.8	

[1] ME = 0.76 × DE for diets containing highly soluble proteins
[2] ME = 0.82 × DE for diets containing considerably protected proteins

bodyweight gain to a final weight at week 44 of 672 kg. Milk production peaked at 36 kg day^{-1} at week 6 and thereafter declined at an average of 3 per cent per week. No allowances were made for any ensuing pregnancies. Metabolizable protein requirements for maintenance of bodyweight and for bodyweight changes were calculated according to the equations proposed by Burroughs, Trenkle and Vetter (1974), assuming a 50 per cent loss due to metabolism, and were found to be similar to those calculated by Hogan (1975) which were based on inescapable losses of nitrogen. The metabolizable protein requirement for milk secretion was calculated to be 46.7 g/kg milk, based on a net protein content of 35 g kg^{-1} and a biological value of 75 which was derived by a comparison of the essential amino acid profiles of protein absorbed from the small intestine of sheep fed a range of forage and cereal diets, and milk protein. Metabolizable energy requirements for maintenance of bodyweight, all bodyweight changes and milk secretion were compiled according to the system proposed by Alderman *et al.* (1974).

Total summated metabolizable protein requirements are given in *Figure 5.3*, and when expressed in relation to metabolizable energy requirements in a similar

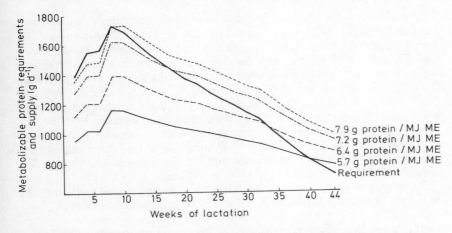

Figure 5.3 The requirements of metabolizable protein for lactation, and the supply from four different concentrates

manner to that adopted by Egan and Walker (1975) values ranged from 8.4 g MJ^{-1} at week 6 to 5.7 g MJ^{-1} at week 44 of lactation. Assuming that all maintenance metabolizable energy (ME) was derived from unwilted grass silage, which was taken to supply 11.50 MJ ME/kg DM and 8.2 g metabolizable protein/MJ ME (*Table 5.6*), the feeding of a concentrate of 12.2 MJ ME/kg DM was fixed at a level sufficient to meet all ME requirements for production. This was found to amount to an average of 3.8 lb/gallon of milk produced. The data presented in *Figure 5.3* indicate the likely total metabolizable protein supply if the concentrate used provided 5.7, 6.4, 7.2 or 7.9 g metabolizable protein/MJ ME and the relationship between supply and demand is clearly illustrated. At almost all levels of potential production, the 5.7 and 6.4 g levels were inadequate and it would appear that, under the conditions examined, the requirement would be for a concentrate supplying 7.9 g metabolizable protein/MJ ME for the first 16 weeks of lactation and one supplying 7.2 g metabolizable protein/MJ ME from week 16 to week 32; thereafter a lower level of 6.43 g metabolizable protein/MJ ME would be adequate. Reliable data on the metabolizable protein supply from concentrates are not available, but if we take the value derived from McMeniman, Ben-Ghadalia and Armstrong (1976) of 4.16 g truly digested metabolizable protein/MJ ME for cereal diets, likely total metabolizable protein supply can be computed. Assuming a total protein content of 16 per cent in the diet (N.B. not simply total N × 6.25) a 10, 20, 30 or 40 per cent protection of the dietary protein, with an assumed 70 per cent digestibility of this protein in the small intestine, would increase metabolizable protein supply to 5.1, 6.0, 6.9 and 7.8 g/MJ ME, provided the reduced availability of protein in the rumen did not depress microbial growth.

Growth requirements

The requirements for the growth of sheep and cattle have been calculated by Egan and Walker (1975) on the basis of the ARC (1965) data. Assuming a biological value of 75 for protein absorbed from the small intestine, most of the diets illustrated in *Table 5.6*, with the exception of wheaten straw, would be adequate to meet the protein requirements of a 40 kg sheep growing at 100 g live weight increase per day (8.13 g protein/MJ ME) and 400 kg cattle at 1 kg d^{-1} (7.89 g/MJ ME), provided sufficient food was consumed to meet the animal's requirement for metabolizable energy. New methods of assessing both the supply and the requirement of ruminants for protein are currently under consideration by the Agricultural Research Council. The inter-relationship of energy concentration and supply with protein supply from microbial and undegraded dietary protein was discussed by Broster and Oldham (1977).

There is evidence (Purser and Buechler, 1966; Bergen, Purser and Cline, 1968) to suggest that the quality of bacterial and protozoal protein as measured by amino acid content, protein quality and *in vitro* digestibility are relatively constant and to a large measure unaffected by the composition of the diet. The amino acid composition of duodenal digesta protein and protein apparently absorbed from the small intestine appears to be relatively constant (Harrison *et al.*, 1973; Beever *et al.*, 1977). However, an elevated leucine content of abomasal digesta of animals fed a high leucine corn-gluten meal has been measured (Poley and Trenkle, 1963).

Single amino acids can be protected from ruminal fermentation and the supply of specific amino acids to the host animal enhanced. Methionine hydroxy analogue (Polan, Chandler and Miller, 1970), the encapsulation of methionine with fat (Mowat and Deelstra, 1970) and the preparation of amino acid copolymers (Ferguson, 1975) are examples. A clearer knowledge of specific amino acid requirements of ruminants is required together with further information on the dietary situations in which advantage may be gained by the use of protected amino acids.

Responses in voluntary food intake to the treatment of forage, prior to ensiling, with formaldehyde have been obtained with sheep (Wilkins, Wilson and

Cook, 1974) growing cattle (Waldo, 1975) and dairy cows (Valentine and Rad-cliffe, 1975). Improved food conversion efficiency has also been measured with young growing cattle (3–6 months of age) (Taylor and Wilkins, 1976) and dairy cows (Valentine and Radcliffe, 1975) fed formaldehyde-treated silage. Verite and Journet (1977) fed rapeseed and soya bean meal treated with formaldehyde with a basal diet of maize silage and measured responses of 1 kg d^{-1} in milk yield.

Conclusions

An examination of the potential of protected proteins for ruminants has shown that:

(1) for many proteins a high proportion of the protein does escape ruminal degradation, even before the imposition of any treatment designed to increase this proportion;

(2) heat treatment, grinding and pelleting and the use of chemical treatment, such as formaldehyde, have been shown to increase the percentage of the dietary protein escaping degradation in the rumen;

(3) the total supply of protein to the ruminant animal can be increased by these measures and, where optimum rates have been satsifactorily deter-mined, over-protection can be avoided.

There are however several qualifications to the protection of protein in the diet of ruminants. Some proteins merit treatment; others do not. Highly soluble proteins where a high proportion of the protein is degraded in the rumen and only a small proportion naturally escapes ruminal degradation are prime candi-dates for treatment, e.g. groundnut meal, soya bean meal and forage, the latter particularly when it is to be conserved as silage. Fish meal and other highly pro-tected sources do not merit treatment. Rumen fermentation and microbial protein synthesis have to be sustained at satisfactory levels of efficiency when protected proteins are fed. Reactions in the rumen dictate to a major extent the nutrient supply to the host animal. Currently available techniques have allowed the quantitative elucidation of degradation and synthesis in the rumen. The use of protected protein in ruminant diets is but part of the interaction of supply to the animal and requirement by the animal for nutrients. Comprehensive modelling should in future refine our knowledge, and also define more precisely situations in which dietary manipulation may be of benefit (Black, Faichney and Graham, 1976). Current assessment would suggest that the early stages of lacta-tion and the early stages of growth, when protein requirements are high, are the situations in which responses to the protection of protein may be obtained.

References

Agricultural Research Council (1965). *The Nutrient Requirements of Farm Livestock, No. 2. Ruminants.* London; HMSO
Alderman, G., Griffiths, J.R., Morgan, D.E., Edwards, R.A., Raven, A.M.,

Holmes, W. and Lessells, W.J. (1974). In *University of Nottingham Nutrition Conference for Feed Manufacturers – 7*, p. 37. Eds. H. Swan and D. Lewis. London; Butterworths

Allison. M.J. (1970). In *Physiology of Digestion and Metabolism in the Ruminant*, p. 456. Ed. A.T. Phillipson. Newcastle-upon-Tyne; Oriel Press

Annison, E.F. (1973). In *University of Nottingham Nutrition Conference for Feed Manufacturers – 6*, p. 2. Eds. H. Swan and D. Lewis. Edinburgh and London; Churchill Livingstone

Armstrong, D.G. (1976). *Übers. Tierarnahrg.*, 4, 1

Armstrong, D.G. and Annison. E.F. (1973). *Proc. Nutr. Soc.*, 32, 107

Armstrong, D.G. and Hutton, K. (1975). In *Digestion and Metabolism in the Ruminant*, p. 432. Eds. I.W. McDonald and A.C.I. Warner. Armidale; University of New England Press

Baldwin, R.L., Lucas, H.L. and Cabrera, R. (1970). In *Physiology of Digestion and Metabolism in the Ruminant*, p. 319. Ed. A.T. Phillipson. Newcastle-upon-Tyne; Oriel Press

Barry, T.N. (1976). *Proc. Nutr. Soc.*, 35, 221

Bauchop, T. and Elsden, S.R. (1960). *J. gen. Microbiol.*, 23, 457

Beever, D.E., Cammell, S.B. and Wallace, Miss A.S. (1974). *Proc. Nutr. Soc.*, 33, 73A

Beever, D.E., Harrison, D.G. and Thomson, D.J. (1972). *Proc. Nutr. Soc.*, 31, 61A

Beever, D.E., Thomson, D.J. and Cammell, S.B. (1976). *J. agric. Sci., Camb.*, 86, 443

Beever, D.E., Thomson, D.J. and Harrison, D.G. (1971). *Proc. Nutr. Soc.*, 30, 86A

Beever, D.E., Thomson, D.J., Cammell, S.B. and Harrison, D.G. (1977). *J. agric. Sci., Camb.*, 88, 61

Bergen, W.G., Purser, D.B. and Cline, H.J. (1968). *J. Anim. Sci.*, 27, 1497

Black, J.L., Faichney, G.J. and Graham, N. McC. (1976). In *Protein Metabolism and Nutrition*, p. 477. Eds. D.J.A. Cole *et al.* London; Butterworths

Blaxter, K.L., Wainman, F.W., Dewey, P.J.S., Davidson, J., Denerly, H. and Gunn, J.B. (1971). *J. agric. Sci., Camb.*, 76, 307

Bray, A.C. and Till, A.R. (1975). In *Digestion and Metabolism in the Ruminant*, p. 243. Eds. I.W. McDonald and A.C.I. Warner. Armidale; University of New England Press

Broster, W.H. and Oldham, J.D. (1977). In *Nutrition and the Climatic Environment*, p. 123. Eds. W. Haresign, H. Swan and D. Lewis. London; Butterworths

Bryant, M.P. and Robinson, I.M. (1962). *J. Bact.*, 84, 605

Burroughs, W., Trenkle, A. and Vetter, R.L. (1974). *Vet. Med., Small Anim. Clinician*, 69, 713

Buttery, P.J. and Annison, E.F. (1973). In *Biological Efficiency of Protein Production*, p. 141. Ed. J.G.W. Jones. Cambridge University Press

Chalmers, M.I., Cuthbertson, D.P. and Synge, R.L.M. (1954). *J. agric. Sci., Camb.*, 44, 254

Chalupa, W. (1975). *J. Dairy Sci.*, 58, 1198

Clark, J.H. (1975). *J. Dairy Sci.*, 58, 1178

Corbett, J.L., Langlands, J.P., McDonald, I. and Pullar, J.D. (1966). *Anim. Prod.*, 8, 13

Egan, A.R. and Walker, D.J. (1975). In *Proc. 3rd World Conf. Anim. Prod.,*
    Melbourne, p. 551. Ed. R.L. Reid. Sydney; Sydney University Press
Ekern, A., Blaxter, K.L. and Sawers, D. (1965). *Br. J. Nutr.,* **19**, 417
Faichney, G.J. (1974). *Aust. J. agric. Res.,* **25**, 583
Ferguson, K.A. (1975). In *Digestion and Metabolism in the Ruminant*, p. 448.
    Eds. I.W. McDonald and A.C.I. Warner. Armidale; University of New England
    Press
Ferguson, K.A., Hemsley, J.A. and Reis, P.J. (1967). *Aust. J. Sci.,* **30**, 215
Fisher, C. (1976). In *Protein Metabolism and Nutrition*, p. 323. Eds. D.J.A Cole
    et al. London; Butterworths
Gawthorn, J.M. and Nader, C.J. (1976). *Br. J. Nutr.,* **35**, 11
Harrison, D.G., Beever, D.E., Thomson, D.J. and Osbourn, D.F. (1973). *J. agric.*
    Sci., Camb., **81**, 391
Hemsley, J.A. and Moir, R.W. (1963). *Aust. J. agric. Res.,* **14**, 509
Hemsley, J.A., Hogan, J.P. and Weston, R.H. In *Proc. 11th Int. Grassl. Cong.,*
    Surfers Paradise, p. 703. Australia
Hemsley, R.A., Reis, P.J. and Downes, A.M. (1973). *Aust. J. Biol. Sci.,* **26**, 961
Hobson, P.N. and Summers, R. (1967). *J. Gen. Microbiol.,* **47**, 53
Hogan, J.P. (1975). *J. Dairy Sci.,* **58**, 1164
Hogan, J.P. and Weston, R.H. (1970). In *Physiology of Digestion and Metabo-*
    lism in the Ruminant, p. 478. Ed. A.T. Phillipson. Newcastle-upon-Tyne;
    Oriel Press
Hume, I.D. (1974). *Aust. J. agric. Res.,* **25**, 155
Hume, I.D. and Purser, D.B. (1974). *Proc. Aust. Soc. Anim. Prod.,* **10**, 399
Hungate, R.E. (1966). In *The Rumen and its Microbes*. New York; Academic
    Press
Hutton, K. and Annison, E.F. (1972). *Proc. Nutr. Soc.,* **31**, 151
JCO (1976). Report No. 2. Protein Feeds for Farm Livestock in the UK
Leng, R.A. (1970). In *Physiology of Digestion and Metabolism in the Ruminant*,
    p. 406. Ed. A.T. Phillipson. Newcastle-upon-Tyne; Oriel Press
Leroy, F., Zelter, S.E. and François, A.C. (1964). *C. r. mensuel Séanc. Acad. Sci.*
    colon., **259**, 1592
Lewis, D. and Mitchell, R.M. (1976). In *Protein Metabolism and Nutrition*,
    p. 417. Eds. D.J.A. Cole *et al.* London; Butterworths
Macrae, J.C., Ulyatt, M.J., Pearce, P.D. and Hendtlass, Jane (1972). *Br. J. Nutr.,*
    27, 39
McDonald, I.W. (1952). *Biochem. J.,* **51**, 86
McDonald, I.W. and Hall, R.J. (1957). *Biochem. J.,* **67**, 400
McLeod, M.N. (1974). *Nutr. Abstrs. Revs.,* **44**, 803
McMeniman, N.P., Ben-Ghadalia, D. and Armstrong, D.G. (1976). In *Protein*
    Metabolism and Nutrition, p. 217. Eds. D.J.A. Cole *et al.* London; Butter-
    worths
Mathison, G.W. and Milligan, L.P. (1971). *Br. J. Nutr.,* **25**, 351
Mercer, J. and Annison, E.F. (1976). In *Protein Metabolism and Nutrition*,
    p. 397. Eds. D.J.A. Cole *et al.* London; Butterworths
Miller, E.L. (1973). *Proc. Nutr. Soc.,* **32**, 79
Mowat, D.N. and Deelstra, K. (1970). *J. Anim. Sci.,* **31**, 1041
Nolan, J.V. (1975). In *Digestion and Metabolism in the Ruminant*, p. 416. Eds.
    I.W. McDonald and A.C.I. Warner. Armidale; University of New England Press

Nolan, J.V. and Leng, R.A. (1972). *Br. J. Nutr.*, **27**, 177

Okorie, A., Buttery, P.J. and Lewis, D. (1977). *Proc. Nutr. Soc.*, **36**, 38A

Osbourn, D.F., Beever, D.E. and Thomson, D.J. (1976). *Proc. Nutr. Soc.*, **35**, 191

Pilgrim, A.F., Gray, F.V., Weller, R.A. and Belling, C.B. (1970). *Br. J. Nutr.*, **24**, 589

Polan, C.E., Chandler, P.T. and Miller, C.N. (1970). *J. Dairy Sci.*, **54**, 607

Poley, G.E. and Trenkle, A.H. (1963). *J. Anim. Sci.*, **22**, 1139

Purser, D.B. and Buechler, S.M. (1966). *J. Dairy Sci.*, **49**, 61

Satter, L.D. and Roffler, R.E. (1975). *J. Dairy Sci.*, **58**, 1219

Satter, L.D. and Slyter, L.L. (1974). *Br. J. Nutr.*, **32**, 199

Smith, R.H. (1975). In *Digestion and Metabolism in the Ruminant*, p. 399. Eds. I.W. McDonald and A.C.I. Warner. Armidale; University of New England Press

Stouthamer, A.H. (1973). *Antonie van Leeuwenhoek*, **39**, 545

Tagari, H., Ascarelli, I. and Bondi, A. (1962). *Br. J. Nutr.*, **16**, 237

Taylor, J.C. and Wilkins, R.J. (1976). In *Principles of Cattle Production*, p. 343. Eds. H. Swan and W.H. Broster. London; Butterworths

Thomson, D.J. and Beever, D.E. (1974). Unpublished data

Ulyatt, M.J., MacRae, J.C., Clarke, R.T.J. and Pearce, P.D. (1975). *J. agric. Sci., Camb.*, **84**, 453

Valentine, S.C. and Radcliffe, J.C. (1975). *Aust. J. agric. Res.*, **26**, 769

Verite, R. and Journet, M. (1977). *Annls. Zootech.*, **26**, 183

Waldo, D.R. (1975). *J. Anim. Sci.*, **41**, 424

Walker, D.J., Egan, A.R., Nader, C.J., Ulyatt, M.J. and Storer, G.B. (1975). *Aust. J. agric. Res.*, **26**, 699

West, J. and Mangan, J.L. (1972). *Proc. Nutr. Soc.*, **31**, 108A

Wilkins, R.J., Wilson, R.F. and Cook, J.E. (1974). *Proc. 12th int. Grassld. Congr.*, p. 277, Moscow

Wilkinson, J.M., Wilson, R.F. and Barry, T.N. (1976). *Outlook on Agriculture*, **9**, 3

6

REDUCING THE RATE OF AMMONIA RELEASE BY THE USE OF ALTERNATIVE NON-PROTEIN NITROGEN SOURCES

E.E. BARTLEY
C.W. DEYOE
Departments of Dairy and Poultry Sciences and Grain Science and Industry, Kansas State University, USA

One of the most serious world shortages is the supply of protein for human and animal consumption. Ruminants do not need to compete with humans or non-ruminants for protein because they have the unique ability to convert non-protein nitrogen (NPN) compounds in their feed to good quality microbial protein. While it has been established that NPN can be used successfully in ruminant rations (National Research Council, 1976; Chalupa, 1968; Helmer and Bartley, 1971; Oltjen, 1969; Tillman and Sidhu, 1969; Virtanen, 1966), there is much more that can and should be done to improve NPN utilisation by ruminants.

In the USA in 1973 approximately 950 000 tons of urea were used in ruminant rations (Anonymous, 1974). It replaced an estimated 6 000 000 tons of soya bean meal. Although urea is the most widely used NPN compound in ruminant rations, several other NPN compounds have been used.

Non-protein nitrogen products for ruminants

The non-protein nitrogen products that have been used in ruminant nutrition include organic and inorganic ammonium salts, ammoniated feeds and by-products, dicyanodiamide, biuret, and urea. Several reviews pertaining to the use of NPN products for ruminants are available (National Research Council, 1976; Helmer and Bartley, 1971; Loosli and McDonald, 1968). Recently Fonnesbeck, Kearl and Harris (1975) reviewed literature on biuret as a protein replacement for ruminants.

Ruminants seem to use organic and inorganic ammonium salts well but economics precludes their wide use. The nitrogen of ammoniated molasses is not used well, and toxic compounds may cause central nervous system disturbances. Ammoniated rice hulls and beet or citrus pulp can be used in small amounts in diets containing some grain. Dicyanodiamide is an interesting compound because it contains 66 per cent N or 412 per cent crude protein and is not toxic for ruminants. However, it has not been well utilised by ruminants as a nitrogen source.

Biuret is palatable, is slowly hydrolysed to ammonia in the rumen and is less toxic than urea. It has been used successfully as a nitrogen supplement by cattle fed low quality roughages. Release of energy from such roughages is relatively slow, conforming to the slow release of ammonia from biuret. Biuret supplementation of diets for full-fed ruminants on high energy diets does not appear to be superior to urea when fed in similar diets (National Research Council, 1976). Animals require from 3 to 8 weeks to adapt to biuret, then they must consume it regularly to maintain the activity of the enzyme biuretase. Biuret costs more than urea and is not currently cleared by the US Food and Drug Administration for cows producing milk for human consumption.

Methods of improving urea utilisation

Problems associated with the use of urea are palatability, toxicity and the efficient utilisation of urea-N in the rumen. The utilisation of urea is influenced greatly by the kind and quantity of energy available in the diet. An understanding of this relationship is outlined in succeeding sections of this chapter.

Many studies (reviewed by Helmer and Bartley, 1971; and National Research Council, 1976) have indicated that animal performance improves with time on urea-containing rations. However, not all investigators have noted this 'adaptation' to urea. In any event, it is undesirable to give ruminants large quantities of urea (say 3 per cent of the ration) before they become accustomed to it. Recommendations in the USA frequently suggest using no more than 1 to 1.5 per cent urea in the grain-concentrate rations for lactating cows.

Several investigators (National Research Council, 1976) have reported improved utilisation of urea by increasing the frequency of feeding. Inadequate mixing can increase the incidence of ammonia toxicity by permitting overconsumption of urea. The addition of urea to forage at ensiling time aids in the mixing of urea. The addition of 0.5 per cent urea on an 'as is' basis to fresh forage (35—40 per cent dry matter) will raise the crude protein of the dry matter four percentage points. Adding higher quantities of urea at ensiling time may buffer acids needed for silage preservation. Using urea in complete diets will dilute the total urea in the diet and reduce problems related to acceptance.

Urea is readily consumed when incorporated in liquid supplements containing molasses and phosphoric acid. The utilisation of urea in liquid supplements is similar to its utilisation in dry supplements. Davidovich, Bartley and Bechtle (1976) observed that liquid supplements with higher concentrations of molasses and phosphoric acid are less toxic than those with lower concentrations of these ingredients. Ammonia toxicity was considerably lower in supplements containing 3 per cent phosphoric acid than in those containing 1 per cent. An explanation for this is provided under the section on ammonia toxicity (*see* p. 106).

Nitrogen metabolism in the rumen

Rumen micro-organisms degrade feed protein in the rumen to peptides, amino acids, and finally ammonia. Ammonia appears to be the major end-product of protein degradation and ammonia is used by the majority of rumen bacteria to synthesize bacterial protein (Allison, 1970; Bryant, 1970). The protozoa engulf and digest bacteria, feed particles, free amino acids, purine and pyrimidine bases from the rumen digesta and synthesize protozoal protein. A major portion of the microbial protein is then enzymatically degraded to amino acids in the small intestine where, after being absorbed, they are available for use by the animal. Non-protein nitrogen compounds in the feed, e.g. urea, are hydrolysed by rumen micro-organisms to ammonia, which is also converted to microbial protein.

Since the majority of rumen bacteria prefer ammonia to organic nitrogen, they should be permitted to produce ammonia but then encouraged to use it more efficiently. There is no indication that high concentrations of ammonia in the rumen inhibit bacterial growth (Smith, 1975). If the ammonia is released too rapidly, considerable quantities can be absorbed through the rumen wall and be subsequently lost to the animal. Consequently numerous attempts have been made to reduce the rate of conversion to ammonia in the rumen. Where an NPN compound or product containing NPN releases ammonia only slowly in the rumen, it is purported to be a good product. However, this is not necessarily a true assumption. Knowing the concentration of ammonia in the rumen is of little value unless it is also shown that more microbial protein is synthesised from the slow-release product. Attempts to reduce the rate at which ammonia is produced in the rumen by coating NPN compounds, by inhibiting the action of urease enzyme or by using less soluble NPN compounds have not been entirely satisfactory, perhaps because they have, in part, prevented conversion of the NPN compounds to ammonia (Helmer and Bartley, 1971). It appears that an abundant supply of ammonia is necessary for maximal microbial protein synthesis.

Edwards and Bartley (1976) compared ammonia concentrations and microbial protein synthesis from isonitrogenous quantities of a mixture of grain and various NPN compounds, extrusion cooked mixtures of grain and some of these NPN compounds, and a commercial slow-release product made by adsorbing the urea on an inert carrier and then coating it with molasses. The data in *Table 6.1* (Experiment 1) show that the slow-release product released less ammonia after 6 h of fermentation *in vitro* than did Starea or a mixture of grain and urea; however, microbial protein synthesis from the slow-release product was less than that from Starea or the mixture of grain and urea. It is clear from the results of Experiment 2 that a low ruminal ammonia concentration is not necessarily an indicator of good microbial protein synthesis. It is generally not realised that the solubility of feed grade urea varies widely and its solubility affects rumen ammonia and microbial protein production (*Table 6.1*, Experiment 2).

Ammonia released from NPN cannot be converted to microbial protein unless a carbon skeleton and source of energy are available. Ration carbohydrate fulfills this function. However, ways in which different carbohydrates work vary widely. The poorest carbohydrate for this purpose is roughage cellulose and the best appears to be starch. Starch is superior to molasses or simple sugars such as glucose, and cooked starch is better than raw starch. In Experiment 3 (*Table 6.1*) Anderson (1976) compared microbial protein synthesis from substrates containing urea and cane molasses, hemicellulose extract (Masonex from Masonite Corporation, Chicago, Illinois) or Starea. The product containing cooked starch (Starea) gave more microbial protein than did molasses or hemicellulose extract.

It is apparent that the rate that energy is released from the carbohydrate

Table 6.1 RUMEN AMMONIA CONCENTRATION AND BACTERIAL PROTEIN SYNTHESIS *IN VITRO* FROM THREE PRODUCTS WITH DIFFERENT AMMONIA RELEASE RATES (EXPERIMENT 1), VARIOUS MIXTURES OF PROCESSED AND UNPROCESSED GRAIN PLUS NPN COMPOUNDS (EXPERIMENT 2), AND THREE CARBOHYDRATE SOURCES (EXPERIMENT 3).

Experiment	Substrates[1]	No. of trials	Ammonia-N (mg/100 ml)	Microbial protein (mg/100 ml)
1	Unprocessed mixture of grain + urea	4	100	16.4
1	Starea	4	89	26.3
1	Slow-release commercial product	4	70	12.5
2	Unprocessed grain +			
	1. soluble urea	2	95	16.3
	2. urea of low solubility	2	108	15.0
	3. urea of very low solubility	2	124	11.9
	4. sulphur-coated urea	2	110	15.0
	5. isobutyl diurea (IBDU)[2]	2	8	0
	6. dicyanodiamide[2]	2	4	4.4
	7. biuret[2]	2	18	0
2	Extrusion processed grain +			
	1. biuret	2	70	26.3
	2. urea (Starea)	2	97	35.6
3	Cane molasses + urea	10	57	14.7
3	Hemicellulose extract + urea	19	56	15.2
3	Starea	8	73	24.5

[1] All substrates contained the same quantity of urea-N
[2] Rumen fluid inoculum from animals not adapted to these compounds

material is crucial. If it is released too slowly, as from cellulose, or if it is released too rapidly as from glucose, then ammonia is converted to microbial protein inefficiently.

Consequently, it appears that conversion of NPN to microbial protein would be maximised by a compound converted to ammonia at a rate similar to the metabolism rate of the carbohydrate source. The quantity of energy available for conversion is also highly important.

Methods for estimating microbial protein in rumen fluid

Determining microbial protein synthesis is a major technical problem, and is important to this discussion because ammonia is of no value to the ruminant unless it is converted to microbial protein. Differential centrifugation has been used (Blackburn and Hobson, 1960). However, with cooked grains, a polysaccharide slime drapes the bacteria and prevents their separation (Barr, Bartley and Meyer, 1975). Protein precipitating agents (trichloroacetic, perchloric, picric, and tungstic acids) have been used. Barr, Bartley and Meyer (1975) have found large variations in the protein precipitated from rumen fluid by these compounds. Source of protein (feed, bacterial and/or protozoal) being precipitated may affect the results when precipitating agents are used to free proteins from solutions. Various intermediate products of precipitated protein may explain differences in quantity of nitrogen precipitated. For example, Bartley and Meyer (1975) have found tri-chloroacetic acid to precipitate three times as much nitrogen from rumen fluid as that precipitated by tungstic acid.

Diaminopimelic acid (an amino acid found only in bacteria) and amino ethyl phosphonic acid (an amino acid found only in protozoa) have been used as markers for bacteria and protozoa. Unfortunately, some rumen bacteria that flourish on high-grain or cooked-grain rations contain little if any diaminopimelic acid. Hutton, Bailey and Annison (1971) have discussed the need to allow for differences in concentrations of the markers among microbial species.

Determinations based on incorporating ^{33}P, ^{35}S, or ^{15}N into the microbes have been developed, but the methods have several limitations. Rates at which microbial cells incorporate the labels can vary with diet and microbial species present (Bucholtz and Bergen, 1973; Hungate, 1966; Smith, 1975; Thomas, 1973; Walker and Nader, 1975).

Smith and McAllan (1970) found that nucleic acids leaving the rumen are almost entirely of microbial origin because nucleic acids in feed are rapidly degraded in the rumen. If the ratio of RNA-nitrogen to total nitrogen is constant in rumen bacteria, it is possible to calculate the amount of bacterial protein synthesized. This method has considerable merit but more information is needed on the ratio of RNA-nitrogen to total nitrogen in rumen bacteria, especially when the diet of the animal contains cooked grains.

Barr, Bartley and Meyer, (1975) have developed a simple method to estimate rumen bacterial and protozoal protein. Centrifuging rumen contents at 25 400 g for 15 min, washing the centrifugate twice with methanol, and determining concentration of the centrifugate gives a quantitative estimate of the nitrogen in a mixture of rumen bacteria and protozoa. The bacteria and proto-zoal fraction was free of urea nitrogen and polysaccharide slime that prevails when the ration contains large quantities of grain, especially cooked grain. Appropriate feed blanks are needed because the methanol removes some of the nitrogen in the feed.

Improved urea utilisation through Starea

Starea[1] is a product that was developed to make energy available to rumen micro-organisms at a rate similar to the rate that urea releases ammonia so the micro-organisms are simultaneously provided with the main components for microbial protein synthesis (Bartley and Deyoe, 1972).

Starea is produced by mixing finely ground grains (corn, barley, wheat, sorghum, etc.) or other economical starch sources with a non-protein nitrogen (NPN) source such as urea. The material is processed by passing it through a cooker—extruder under moisture, temperature and pressure conditions that cause the starch to gelatinise. Very careful attention must be paid to processing procedures or the product will not have good biological activity. Unfortunately, many products that did not meet quality specifications for Starea have been tested and reported as Starea. Several workers (Barr, 1974; Males and Johnson, 1974;

[1] Starea – registered trademark 860255, US Patent No. 3642489, patent assigned to Kansas State University Research Foundation, Manhattan, Kansas, USA

Table 6.2 AMMONIA NITROGEN CONCENTRATION AND MICROBIAL PROTEIN SYNTHESIS *IN VITRO* AND *IN VIVO* FROM UNPROCESSED GRAIN PLUS UREA OR STAREA SUBSTRATES

Investigator	System	Urea (%)	Ammonia N		Microbial protein	
			Grain + urea	Starea	Grain + urea	Starea
			(mg/100 ml)		(mg/100 ml)	
Helmer *et al.* (1970)	*In vitro*[1]	13	114[a]	81[b]	27[a]	50[b]
Helmer *et al.* (1970)	*In vitro*[1]	13	156[a]	124[b]	42[a]	64[b]
Barr (1974)	*In vitro*[1]	13	132[a]	122[b]	31[a]	43[b]
Barr (1974)	*In vitro*[1]	13	121[a]	93[b]	31[a]	63[b]
Stiles *et al.* (1970)	*In vivo*[2]	5	14[a]g	16[a]g	42[a]g	93[b]g

[a,b]Values between treatments with different letters differ significantly ($P < 0.05$)
[1] Results after 4 h fermentation. TCA precipitable bacterial protein measured
[2] Average of samples collected during 8 h after feeding. Quantities in rumen based on polyethylene glycol volume. Bacterial and protozoal protein by differential centrifugation techniques.

Table 6.3 EFFECT OF DEGREE OF STARCH DAMAGE ON GAS PRODUCTION AND MICROBIAL PROTEIN SYNTHESIS *IN VITRO*

Investigator	Urea (%)	Starch[1] damage (%)	Gas production		Microbial protein	
			Grain + urea (ml)	Starea (ml)	Grain + urea (mg/100 ml)	Starea (mg/100 ml)
Helmer (1969)	15	10				32
	15	100				105
Barr (1974)	22	68	47[a]	127[b]	7[a]	33[b]
	22	80	47[a]	167[b]	7[a]	61[b]
	22	82	47[a]	169[b]	7[a]	62[b]

[a,b]Values between treatments with different letters differ significantly ($P < 0.05$)
[1] Determined by β-amylase (Anstaett *et al.*, 1969)

Shiehzadeh and Harbers, 1974; Stiles *et al.*, 1970; Thompson *et al.*, 1972) have shown that Starea lowers ammonia concentration in the rumen compared with urea. What is more important, however, is the effect of Starea on microbial protein synthesis. In repeated *in vitro* studies (*Tables 6.2* and *6.3*) with a variety of techniques, several workers have shown that microbial protein synthesis is always greater when using Starea as a substrate than when using an unprocessed mixture of grain and urea.

Data in *Table 6.3* show the effects of starch alteration on fermentability of the product and microbial protein synthesis. Generally, the greater the degree of cooking (greater starch alteration), the more fermentable the product is (as demonstrated by the amount of gas produced during fermentation) and the greater the quantity of microbial protein synthesized. While microbial protein synthesis is an excellent estimate of the quality of the product, gas production and the extent to which starch is altered also can be used as indicators of Starea quality.

It is clear that more microbial protein is synthesized from Starea than from unprocessed mixtures of grain and urea. The question of whether the microbial

Table 6.4 NITROGEN RETENTION BY LAMBS OR STEERS FED RATIONS
CONTAINING STAREA, UREA OR SOYA BEAN MEAL

| | | | Nitrogen | |
Investigator	*Nitrogen supplement*	*Urea content of ration (%)*	*Retained (g)*	*Retained (% of intake)*
Shiehzadeh and	Soya bean meal[1]		2.9[3]	14.7[a]
Harbers (1974)	Starea 44[1]	2.0	3.1[3]	14.0[a]
Shiehzadeh and	Starea 44[1]	2.0	1.2[3]	5.3[a]
Harbers (1974)	Starea 70[1]	2.0	1.1[3]	4.6[a]
	Urea[1]	2.0	0.6[3]	2.5[b]
Griffel and	Soya bean meal[2]		29.5[4]	32.1[a]
Bartley (1975)	Starea 44[2]	1.6	18.4[4]	20.0[a]
	Urea[2]	1.6	12.1[4]	12.5[b]
Griffel and	Soya bean meal[2]		26.0[4]	21.0[a]
Bartley (1975)	Starea 70[2]	1.6	31.0[4]	25.4[a]
	Urea[2]	1.6	14.6[4]	11.8[b]

[a,b]Values among treatments with different letters differ significantly (*P* <0.05)
[1] Ration fed to wether lambs (29 kg) contained 60 per cent prairie (grass) hay, 22.85 per
cent sorghum grain, 15.90 per cent protein supplement (10 per cent when Starea 70 was
used), 1.25 per cent mineral-vitamin supplement.
[2] Ration fed to steers (155–165 kg) contained 60 per cent prairie (grass) hay, 27.1 per cent
sorghum grain, 12.4 per cent protein supplement (7.4 per cent when Starea 70 was used),
0.5 per cent mineral-vitamin supplement.
[3] Average of 5 lambs
[4] Average of 6 steers

protein resulting from Starea is useful in meeting an animal's protein requirements can be answered by nitrogen balance and animal performance studies.

Shiehzadeh and Harbers (1974) compared soya bean meal, Starea and urea as
nitrogen supplements to high-roughage rations fed to lambs (*Table 6.4*). In one
experiment Starea containing 44 per cent crude protein was compared with soya
bean meal. The nitrogen balance was the same for both supplements. In a second
experiment urea was compared with Starea containing 44 or 70 per cent crude
protein. The nitrogen balance when Starea was fed was twice that when urea was
fed. Similar studies were conducted by Griffel and Bartley (1975) using steers
instead of lambs. Nitrogen balances were very similar for the Starea and soya
bean meal supplements, and twice that with urea as the supplement. These data
show that the increased microbial protein synthesized from Starea (compared
with that from urea) is utilised by the animal.

A number of studies (Bartley and Deyoe, 1975) have compared Starea with
urea or a natural protein supplement (usually soya bean meal) for lactating dairy
cows. While the quality of Starea used in some of the experiments was either low
or unknown, information from all known experiments was compared to avoid
bias that might result from selecting data. Milk production was significantly
higher in 7 of 10 experiments that compared Starea and urea.

Starea was compared with a natural protein supplement in 16 experiments. In
only two was production from the natural protein supplement significantly
different from that with Starea; however, in the majority of the experiments
production from the cows supplemented with natural protein was slightly higher

than from cows supplemented with Starea. In the 10 comparisons between Starea and urea, grain intake was higher with Starea in all but one. There were no statistically significant differences in intake between animals given either Starea or natural protein supplements. It is apparent that Starea supplementation significantly improves grain intake and milk production over urea supplementation and Starea is almost equal to natural protein supplements.

Burt *et al.* (1972) reported on-farm trials where the nitrogen supplements were soya bean meal, urea (2.5 per cent), urea plus extrusion-cooked barley, or Starea of unknown quality. Milk yield was depressed by urea and increased by gelatinised barley, with no difference in the response of milk yield between gelatinised barley plus urea and Starea.

Starea has been fed to the majority of lactating cows (approximately 100) in the Kansas State University dairy herd continuously since November, 1970. It replaced 66.6 per cent of the supplemental natural protein (soya bean meal) in the grain ration (equivalent to 1.6 per cent urea). Average milk production (2 × 305 day mature equivalents (ME)) in 1968 and 1969, before Starea was fed, was 5783 kg per cow. In 1974 the average milk production was 6914 kg. Health and reproductive performance has not been impaired during the four years with Starea. That is not to infer that the improved performance resulted from Starea; however, the results demonstrate that Starea feeding did not have a deleterious effect on the herd. The average milk production (2 × 305 ME) for the top 50 lactations during the four years with Starea was 9336 kg. It is apparent that high milk production can be obtained from cows receiving Starea.

For growing or finishing cattle, Starea (compared with urea) has improved rate of gain and feed efficiency, particularly during the first 28 to 63 days on feed (Bartley and Deyoe, 1975). Cattle receiving Starea go on feed faster and require less time to adapt to high-energy, urea-containing rations. Starea for wintering cattle is superior to urea and approximately equal to natural protein judged by cow weights and weaning weights of their calves. Yearling cattle wintered on dry grass gain faster when receiving Starea than when receiving mixtures of grain and urea or molasses and urea. Starea has been successfully used in sheep growing and finishing rations.

Rumen ammonia concentration and its relation to ammonia toxicity

It is well known that dietary urea consumed in large quantities in a short time can be toxic (Helmer and Bartley, 1971); 244 cattle were given 0.5 g urea per kilogram bodyweight (Bartley *et al.*, 1976) and this amount proved toxic to 125 of them. In the toxic cases, blood ammonia was elevated to 0.9 mg per 100 ml blood in 60 min; in the non-toxic cases blood ammonia was significantly lower (0.5 mg per 100 ml in 60 min). Blood ammonia and toxicity were strongly correlated ($r = 0.707$).

In toxic cases, rumen pH (*Table 6.5*) was elevated to 7.41 in 60 min, significantly higher than 7.16 for the non-toxic cases. Rumen pH correlated with toxicity at $r = 0.317$. However, rumen ammonia concentration was the same for toxic and non-toxic cases (*c.* 80 mg per 100 ml rumen fluid) and did not correlate with toxicity ($r = 0.309$).

Table 6.5 AVERAGE CONCENTRATIONS OF RUMEN pH, RUMEN AMMONIA-N, BLOOD AMMONIA-N AND BLOOD UREA IN CATTLE FED TOXIC AND NON-TOXIC COMBINATIONS OF GRAIN AND UREA (BARTLEY ET AL., 1976)

Time after dosing (min)	Non-toxic samples					Toxic samples				
	Rumen pH[1]	Free NH$_3$ at pK'a 9.02 (%)	Rumen ammonia-N[1]	Blood ammonia-N[1] (mg/100 ml)	Blood urea-N[2]	Rumen pH[3]	Free NH$_3$ at pK'a 9.02 (%)	Rumen ammonia-N[3]	Blood ammonia-N[3] (mg/100 ml)	Blood urea-N[4]
0	6.58	0.34	7.63	0.14	5.12	6.70	0.42	5.60	0.14	4.40
30	7.03	0.86	61.10	0.44	5.93	7.34	1.92	66.99	0.80	5.37
60	7.16	1.05	81.18	0.53	6.91	7.41	2.49	76.79	0.89	6.14
90	7.15	1.80	89.54	0.58	7.44	7.39	2.25	90.67	0.85	6.93
120	7.08	1.00	93.54	0.61	8.62	7.38	2.20	95.43	0.92	–
180	6.93	0.75	91.12	0.62	10.16	7.37	2.15	101.50	1.04	–
240	6.77	0.90	83.19	0.53	11.41	–	–	–	–	–

[1] Mean of 119 observations
[2] Mean of 48 observations
[3] Mean of 125 observations at 0 and 30 min, 58 at 60 min, 19 at 90 min, 12 at 120 min, and 3 at 180 min
[4] Mean of 35 observations at 0 and 30 min, 15 at 60 min, 5 at 90 min

High concentrations of rumen ammonia obviously do not necessarily indicate ammonia toxicity; high rumen ammonia concentration commensurate with high rumen pH, however, would indicate toxicity because the free NH_3 concentration would be much higher at high pH than at low pH. Ammonia exists as free NH_3 at high pH but as the ammonium ion (NH_4^+) at lower pH. Because tissue membranes are permeable to the lipid soluble NH_3 form but impermeable to the charged NH_4^+ form, more ammonia is absorbed at high pH than at low pH.

The significance of this is that a large ammonia pool can be maintained in the rumen for microbial protein synthesis by maintaining low rumen pH. Readily available starch, such as the cooked starch in Starea, is rapidly fermented to volatile fatty acids, which help maintain low rumen pH.

Smith (1974) presented the following view on nitrogen metabolism in the rumen in an invitational paper at the Fourth International Symposium on Ruminant Physiology, Sydney, Australia:

'It is generally considered that, even moderate, non-toxic elevation of rumen ammonia is undesirable as it may lead to wastage of ammonia by absorption across the rumen wall. Evidence of the practical importance of this is, however, meagre and it appears, rather, that after feeding urea, fairly high concentrations of ammonia in the rumen may persist for many hours and provide a reservoir of nitrogenous nutrient for bacterial growth. Under these conditions a reduction of the rate of ammonia formation by such means as giving urea in frequent small amounts, chemically modifying it or inhibiting urease activity would be expected to reduce the danger of toxicity but not to improve N utilisation greatly. Most attempts which have been made to demonstrate such an improvement have, in fact, failed. It seems more sensible to control urea toxicity by ensuring an adequate matched supply of available energy than to replace urea with other, more expensive, kinds of NPN.'

Starea makes energy available to the rumen micro-organisms at a rate similar to the rate urea releases ammonia so that the micro-organisms are simultaneously provided with the main components for microbial protein synthesis.

Starea has been shown to be less toxic than mixtures of grain and urea (Stiles *et al.*, 1970; Davidovich, Bartley and Bechtle, 1976). Mixtures of ground grain and urea were usually toxic while high quality Starea was non-toxic (*Table 6.6*).

Table 6.6 RELATION OF DEGREE OF STARCH DAMAGE TO BLOOD AMMONIA CONCENTRATION AND CLINICAL SIGNS OF TOXICITY

Product	Starch damage (%)	Urea content (%)	Blood NH_3-N Avg. (mg/100 ml)	Range	Toxicity no. toxic/ no. tested
Grain plus urea unprocessed	0	22.0	0.94	(0.78–1.07)	4/4
Grain plus urea extruded ⎱	58.0	12.1	0.74	(0.71–0.93)	3/3
at low temperature ⎰	73.2	10.6	0.74	(0.66–0.82)	2/2
Grain sorghum Starea	86.7	11.6	0.68	(0.55–0.72)	0/3
Grain sorghum Starea	92.9	20.8	0.43	(0.34–0.51)	0/2
Grain sorghum Starea	86.7	18.3	0.19	(0.11–0.28)	0/2
Barley grain Starea	75.4	9.77	0.62	(0.53–0.74)	0/3

Poorly processed Starea was frequently toxic. There was an inverse, though not perfect, relationship between degree of starch alteration and toxicity. However, in all instances, Starea samples that exhibited urea in an amorphous form under a scanning electron microscope were non-toxic (Behnke *et al.*, 1973). When the urea was in a crystalline form, the material was toxic. Urea in its native crystalline structure is likely to be more readily available to bacterial urease attack than it is in other structures. Urea seems to be more thoroughly incorporated into the starch material when starch damage is high, thus encouraging the formation of non-crystalline structures found in non-toxic Starea products. High starch damage also results in a more fermentable product which lowers rumen pH and slows absorption of ammonia. We have concluded that formation of an amorphous structure and high starch damage are involved in producing the highest quality Starea products, i.e. products that supply high concentrated rumen ammonia nitrogen for maximal microbial protein synthesis without the danger of toxicity.

Comparative ammonia release curves for extrusion-processed and unprocessed mixtures of grain and urea, biuret or dicyanodiamide (Davidovich, Bartley and Bechtle, 1976) are shown in *Table 6.7*. It is apparent that biuret and dicyanodiamide are slowly hydrolysed to ammonia in the rumen. Extrusion cooking of grain and biuret markedly elevated rumen and blood ammonia concentrations. The extrusion-cooked mixture of grain and biuret contained considerable urea, indicating that the extrusion cooking process converts biuret to urea. Extrusion cooking did not affect dicyanodiamide.

Table 6.7 EFFECT OF EXTRUSION-PROCESSED OR UNPROCESSED MIXTURES OF GRAIN AND UREA, BIURET OR DICYANODIAMIDE ON RUMEN pH, RUMEN AMMONIA, AND BLOOD AMMONIA CONCENTRATION[1]

Product	Time after test mixtures administered (min)							
	0	30	60	90	120	180	240	360
Rumen pH								
Cracked grain + urea	6.8	7.8	Toxicity occurred					
Extruded grain + urea	6.8	7.2	7.4	7.4	7.3	7.1	6.9	
Cracked grain + biuret	6.9	6.9	6.9	6.8	6.8	6.8	6.8	6.8
Extruded grain + biuret	6.9	7.4	7.7	7.8	7.7	7.6	7.2	6.6
Extruded grain + DCN	6.4	6.6	6.5	6.4	6.3	6.3	6.3	6.4
Rumen NH_3-N (mg/100 ml)								
Cracked grain + urea	6.7	58.9	Toxicity occurred					
Extruded grain + urea	8.2	50.2	71.5	84.9	88.9	91.3	87.4	
Cracked grain + biuret	3.8	17.2	17.5	14.5	12.5	11.5	11.1	5.6
Extruded grain + biuret	4.5	61.2	95.1	110.0	117.9	104.0	91.7	66.5
Extruded grain + DCN	7.2	11.3	9.0	8.0	5.9	3.7	2.9	2.4
Blood NH_3-N (mg/100 ml)								
Cracked grain + urea	0.12	1.05	Toxicity occurred					
Extruded grain + urea	0.11	0.40	0.46	0.53	0.56	0.53	0.47	
Cracked grain + biuret	0.07	0.15	0.13	0.11	0.12	0.21	0.13	0.08
Extruded grain + biuret	0.11	0.56	0.60	0.83	0.83	0.79	0.59	0.37
Extruded grain + DCN	0.12	0.13	0.23	0.24	0.16	0.15	0.11	0.11

[1] Dose of biuret or dicyanodiamide was equivalent to 0.5 g urea per kilogram bodyweight

Relation of rumen ammonia concentration to protein synthesis

As stated earlier, maximum microbial protein synthesis may be obtained in the rumen if there is a large concentration of nitrogen (ammonia) present with a matched supply of available energy. Toxicity will not occur when the energy supply lowers rumen pH to the point where ammonia will not be absorbed. However, recently Satter and Roffler (1975) stated: '(*a*) Maintenance of ruminal ammonia nitrogen in excess of 5 mg/100 ml rumen fluid has no effect on microbial protein. (*b*) Supplemental non-protein nitrogen is not utilised in typical dairy and feedlot rations containing not more than 12 to 13 per cent crude protein.' Using an *in vitro* fermentation system, Satter and Slyter (1974) established that maximal microbial protein synthesis is reached near 2 mg ammonia N per 100 ml rumen fluid and recommended 5 mg because 'higher value gives a slight margin of excess'. Because rations containing 12 to 13 per cent natural protein would raise the ammonia N concentration to 5 mg, they concluded that rumen micro-organisms cannot use urea in a ration already containing 12 to 13 per cent protein. Satter and Slyter (1974) infused their fermentors continuously with soluble starch and urea. That would depress ammonia concentration by providing readily available energy whenever urea was being hydrolysed by the micro-organisms. Unfortunately the cow does not consume continuously soluble starch and urea.

The data with Starea clearly indicate that 5 mg is not the maximum concentration of ruminal ammonia N and that protein synthesis will occur with concentrations much higher. It is apparent from the results of the *in vitro* experiments (*Table 6.2*) that even when concentrations of ruminal ammonia N ranged from 81 to 124 mg (approximately 20 times 5 mg) the microbial protein synthesis was greater for some urea-containing substrates than for others. This demonstrates clearly that 5 mg of ruminal ammonia N is not the limit for microbial protein synthesis. The *in vivo* experiments of Stiles *et al.* (1970) show (*Table 6.2*) that results similar to those obtained *in vitro* can be obtained *in vivo*.

In practical feeding situations, rumen ammonia concentrations increase after feeding, and the extent of the increase is determined by the solubility of the protein or NPN source (which governs how rapidly it is hydrolysed to ammonia), and the form of energy substrate (which governs the rate at which ammonia is converted to microbial protein and the rate at which ammonia is absorbed). If a soluble protein or NPN compound is fed in a ration whose energy is not readily available to the micro-organisms, a rapid increase in ruminal ammonia concentration can be expected, and microbial protein production will be low. However, if the same soluble protein or NPN compound is fed in a ration where the energy substrate is readily available, an increase in ruminal ammonia concentration can be expected, but the increase will be much less than when the energy substrate is not so available. Also, more microbial protein will be produced. A low ammonia concentration could mean more, and a high ammonia concentration could mean less, microbial protein synthesis. However, that relationship is not always true. It is if an available energy substrate is used with a soluble protein, but it is not if the energy substrate is available but the protein source is not readily degraded to ammonia. In the latter instance both the ammonia concentration and the microbial protein production would be low. Consequently, a fixed ruminal ammonia-N concentration of 5 mg has little to do with microbial synthesis and is too simple an approach to a complex problem.

Meyer *et al.* (1967) fed one member of sets of identical twin cattle a ration consisting of long alfalfa hay and cracked sorghum grain (1:1). The other twin received the same ration except that the alfalfa hay was ground finely and the grain was expanded through an extrusion process to achieve 100 per cent gelatinisation of starch. The processed feed lowered ruminal ammonia N 50 per cent and increased bacterial nitrogen 50 per cent (*Figure 6.1*). The ruminal ammonia nitrogen (mg/100 ml) was 9.8 for the unprocessed ration and 5.2 for the processed ration. The ingredients of the two rations were identical and their protein

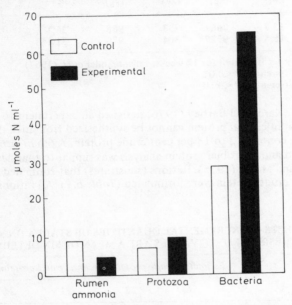

Figure 6.1 Relative concentrations of rumen ammonia nitrogen and microbial amino acid nitrogen in rumen contents of twins fed cracked sorghum grain and chopped alfalfa hay (control) and extrusion processed sorghum grain and finely ground alfalfa hay (experimental)

contents were identical, yet the quantity of microbial protein synthesised was twice as great for the processed ration as for the unprocessed ration.

When Colenbrander *et al.* (1967) fed the processed alfalfa and sorghum grain ration to milking cows, significantly more milk and milk protein were produced than when the same ingredients were fed in the unprocessed form (*Table 6.8*). Satter and Roffler (1975) considered the way in which ration energy concentration limits NPN utilisation in relation to protein content of the unsupplemented ration (they recommended not using urea in rations already containing 13 per cent crude protein and 80 per cent total digestible nutrients), but they did not consider the profound effects that ration processing can have on microbial synthesis.

Several studies (Conrad, Hibbs and Neuhardt, 1969; Huber, 1975; Ramage and Woolf, 1970, 1973) have shown that high producing cows can benefit from urea additions to rations containing natural protein in excess of 11 to 12 per cent.

Table 6.8 MILK AND MILK PROTEIN FROM COWS FED CRACKED SORGHUM GRAIN AND CHOPPED ALFALFA HAY (CONTROL) AND FROM THOSE RECEIVING EXTRUSION COOKED SORGHUM GRAIN AND FINELY GROUND ALFALFA HAY (EXPERIMENTAL)[1]

Treatment	Ration protein (%)	Milk[1] (kg)	Milk protein[1] (kg)	Feed protein[1] (kg)	Milk protein to feed protein conversion (%)	Mean ruminal ammonia N (mg/100 ml)
Control	15.7	7661	253	968	26.1	9.4
Experimental	15.5	9727[2]	304[3]	976	31.1[2]	2.9[2]

[1] Total of 6 cows per treatment for 12 weeks. Colenbrander *et al.* (1967)
[2] Significantly different at $P < 0.01$
[3] Significantly different at $P < 0.10$

Recently Edwards and Bartley (1976) designed an experiment to test the hypothesis that microbial protein cannot be synthesized from urea if it is added to rations that contain 12 to 13 per cent crude protein. A 6 h *in vitro* fermentation was used and microbial protein analysis was similar to that described by Barr, Bartley and Meyer (1975). Rations (substrates) that contained from 12 to 27 per cent crude protein were formulated (*Table 6.9*). All rations contained

Table 6.9 EFFECTS OF INCREMENTAL QUANTITIES OF STAREA ON MICROBIAL PROTEIN SYNTHESIS *IN VITRO* (VALUES ARE A MEAN OF SIX DETERMINATIONS)

Substrate ingredients (%)	Estimated crude protein percentage and protein source					
	12	15	18	21	24	27
Brome hay	25.0	25.0	25.0	25.0	25.0	25.0
Sorghum grain	65.5	57.6	49.8	42.0	34.1	26.3
Soya bean meal	9.5	9.5	9.5	9.5	9.5	9.5
Starea	–	7.9	15.7	23.5	31.4	39.2
Actual crude protein (%)	11.8	15.0	18.0	20.5	24.0	26.9
Microbial protein synthesized (mg g^{-1})	14.2	12.4	15.7	17.5	19.6	23.0
Final rumen NH_3-N (mg N/100 ml)	4.7	15.2	29.0	43.8	60.3	75.7

brome grass hay, sorghum grain and soya bean meal or Starea. The quantity of Starea added to the basal ration (12 per cent crude protein) to increase the protein content of the experimental rations was at the expense of sorghum grain. All rations contained 25 per cent brome grass hay.

It is apparent from the data in *Table 6.9* that the production of microbial protein increased steadily as the protein content of the substrates was increased from 15 to 27 per cent by using Starea. Obviously the urea in Starea was used although the rations contained considerably more than 12 per cent natural protein and the rumen ammonia-N concentrations greatly exceeded 5 mg. The test was repeated six times and the microbial protein production ranked the same each time.

References

Allison, M.J. (1970). In *Physiology of Digestion and Metabolism in the Ruminant*, p. 456. Ed. A.T. Phillipson. Newcastle-upon-Tyne; Oriel Press

Anderson, W.L. (1976). MS Thesis, Kansas State University

Anonymous (1974). *Feed Situation* No. 252, February Economic Research Service, United States Department of Agriculture

Anstaett, F.R., Sung, A.C., Pfost, H.B. and Deyoe, C.W. (1969). *Feedstuffs*, **41**, 19

Barr, G.W. (1974). PhD Thesis, Kansas State University

Barr, G.W., Bartley, E.E. and Meyer, R.M. (1975). *J. Dairy Sci.*, **58**, 1308

Bartley, E.E., Davidovich, A.D., Barr, G.W., Griffel, G.W., Dayton, A.D., Deyoe, C.W. and Bechtle, R.M. (1976). *J. Anim. Sci.*, **43**, 835

Bartley, E.E. and Deyoe, C.W. (1972). US Patent No. 3 642 489

Bartley, E.E. and Deyoe, C.W. (1975). *Feedstuffs*, **47**, 42

Behnke, K.C., Deyoe, C.W., Bartley, E.E. and Griffel, G.W. (1973). *Feedstuffs*, **45**, 25

Blackburn, T.H. and Hobson, P.N. (1960). *Br. J. Nutr.*, **14**, 445

Bryant, M.P. (1970). *Am. J. clin. Nutr.*, **23**, 1440

Bucholtz, H.F. and Bergen, W.G. (1973). *Appl. Micro.*, **25**, 504

Burt, A.W.A., Dunton, C.R., Atkinson, W., Bush, T.J., Thomson, I., Durran, A.A., Whiteley, K.B. and Aspinall, L.J. (1972). *Proc. Br. Soc. Anim. Prod.*, p. 129

Chalupa, W. (1968). *J. Anim. Sci.*, **27**, 207

Colenbrander, V.F., Bartley, E.E., Morrill, J.L., Deyoe, C.W. and Pfost, H.B. (1967). *J. Dairy Sci.*, **50**, 1966

Conrad, H.R., Hibbs, J.W. and Neuhardt, V.A. (1969). Ohio Agric. Res. Dev. Center, *Dairy Sci. Res. Summ.* No. 39

Davidovich, A., Bartley, E.E. and Bechtle, R.M. (1976). Unpublished data

Edwards, J. and Bartley, E.E. (1976). Unpublished data

Fonnesbeck, P.V., Kearl, L.C. and Harris, L.E. (1975). *J. Anim. Sci.*, **40**, 1150

Griffel, G.W. and Bartley, E.E. (1975). Unpublished data

Helmer, L.G. (1969). PhD Thesis, Kansas State University

Helmer, L.G. and Bartley, E.E. (1971). *J. Dairy Sci.*, **54**, 25

Helmer, L.G., Bartley, E.E., Deyoe, C.W., Meyer, R.M. and Pfost, H.B. (1970). *J. Dairy Sci.*, **53**, 330

Huber, J.T. (1975). *J. Anim. Sci.*, **48**, 954

Hungate, R.E. (1966). *The Rumen and its Microbes.* New York; Academic Press

Hutton, K., Bailey, F.J. and Annison, E.F. (1971). *Br. J. Nutr.*, **25**, 165

Loosli, J.K. and McDonald, I.W. (1968). *Non-protein Nitrogen in the Nutrition of Ruminants.* FAO Agric. Stud. 75. Rome; FAO

Males, R. and Johnson, R.R. (1974). *J. Anim. Sci.*, **39**, 245

Meyer, R.M., Bartley, E.E., Deyoe, C.W. and Colenbrander, V.F. (1967). *J. Dairy Sci.*, **50**, 1966

National Research Council (1976). *Urea and Other Non-protein Nitrogen Compounds in Animal Nutrition.* Washington, D.C.; National Academy of Sciences

Oltjen, R.R. (1969). *J. Anim. Sci.*, **28**, 673

Ramage, C.H. and Woolf, H.D. (1970). *J. Dairy Sci.*, **53**, 667

Ramage, C.H. and Woolf, H.D. (1973). *J. Dairy Sci.,* **56**, 649
Satter, L.D. and Roffler, R.E. (1975). *J. Dairy Sci.,* **58**, 1219
Satter, L.D. and Slyter, L.L. (1974). *Br. J. Nutr.,* **32**, 199
Shiehzadeh, S.A. and Harbers, L.H. (1974). *J. Anim. Sci.,* **38**, 206
Smith, R.H. (1974). Personal communication
Smith, R.H. (1975). In *Digestion and Metabolism in the Ruminant*, p. 399. Eds.
    I.W. McDonald and A.C.I. Warner. Armidale; University of New England
    Publishing Unit
Smith, R.H. and McAllan, A.B. (1970). *Br. J. Nutr.,* **24**, 545
Stiles, D.A., Bartley, E.E., Meyer, R.M., Deyoe, C.W. and Pfost, H.B. (1970).
    J. Dairy Sci., **53**, 1436
Thomas, P.C. (1973). *Proc. Nutr. Soc.,* **32**, 85
Thompson, L.H., Wise, M.B., Harvey, R.W. and Barrick, E.R. (1972). *J. Anim.*
    Sci., **35**, 474
Tillman, A.D. and Sidhu, K.S. (1969). *J. Anim. Sci.,* **28**, 689
Virtanen, A.I. (1966). *Science,* **153**, 1603
Walker, D.J. and Nader, C.J. (1975). *Aust. J. agric. Res.,* **26**, 689

7

INFLUENCE OF NITROGEN AND CARBOHYDRATE INPUTS ON RUMEN FERMENTATION

L.D. SATTER
R.E. ROFFLER*
Department of Dairy Science, University of Wisconsin, USA

Introduction

The rumen micro-organisms have a profound influence on the amino acid nutrition of ruminant animals. They enable ruminants to utilise dietary non-protein nitrogen (NPN) efficiently, and to survive on low intakes of dietary nitrogen by utilising nitrogen recycled into the reticulorumen via saliva. In addition, the rumen microbes enable an upgrading of low quality dietary protein to high quality microbial protein. These advantages are accompanied, however, by the important disadvantage that under some conditions more protein may be destroyed than synthesized by the rumen microbes, resulting in a net loss of dietary protein to the host animal. This becomes a major consideration when high protein rations are fed to lactating dairy cows.

Despite the general understanding and acceptance of these major features of nitrogen utilisation by ruminants, little effort has been made to utilise this information in a quantitative evaluation of protein and non-protein nitrogen, or in establishing or expressing protein requirements for domestic ruminants. Most feeding standards have relied upon crude protein (nitrogen × 6.25) or apparent digestible crude protein. It has been assumed that all sources of nitrogen were equivalent for ruminants as long as supplemental NPN did not exceed certain absolute or fractional amounts of dietary nitrogen intake. This assumption can lead to serious error, and the purpose of this paper is to outline a scheme that can be used to evaluate protein and NPN utilisation by ruminants. Special emphasis will be placed on the utilisation of NPN, and when or when not to expect benefit from including it in the ruminant ration.

Utilisation of ammonia by rumen micro-organisms

A schematic summary of nitrogen utilisation by ruminants is shown in *Figure 7.1*. Ingested true protein may be degraded by ruminal micro-organisms or may

*Present Address: Department of Animal Industries, University of Idaho, Moscow, Idaho, USA

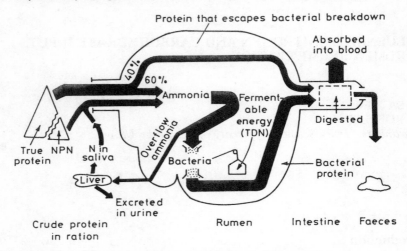

Figure 7.1 Schematic summary of nitrogen utilisation by the ruminant

escape degradation and pass to the lower gut to be digested or excreted in the faeces. The amount of true protein that escapes degradation may vary considerably, but with most management and feeding conditions in the dairy and feedlot industry, an escape rate of 40 per cent for dietary protein probably represents an acceptable average. The remaining 60 per cent of dietary protein is degraded almost entirely to ammonia.

Dietary NPN, salivary nitrogen and possibly a small amount of urea entering across the rumen wall are converted almost totally to ammonia. Several nitrogen sources, therefore, contribute to ruminal ammonia production.

The amount of ammonia that can be utilised by bacteria will depend on the number of bacteria and how rapidly they are growing. In other words, it will depend on the amount of energy available for the bacteria or the amount of fermentable feed consumed. Rations high in grain or digestible dry matter are more fermentable than high forage rations. Therefore, more ammonia (NPN) can be utilised with rations high in digestible dry matter. This is illustrated in *Figure 7.1* where an increase in total digestible nutrients (TDN) 'opens the gate' and allows more ammonia use by supporting greater bacterial numbers.

Figure 7.1 presents a situation where bacteria are unable to utilise all of the ammonia produced, and there is an 'ammonia overflow'. This excess ammonia is absorbed from the reticulorumen, or passed to the lower gut, where it is absorbed and eventually converted to urea by the liver. A fraction of this urea may be recycled via saliva to the rumen, but the majority is excreted in the urine.

Figure 7.1 suggests that it does not make much difference whether dietary true protein is degraded as long as the rumen bacteria are able to utilise all of the ammonia produced. Either way, dietary or recycled nitrogen ultimately ends up as protein presented to the intestine for absorption. This is not true, however, when ammonia production exceeds the ability of rumen bacteria to convert the ammonia to microbial protein. In this situation, only dietary true protein that escapes ruminal degradation will contribute to the amino acid nutrition of the host. The ammonia derived from NPN and from degraded true protein will not be of any value.

Being able to predict the point of 'ammonia overflow' in the rumen would be helpful in determining when or when not to expect benefit from addition of NPN to the ration. To develop some means by which the point of 'ammonia overflow' could be predicted, two pieces of information seemed essential. The first was to determine the concentration of ruminal ammonia necessary to support maximal growth rates of rumen bacteria. In other words, at what concentration would ruminal ammonia cease to be rate limiting for bacterial growth? Knowing this, it then was necessary to know the mean or prevailing concentration of ruminal ammonia under typical feeding and management conditions. The desired objective, therefore, was to relate mean ruminal ammonia concentration to readily measured and understood characteristics of the ration, namely crude protein and digestibility, and further to use this in predicting when ruminal ammonia production would be in excess of bacterial need.

EFFECT OF AMMONIA CONCENTRATION ON MICROBIAL PROTEIN PRODUCTION *IN VITRO*

The effect of ammonia concentration on microbial protein production was determined in continuous culture fermentors charged with ruminal contents from steers fed on either a protein-free purified diet, a corn-based all-concentrate diet or a forage concentrate (23:77) diet (Satter and Slyter, 1974). Feed mixes of similar nutrient composition were added to the fermentors either two or four times daily. Urea was infused into the fermentors to maintain various concentrations of ammonia in the incubating mixtures. During each experiment, at least two of six fermentors were supplied with sufficient urea to maintain ammonia concentrations in excess of microbial needs. Protein content of the effluent, measured as tungstic acid precipitable nitrogen (TAPN), from these fermentors served as the control with which protein output of fermentors with inadequate urea supplementation could be compared.

Figure 7.2 shows the relationship between crude protein content of the mixture added to the fermentor (dry matter (DM) basis), the TAPN output of the fermentor and ammonia concentration of the incubation mixture. Each point is an average of two composite samples from one fermentor during the last four days of each nine-day experiment. Protein output by the fermentors increased as urea supplementation was increased, and then leveled off. Further increases in the amount of supplemental urea were without effect on protein output. The leveling off of protein output coincided with the point when ammonia began to accumulate. Ammonia nitrogen in excess of 5 mg/100 ml had no effect on protein content of the fermentor effluent, even when ammonia concentration was in excess of 80 mg NH_3-N/100 ml.

Intercepts for TAPN and ammonia plots were at 12.0 and 11.9, 13.5 and 14.2, and 14.7 and 15.0 per cent crude protein of ration dry matter for the purified, forage—concentrate, and concentrate rations. This agreement underscores the close relationship between achievement of maximum TAPN production and the start of ammonia accumulation. Intercepts on the ammonia nitrogen plot for each of the three rations occurred at 1.9, 2.0, and 1.7 mg NH_3-N/100 ml rumen fluid, suggesting that the bacteria actually were being satisfied

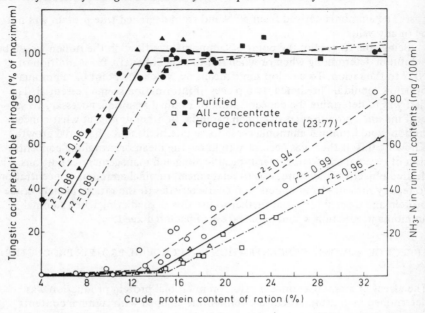

Figure 7.2 Relationship between ammonia concentration of continuous culture fermentor contents and output of tungstic acid precipitable nitrogen when either a purified, all-concentrate, or forage-concentrate (23:77) mixture was added to the fermentor (Satter and Slyter, 1974)

with an ammonia nitrogen concentration at somewhat less than 5 mg/100 ml. The choice of 5 mg NH_3-N/100 ml as being the point of ammonia accumulation therefore, allows for a small margin of excess.

Under *in vitro* conditions and with diets in these experiments, ammonia started to accumulate when nitrogen equivalent to 12–15 per cent dietary crude protein (DM basis) was added. As expected, ammonia accumulated earlier with the purified diet than with the natural diets because virtually all of the nitrogen in the purified diet would go through the ammonia pool, whereas some of the protein in the natural diet escaped degradation and was not deaminated to ammonia. Because there is neither absorption nor recycling of nitrogen *in vitro* as would occur *in vivo*, it does not necessarily mean that ammonia would start to accumulate at this same dietary protein level *in vivo*.

Since the majority of rumen bacteria use ammonia as a nitrogen source (Bryant and Robinson, 1962), it follows that availability of ammonia will be an important determinant of microbial protein production. It is essential to know what concentration of ammonia will support maximal microbial growth to make judgments regarding utilisation of dietary nitrogen. It appears that once ammonia starts to accumulate in the rumen and exceeds 5 mg NH_3-N/100 ml rumen fluid, nothing is gained by further supplementation with NPN. Likewise, that fraction of dietary true protein which is degraded to ammonia is not utilised when ruminal ammonia nitrogen is in excess of 5 mg/100 ml.

EFFECT OF RATION COMPOSITION ON RUMINAL AMMONIA CONCENTRATION IN CATTLE

Having established the minimal concentration of ammonia necessary to support maximal microbial growth rates, it then became necessary to know the mean or prevailing concentration of ruminal ammonia in cattle fed a variety of rations. To study the influence of ration composition on mean ruminal ammonia concentration, over 1000 ruminal ingesta samples were collected from 211 cattle fed rations containing one or more of the following major ingredients: maize, oats, soya bean meal, maize silage, and alfalfa-grass hay or silage (Roffler and Satter, 1975a). Animals were sampled at least four times during the day to obtain an average ruminal ammonia concentration. Thirty-five different rations, each fed to an average of six cows, varied in crude protein (CP) (N × 6.25) content from 8 to 24 per cent and in total digestible nutrient content from 53 to 85 per cent. Crude protein content of each ration was determined by Kjeldahl analysis, and ration TDN content was established from National Research Council tabular values (National Research Council, 1971). All 35 rations were formulated with only natural protein sources. Simple and multiple regression equations relating mean ruminal ammonia concentration to ration composition were computed.

Mean ruminal ammonia nitrogen concentrations ranged from 0.8 to 56.1 mg/100 ml rumen fluid, increasing with per cent of dietary crude protein. The relationship between mean ruminal ammonia concentration and per cent dietary crude protein is described by the equation:

$$\text{NH}_3\text{-N (mg/100 ml)} = 10.57 - 2.5 \text{ \%CP} + 0.159 \text{ \%CP}^2 \, ; r^2 = 0.88$$

Mean ruminal ammonia concentration reached 5 mg NH_3-N/100 ml at approximately 13 per cent dietary crude protein (DM basis). Above this concentration, ruminal ammonia increased rapidly with increasing protein.

The amount of fermentable energy available to ruminal bacteria influences their growth rate and, consequently, the quantity of ammonia converted to microbial protein. Therefore, some measure of fermentable energy must be considered in predicting mean ruminal ammonia concentration. Originally (Roffler and Satter, 1975a), TDN was chosen as a practical measure of dietary energy because values are readily available and understood by livestock producers in North America. In this presentation, digestible dry matter (DDM) values are included as an alternative measure of fermentable energy. Relationships between expressions of energy value of feeds for lactating cattle were used to convert TDN to DDM (Moe, Flatt and Tyrrell, 1972).

The following multiple regression equation, which considers ration TDN as well as crude protein, improved the precision of predicting mean ruminal ammonia concentration:

$$\text{NH}_3\text{-N (mg/100 ml)} = 38.73 - 3.04 \text{ \%CP} + 0.171 \text{ \%CP}^2 - 0.49 \text{ \%TDN} + 0.0024 \text{ \%TDN}^2 \, ; r^2 = 0.92$$

From this equation came mean ruminal ammonia values expected when rations differing in TDN content were fed (*Table 7.1*). With increasing dietary protein, ruminal ammonia nitrogen either exceeds or reaches 5 mg/100 ml

Table 7.1 INFLUENCE OF RATION COMPOSITION ON MEAN RUMINAL AMMONIA CONCENTRATION AND NON-PROTEIN NITROGEN UTILISATION

% Crude protein in ration dry matter		55	60	65	70	75	80	85	Non-protein nitrogen utilisation (%)
	TDN[1] DDM[2]	55 59	60 63	65 68	70 72	75 76	80 81	85 85	
		Ruminal NH₃ concentration (mg/100 ml)[3]							
8		6	5	4	3	2	2	1	
9		6	5	4	3	2	2	1	
10		6	5	4	3	2	2	1	>90
11		6	5	4	3	3	2	2	
12		7	6	5	4	4	3	3	
13		8	7	6	6	5	4	4	0–90
14		10	9	8	7	6	6	5	
15		12	11	10	9	8	8	7	
16		14	13	12	11	10	10	10	
17		17	16	15	14	13	13	12	
18		20	19	18	17	16	16	15	0
19		23	22	21	20	19	19	18	
20		27	26	25	24	23	23	22	

[1] National Research Council tabular values; expressed as percentage of ration dry matter
[2] Calculated from regression equations proposed by Moe, Flatt and Tyrell (1972); expressed as percentage of ration dry matter
[3] Predicted from the equation discussed on page 119.

sooner with low energy rations than with high energy rations. Dietary protein and energy combinations have been divided into three groups: (*a*) those crude protein and TDN/DDM combinations where added NPN would be utilised efficiently; (*b*) those combinations where NPN would be partially utilised, and (*c*) those where added NPN would not be utilised. Contents of *Table 7.1* agree with what has been long recognised, namely that NPN is utilised well in low protein, high energy rations and poorly utilised in high protein, low energy rations. When ruminal ammonia nitrogen concentration is 2 mg/100 ml or less, NPN utilisation is probably in excess of 90 per cent. As ammonia nitrogen begins to accumulate (3 to 5 mg/100 ml), utilisation of added NPN would be variable, ranging between 0 and approximately 90 per cent. Above 5 mg NH₃-N/100 ml, utilisation of added NPN would be nil.

In addition to effects of dietary crude protein and ration digestibility on ruminal ammonia concentration, provision must be made for another important factor influencing ruminal ammonia concentration, that of substituting NPN for dietary true protein. When part of the ration protein is replaced by NPN, the amount of true dietary protein escaping ruminal degradation is reduced, and the fractional amount of dietary nitrogen going through the ruminal ammonia pool is increased. As the amount of NPN in the ration increases, the point of zero utilisation of NPN is reached at corresponding lower ration protein. The point of excessive ammonia accumulation in the rumen, therefore, is affected by amount of NPN added to the ration as well as digestibility and total protein content of the unsupplemented ration. Details of calculations are discussed elsewhere (Roffler and Satter, 1975a).

Integration of effects caused by dietary crude protein and ration digestibility,

Table 7.2 UPPER LIMIT FOR NON-PROTEIN NITROGEN UTILISATION

% Crude protein in ration dry matter before non-protein nitrogen addition		% Crude protein after non-protein nitrogen addition					
	TDN[1] 55–60	60–65	65–70	70–75	75–80	80–85	
	DDM[2] 59–63	63–68	68–72	72–76	76–81	81–85	
8	No[3]	10.0	10.5	10.9	11.2	11.4
9	No[3]	10.4	10.9	11.3	11.6	11.8
10	No[3]	10.8	11.3	11.7	12.0	12.2
11	No[3]	11.2	11.7	12.1	12.4	12.6
12	No[3]	No[3]	12.1	12.5	12.8	13.0
—	—	11.4[4]	12.2[4]	12.8[4]	13.3[4]	13.6[4]

[1] See footnote (1) in *Table 7.1*
[2] See footnote (2) in *Table 7.1*
[3] The upper limit for non-protein nitrogen utilisation is below the crude protein content of the unsupplemented ration, and no benefit from non-protein nitrogen supplementation would be expected
[4] Dietary crude protein where ruminal ammonia begins to accumulate when only plant protein is in the ration

as well as NPN substitution for true protein on ruminal ammonia, is given in *Table 7.2*. Values in this table represent the per cent of dietary crude protein at which mean ruminal ammonia nitrogen reaches 5 mg/100 ml with rations containing variable amounts of TDN/DDM and added NPN. In other words, these values are the upper limit to which total ration crude protein (DM basis) justifiably can be raised by adding NPN. Utilisation of NPN added above this point is nil.

DDM and TDN are used as measures of ration fermentability in *Tables 7.1* and *7.2*. Alternative expressions, such as digestible energy, digestible organic matter, or metabolizable energy, could be substituted when they are more convenient or accurate. Disadvantages of TDN are: (*a*) it overestimates fermentability of rations high in fat or oil and (*b*) it assumes all carbohydrate sources to be isofermentable. Numerous other factors can influence ruminal ammonia concentration, including frequency of feeding, type of dietary carbohydrate, the extent of dietary protein degradation and rumen pH. The majority of dairy and feedlot animals in North America are fed *ad libitum* rations consisting primarily of feed grains, maize silage, or grass or legume forage. Therefore, these were the rations chosen for developing relationships between ruminal ammonia concentrations and identifiable ration characteristics. When these types of rations were fed under typical husbandry conditions, then ration crude protein and TDN accounted for 92 per cent of the variation in mean ruminal ammonia (Roffler and Satter, 1975a). This suggested that under these conditions the net effect of other factors which influenced ruminal ammonia concentration was small.

It is obvious, however, that care must be exercised in applying the information contained in *Tables 7.1* and *7.2* to feeding and management conditions that differ from those used to develop the information. When diets contain primarily readily degradable protein such as contained in fresh, immature grass (Egan,

1974), or relatively resistant protein such as in fish meal or dried brewers' grains (Chalupa, 1975; Li-Pun, Beardsley and Satter, 1975), estimates of ruminal ammonia concentration may be underestimated or overestimated, respectively, by the predictive equation. In particular, rations containing large amounts of by-product or processed feeds which have been exposed to heat or leaching of soluble protein may differ. Predictive equations may have to be developed for some special feeding and management conditions. Though the predictive equation presented can be generally applied to cattle fed feed grains and stored forage, it does not apply to grazing cattle. A cooperative study with the University of Rio Grande Do Sul (Brazil) is being conducted to develop similar information with grazing cattle and sheep.

Ruminal ammonia concentration normally fluctuates, reaching a peak concentration about one to two hours following feeding, and then decreasing. It was found that cattle fed a minimum of twice daily, with both low and high protein ration ingredients balanced between feedings, usually fluctuated between 3 and 8 mg NH_3-N/100 ml rumen fluid when fed to maintain a mean concentration of 5 mg. As pointed out earlier, the critical concentration of NH_3-N for maintaining maximum rumen microbial growth is about 2 mg/100 ml. As illustrated schematically in *Figure 7.3* by the solid line, normal fluctuation about a

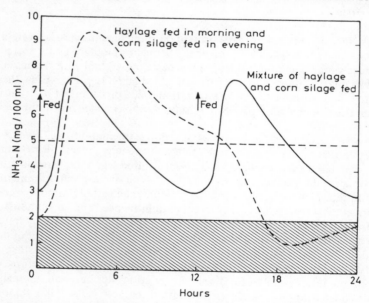

Figure 7.3 Schematic illustration of how ruminal ammonia concentration may fluctuate with normal twice-daily feeding (—) or when the high protein ration ingredient (haylage) is fed in the morning and the low protein ingredient (corn silage) is fed in the evening (---)

mean concentration of 5 mg NH_3-N/100 ml would not impair microbial growth. An unequal distribution of high and low protein ingredients between feedings, such as would occur if high protein hay (or grass silage) were fed in the morning, and low protein corn silage in the evening, can cause a distorted curve as illustrated by the dotted line in *Figure 7.3*. Maintaining a mean concentration of

5 mg NH$_3$-N/100 ml may not be enough in this situation to keep the concentration from dropping below 2 mg during part of the day. If maximum microbial growth is desired under such conditions, then mean ruminal ammonia concentration would have to be maintained above 5 mg/100 ml. This would be nutritionally favourable but probably uneconomical.

The limited potential for a slow-release NPN supplement is illustrated in *Figures 7.4* and *7.5*. Levelling out the 'peaks and valleys' of ruminal ammonia

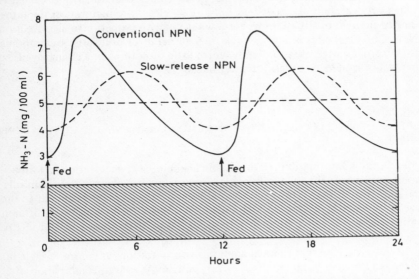

Figure 7.4 Schematic illustration of a situation where a slow-release NPN product would have little or no advantage over a conventional NPN source

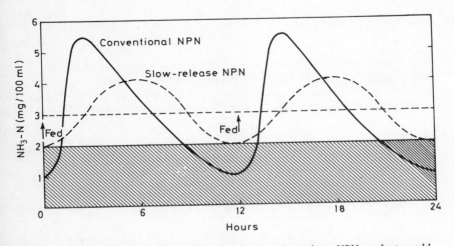

Figure 7.5 Schematic illustration of a situation where a slow-release NPN product would have some advantage over a conventional NPN source

concentration with a slow-release NPN supplement would have no beneficial effect in the situation illustrated in *Figure 7.4*. In this example the ammonia did not drop below the critical concentration of 2 mg NH_3-N/100 ml, even with the conventional product. *Figure 7.5* illustrates a situation where ruminal ammonia concentration dips too low with the conventional product, thus impairing microbial growth, but remains at adequate concentrations with the slow-release product. Simply feeding a little more of the conventional product, however, would assure adequate ammonia for the rumen bacteria. Thus, one has to weigh very carefully the added cost of a slow-release product against the rather limited number of situations where it will actually be superior to a conventional NPN source. Of course, the slow-release material involves less risk of ammonia toxicity. This attribute is probably worth little or nothing in well managed herds, but is of value to less attentive managers.

EFFECT OF RATION COMPOSITION ON RUMINAL AMMONIA CONCENTRATION IN SHEEP

All preceding information relating ruminal ammonia concentration to ration composition was obtained with cattle. Similar data have been obtained in this laboratory with sheep. In general, experimental procedures were similar to those used in the cattle studies. Both lambs and ewes were used to study 31 different rations ranging in crude protein content from 4 to 26 per cent and 44 to 81 per cent TDN.

Results indicate that ruminal ammonia concentrations are more variable in sheep, and predictive equations seem less precise. At a given combination of dietary protein and energy, sheep maintain higher concentrations of ruminal ammonia than cattle. The following multiple regression equation predicts sheep ruminal ammonia concentration:

$$NH_3\text{-N (mg/100 ml)} = 3.17 + 0.453 \,\%CP + 0.032 \,\%CP^2 - 0.091 \,\%TDN;$$
$$r^2 = 0.86$$

Note that TDN is an NRC tabular value determined with sheep (National Research Council, 1975), and that CP is on a dry matter basis.

Use of this equation for sheep, and the one developed earlier for cattle, enables comparison of the two species (*Table 7.3*). The dietary crude protein

Table 7.3 DIETARY CRUDE PROTEIN CONTENT WHERE RUMINAL AMMONIA NITROGEN EQUALS 5mg/100 ml RUMEN FLUID IN CATTLE AND SHEEP

	Percentage TDN[1]			
Species	60–65	65–70	70–75	75–80
Cattle	11.4	12.2	12.8	13.3
Sheep	9.8	10.2	10.6	11.0

[1] In diets containing only plant protein; TDN values are NRC tabular values

level where ruminal ammonia begins to accumulate (5 mg NH_3-N/100 ml) in sheep is about 2 percentage units lower than in cattle fed similar rations. Thus, sheep would be less likely to benefit from NPN supplementation than cattle.

A review (Roffler and Satter, 1976) of published studies comparing the performance of lactating cattle or growing sheep fed rations supplemented with isonitrogenous amounts of urea or plant protein clearly showed that sheep, compared to cattle, did relatively poorly on the NPN supplemented rations. In 41 comparisons involving over 300 lactating cows, NPN supported milk production 97 per cent as well as plant protein. In 67 comparisons involving more than 800 growing sheep, those fed NPN performed only 86 per cent as well as those fed plant protein.

The difference between sheep and cattle is probably even greater in grazing animals. Sheep are more effective in selectively grazing the higher quality forage than cattle are, and this would tend to further increase an already higher concentration of ruminal ammonia in sheep. Loosli and McDonald, in a review of literature regarding NPN nutrition of ruminants, concluded that sheep often do not respond to urea supplementation of low quality roughage as efficiently as cattle (Loosli and McDonald, 1968).

UTILISATION OF NPN IN RELATION TO RUMINAL AMMONIA CONCENTRATION

Several lines of independent evidence were developed to support the concept that NPN is not utilised when supplemented to animals maintaining ruminal NH_3-N in excess of 5 mg/100 ml.

Ruminal ammonia accumulation

This experiment postulated that a plot of ruminal ammonia concentration as a function of urea intake would be linear beyond the point of ammonia accumulation (5 mg NH_3-N/100 ml) if total ammonia uptake by the microbes was unaffected by ammonia in excess of this concentration. This assumes that ammonia absorption and passage out of the rumen are directly proportional to concentration of ammonia (Chalmers, Jaffray and White, 1971). A curvilinear plot would suggest a changing extraction rate by the microbes and would constitute indirect evidence that ammonia nitrogen concentrations in excess of 5 mg/100 ml were influencing total ammonia uptake by the microbes.

Results from a series of three trials where incremental amounts of urea were infused intraruminally are shown in *Figures 7.6, 7.7* and *7.8* (Roffler, Schwab and Satter, 1976). Crude protein and TDN content of the basal ration for each of the trials are shown in the figures. The absolute linearity of the curve of ammonia concentration above a concentration of approximately 5 mg NH_3-N/ 100 ml suggests ammonia uptake by rumen micro-organisms and/or loss from the rumen was occurring at a constant rate. In other words, a constant fraction of the ammonia in the rumen was being removed over the linear part of the curve. Two possibilities for ammonia uptake by rumen microbes would be consistent with the linear nature of ammonia accumulation in *Figures 7.6,*

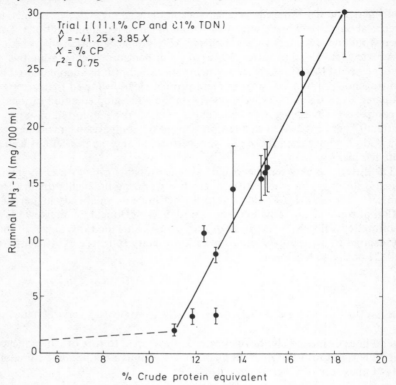

Figure 7.6 Relationship between dietary crude protein (CP) equivalent and ruminal ammonia concentration when the basal ration contained 11.1 per cent CP and 81 per cent total digestible nutrients (TDN)

7.7 and *7.8*. Either ammonia uptake by rumen micro-organisms is directly proportional to concentration of ammonia, and remains so without change over an extremely large range of concentrations, or total uptake of ammonia by rumen micro-organisms remains static and is unaffected by a change in concentration of ammonia over the linear part of the curve. The latter alternative is consistent with other evidence discussed below.

Flow of non-ammonia nitrogen through the abomasum

Published experiments were reviewed where flow of non-ammonia nitrogen (NAN) through the abomasum or small intestine of sheep was measured (Roffler and Satter, 1975b). There were 24 rations where NPN was the source of supplemental nitrogen and 36 rations where protein was the source of nitrogen. The flow of non-ammonia nitrogen through the abomasum when NPN was the source of supplemental nitrogen was plotted and was equal for all rations ranging between approximately 10 and 24 per cent crude protein (*Figure 7.9*). This suggests that the high nitrogen rations containing NPN were no better than the

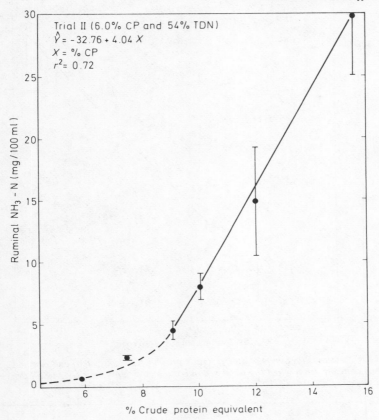

Figure 7.7 Relationship between dietary crude protein (CP) equivalent and ruminal ammonia concentration when the basal ration contained 6 per cent CP and 54 per cent total digestible nutrients (TDN)

low nitrogen rations containing NPN in terms of protein flow through the abomasum. With rations supplemented with true protein, however, there was a continued increase in the flow of non-ammonia nitrogen through the abomasum as dietary protein was increased to as high as 26 per cent of the ration (*Figure 7.10*). This incremental increase in flow of protein through the abomasum presumably represents that portion of the dietary protein which escaped ruminal degradation.

Growth rate of feedlot beef cattle supplemented with either urea or soya bean meal

A third line of evidence, using growth of feedlot cattle as the measured response, is available from the studies of Burroughs, Trenkle and Vetter (1973) (*Figure 7.11*). Experiments in this group of studies were well designed, having four treatment groups consisting of: (*a*) a low protein basal ration; (*b*) a basal ration plus low NPN; (*c*) a basal ration plus high NPN; and (*d*) a basal ration plus plant

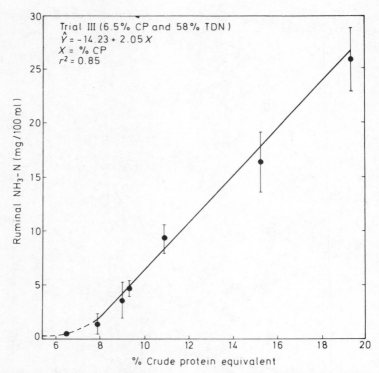

Figure 7.8 Relationship between dietary crude protein (CP) equivalent and ruminal ammonia concentration when the basal ration contained 6.5 per cent CP and 58 per cent total digestible nutrients (TDN)

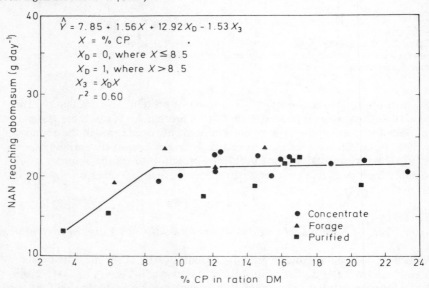

Figure 7.9 Influence of NPN supplementation on the quantity of non-ammonia nitrogen (NAN) flowing through the abomasum of sheep fitted with omasal, abomasal or duodenal cannulae

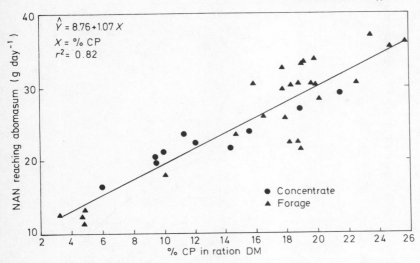

Figure 7.10 Influence of protein supplementation on the quantity of non-ammonia nitrogen (NAN) flowing through the abomasum of sheep fitted with omasal, abomasal or duodenal cannulae

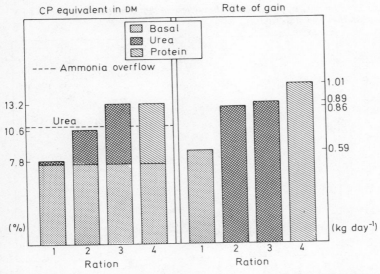

Figure 7.11 Growth response from plant protein or NPN supplementation of feedlot rations (Burroughs, Trenkle and Vetter, 1973)

protein isonitrogenous with treatment (c). The point of ammonia accumulation, as predicted from the regression equation (*see* p. 119) is illustrated by the dotted line in *Figure 7.11*. The conclusion reached from this experimentation was that addition of NPN to appropriate low protein rations could result in an increase in growth rate, but that further additions would be without benefit, even though

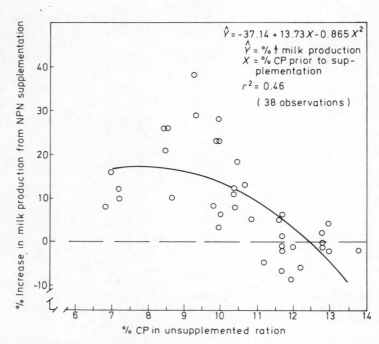

Figure 7.12 Summary of published studies where milk production response to NPN supplementation was measured

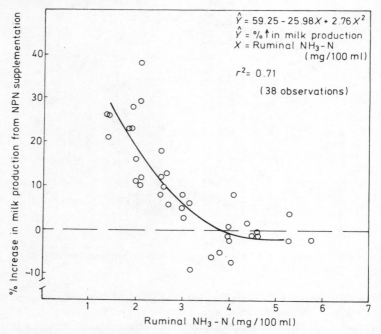

Figure 7.13 Summary of published studies where milk production response to NPN supplementation is plotted vs. predicted ruminal ammonia concentration prior to NPN supplementation

the animal needed additional protein as evidenced by superior performance of the plant protein-supplemented group. The point of predicted ruminal ammonia accumulation agrees with the observed growth performance.

Effect of urea supplementation on milk production

A fourth line of evidence regarding ineffectiveness of NPN in dairy rations containing more than 12 to 13 per cent crude protein was obtained using data from published lactation trials involving 38 comparisons of NPN-supplemented rations to unsupplemented negative control rations (Roffler and Satter, 1975b). These comparisons involved 406 cows. A simple regression equation was computed relating percentage improvement in milk production following NPN supplementation to ration protein content prior to supplementation (*Figure 7.12*). Addition of NPN to low protein rations caused a substantial increase in milk production. The milk production response diminished progressively as the protein content of the ration prior to NPN supplementation was increased. The point of zero response in milk production to NPN supplementation occurred when the rations contained, prior to supplementation, about 12.5 per cent crude protein. This line of evidence is somewhat equivocal, for many of the cows used in these experiments probably had a dietary protein requirement of 12.5 per cent or less, and therefore would not have been able to respond to either NPN or plant protein supplementation in excess of this amount.

Another noteworthy observation drawn from this group of experiments deals with the relationship between predicted ruminal ammonia concentration and milk production response. Estimates of ruminal ammonia concentration for cows in each of the published studies were obtained by using the equation discussed earlier to predict ammonia concentration from ration protein and TDN content. A regression of milk production response on predicted ruminal ammonia ($r^2 = 0.71$) indicated zero response with ruminal ammonia nitrogen concentration in excess of 4 mg/100 ml (*Figure 7.13*). This agrees closely with the value of 5 mg NH_3-N/100 ml previously demonstrated to be adequate for maximal microbial growth rates.

Calculation of metabolizable protein

Burroughs, Nelson and Mertens (1975) have used the term 'metabolizable protein'. It is analogous to metabolizable energy and represents that portion of the dietary crude protein intake available in α-amino form for metabolism by the host.

Crude protein (N × 6.25) has been the favoured terminology for expressing protein composition of feeds and animal protein requirements. This is particularly true for ruminants since NPN may have nearly the same nutritive value as α-amino nitrogen under some conditions. From the preceding discussion, however, the amount of metabolizable or absorbable protein is not related linearly to dietary crude protein intake for a wide range of protein intakes. In other words, the amount of metabolizable protein per unit of crude protein intake is much higher under conditions where ruminal ammonia is utilised totally for microbial

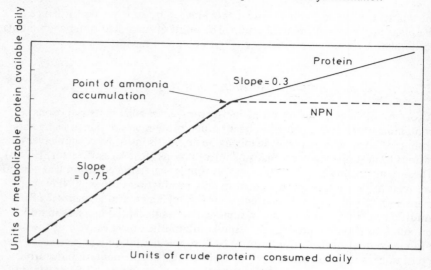

Figure 7.14 Schematic relationship between metabolizable protein, crude protein and NPN

protein production than under conditions where ruminal ammonia is in excess. This is illustrated schematically in *Figure 7.14*. Below the point of ammonia accumulation in the rumen, all nitrogen sources are approximately equal for the ruminant in providing metabolizable protein. Above the point of ammonia accumulation, however, additional NPN contributes nothing to the amount of protein available for absorption. Additional true dietary protein adds to the amount of protein available for absorption to the extent that it escapes ruminal degradation and is digested. From this discussion it is seen that the amount of metabolizable protein from a given amount of crude protein is less when high protein rations are fed compared to when low protein rations are fed.

There is unquestioned need for some method that relates absorbable (metabolizable) protein to readily measured features of a feed or ration, such as crude protein or TDN/DDM content. The discussion that follows outlines the approach to a method for calculating metabolizable protein. It is simple and may be readily modified to accommodate more accurate information as it becomes available. Assumptions and values derived therefrom must be considered tentative. It is hoped that this approach may provide a framework within which more definitive experimentation can be planned and that it ultimately may be useful as a vehicle for expressing recommendations regarding protein supplementation of ruminants.

The following assumptions form the basis for estimating metabolizable protein. Some can be documented well with evidence; others must be considered tentative. All values are averages, some of which are associated with high variance. Assumptions are: (*a*) the amount of nitrogen recycled into the reticulo-rumen is equal to 12 per cent of the dietary nitrogen intake; (*b*) 85 per cent of the dietary nitrogen intake with typical ruminant rations is in true protein form and 15 per cent in natural NPN form; (*c*) 40 per cent of the true dietary protein escapes degradation in the rumen and goes to the intestine while all of the dietary NPN and recycled nitrogen passes through the ruminal ammonia pool;

(*d*) 90 per cent of all ruminal ammonia produced is incorporated into microbial nitrogen when the ration fed does not exceed the 'upper limit' value for crude protein given in *Table 7.2* (*see* p. 121); (*e*) no ruminal ammonia derived from dietary crude protein fed in excess of the 'upper limit' value for dietary crude protein (*Table 7.2*) is incorporated into microbial nitrogen; (*f*) 80 per cent of microbial nitrogen is in true protein form, and 20 per cent is in a non-utilisable NPN form; (*g*) 80 per cent of the microbial true protein will be absorbed (metabolizable protein); and (*h*) 87 per cent of the dietary true protein that escapes degradation in the rumen will be absorbed (metabolizable protein). A more detailed discussion of the evidence behind each assumption is available (Satter and Roffler, 1975).

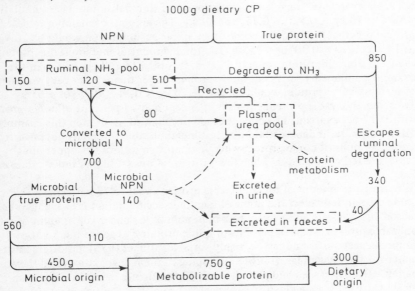

Figure 7.15 Schematic summary of metabolizable protein calculations

Application of the above assumptions to the calculation of metabolizable protein is illustrated in *Figure 7.15*. Under conditions where ruminal ammonia production is not in excess of microbial need, 1 kg of dietary protein results in approximately 750 g of metabolizable protein. Of this amount, 450 g is of microbial origin and 300 g of dietary origin. In other words, whenever the crude protein content of a ration is equal to or less than the 'upper limit' values of *Table 7.2*, the amount of metabolizable protein will equal approximately 75 per cent of the crude protein consumed. For simplicity, all forms of dietary nitrogen are considered equal when dietary protein does not exceed the 'upper limit'. This is not true to the extent that microbial nitrogen derived from dietary NPN does not provide quite the amount of absorbable amino acids as would be supplied by the equivalent amount of dietary true protein. The difference is small and may be ignored. Likewise, differences in amino acid composition between dietary protein and microbial protein are overlooked. Ultimately, recognition of amino acid content is necessary.

When dietary crude protein is fed in excess of the 'upper limit' value of *Table*

7.2, a two-step calculation is needed. Above the point of ammonia accumulation in the rumen, only escaped dietary true protein will contribute to metabolizable protein. One kilogram of protein supplemented under these conditions and in this example results in only about 0.3 kg of metabolizable protein (*Figure 7.15*). Therefore, the total amount of metabolizable protein available from a high protein ration (> 'upper limit' value) will equal the sum of 75 per cent of dietary crude protein fed to the 'upper limit' value and 30 per cent of the dietary crude protein (assuming only plant protein is fed) of that portion fed above the 'upper limit' value. If a cow were consuming 20 kg of a ration containing 72 per cent TDN and 17 per cent crude protein (DM basis and no added NPN), the 'upper limit' would be 12.8 per cent crude protein (*Table 7.2*). The amount of metabolizable protein obtainable below the point of ruminal ammonia accumulation would be 20 kg $\times$ 0.128 $\times$ 0.75, or 1.92 kg. The amount of metabolizable protein obtainable above the point of ammonia accumulation would be 20 kg $\times$ (0.17 − 0.128) $\times$ 0.30, or 0.25 kg. The total amount of metabolizable protein available from this ration equals 1.92 + 0.25, or 2.17 kg. If the ration in the example contained 11 per cent crude protein rather than 17 per cent, calculation of metabolizable protein would simply be 20 kg $\times$ 0.11 $\times$ 0.75, or 1.65 kg. Thus, metabolizable protein equals 64 per cent and 75 per cent of crude protein for the 17 per cent and 11 per cent crude protein rations used in this example. These calculations demonstrate that less metabolizable protein is obtained from a given amount of crude protein when high protein rations (> 'upper limit' value) are fed compared to when low protein rations (< 'upper limit' value) are fed.

Setting the amount of metabolizable protein equal to 75 per cent of the crude protein fed below the point of ammonia accumulation is thought to be reasonably accurate and subject to a minimum of variance. The amount of metabolizable protein available per unit of crude protein fed above the point of ammonia accumulation may be highly variable. Miller (1973) has offered estimates for the percentage of protein escaping ruminal degradation, and they are: barley, 10; cotton seed and peanut meal, 20; sunflower meal, 25; soya bean meal, 45; dried grass and white fish meal, 50; and Peruvian fish meal, 70. In view of other experimental evidence (Chalupa, 1975), it appears that the extent of degradation of a given protein source may be quite variable, and caution must be used in assigning an arbitrary value to a protein source. On the other hand, it will be of important nutritional and economic value to know the average relative resistance each major protein supplement has to microbial breakdown.

One might think that the level of dietary protein at which ruminal ammonia begins to accumulate would be highly variable in view of the large differences between protein sources and their resistance to degradation. We have been generally surprised at how well we seem able to predict the point of ruminal ammonia accumulation when typical dairy and feedlot rations consisting of unprocessed feed grains, hay, and corn or grass silage are fed on an *ad libitum* basis. More information is needed, however, with rations containing large amounts of relatively resistant protein, such as dried brewers and distillers grains. In all probability, the point of ammonia accumulation will occur at a higher protein level when large amounts of these feedstuffs are present in the ration.

We should not become preoccupied with obtaining difficult and inaccurate estimates of protein degradation for each and every ration constituent. It is hazardous to assume that these values can simply be added together in a linear fashion along with an estimate of microbial protein production to obtain an accurate estimate of metabolizable protein for the entire ration. It is natural for nutritionists to want a description of each ration ingredient, and to assume that the nutritive value of each ration component can be added to obtain a value for the overall ration. It would appear that a metabolizable protein system relying on estimates of protein escape rate for each ration component (Burroughs, Nelson and Mertens, 1975) is subject to considerable additive error, particularly in view of the variable estimates of protein degradation in the rumen. Ruminal ammonia concentration, reflecting both synthesis and degradation of protein as well as nitrogen recycling, absorption and passage from the reticulorumen provides more comprehensive information. It reflects, for example, the effect that ration digestibility has on rumen pH, and consequently the loss of ammonia by absorption from the rumen. Furthermore, ruminal ammonia concentration is much easier to obtain than are estimates of protein degradation in the rumen. For this reason the point of ruminal ammonia concentration is best used as a benchmark or point of departure for calculating metabolizable protein. Research is needed to provide more accurate estimates of degradation of the high protein supplements commonly used to raise dietary protein levels above 11–13 per cent, the point of ruminal ammonia accumulation in most dairy rations. Measurement of ruminal protein degradation should be focused on the relatively few high protein supplements commonly used in ruminant rations. The by-product feeds are also deserving of closer observation, because many of them have undergone some processing which may have rendered the protein more resistant.

A feeding standard based upon metabolizable protein

A brief outline of how a metabolizable protein scheme can be applied will be discussed. A more thorough discussion is available elsewhere (Satter and Roffler, 1975). Simply stated, it involves making an allocation of metabolizable protein for maintenance and for milk production. A lactating cow losing weight is credited with the mobilised protein, and a lactating cow gaining weight has the added requirement for the tissue protein deposited. The following assumptions are involved:

(1) The maintenance requirement for metabolizable protein is 2.4 g $kg^{-0.75}$. This was calculated from the digestible protein requirement for maintenance of 1.6 g $kg^{-0.75}$ for cattle as suggested by Preston (1972) in a review of protein requirements of cattle. Under most maintenance feeding conditions, 1 g of apparent digestible protein would be equivalent to about 1.5 g of metabolizable protein. This follows if one uses as an example a ration that meets maintenance requirements for digestible protein (1.6 g $kg^{-0.75}$). Converting digestible protein to CP with the regression of Knight and Harris (1966) (Digestible protein = 0.877 (%CP) − 2.64) and knowing that metabolizable protein is equal to about 75 per cent of CP when low protein rations are fed, it can be shown that metabolizable protein is approximately 1.5 times the amount

of digestible protein under maintenance feeding conditions, or 2.4 g $kg^{-0.75}$.

(2) The protein content of a kg of bodyweight loss or gain is 0.15 kg. During early lactation each kg of bodyweight loss would contribute 0.15 kg metabolizable protein to the overall supply, and during later lactation when body reserves are being replenished and fetal growth is occurring, each kg of bodyweight gain would result in deposition of 0.15 kg protein. Using these values together with typical weight changes (Everson, 1973; Swanson, Hinton and Miles, 1967; Trimberger *et al.*, 1972) results in a larger amount of metabolizable protein than suggested by Coppock *et al.* (1968), but somewhat less than suggested by Paquay, DeBaere and Lousse (1972). The latter suggested that the mature cow is able to store and then lose 15 kg or more of body protein, but some of their observations were made with atypically large weight changes, and it is questionable whether these apply to the lactating cow. The assumption that 15 per cent of bodyweight is protein essentially agrees with body composition data from studies with cows (Reid, Wellington and Dunn, 1955).

(3) Milk contains 3 per cent true protein. This is a good value for milk from Holsteins, but may be low for other breeds.

(4) The efficiency with which metabolizable protein is utilised for milk production and bodyweight gain is 60 per cent. In other words, synthesis of 1 kg of milk containing 30 g of protein would require 50 g of metabolizable protein. This is an estimate, but it seems quite reasonable in view of some unpublished lactation data.

With these assumptions, the amount of metabolizable protein required is calculated by summing the amount needed for maintenance, milk production and body deposition. If there is a loss in bodyweight, protein mobilised is credited to the supply of metabolizable protein.

When these assumptions are applied to cows producing approximately 7000 kg of milk per 305 days (Everson, 1973; Swanson, Hinton and Miles, 1967; Trimberger *et al.*, 1972), the required level of dietary crude protein in early lactation is about 16 per cent (whole ration − dry matter basis). By week 14 of lactation, a dietary crude protein level of 12−13 per cent is adequate, and continues to decrease to about 10 per cent crude protein at the end of lactation.

To understand why the dietary crude protein is so high in early lactation, milk production, feed intake and bodyweight change during the lactation must be related. The typical lactating cow in her second or subsequent lactation will reach peak milk production at about 5−7 weeks, but dry matter consumption will not reach a peak until 9−11 weeks (Everson, 1973; Swanson, Hinton and Miles, 1967; Trimberger *et al.*, 1972). Bodyweight loss occurs during the first 6 weeks, followed by a stabilisation period of about 2 weeks, after which gradual weight gains occur. The crucial period, from a protein nutrition point of view, is during the first 9−11 weeks of lactation. Unless a cow can mobilise protein and energy proportionate to need, the ration will have to be enriched with protein. Available evidence suggests that the ability of cows to mobilise tissue protein for the synthesis of milk is quite small relative to the ability to mobilise energy (Coppock *et al.*, 1968). Therefore, dietary protein must be proportionately higher during early lactation if protein requirements of the cow are to be met.

At 9–11 weeks, energy intake has reached a maximum, and milk production is on the decline. In contrast to the first few weeks of lactation when low protein, high energy body reserves were contributing to milk synthesis, the situation beyond 11 weeks is reversed, with deposition of body tissue low in protein and high in energy taking place. A cow producing 30 kg milk on the ascending portion of the lactation curve has quite different dietary requirements for protein than the same cow producing 30 kg milk on the descending portion of the lactation curve. Present feeding standards do not recognize this point.

The important effect that level of feed intake may have on the required percentage of dietary protein, combined with the effect of inefficient protein utilisation in high protein rations (> 12–13 per cent CP), results in potentially high dietary CP requirements for cows in early lactation. True protein (plant protein) must be used in early lactation if the higher levels of supplementation are to be effectively achieved. Non-protein nitrogen may be the major, if not sole, source of supplemental nitrogen during the last two-thirds of lactation when the required CP content of the ration is 12–13 per cent or less.

It appears from a study recently completed that first lactation heifers do not respond to an increase in dietary protein from about 12 to 15 per cent as do older cows. Interestingly, first lactation heifers do not reach a peak in milk production as quickly nor to the extent that older cows do. They do not need to mobilise as much low protein, high energy tissue during early lactation when dry matter intake is trying to catch up, and consequently the dietary level of protein required appears to be lowered. There may be an opportunity to use a limited amount of NPN in early lactation with first lactation heifers.

The suggested level of supplementation is maintained at a minimum of 12–13 per cent dietary crude protein, even though the actual requirement may drop to as low as 10 per cent crude protein. The reason for this is to provide the rumen micro-organisms with enough ammonia to maintain maximum growth potential. This can be done rather inexpensively with an NPN source, and may prevent a depression in ration digestibility. More research is needed to determine whether there would be a significant reduction in digestibility by going to as low as 10 per cent dietary CP, but it is conceivable that digestibility of cellulose in high forage rations could be reduced. This point would not be as important with feedlot cattle fed high concentrate rations, for a reduction of starch digestibility in the rumen may be compensated for by increased starch digestion in the intestine.

An attempt was made to get some measure of how much better a protein requirement scheme based upon metabolizable protein would be than the present system based upon CP (N × 6.25). A regression analysis was made of milk production and protein intake on data from published studies comparing milk production when either a negative control (low protein) or treatment (added NPN or protein) ration was fed (Satter and Roffler, 1975). The results are shown in *Table 7.4*. When plant protein was fed, use of metabolizable protein instead of CP improved the r^2 value of the regression from 0.34 to 0.42. When NPN was supplemented, use of metabolizable protein instead of CP increased the r^2 value from 0.15 to 0.34. A number of factors other than per cent dietary protein were affecting milk production in this diverse group of studies; hence the low r^2 values. The significant improvement in the regression obtained by using metabolizable protein instead of CP, particularly when NPN was the source of supplemental nitrogen, suggests that use of the term is worthy of consideration.

Table 7.4 RELATIONSHIP BETWEEN PER CENT INCREASE IN MILK PRODUCTION (Y) AND PER CENT INCREASE IN DIETARY CRUDE PROTEIN (CP) OR METABOLIZABLE PROTEIN (MP)

Type of supplement	Number of observations	Predictive equation	r^2
Non-protein nitrogen	38	$Y = -0.76 + 0.36$ CP	0.15
	38	$Y = 1.24 + 0.52$ MP	0.34
Protein	51	$Y = -0.18 + 0.39$ CP	0.34
	51	$Y = 0.85 + 0.44$ MP	0.42
Combined	89	$Y = -0.32 + 0.37$ CP	0.23
	89	$Y = 1.10 + 0.47$ MP	0.37

The regression should be further improved with substitution of more accurate values, as they become available, for the amount of metabolizable protein obtained per unit of protein fed above the point of ammonia accumulation.

The calculation of protein requirements in terms of metabolizable protein, with final expression in terms of CP, improves accuracy yet retains the simplicity of the CP designation. It is an approach that recognises the nitrogen needs of the rumen bacteria, as well as the host ruminant, and has the requisite features of being easily understood by people in the livestock and feed industry.

Implications for the feed industry

If dairy farmers adopt feeding practices that would be implied from the foregoing discussion, the feed industry will need to supply largely two types of nitrogen supplements. One would be all-plant protein, the other largely, if not all, non-protein nitrogen. The demand for supplements where 15–40 per cent of the nitrogen is non-protein nitrogen should diminish greatly.

Feed suppliers will need to be aware of when or when not to expect benefit from non-protein nitrogen supplementation. When liberal amounts of grain and good quality forage are fed to lactating cows or fattening cattle, then NPN can be utilised in rations containing not more than 12–13 per cent crude protein (dry basis). For cattle receiving only small amounts of grain, the upper limit for NPN utilisation will be around 10–11 per cent crude protein. Cattle that are grazing, or fed only low energy forages, will utilise urea only in rations containing less than 9–10 per cent crude protein. Sheep will reach the upper limit for NPN utilisation at dietary protein levels about two percentage points lower than those described for cattle.

References

Bryant, M.P. and Robinson, I.M. (1962). *J. Bacteriol.*, **84**, 605
Burroughs, W., Trenkle, A.J. and Vetter, R.L. (1973). IAS Leaflet R 173. Ames, Iowa; Iowa State University
Burroughs, W., Nelson, D.K. and Mertens, D.R. (1975). *J. Anim. Sci.*, **41**, 933
Chalmers, M.I., Jaffray, A.E. and White, F. (1971). *Proc. Nutr. Soc.*, **30**, 7
Chalupa, W. (1975). *J. Dairy Sci.*, **58**, 1198

Coppock, E.C., Tyrrell, H.F., Merrill, W.G. and Reid, J.T. (1968). Proc. Cornell Nutrition Conference. Ithaca, New York; Cornell University

Egan, A.R. (1974). *Aust. J. Agric. Res., 25*, 613

Everson, R.A. (1973). PhD Thesis. University of Wisconsin, Madison, Wisconsin

Knight, A.D. and Harris, L.E. (1966). *J. Anim. Sci., 25*, 593

Li-Pun, H.H., Beardsley, G.L. and Satter, L.D. (1975). Unpublished data

Loosli, J.K. and McDonald, I.W. (1968). FAO Agricultural Studies Publication No. 75

Miller, E.L. (1973). *Proc. Nutr. Soc., 32*, 79

Moe, P.W., Flatt, W.P. and Tyrrell, H.F. (1972). *J. Dairy Sci., 55*, 945

National Research Council (1971). *Nutrient Requirements of Dairy Cattle.* Washington, D.C.; National Academy of Sciences

National Research Council (1975). *Nutrient Requirements of Sheep.* Washington, D.C.; National Academy of Sciences

Paquay, R., DeBaere, R. and Lousse, A. (1972). *Br. J. Nutr., 27*, 27

Preston, R.L. (1972). In *University of Nottingham Nutrition Conference for Feed Manufacturers – 6*, p. 22. Eds. H. Swan and D. Lewis. Edinburgh and London; Churchill Livingstone

Reid, J.T., Wellington, G.H. and Dunn, H.O. (1955). *J. Dairy Sci., 38*, 1344

Roffler, R.E. and Satter, L.D. (1975a). *J. Dairy Sci., 58*, 1880

Roffler, R.E. and Satter, L.D. (1975b). *J. Dairy Sci., 58*, 1889

Roffler, R.E. and Satter, L.D. (1976). Unpublished data

Roffler, R.E., Schwab, C.C. and Satter, L.D. (1976). *J. Dairy Sci., 59*, 80

Satter, L.D. and Roffler, R.E. (1975). *J. Dairy Sci., 58*, 1219

Satter, L.D. and Slyter, L.L. (1974). *Br. J. Nutr., 32*, 199

Swanson, E.W., Hinton, S.A. and Miles, J.T. (1967). *J. Dairy Sci., 50*, 1147

Tilley, J.M.A. and Terry, R.A. (1963). *J. Br. Grassland Soc., 18*, 104

Trimberger, G.W., Tyrrell, H.F., Morrow, D.A., Reid, J.T., Wright, M.J., Shipe, W.F., Merrill, W.G., Loosli, J.K., Coppock, C.E., Moore, L.A. and Gordon, C.H. (1972). *New York's Food & Life Sci. Bull.* No. 8. Ithaca, New York; Cornell University

8

ASPECTS OF THE BIOCHEMISTRY OF RUMEN FERMENTATION AND THEIR IMPLICATION IN RUMINANT PRODUCTIVITY

P.J. BUTTERY
University of Nottingham School of Agriculture

Introduction

In this chapter it is hoped to provide a background for the subsequent chapters. The selection of the material to be covered must be rather arbitrary, as must the depth with which each topic is discussed. It is to be hoped that the reader will not be offended by the generalisations nor the omissions which have had to be made to complete the picture in the space available.

The approach adopted has been to consider the breakdown of the diet and the subsequent utilisation of the products for the synthesis of microbial protein, special attention being given to the role of ammonia. Some consequences of the processes to the animal will also be considered. The utilisation of the protein reaching the duodenum is also briefly mentioned.

The breakdown of dietary nitrogenous materials

Although a proportion of dietary protein is broken down in the rumen the rest leaves the rumen largely unaltered (*Figure 8.1*). In order to advance the precision with which it might be possible to feed a ruminant it would be ideal to be able to predict the extent of these two processes. Several techniques are available to determine what proportion of the protein reaching the duodenum is of microbial origin and by difference the extent to which dietary protein escapes fermentation. Ideally the contribution of the digestive juices to the protein flow should also be considered. All these techniques rely on the assay of a constituent peculiar to the microbial fraction in the duodenal contents and on a determination of the ratio of the constituent to microbial protein in an isolated microbial fraction. The methods currently used are summarised in *Table 8.1* and a selection of the results obtained are given in *Table 8.2*. A different approach is to determine the amino acid profile of the duodenal digesta, protozoal protein, bacterial protein, digestive juices and feed protein and from the solution of a series of simultaneous equations to give the source of the protein reaching the duodenum (Evans, Axford and Offer, 1975). The latter method gives the most complete picture

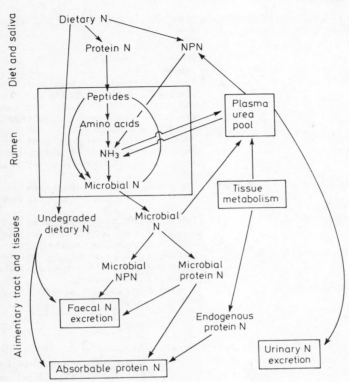

Figure 8.1 The metabolism of nitrogen in the ruminant (from Ling, 1976)

but does require accurate amino acid analyses. Although all these techniques are beset with difficulties and can give some erroneous results, it is to be hoped that progress in this field will not be hampered by a quest for precision without due consideration of the problems the techniques were established to solve. Confidence in the techniques can be obtained from the correlation between the results obtained by using different techniques on the same animal under one dietary situation (*see* data of Ling and Buttery, 1977 in *Table 8.2*) although there are at present no techniques which can provide data to confirm the absolute accuracy of the results.

To illustrate the potential of such techniques the amino acid supply at the duodenum of sheep fed a diet of urea plus barley, and fishmeal plus barley, has been partitioned by Ling (1976) into bacterial, protozoal and undegraded feedstuff. Unfortunately a slight error is introduced since no account could be taken of the contribution of endogenous nitrogenous excretion (*Figure 8.2*). The extent to which a protein is broken down depends on many factors, for example its solubility (Henderickx and Martin, 1963); its rate of passage through the rumen (Ørskov and Fraser, 1973); and the preparation of the diet, e.g. screw pressing, steam pelleting (Mercer and Annison, 1976).

Proteins are degraded in the rumen by the action of proteases of microbial origin. Not all the microbial population possess exopeptidases; indeed only 10

Table 8.1 SOME METHODS FOR DETERMINING FRACTION OF UNDEGRADED FEED IN DUODENAL DIGESTA

Method	Principle of operation
$^{35}SO_4$ incorporation	Bacterial and protozoal sulphur amino acids labelled. Requires separation of microbial fraction and assay of radioactivity in (*a*) methionine; (*b*) cysteine; or (*c*) organic sulphur of microbial fraction and duodenal digesta.
$^{32}PO_4$ incorporation	Bacterial and protozoal nucleic acids labelled. Requires assay of activity in digesta and microbial nucleic acids. Activity of ^{32}P prevents widespread use.
^{15}N incorporation	Bacterial and protozoal nitrogen labelled. Need to isolate a microbial fraction from the digesta. ^{15}N difficult to assay.
Diaminopimelic acid (DAPA)	This amino acid occurs in the cell walls of some bacteria. Does not occur in feed. Requires assay of DAPA in microbial fraction and digesta.
Aminoethylphosphonic acid	This amino acid occurs in the lipid fraction of some protozoa. May occur in some feeds. Can be difficult to assay. Occurs in bacteria.
Constrained optimisation of amino acid profile	Requires amino acid analysis of feed, microbial and digesta fractions.

per cent of bacterial isolates studied by Abou Akkada and Blackburn (1963) showed proteolytic activity. Data from the bovine rumen indicate that this may be an underestimate: Fulghum and Moore (1963) reported that 38 per cent of bovine rumen bacteria had proteolytic activity. Although the proteolytic enzymes are extracellular there is little proteolytic activity in the rumen fluid (Isaacs and Owens, 1971). Protozoa have the ability to engulf protein particles and are equipped with powerful intracellular proteases (Kudo, 1966).

The peptides released by protease activity are further catabolised to yield amino acids and ammonia. The ammonia concentration in the rumen is normally in the order of $10^{-2}M$ while that of the free amino acids is much lower (2.6–65 $\times 10^{-5}M$) (Wright, 1967).

Breakdown of carbohydrate and carbon skeletons of amino acids

Glucose is the major breakdown product of starch and cellulose whilst hemicelluloses mainly yield pentoses. The pentoses are converted to hexoses before further catabolism. The great majority of dietary carbohydrate metabolism thus proceeds via hexose which is then fermented to yield pyruvate, lactate and subsequently CO_2, volatile fatty acids, methane and of course ATP (*Figure 8.3*). A simple scheme for these reactions (*see* Baldwin, Lucas and Cabrera, 1970) is:

$$\text{Hexose} \longrightarrow 2 \text{ pyruvate} + 4H + 2ATP$$
$$\text{Pyruvate} + H_2O \longrightarrow \text{acetate} + CO_2 + 2H + ATP$$
$$\text{Pyruvate} + 4H \longrightarrow \text{propionate} + H_2O + ATP$$
$$2 \text{ Pyruvate} \longrightarrow \text{butyrate} + 2CO_2 + 2ATP$$

Table 8.2 FRACTION OF DUODENAL DIGESTA OF MICROBIAL ORIGIN (A SELECTION OF VALUES ADAPTED FROM SMITH, 1975)

Animal	Method	Main diet	MN:NA-N[1]		References
Sheep	DAP	Dried ryegrass	0.54	–	Hogan and
		Dried phalaris	0.51		Weston (1970)
		Dried subterranean clover	0.44		
		Dried berseem clover	0.32		
Sheep	Nucleic acid	Dried grass	0.85	–	Coelho da Silva *et al.* (1972a)
		Pelleted, dried grass	0.69	–	
		Dried lucerne	0.46		Coelho da Silva
		Pelleted, dried lucerne	0.32		*et al.* (1972b)
Sheep	³⁵S	Dried sainfoin	0.34	–	Beever, Harrison and Thomson (1972)
Sheep	DAP	Pelleted hay	0.85	–	Harrison *et al.* (1973)
		Dried lucerne	0.79		
		Dried sainfoin	0.37		
		Pelleted, dried red clover	0.40		
		Fresh red clover	0.66		
Sheep	³⁵S	Dried subterranean clover	0.43	–	Hume (1975)
		Fresh subterranean clover	0.73		
Sheep	³⁵S	Straw + lucerne meal	0.59	–	Leibholz (1972)
		Straw + lucerne meal + casein	0.61		
		Straw + purified diet (low-N)	0.99		
		Straw + purified diet + casein	0.75		
		Straw + purified diet + wheat gluten	0.84		
Sheep	³⁵S	Semipurified diet + fishmeal	0.40	–	Hume (1975)
		Semipurified diet + groundnut meal	0.60		
		Semipurified diet + soya bean meal	0.50		
Sheep	³⁵S	Semipurified diet + lupin meal	0.60		
Sheep	RNA	Fishmeal + barley	0.56	–	Ling and Buttery (1977)
		Soya bean meal + barley	0.7		
		Urea + barley	0.98		
	³⁵S	Fish meal + barley	0.54	–	Ling and Buttery (1977)
		Soya bean meal + barley	0.64		
		Urea + barley	0.92		
	DAP	Fishmeal + barley	0.42	–	Ling and Buttery (1977)
		Soya bean meal + barley	0.47		
		Urea + barley	0.80		
Cow	DAP	Straw + concentrates	0.50	–	Hutton, Bailey and Annison (1971)
	DAP	Hay + cereal + soya bean meal	0.60	–	Hagemeister and Pfeffer (1973)
		Hay + cereal + HCHO-casein	0.40		
		Hay + cereal + urea	0.73		
Cow	RNA	Hay + concentrates	0.78	–	McAllan and
	DAP	Hay + concentrates	0.40		Smith (1974)

[1] MN:NA-N = microbial nitrogen: total non-ammonia nitrogen at the duodenum

This simplistic view suggests the pattern of VFA production does not affect the amount of ATP generated; however, following a much more detailed consideration of the problem, Harrison *et al.* (1973) suggested that acetate production is associated with the production of 4.25 moles of ATP per mole hexose fermented while propionate is associated with 4 moles of ATP and butyrate

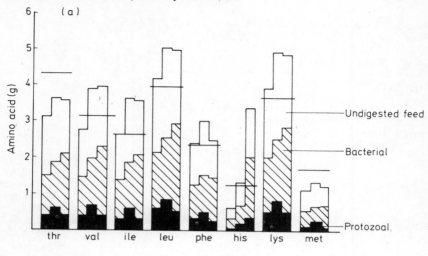

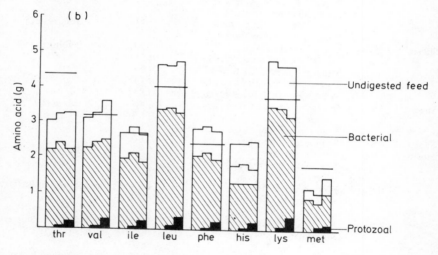

Figure 8.2 Partition of protein reaching the duodenum of sheep fed (a) a fishmeal + barley diet; (b) urea + barley diet. Data are results from three individual sheep. The bar represents the predicted requirement for the animal (see Wakeling, 1970) (data taken from Ling, 1976)

3 moles of ATP. It is this difference which, among other things, gives encouragement for other attempts to manipulate rumen fermentation (*see Chapter 9*). Since in an anaerobic fermentation, excess reducing power cannot be combined with oxygen to form water, products of the fermentation have to be reduced (e.g. the production of propionate, useful to the ruminant, or methane which is lost).

The routes of amino acid catabolism by rumen micro-organisms have not been fully elucidated although for nearly 25 years it has been known that they also yield VFAs (El-Shazly, 1952). Free amino acids are rapidly catabolised in the rumen, e.g. 5 g of methionine introduced into the rumen of a sheep have a

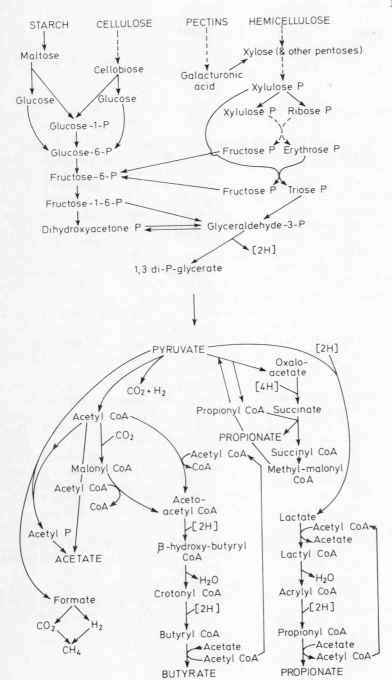

Figure 8.3 Pathway of carbohydrate metabolism in the rumen (adapted from Leng, 1970)

half-life of 2.5 h (Lewis, 1971). Methionine would appear to be one of the more stable amino acids (Chalupa, 1976). The models to describe rumen nitrogen metabolism developed by Nolan and Leng (1972) do suggest that there is a direct incorporation of amino acids into microbial protein.

Protein synthesis in the rumen

The major source of nitrogen for microbial protein synthesis is ammonia. Nolan and Leng (1972) calculated that for a sheep fed 800 g lucerne per day, 80 per cent of microbial nitrogen passed through the rumen ammonia pool. Pilgrim *et al.* (1970), for a similar situation, suggested that 63 per cent of the bacterial and 37 per cent of the protozoal nitrogen pass through this pool. Many bacteria have an absolute requirement for ammonia while others readily use it, even in the presence of a ready supply of amino acids (Bryant and Robinson, 1961). Ciliate protozoa cannot utilise ammonia (Smith, 1975). Little is known about the initial steps of ammonia fixation by rumen micro-organisms; however, sufficient general biochemical information is available to speculate on possible metabolic pathways (Buttery, 1976; Buttery and Lewis, 1976). One striking observation of a study of the enzymes which are likely candidates for the initial reactions is that they all have high affinities for ammonia (*Table 8.3*) and this coupled with the probable ability of the rumen bacteria to concentrate ammonia (Lund, Brosnan and Eggleston, 1970; Pribil and Kotyk, 1970) suggests that the requirement of the bacteria is satisfied at a relatively low rumen ammonia concentration, a feature that will be further considered.

Ammonia can of course be supplied from non-protein sources, e.g. urea, and the catabolism of urea to ammonia is very rapid. Some early data illustrate this point: Pearson and Smith (1943) demonstrated that 100 g of rumen contents can hydrolyse 100 mg urea per hour, this being some four times greater than the maximum rate with which the rumen micro-organisms can incorporate ammonia into protein (Baunstark *et al.*, 1960). Not all rumen bacteria possess urease activity; i.e. 30 per cent of species in sheep (Jones, MacLeod and Blackwood, 1964). The total activity of urease in the rumen can be affected by the diet (Clifford, Bourdette and Tillman, 1968; Wortham *et al.*, 1968). Protozoa, on the other hand, possess little if any urease activity (Jones, MacLeod and Blackwood, 1964).

The synthesis of methionine and cysteine by rumen micro-organisms requires sulphur and its intake may limit protein synthesis when large amounts of non-protein nitrogen are used. Normally a nitrogen to sulphur ratio of less than about 10 is necessary (see for example Bouchard and Conrad, 1973; Chalupa, Oltjen and Dinius, 1973). The synthesis of the nucleic acid involved in protein synthesis requires phosphorus and it is therefore also essential to ensure an adequate supply in the diet.

Protozoa

Coleman (1975) presents some interesting data on the inter-relationship between protozoa and bacteria in the rumen. One startling point is that, for a heifer on a

Table 8.3 THE CHARACTERISTICS OF SOME POSSIBLE ENZYMES INVOLVED IN AMMONIA FIXATION BY RUMEN BACTERIA (DATA TAKEN FROM BARMAN, 1969)

Enzyme	Source	Reaction catalysed	K_m for ammonia
Alanine dehydrogenase	B. subtilis	Pyruvate + NH_3 + NADH $\rightleftharpoons$ L-alanine + NAD^+ + H_2O	3.8×10^{-2} M
Glutamate dehydrogenase	Yeast	2-oxoglutarate + NH_3 + H^+ + NADH (NADPH) $\rightarrow$ L-glutamate + NAD^+ + H_2O ($NADP^+$)	5.0×10^{-4} M
Aspartase	B. cadaveris	Fumarate + NH_3 $\rightarrow$ L-aspartate	3.0×10^{-2} M
Asparagine synthetase	S. bovis	L-aspartate + ATP + NH_3 $\rightarrow$ L-asparagine + ADP + Pi	4×10^{-3} M
Glutamine synthetase	E. coli	L-glutamate + NH_3 + ATP $\rightarrow$ L-glutamine + ADP + Pi	1.8×10^{-3} M
Carbamoyl phosphate synthetase	E. coli	L-glutamine + CO_2 + ATP $\rightarrow$ carbamoyl $- PO_4$ + ADP + L-glutamate	1.2×10^{-2} M

restricted grain ration, each ml of rumen liquor contains the following volume of protozoa: epidinia 0.03 ml, entodinia 0.07 ml, isotrichs 0.05 ml and medium-sized protozoa 0.03 ml while the volume occupied by the bacteria is only 0.03 ml (i.e. 20 per cent of the total volume of the micro-organisms). However, the surface area presented to the rumen liquor by the rumen bacteria is four times that of the protozoa and since the metabolic rate is related to surface area the bacteria are metabolically more important. Coleman (1975) further discusses the engulfment of bacteria by protozoa and calculates that each day in a sheep 90 g of bacteria are engulfed by protozoa. This can be compared with a dry matter flow from the rumen on a readily degradable diet of approximately 500 g day^{-1}.

The protozoa do however have a marked influence on rumen fermentation. For example, in a rumen with a typical protozoal population there is a tendency to a much higher rumen ammonia concentration than with de-faunated animals (Eadie *et al.*, 1970). Protozoa also influence rumen volatile fatty acid patterns by ingesting starch granules, which results in a reduction in the concentration of the volatile fatty acids and an increase in the butyrate:propionate ratio (Whitelaw *et al.*, 1972).

Current information indicates that the proportion of microbial protein entering the duodenum which is of protozoal origin is less than that expected when comparing the ratio of bacterial to protozoal protein in the rumen. Weller and Pilgrim (1974) counted the protozoa passing into the omasal canal and found the concentration to be less than one-fifth of that found in the rumen. Although protozoa may not have a marked influence on the amino acid composition of the duodenal digesta, the differences between the amino acid profiles of bacteria and protozoa (*Table 8.4*) and the higher digestibility of protozoa make it desirable to develop techniques of measuring protozoal flow at the duodenum.

Table 8.4 THE AMINO ACID COMPOSITION OF BACTERIAL AND PROTOZOAL PROTEIN ISOLATED FROM SHEEP (DATA TAKEN FROM LING, 1976)

	Bacteria (g AA/16 g N)*	*Protozoa* (g AA/16 g N)*
Thr	5.37 ± 0.39	5.07 ± 0.48
Val	5.49 ± 0.35	5.24 ± 0.60
Ile	4.68 ± 0.20	5.80 ± 0.54
Leu	6.47 ± 0.30	7.18 ± 0.66
Phe	3.98 ± 0.18	5.29 ± 0.51
His	1.49 ± 0.11	1.79 ± 0.15
Lys	6.99 ± 0.37	10.14 ± 0.60
Arg	4.09 ± 0.25	4.58 ± 0.31
Met	1.78 ± 0.09	1.65 ± 0.16
Asp	12.10 ± 0.56	12.62 ± 1.24
Ser	4.24 ± 0.23	4.10 ± 0.37
Glu	11.98 ± 0.59	13.81 ± 1.62
Gly	4.85 ± 0.34	3.61 ± 0.46
Ala	6.12 ± 0.37	3.48 ± 0.40
Tyr	3.94 ± 0.19	4.49 ± 0.48

*Mean of 10 observations ± s.e. mean

Energy cost of bacterial protein synthesis

Protein synthesis in the rumen is of course closely associated with microbial growth, which is naturally dependent upon the supply of energy-yielding substances, e.g. ATP. Bauchop and Elsden (1960) suggested for a series of anaerobic bacteria that on average 10.5 g of cellular dry matter were produced per mole of ATP generated (the so-called Y-ATP value). There are however many exceptions to this norm, for example, Hobson and Summers (1967) produced data from studies with *Selenomonas rumenantium* which suggested a Y-ATP value of 20. Mixed cultures of bacteria yield higher Y-ATP values than pure cultures, indicating that the mixed culture, as is found in the rumen, is more efficient (Bryant, 1970; Hungate, Reichl and Prins, 1971). It is also possible to describe the energetics of protein synthesis in the rumen using other conventions, for example g microbial crude protein per 100 g apparently digested organic matter. A wide range of values can be found in the literature; a mean value of around 20 g microbial protein per 100 g apparently digested organic matter has been suggested (Ling and Buttery, 1977). One feature that must be emphasised in this context is that for an efficient fermentation to occur energy and nitrogen supply must be balanced. Too little nitrogen will induce uncoupled fermentation (i.e., fermentation without useful ATP production) whilst too much nitrogen and not enough available energy will result in an inefficient use of the nitrogen. It is not appropriate to discuss this matter at length but it is interesting to note that using simulation techniques, Baldwin, Lucas and Cabrera (1970) predicted that the microbial yield would fall when rumen ammonia concentrations were low, i.e. when low protein diets were considered. This is a prediction that has been demonstrated to occur in practice in several instances.

Ammonia supply and protein synthesis

As already mentioned it would appear from theoretical considerations that the concentration of ammonia in the rumen which saturates the capacity of the micro-organisms to synthesize protein is 'relatively low'. This is borne out by much experimental data. Henderson, Hobson and Summers (1969) showed that in continuous culture, ammonia became limiting for growth of *Bacteroides amylophilus* only when its concentration fell below 6×10^{-3} M and that growth rate increased linearly when the ammonia concentration was raised from 1×10^{-3} to 5×10^{-3} M. Allison (1970) also showed that the growth of *B. amylophilus* was restricted when ammonia concentrations fell below 4.6×10^{-3} M. The *in vitro* results of Nikolic, Janovic and Filipovic (1974) and Satter and Slyter (1974) also suggest an optimal level of rumen ammonia of about 5×10^{-3} M.

In vivo data tend to be conflicting. Hume, Moir and Somers (1970) fed sheep purified diets based upon purified ingredients and observed that rumen protein concentrations attained a maximum level when rumen ammonia concentration reached 6.4×10^{-3} M although maximal flow of protein from the duodenum occurred when the rumen ammonia concentration reached 9×10^{-3} M. When the abomasal ammonia concentration in lambs was raised above 6.3×10^{-3} M by adding more urea to a rolled barley diet Ørskov, Fraser and McDonald (1972)

were unable to detect any increase in the passage of protein through the duodenum. In contrast to this Miller (1973) suggested that maximal non-ammonia
nitrogen passage from the rumen occurs when rumen ammonia concentrations
reach 13×10^{-3} M. Recent *in vivo* studies (Okorie, Buttery and Lewis, 1977)
again suggest that rumen protein synthesis attains a maximum level when rumen
ammonia concentrations reach 5×10^{-3} M. In these studies sheep (~40 kg) were
fed a high energy, low protein diet and urea was continuously infused into the
rumen. With increasing total nitrogen intake there was a gradual increase in
rumen ammonia concentration followed by a marked increase when the daily
nitrogen intake reached 10 g, i.e. when the nitrogen supply exceeded the availability of energy. Total microbial protein passage from the rumen, assessed by the
^{35}S technique (*see Table 8.1*), attained a maximum rate when the ammonia concentration reached approximately 5 mM (*Figure 8.4*). The energetic efficiency
of protein production, as predicted by Baldwin, Lucas and Cabrera (1970) was
reduced at low ammonia concentration. The saturation of protein production in
the rumen when there is an ammonia concentration in the region of 5 mM is in
agreement with the findings of Satter and Roffler (*see Chapter 7*).

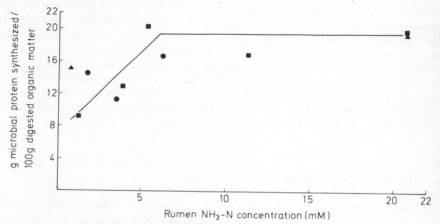

*Figure 8.4 Protein production by the rumen of sheep fed a semisynthetic diet – the effect
of increasing ammonia concentration (from Okorie, Buttery and Lewis, 1977).* ▲, ●, ■
different animals

Excess ammonia would appear to have little adverse effect upon rumen
micro-organisms (see for example Smith, 1975); however, as discussed in several
reports it can pass through the rumen wall and enter the peripheral circulation
(Chalmers, Jaffray and White, 1971). Assuming that the hydrophobic form of
ammonia (NH_3) is the main form in which ammonia passes through cell membranes it can be calculated that, assuming a rumen pH of 6.5, even without
implicating any energy-linked transport processes, there will be a loss of
ammonia from the rumen at concentrations as low as 0.4×10^{-3} M (Lewis and
Buttery, 1973).

Effects of ammonia on tissue metabolism

Ammonia, as is well known, can be very toxic and all terrestrial animals have
elaborate mechanisms to convert it to a less toxic form (e.g. urea or uric acid).

The accumulation of ammonia in tissues can result in many marked derangements in metabolism. It has been suggested, for example, that ammonia exerts its toxic action by interfering with energy metabolism within the cell (Hindfelt and Siesjo, 1971a, b). The ammonia may also act by depleting 2-oxoglutarate in the cell as a result of the formation of L-glutamate or it could promote glutamine synthesis and thereby deplete intracellular ATP. It is also likely that the resting potential across the plasma membrane in the brain is altered by a stimulation of the Na^+-K^+ ATPase, the system responsible for the maintenance of the Na^+ and K^+ gradients found across cell membranes. Perhaps the key to these effects is that the NH_4^+ form of ammonia is very similar in size to the hydrated K^+ ion and indeed, *in vitro* at least, NH_4^+ will often mimic many of the effects of K^+. The problem however is that although the NH_4^+ can be pumped into a cell a proportion of it will be converted to the NH_3 form which would then readily diffuse out through the cell membrane. Following discussion of the biochemistry of ammonia metabolism Tager *et al.* (1975) concluded that the results of their studies with isolated rat liver cells indicates that the presence of ammonia imposed upon the cell an energy demand over and above that required for urea synthesis. This increased energy demand may play a role in the pathogenesis of ammonia toxicity. Whatever the metabolic explanation for ammonia toxicity both infusion of ammonium acetate into the jugular vein and the feeding of urea to sheep causes marked changes in plasma K^+ concentration (Soar, Buttery and Lewis, 1973; Leonard, Buttery and Lewis, 1977). High ammonia concentrations also effect carbohydrate metabolism (see for example Prior, 1976). It is however a matter of debate whether this effect substantially accounts for the depressions of growth rate or food intake seen in animals where a large proportion of the dietary protein is replaced by non-protein nitrogen (Jackson, 1974). It has been suggested that some of the bacteria require preformed peptides; however, it is difficult to accept that this is so important when peptides are continually being generated during the hydrolysis of the protein from lysed micro-organisms and sloughed rumen wall cells. It has also been suggested that there may be a deficiency of the branched chain fatty acids required for the synthesis of certain amino acids in animals fed high urea diets. Oltjen *et al.* (1971) were able to demonstrate a stimulation of rumen protein production when branched chain fatty acids were infused into the rumen of steers fed urea-supplemented diets.

Microbial protein as a source of protein for the ruminant

The apparent digestibility of amino acids in the small intestine of the ruminant is only 50 to 80 per cent (Coelho da Silva *et al.*, 1972b; Salter and Smith, 1974). The digestibility of the individual amino acids varies and there is some evidence that essential amino acids are preferentially absorbed by sheep (Ben-Ghedalia *et al.*, 1974) and cows (van't Klooster and Boekholt, 1972). Data for microbial protein indicate an apparent digestibility of 70–80 per cent (Hoogenraad *et al.*, 1970; Bird, 1972) although a much wider range (49–79 per cent) has been reported by Salter and Smith (1974).

Various methods are available for the determination of the amino acid requirement of the ruminant. Since there is no reason to believe that the metabolism of amino acids in the ruminant differs from the non-ruminant it is, therefore, perhaps acceptable to extrapolate data obtained for animals like the pig to the ruminant (see for example the use of the pig data to calculate the amino acid requirements of the steer by Hutton and Annison, 1972). The use of animals fitted with duodenal cannulae also enables the use of plasma concentration or oxidation rates of amino acids as a basis for assessing requirement (Lewis and Mitchell, 1976). Generally, it is accepted that methionine is the first-limiting amino acid in the sheep and probably the steer. The situation with the dairy cow is unfortunately not at all clear: lysine, methionine, histidine and leucine have all been cited (Schelling and Hatfield, 1968; Brown, 1969; Mepham, 1971; Clark, 1975) as possible first-limiting amino acids.

When the precise amino acid requirements of ruminants have been established it should be possible to manipulate the amino acid flow at the duodenum to meet these requirements. Amongst the ways which should be useful in this exercise are the use of protected protein (*see Chapter 5*); the use of protected amino acids (Langar, Buttery and Lewis, 1975; Ferguson, 1975); the use of protein sources relatively stable against breakdown in the rumen; and adjustments in dietary nutrient balance to achieve a particular post-duodenal supply (Ling, 1976).

Utilisation of absorbed amino acids

A picture of overall metabolism of amino acids in the ruminant is difficult to achieve since studies on such animals are hampered by two main factors: (*a*) the modification of the amino acid supply at the duodenum; and (*b*) the size of the animal which makes the use of isotopic tracers rather expensive. If data from pigs can be applied to the ruminant it would appear that even when an amino acid limits growth then a surprisingly small proportion (~50 per cent) is incorporated into the carcass (Lewis, Boorman and Buttery, 1976). Recently we have conducted similar experiments with the rapidly growing lamb and although there are many assumptions it would appear that the retention of lysine is again only 50 per cent (Buttery, Lubbock and Beckerton, 1977). It is interesting to speculate on some of the reasons for this. Protein like most other animal constituents is continually being turned over. In a 50 kg sheep mixed muscle protein of the *l. dorsi* muscle has a fractional synthetic rate of 0.018 day^{-1} (Buttery *et al.,* 1975) which indicates that in a sheep of this size 86 g (dry wt) of skeletal muscle are synthesized per day whilst the net deposition of protein would only be expected to be a few grams. This contrasts with the rapidly growing cockerel where 6.8 g of skeletal muscle are synthesized per day but there is still a protein deposition of 3.9 g day^{-1} (Buttery, Boorman and Barratt, 1973). This continual turnover of tissue protein accentuates any inefficiency that might exist in the incorporation of amino acids into protein. This can be illustrated by considering some data from the rat (Millward, Nnanyelugo and Garlick, 1975) which indicates that between one-third and one-fifth of the total body protein is turned over per day. Neale and Waterlow (1974) showed that in rats fed a low-protein diet, 2.75 per cent and 1.75 per cent of body lysine and leucine respectively are lost per day. If this data is used to calculate the efficiency of re-incorporation of lysine and leucine, released from protein, values of 87–92 per cent, and 91–95 per cent for lysine and leucine are obtained (Buttery and Annison, 1977). Thus, in an animal in which the ratio of protein synthesis to protein deposition is high, there would be a tendency for a lower efficiency of incorporation of dietary amino acid than in an animal where the synthesis to deposition ratio is lower, e.g. the broiler chicken. It is interesting to note the efficiency of incorporation of amino acids taken up by the udder into milk for several amino acids reaches 100 per cent (Derrig, Clark and Davis, 1974). There would appear to be little, if any, turnover of milk protein.

The continual turnover of protein must also put a substantial energy demand on the animal (Buttery and Boorman, 1976). It would, therefore, appear to be beneficial if the turnover of protein could be reduced without affecting the rate of net protein deposition. In this context it is relevant to consider the mode of action of some of the anabolic agents currently used in animal production. One such compound, trienbolone acetate, has recently been examined in this respect (Vernon and Buttery, 1977). This compound, at least with the rat, reduced the rate of protein synthesis and the rate of protein degradation whilst also stimulating growth. It may well be that this reduction could account at least in part for the increased production performance of farm animals, treated with this compound (see for example Chan, Heitzman and Kitchenham, 1975).

Amino acids serve other functions than protein synthesis; for example, they may contribute to the glucose produced by ruminant tissues. In the ruminant little or no glucose is absorbed from the gut. From a selection of the data obtained with ruminants (Lindsay, 1976), it appears that up to 20 per cent of the absorbed protein is incorporated into glucose. It is interesting to note that amongst the amino acids which are readily incorporated into glucose is threonine (see for example Morton, Buttery and Lindsay, 1977) and that the supply of this amino acid *may* be inadequate on certain diets (Lewis and Mitchell, 1976). The situation regarding the relative supply and demand for amino acids is by no means entirely resolved and conclusions come to depend largely upon the methods used to assess requirement (Armstrong and Annison, 1973).

Conclusions

With the increasing amount of information available on the quantitative pathways of nitrogen metabolism both in the rumen and in ruminant tissues, the time is approaching when it will be possible to feed a ruminant with the precision normally associated with the broiler chicken.

References

Abou Akkada, A.R. and Blackburn, T.H. (1963). *J. gen. Microbiol.*, **31**, 461

Allison, M.J. (1969). In *Physiology of Digestion and Metabolism in the Ruminant*: Symposium Proceedings, p. 456. Ed. A.T. Phillipson. Newcastle-upon-Tyne; Oriel Press

Armstrong, D.G. and Annison, E.F. (1973). *Proc. Nutr. Soc.*, **32**, 107

Baldwin, R.L., Lucas, H.L. and Cabrera, R. (1969). In *Physiology of Digestion and Metabolism in the Ruminant*: Symposium Proceedings, p. 319. Ed. A.T. Phillipson. Newcastle-upon-Tyne; Oriel Press

Barman, T.E. (1969). *Enzyme Handbook I and II*. Berlin, Heidelberg, New York; Springer-Verlag

Bauchop, T. and Elsden, S.R. (1960). *J. gen. Microbiol.*, **23**, 457

Baunstark, J.S., Bloomfield, R.A., Garner, G.B. and Muhrer, M.E. (1960). *J. Anim. Sci.*, **19**, 1248 (Abstr)

Beever, D.E., Harrison, D.G. and Thomson, D.J. (1972). *Proc. Nutr. Soc.*, **31**, 61A

Ben-Ghedalia, D., Tagari, H., Bondi, A. and Tadmor, A. (1974). *Br. J. Nutr.*, **31**, 125

Bird, P.R. (1972). *Aust. J. biol. Sci.*, **25**, 195

Bouchard, R. and Conrad, H.R. (1973). *J. Dairy Sci.*, **56**, 1429

Brown, R.E. (1969). In *University of Nottingham Nutrition Conference for Feed Manufacturers – 3*, p. 23. Eds. H. Swan and D. Lewis. London; J. & A. Churchill

Bryant, M.P. (1970). *Am. J. clin. Nutr.*, **23**, 1440

Bryant, M.P. and Robinson, I.M. (1961). *Appl. Microbiol.*, **9**, 96

Buttery, P.J. (1976). In *Principles of Cattle Production*, p. 145. Eds. H. Swan and W.H. Broster. London; Butterworths

Buttery, P.J. and Annison, E.F. (1977). In *Reviews of Rural Science*, p. 111. Ed. T.A. Sutherland. Australia; University of New England

Buttery, P.J. and Boorman, K.N. (1976). In *Protein Metabolism and Nutrition*, p. 197. Eds. D.J.A. Cole, K.N. Boorman, P.J. Buttery, D. Lewis, R.J. Neale and H. Swan. London; Butterworths

Buttery, P.J. and Lewis, D. (1976). In *Nuclear Techniques in Animal Production and Health*, p. 271. Vienna; FAO and IAEA

Buttery, P.J., Boorman, K.N. and Barratt, B. (1973). *Proc. Nutr. Soc.*, **32**, 80A

Buttery, P.J., Lubbock, M.H. and Beckerton, A. (1977). In *Proc. 2nd International Symposium on Protein Metabolism and Nutrition*. EAAP

Buttery, P.J., Beckerton, A.B., Mitchell, R.M., Davis, K. and Annison, E.F. (1975). *Proc. Nutr. Soc.*, **34**, 21A

Chalmers, M.I., Jaffray, A.E. and White, F. (1971). *Proc. Nutr. Soc.*, **30**, 7

Chalupa, W. (1976). *J. Anim. Sci.*, **43**, 828

Chalupa, W., Oltjen, R.R. and Dinius, D.A. (1973). *J. Anim. Sci.*, **37**, 340

Chan, K.H., Heitzman, R.J. and Kitchenham, B.A. (1975). *Br. Vet. J.*, **131**, 170

Clark, J.H. (1975). *J. Dairy Sci.*, **58**, 1178

Clifford, A.J., Bourdette, J.R. and Tillman, A.D. (1968). *J. Anim. Sci.*, **27**, 814

Coelho da Silva, J.F., Seeley, R.C., Thomson, D.J., Beever, D.E. and Armstrong, D.G. (1972a). *Br. J. Nutr.*, **28**, 43

Coelho da Silva, J.F., Seeley, R.C., Beever, D.E., Prescott, J.H.D. and Armstrong, D.G. (1972b). *Br. J. Nutr.*, **28**, 357

Coleman, G.S. (1975). In *Physiology and Digestion in the Ruminant*, p. 149. Eds. I.W. McDonald and A.C.I. Warner. Australia; University of New England

Derrig, R.G., Clark, J.H. and Davis, C.L. (1974). *J. Nutr.*, **104**, 151

Eadie, J.M., Hyldgaard-Jensen, J., Mann, S.O., Reid, R.S. and Whitelaw, F.G. (1970). *Br. J. Nutr.*, **24**, 157

El-Shazly, K. (1952). *Biochem. J.*, **51**, 640

Evans, R.A., Axford, R.F.E. and Offer, N.W. (1975). *Proc. Nutr. Soc.*, **34**, 65A

Ferguson, K.A. (1975). In *Digestion and Metabolism in the Ruminant*, p. 448. Eds. I.W. McDonald and A.C.I. Warner. Australia; University of New England

Fulghum, R.S. and Moore, W.E.C. (1963). *J. Bact.*, **85**, 808

Hagemeister, H. and Pfeffer, E. (1973). *Z. Tierphysiol. Tierernähr. Futtermittelk*, **31**, 275

Harrison, D.G., Beever, D.E., Thomson, D.J. and Osbourn, D.F. (1973). *J. agric. Sci., Camb.*, **81**, 391

Henderson, C., Hobson, P.N. and Summers, R. (1969). In *Proceedings 4th International Symposium on Continuous Culture of Micro-organisms*, p. 189. Prague; Czechoslovak Acad. Sci.

Henderickx, H. and Martin, J. (1963). *C.r. Rech. Inst. Encour. Rech. scient. Ind. Agric.*, **31**, 110

Hindfelt, B. and Siesjo, B.K. (1971a). *Scand. J. clin. Lab. Invest.*, **28**, 353

Hindfelt, B. and Siesjo, B.K. (1971b). *Scand. J. clin. Lab. Invest.*, **28**, 363

Hobson, P.N. and Summers, R. (1967). *J. gen. Microbiol.*, **47**, 53

Hogan, J.P. and Weston, R.H. (1970). In *Physiology of Digestion and Metabolism in the Ruminant*, p. 478. Ed. A.T. Phillipson. Newcastle-upon-Tyne; Oriel Press

Hoogenraad, N.J., Hird, F.J.R., White, R.G. and Leng, R.A. (1970). *Br. J. Nutr.*, **24**, 129

Hume, I.D. (1975). In *Tracer Techniques in Studies on the Use of Non-protein Nitrogen in Ruminants*, p. 1. Vienna; International Atomic Energy Agency

Hume, I.D., Moir, R.J. and Somers, M. (1970). *Aust. J. agric. Res.*, **21**, 283

Hungate, R.E., Reichl, J. and Prins, R. (1971). *Appl. Microbiol.*, **22**, 1104

Hutton, K. and Annison, E.F. (1972). *Proc. Nutr. Soc.*, **31**, 151

Hutton, K., Bailey, F.J. and Annison, E.F. (1971). *Br. J. Nutr.*, **25**, 165

Isaacs, J. and Owens, F.N. (1971). *J. Anim. Sci.*, **33**, 287

Jackson, P. (1974). In *University of Nottingham Nutrition Conference For Feed Manufacturers – 8*, p. 123. Eds. H. Swan and D. Lewis. London; Butterworths

Jones, G.A., MacLeod, R.A. and Blackwood, A.C. (1964). *Can. J. Microbiol.*, **10**, 371

Kudo, R.R. (1966). *Protozoology*. Springfield, Illinois; Charles C. Thomas

Langar, P.N., Buttery, P.J. and Lewis, D. (1975). *J. Anim. Sci.*, **41**, 409

Leibholz, J. (1972). *Aust. J. agric. Res.*, **22**, 1073

Leng, R.A. (1970). In *Physiology of Digestion and Metabolism in the Ruminant*, p. 406. Ed. A.T. Phillipson. Newcastle-upon-Tyne; Oriel Press

Leonard, M.C., Buttery, P.J. and Lewis, D. (1977). *Br. J. Nutr.*, **38**, 455

Lewis, A.J. (1971). PhD Thesis, University of Nottingham

Lewis, D. and Buttery, P.J. (1973). In *Production Disease in Farm Livestock*, p. 201. Eds. J.M. Payne, K.G. Hibbitt and B.F. Sansom. London; Baillière Tindall

Lewis, D. and Mitchell, R.M. (1976). In *Protein Metabolism and Nutrition*, p. 417. Eds. D.J.A. Cole, K.N. Boorman, P.J. Buttery, D. Lewis, R.J. Neale and H. Swan. London; Butterworths

Lewis, D., Boorman, K.N. and Buttery, P.J. (1976). In *Meat Animals – Growth and Productivity*, p. 103. Eds. D. Lister, D.N. Rhodes, V.R. Fowler and M. Fuller. London; Plenum Press

Ling, J.R. (1976). PhD Thesis, University of Nottingham

Ling, J.R. and Buttery, P.J. (1977). *Br. J. Nutr.*, **39**, 165

Lindsay, D.B. (1976). In *Protein Metabolism and Nutrition*. Eds. D.J.A. Cole, K.N. Boorman, P.J. Buttery, D. Lewis, R.J. Neale and H. Swan. London; Butterworths

Lund, P., Brosnan, J.T. and Eggleston, L.V. (197.). In *Essays in Cell Metabolism* p. 167. Eds. W. Bartley, H.L. Komberg and R.J. Quale. London; Wiley-Interscience

McAllan, A.B. and Smith, R.H. (1974). *Proc. Nutr. Soc.,* **33**, 41A

Mepham, T.B. (1971). In *Lactation*, p. 297. Ed. I. Falconer. London; Butterworths

Mercer, J.R. and Annison, E.F. (1976). In *Protein Metabolism and Nutrition*, p. 397. Eds. D.J.A. Cole, K.N. Boorman, P.J. Buttery, D. Lewis, R.J. Neale and H. Swan. London; Butterworths

Miller, E.L. (1973). *Proc. Nutr. Soc.,* **32**, 79

Millward, D.J., Nnanyelugo, D.O. and Garlick, P.J. (1975). *Proc. Nutr. Soc.,* **34**, 334

Morton, J.L., Buttery, P.J. and Lindsay, D.B. (1977). *Proc. Nutr. Soc.,* **36**, 20A

Neale, R.J. and Waterlow, J.C. (1975). *Br. J. Nutr.,* **32**, 257

Nikolic, J.A., Janovic, M. and Filipovic, R. (1974). In *Tracer Studies on Nonprotein Nitrogen for Ruminants*, p. 14. Vienna; FAO and IAEA

Nolan, J.V. and Leng, R.A. (1972). *Br. J. Nutr.,* **27**, 177

Okorie, A.U., Buttery, P.J. and Lewis, D. (1977). *Proc. Nutr. Soc.,* **36**, 38A

Oltjen, R.R., Slyter, L.L., Williams, E.E. Jr. and Kern, D.L. (1971). *J. Nutr.,* **101**, 101

Ørskov, E.R. and Fraser, C. (1973). *Proc. Nutr. Soc.,* **32**, 68A

Ørskov, E.R., Fraser, C. and McDonald, I. (1972). *Br. J. Nutr.,* **27**, 491

Pearson, R.M. and Smith, J.A.B. (1943). *Biochem. J.,* **37**, 148

Pilgrim, A.F., Gray, F.V., Weller, R.A. and Belling, C.B. (1970). *Br. J. Nutr.,* **24**, 589

Pribil, S. and Kotyk, K.A. (1970). *Biochim. Biophys. Acta,* **219**, 242

Prior, R.L. (1976). *J. Anim. Sci.,* **42**, 160

Salter, D.N. and Smith, R.H. (1974). *Proc. Nutr. Soc.,* **33**, 42A

Satter, L.D. and Slyter, L.L. (1974). *Br. J. Nutr.,* **32**, 199

Schelling, G.T. and Hatfield, E.E. (1968). *J. Nutr.,* **96**, 319

Smith, R.H. (1975). In *Digestion and Metabolism in the Ruminant*, p. 399. Eds. I.N. MacDonald and A.C.I. Warner. Australia; University of New England

Soar, J.B., Buttery, P.J. and Lewis, D. (1973). *Proc. Nutr. Soc.,* **82**, 77A

Tager, J.M., Akerboom, T.P.M., Hoek, J.B., Meijer, A.J., Vaartjes, W., Eruster, I and Williamson, J.R. (1975). In *Normal and Pathological Development of Energy Metabolism*, p. 63. Eds. F.A. Holmes and C.V. Vander Berg. London and New York; Academic Press

van't Klooster, A.Th. and Boekholt, H.A. (1972). *Neth. J. agric. Sci.,* **20**, 272

Vernon, B.G. and Buttery, P.J. (1977). *Br. J. Nutr.,* **36**, 575

Wakeling, A.E. (1970). PhD Thesis, University of Nottingham

Weller, R.A. and Pilgrim, A.F. (1974). *Br. J. Nutr.,* **32**, 341

Whitelaw, F.G., Eadie, J.M., Mann, S.O. and Reid, R.S. (1972). *Br. J. Nutr.,* **27**, 425

Wortham, J.S., Wilson, B.B., Knight, W.M., Holland, B.F. and Scheirer, D.E. (1968). *J. Anim. Sci.,* **27**, 1180 (abstr.)

Wright, D.E. (1967). *Appl. Microbiol.,* **15**, 547

9

MANIPULATION OF RUMEN FERMENTATION

P.C. THOMAS
J.A.F. ROOK
Hannah Research Institute, Ayr, Scotland

Manipulation of diet, through the selection of feed constituents and the control of their relative proportions, is a traditional part of animal management. To predict accurately the performance of an individual animal on the basis of diet composition and amount is not possible, however, even when the composition is defined in precise chemical terms. Knowledge of the interactions between nutrients in their effect on feed utilisation is far from complete and there is considerable individual variation in the interaction between an animal and its feed supply, reflecting quantitative differences in the physiology of digestion and metabolism. Within ruminants, there is a further major source of variation in digestion due to the complex inter-relationship between diet, symbiotic microbes (mainly of the reticulorumen but also of the caecum) and gut physiology. Evidence on the quantitative importance of this variation is now extensive and a variety of attempts have been made, by dietary means, to regulate fermentation within the rumen with a view to improving animal performance. The purpose of this chapter is to review present evidence on the nature and extent of variations in rumen fermentation and of possible consequences for animal production, and then to examine the various techniques which have been suggested for the manipulation of rumen fermentation and to evaluate their effects.

Variation in the efficiency of utilisation of energy and nitrogen at different stages of digestion and metabolism

Differences in digestibility are a main source of the variation between feeds in the efficiency with which they are converted to animal products but there is little possibility of increasing digestibility through events within the rumen except where there are deficiencies in the supply of nutrients to the rumen micro-organisms. The extent and nature of rumen fermentation have a more profound effect on the efficiency of use of digested nutrients and observed variation in this efficiency may be seen as the limit of the benefits that could come from rumen fermentation. For typical farm diets, the partial efficiency of utilisation of digestible energy for maintenance varies from about 53 to 66 per cent, and the corresponding partial efficiencies for fattening are 26 to 54 per cent, and for lactation 53 to 65 per cent. Since in animals fed for production, a change in the efficiency of utilisation of energy for maintenance affects the level of feeding, the potential variation in production efficiency may be greater but only in the fattening animal does there appear to be scope to alter production by more than 25 per cent. It is more difficult to assess the extent of variation in the efficiency of utilisation of dietary protein, because of the interaction between dietary energy and protein and of the problem of distinguishing between the use of amino acids for maintenance and for production. Conventional balance studies with diets adequate in energy suggest that the efficiency of utilisation of digestible crude protein in the growing animal varies from 35 to 60 per cent, but much of this variation can be linked to variation in the dietary ratio of energy: protein and variations due to the type of dietary protein are much smaller (Ørskov, Fraser and Corse, 1970; Broster, 1972).

The sites of digestion of dietary constituents

Wide variations in the sites of disappearance of energy are related to the chemical composition of the diet, the type and degree of processing, the level of feeding and other factors. In a summary of published work, Thomas and Clapperton (1972) concluded that the energy digested in the rumen could account for 23 to 87 per cent of the total energy digested, and the corresponding figures for the small intestine and for the caecum and colon were 17 to 51 per cent and 4 to 26 per cent.

For medium-quality diets of fresh or sun-dried grass given at moderate levels of feeding in long or chopped form, 65–70 per cent of the digestible energy 'disappears' in the stomach, 20–25 per cent in the small intestine and 13–15 per cent in the caecum and colon (*Table 9.1*, a). There is an almost complete ruminal degradation of dietary sugars (Beever *et al.*, 1971) and a very extensive digestion of starchy carbohydrates (MacRae and Armstrong, 1969). About 90–95 per cent of the digestible cellulose is also fermented within the rumen, together with a slightly smaller proportion of the digestible hemicellulose. The undigested starchy and fibrous carbohydrates, long-chain fatty acids, partially digested food protein and microbial bodies pass to the small intestine, where they may be digested and the products absorbed; the digestion of fibrous carbohydrates is, however, low and most of those entering the duodenum pass, with other residues of intestinal digestion, to the caecum and colon where they are subject to further fermentation. Distinct differences in the quantitative importance of the various sites of digestion have been observed between varieties of grasses and between grass and other types of forage (*Table 9.1*, b).

As forages mature and become more heavily lignified, ruminal digestion of the cell wall constituents tends to be depressed, and there are associated decreases in the digestion of dietary and microbial material in the small intestine and increases in the fermentation in the caecum and colon (*Table 9.1*, c). Reduced ruminal digestion of the cell wall materials is also sometimes observed when the level of feeding is raised (*Table 9.1*, c) and always when the diet is provided in a finely ground form. Under these conditions, the non-fibrous constituents of the diet are also affected and digestion is increased in the small intestine and in the caecum and colon (*Table 9.1*, c). Digestion in the small intestine is also enhanced when forages are artificially dried (*Table 9.1*, a).

Table 9.1 THE APPARENT DIGESTIBILITY OF ENERGY AND THE DISAPPEARANCE OF APPARENTLY DIGESTED ENERGY IN THE RUMEN, SMALL INTESTINE, AND CAECUM AND COLON IN SHEEP OR COWS GIVEN A VARIETY OF DIETS

Diet	Apparent digestibility (%) of gross energy	Proportion of apparently digested energy disappearing in the:			Reference
		Rumen	Small intestine	Caecum and colon	
Fresh grass	67.4	63.0	23.6	13.4	(a) Beever *et al.* (1971)
Artificially dried grass	68.1	53.4	30.2	16.3	
Ruanui ryegrass	76.6	53.4	31.8	14.7	(b) Ulyatt and MacRae (1974)
Manawi ryegrass	71.5	44.4	41.0	14.6	
White clover	80.4	58.9	26.3	14.8	
Early-cut ryegrass – chopped low level of feeding	83.3	64.4	29.4	4.2	(c) Beever *et al.* (1972)
Medium-cut ryegrass – chopped low level of feeding	73.4	60.3	26.3	13.4	
Early-cut ryegrass – chopped high level of feeding	83.3	61.9	32.7	5.4	
Early-cut ryegrass – pelleted low level of feeding	81.0	56.2	33.7	10.1	
Hay (100%)	59.3	67.1	21.2	11.8	(d) MacRae and Armstrong (1969)
Hay (33%), barley (66%)	71.8	62.3	29.4	8.2	
Dried grass, rolled barley	73.7	64.5	19.1	16.5	(e) Watson, Savage and Armstrong (1972)
Dried grass, ground and pelleted maize	74.8	53.4	34.7	12.0	
Hay, barley, flaked maize propionic acid	80.1	74.1	25.9		(f) Ishaque, Thomas and Rook (1971)
Hay, barley, flaked maize butyric acid fermentation	85.2	87.5	12.5		

Substitution of starchy cereals for dietary forages causes a depression in ruminal cellulose digestion but an increase in the flow of starch to the intestine and its digestion there (*Table 9.1*, d); the effects, however, are very variable and are markedly influenced by the type and form of the cereal inclusion (Armstrong and Beever, 1969; *Table 9.1*, e). Furthermore, under certain dietary conditions, rumen fermentation may vary independently of diet and affect the extent of digestion within the rumen. When the fermentation is characterised by a high molar proportion of propionic acid the extent of ruminal digestion tends to be depressed and digestion in the intestine increased (*Table 9.1*, f).

The energetics of rumen fermentation

Measurement of the 'disappearance' of energy in the rumen underestimates the significance of rumen digestion to the host animal since a substantial part of the products of the ruminal degradation of dietary constituents may be incorporated into microbial cells and pass to the intestine. The 'disappearance' of energy does, however, provide a measure of the microbial wastes, the short-chain fatty acids, methane and the fermentation heat loss. Of these, only the short-chain fatty acids are absorbed and utilised; the methane and, in a thermoneutral environment, the heat of fermentation represent an energy loss to the host.

Respiration calorimetry experiments have provided comprehensive data on energy lost as methane. The loss can vary from 8 to 15 per cent of the digestible energy of the diet, being high for forage diets and, generally, low for diets rich in starchy carbohydrates (Clapperton and Blaxter, 1965). The extent of the loss is roughly proportional to the amount of energy fermented but since the formation of both methane and propionic acid requires hydrogen (Hungate, 1966), methane production also varies with the composition of the mixture of fermentation acids, and is low when the proportion of propionic acid is high.

There is only limited information on the heat of fermentation. *In vitro*, heat losses as high as 13 per cent of the substrate fermented have been observed in some experiments (Menke and Ehrensvaard, 1974) but more usual values are about 6 per cent (Marston, 1948; Houpt, 1968; Hersberger and Hartsook, 1970). *In vivo*, the heat of fermentation is difficult to determine, but Webster *et al.* (1975) have developed a technique based on the measurement of portal blood flow and of the difference in temperature and oxygen content between arterial and portal venous blood. Using this method in sheep given diets of barley, of dried grass and of dried lucerne, they have estimated heat of fermentation to be 2.2–7.6 per cent of the digestible energy or about 7.5 per cent of the energy of the substrate fermented in the rumen.

These observations collectively indicate that the major proportion of the fermentation wastes is in the form of short-chain fatty acids and this is confirmed by the rates of fatty acid production as measured using ^{14}C-labelled acids, which show that 53–62 per cent of the digestible energy of the diet may be absorbed as acetic, propionic and butyric acids (Whitelaw *et al.*, 1970).

On the basis of information on short-chain fatty acid, methane and fermentation heat production, Thomas and Clapperton (1972) calculated that, of the energy disappearing in the rumen, 75–88 per cent is absorbed as fatty acids, 9–18 per cent is lost by eructation as methane and that 3–7 per cent is lost as heat. These estimates may be unreliable since, in recent experiments in which energy disappearance and short-chain fatty acid production were determined simultaneously, the short-chain fatty acids accounted for 61–93 per cent of the energy loss in the fermentation wastes (Beever, Thomson and Cammell, 1976). It appears that under some circumstances, variation in microbial metabolism may cause a substantial change in the partition of energy between the short-chain fatty acids, methane and heat of fermentation, although part of the observed variation could be the result of the lack of precision of the methods available for the measurement of energy disappearance and fatty acid production.

The composition of the ruminal mixture of short-chain fatty acids

The rates of ruminal production of short-chain fatty acids, as measured using ^{14}C-acids, have been determined for only a limited number of diets. The results available, however, suggest that the relative rates of production are broadly reflected by the molar proportions of the acids in rumen liquor. The relationship is especially good with forage diets, but with mixtures of forages and cereals, use of the molar proportions of the fatty acids may underestimate slightly the contribution of acetic acid to the mixture of acids absorbed (Leng and Brett, 1966).

Typically, diets composed solely of forages give rise to mixtures containing, on a molar basis, 65–74 per cent acetic acid, 15–20 per cent propionic acid and 8–16 per cent butyric acid, although with high-quality forage fine-grinding can cause a reduction in the proportion of acetic acid and an increase in that of propionic acid, butyric acid or both. Substitution of starchy concentrates for forage, or supplementation of forage with concentrates, generally, although not invariably, results in a decrease in the proportion of acetic acid and, where the concentrate forms a moderate proportion of the diet (or even a high proportion if the level of dry matter intake is not too high), moderately high proportion of propionic acid or butyric acid or both (*Figure 9.1*). When the concentrate forms a

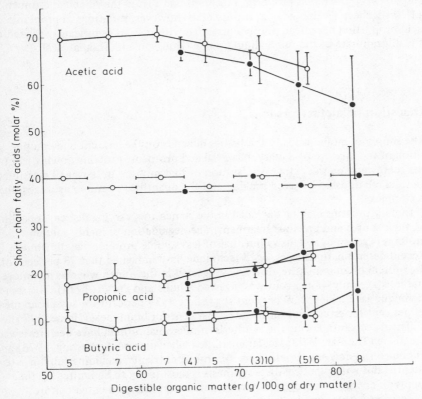

Figure 9.1 The relationship between the molar proportion of acetic, propionic and butyric acids in the rumen and the concentration of digestible organic matter (DOM) in the diet in animals given forage diets (○) or concentrate and mixed forage and concentrate diets (●). Vertical bars show the extreme values included in each mean value. Horizontal bars show the range of DOM contents included in each mean value. Number of observations in each mean are given at the foot of the figure; values in parentheses refer to the concentrate and mixed forage and concentrate diets. Each observation represents a mean for at least two animals. All forages are in the long or chopped form. No allowance has been made for effects due to level of feeding

large proportion of the diet and the dry matter intake is high, the fermentation pattern tends to be more constant and to be characterised by a very high proportion of propionic acid (more than 30 per cent) and low proportions of acetic and butyric acids.

The links between the composition of the mixture of short-chain fatty acids and the chemical composition of the diet are often not close, because the composition of the mixture of fatty acids produced reflects not only the composition of the substrate fermented but also the metabolic activity of the rumen microbes (Sutton, 1968, 1969). The composition and metabolism of the microbial population is dependent on the chemical composition of the diet but is also influenced by a wide range of other dietary and non-dietary factors which are important because of their effect on the environment within the rumen, and the effects of these factors are difficult to predict. For example, Sutton and Johnson (1969) have shown that in cows given high concentrate diets there is an inverse relationship between the molar proportion of propionic acid in the rumen and rumen pH. With sheep given high concentrate diets, however, variations in propionic acid proportion have been poorly correlated with pH but significantly related to the dilution rate of the rumen liquid phase (Hodgson and Thomas, 1975).

Digestion of dietary protein

The supply of amino acids to the tissues depends on the amount and composition of the mixture of dietary, bacterial and protozoal proteins flowing from the rumen and on the extent of digestion of that mixture in the small intestine; and the relationship between the diet and the quantities of amino acids absorbed is complex.

Dietary proteins may be degraded in the rumen to a varying degree, depending on their source and previous treatment. The degradation of highly soluble proteins is generally extensive but that of less soluble proteins may be limited. Recent determinations using a ^{35}S technique have indicated that 73 per cent of the protein of an immature clover was digested in the rumen whereas at a more mature stage only 43 per cent was digested (Hume and Purser, 1974). The same technique gave values of 29 per cent for fishmeal, 39 per cent for soya bean meal, 63 per cent for groundnut meal and 65 per cent for lupin meal (Hume, 1974).

The factors influencing the synthesis of microbial protein have been reviewed elsewhere (Thomas, 1973; McMeniman, Ben-Ghedalia and Armstrong, 1976) and will be considered only briefly here. Microbial nutrients, including sulphur, are essential but with practical diets synthesis is most likely to be limited by the supply of energy or nitrogen. Under optimum conditions in batch culture, bacterial growth generally yields about 10.5 g of dry matter per mole of ATP formed from substrate fermentation. This figure, which corresponds to about 23 g of bacterial crude protein per 100 g organic matter converted to microbial wastes, has been used as a basis for judging the efficiency of bacterial protein synthesis in the rumen. The agreement between this *in vitro* efficiency and that measured *in vivo* is fairly good for forage diets (*Figure 9.2a*) but for concentrate and mixed forage and concentrate diets, the *in vivo* efficiencies are variable and

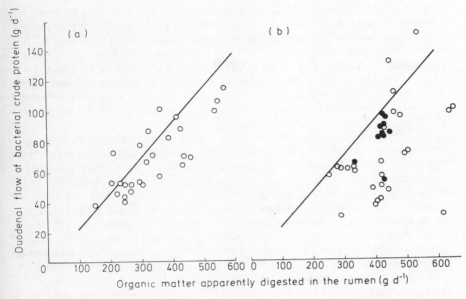

Figure 9.2 The relationship between the duodenal flow of bacterial crude protein and the amount of organic matter apparently digested in the rumen in sheep (O) and cattle (●) given (a) forage and (b) concentrate or mixed forage and concentrate diets. Values are estimated mainly using the duodenal concentration of Σ-diaminopimelic acid (Chamberlain and Thomas, unpublished; Chamberlain, Thomas and Wilson, 1976; Hagemeister, Kaufmann and Pfeffer, 1976; Hogan and Weston, 1969, 1971; Ishaque, Thomas and Rook, 1971; Jackson, Rook and Towers, 1970; Leibholz and Hartmann, 1972; Ørskov, Fraser and McDonald, 1972; Weston and Hogan, 1968, 1971). Values for cows have been divided by 10. The solid line represents a rate of synthesis of 23 g bacterial crude protein/100 g organic matter apparently digested in the rumen (see text)

often low (*Figure 9.2b*). For some diets a low efficiency is due to a less than optimal supply of nitrogen, as reflected in low rumen concentrations of ammonia, with a consequent restriction on protein synthesis. Low efficiency may still arise, however, in the presence of adequate nitrogen. There is a positive correlation between microbial protein synthesis and the dilution rate of the liquid phase in the rumen (Kennedy, Christopherson and Milligan, 1976; Harrison *et al.*, 1976), and with high-concentrate diets the dilution rate is generally low.

Also, with starch diets under some circumstances the rumen protozoa form a large part of the total microbial population (Eadie *et al.*, 1970). Only a small proportion of the protozoa present in the rumen flow freely with the digesta into the intestine (Weller and Pilgrim, 1974) and as the protozoa engulf bacteria and increase the recycling of nitrogen, when protozoal numbers are high the efficiency of bacterial synthesis is reduced and there is little compensatory increase in the flow of protozoa to the intestine. Recycling of nitrogen may also occur with wholly bacterial populations if they are subjected to conditions which induce a high degree of lysis.

The importance of protozoa and of bacterial lysis in reducing the efficiency of ruminal protein synthesis in animals receiving concentrate diets is difficult to judge. Lindsay and Hogan (1972) have demonstrated that with animals receiving forage diets defaunation increases the efficiency of rumen protein synthesis, and with sheep receiving high-concentrate diets exceptionally low efficiencies of synthesis have been observed in some experiments (Jackson, Rook and Towers, 1971; Ishaque, Thomas and Rook, 1971). These low efficiencies were linked with high rumen ammonia concentrations and a large proportion of butyric acid in the mixture of short-chain fatty acids, both of which are consistent with the presence of substantial protozoal populations (Eadie *et al.*, 1970; Abe *et al.*, 1973).

The effect of the composition of the mixture of duodenal nitrogen compounds on the uptake of nitrogen in the small intestine is difficult to judge; the digestibility of the mixture, the proportion of amino acids to nucleic acids and the composition of the amino acid mixture are all factors to be taken into account. The digestibility of the bacteria is high, about 70 per cent, although less than that of the protozoa (Hungate, 1966). Since the protozoal contribution to nitrogen entering the intestine is normally relatively small (Weller and Pilgrim, 1974) the microbial material will have a fairly constant digestibility. On the other hand, the digestibility of unfermented dietary protein in the small intestine may vary considerably, especially if the protein has been processed to reduce its availability in the rumen. If intestinal digestibility is low, then fermentation in the caecum and colon will lead to a wasteful loss of nitrogen as ammonia.

The digestibility of total nitrogen in the small intestine varies from about 60 per cent to 70 per cent, this representing a composite value for the poor digestibility of the microbial cell walls and some of the resistant plant materials and the high digestibility of the nucleic acids and the digestible protein. The amino acid composition of mixed rumen organisms is fairly constant (Purser and Buechler, 1966) and because the duodenal digesta contains a large proportion of microbial protein, changes in the composition of the diet can have relatively little effect on the mixture of amino acids entering the small intestine (*Figure 9.3*). Significant differences between diets have, however, been reported (Harrison *et al.*, 1973) and in some instances these are apparently coupled with differences in the digestibility of individual amino acids in the small intestine. Under those circumstances there could be important differences not only in the total quantity of amino acids absorbed but also in their composition. A significant part of some of the microbial amino acids is in the form of the D isomer but the nutritional importance of this is still to be assessed.

The relationship between the composition of the mixture of substrates absorbed and the efficiency of utilisation of dietary energy

MAINTENANCE

Blaxter (1962) reported a technique based on the intraruminal or intra-abomasal infusion of substrates to study calorimetrically the metabolism of substrates and their interactions. The results with fasting sheep indicated that acetic acid, when infused into the rumen, was used for maintenance with an efficiency of 59 per cent. Corresponding figures for infusions of propionic acid and butyric

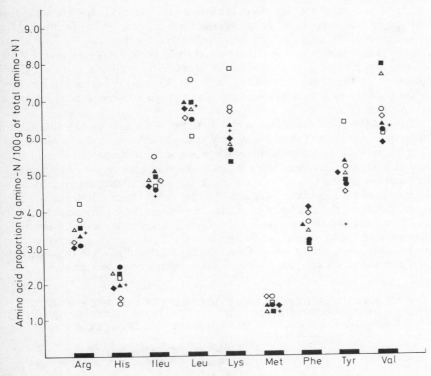

Figure 9.3 The proportion (g amino acid-N/100 g of total amino-N) of 'essential' amino acids in the duodenal digesta of cattle given diets consisting of hay (30–40 per cent), barley and oats (25–30 per cent), tapioca (0–30 per cent) and up to 30 per cent of a protein supplement supplying 45–50 per cent of the dietary nitrogen in the form of soya bean meal (○); fish meal (●); yeast (□); rapeseed meal (■); groundnut meal (△); casein (▲); or urea (◇); together with corresponding values for diets of ryegrass (+) and a grass/clover mixture (♦). Values are taken from Hagemeister, Kaufmann and Pfeffer (1976)

acid were 86 per cent and 76 per cent respectively. When the acids were infused as mixtures, as would occur naturally in the rumen, the efficiency varied only from 83 to 87 per cent. Glucose infused into the abomasum was used for maintenance with an efficiency of 100 per cent and the corresponding value for casein was 81 per cent. The results for the short-chain fatty acids have been confirmed in studies with cows (Holter, Heald and Colovos, 1970) and there is agreement between the efficiencies determined experimentally and those calculated from the results of calorimetric studies with natural diets or theoretically from biochemical considerations.

FATTENING AND GROWTH

When animals are receiving food the interpretation of results obtained with the intraruminal substrate infusion technique is less certain. The infused substrate may affect fermentation of the basal diet and the amount of substrate has to be restricted, and errors are high. Also, the infused substrate is utilised in admixture with the substrates produced naturally, and there is limited scope for varying the composition of the mixture of absorbed substrates. Furthermore, when the basal diet meets the maintenance requirements, the additional energy provided by the infusate may be used to promote both protein and fat synthesis, and since the efficiencies of these processes differ (Pullar and Webster, 1974) variation in the partition of energy between fat and protein synthesis influences the efficiency of energy utilisation.

Blaxter (1962) indicated that in mature sheep, the efficiency of utilisation for fattening of mixtures of short-chain fatty acids absorbed from the rumen varied from 56 and 62 per cent respectively when propionic acid and butyric acid were infused singly to 33 per cent when acetic acid was infused singly, and was less than that for glucose (72 per cent) or casein (65 per cent) introduced into the abomasum or for long-chain fatty acids (80 per cent). Other calorimetric measurements of the efficiency of utilisation of short-chain fatty acids for growth or fattening are summarised in *Table 9.2*. They confirm that when the mixture of absorbed acids is rich in acetic acid, the efficiency of utilisation is low but only in the recent work of Tyrrell, Reynolds and Moe (1976), where the basal diet was alfalfa hay, has a value as low as 30 per cent been observed.

Table 9.2 THE APPARENT EFFICIENCY OF UTILISATION OF THE ENERGY OF ACETIC, PROPIONIC AND BUTYRIC ACIDS FOR FATTENING IN SHEEP OR CATTLE GIVEN BASAL DIETS SUPPLEMENTED WITH SHORT-CHAIN FATTY ACIDS

Basal diet	*Acid*	*Efficiency of utilisation of energy for fattening* (%)	*Reference*
Chopped dried grass	Acetic acid	33	Armstrong and Blaxter
	Propionic acid	56	(1957)
	Butyric acid	62	
Ground-pelleted hay	Acetic acid	70	Lawrence and Thomas
	Propionic acid	84	(1972)
	Butyric acid	86	
Ground-pelleted lucerne	Acetic acid[1,4]	70	Bull, Reid and Johnson (1970)
Shelled corn	Acetic acid[4]	67	Johnson (1972)
Ground-pelleted lucerne	Acetic acid	63 (52)[2]	Robb and Reid (1972)
		68 (58)[2]	
Barley concentrate diet	Acetic acid[3,4]	54	Hovell, Greenhalgh and Wainman (1976)
Alfalfa hay	Acetic acid[5]	27	Tyrell, Reynolds and
Maize meal and alfalfa high-concentrate diet		69	Moe (1976)

[1] Given as triacetin
[2] Values in parenthesis are for a rapid infusion over a period of 1 hour after feeding as opposed to a continuous infusion
[3] Given as sodium, potassium and calcium acetate
[4] Animals with considerable potential for growth and consequent protein deposition
[5] Experiments undertaken in mature cows

Comparative slaughter trials with lambs in which acids were included in the diet as sodium and calcium salts and the assessment was based on carcass weight gain have shown no significant difference between the acids (Ørskov and Allen, 1966a, b, c; Ørskov, Hovell and Allen, 1966; Poole and Allen, 1970). These results are inconclusive, however, since there is evidence that acetic acid may enhance tissue protein synthesis and reduce the caloric content of carcass gain. Recent trials based on carcass energy measurements have given values as low as 3–10 per cent for the efficiency of utilisation of acetate (Hovell, Greenhalgh and Wainman, 1976).

The explanation for the low and variable efficiency of utilisation of acetic acid is not certain but there does appear to be synergism between acetic acid and the other absorbed substrates. It has been suggested that an adequate supply of glucogenic materials may be required for the efficient metabolism of acetate but this has yet to be substantiated; intra-abomasal infusions of glucose or casein in animals receiving forage diets do not show unusually high efficiencies. If the supply of glucogenic materials is important the effect may not be direct but mediated through effects on hormone balance.

LACTATION

The results of intraruminal infusion experiments with lactating goats (Armstrong and Blaxter, 1965) and cattle (Ørskov *et al.*, 1969) have shown little difference between acetate and propionate in their efficiency of utilisation for milk synthesis, but propionate promotes deposition of energy in body tissue and acetate has the opposite effect. These results have also shown that fattening is a more efficient process in the lactating than in the non-lactating animal.

Intraruminal infusion experiments have also demonstrated distinct effects on milk composition (*Figure 9.4*). With acetic acid there is an increase in milk yield and in the yields of all major constituents, a specific increase in milk-fat content and a tendency for milk-protein content to be depressed. With propionic acid, fat content is depressed and protein content increased, and with butyric acid fat content is increased.

The relationship between the composition of the mixture of nitrogen compounds absorbed and the efficiency of utilisation of dietary protein

The complex pathways of absorption, metabolism and recycling of nitrogen in the ruminant (Nolan, 1976) present difficulties in any analysis of the utilisation of dietary nitrogen. In simple net terms, the main nitrogenous end-products of digestion are ammonia absorbed from the rumen and caecum, together with amino acids, and purine and pyrimidine bases from nucleic acids, absorbed in the small intestine. Only the amino acids have an established quantitative importance in the nutrition of the host; there may be some utilisation of ammonia and nitrogenous bases for tissue synthesis but they are largely waste products (Smith, 1969). The factors that affect the flow of nitrogen to the small intestine have been considered previously and these same factors influence the partition of

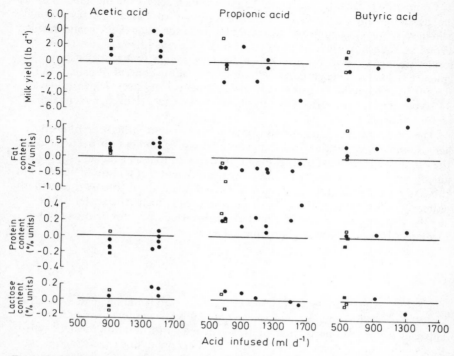

Figure 9.4 Responses in milk yield and composition to continuous intraruminal infusions of acetic, propionic or butyric acids. The values are a mean response, at the end of a 3- or 4-week infusion period, as determined according to a Latin square design. (●) The results of Rook and Balch (1961) and Rook, Balch and Johnson (1965). (■), (□) The results of Kitchen (1974) for animals that were fed to Woodman's standards, or to 80–90 per cent of those standards respectively.

nitrogen absorbed in the rumen and the small intestine. Cuthbertson and Chalmers (1959) demonstrated that the efficiency of utilisation of dietary nitrogen for tissue synthesis was proportional to the nitrogen entering the small intestine by infusing casein either into the rumen or the abomasum. The same considerations apply under normal dietary situations, when differences in the composition of the diet affect the duodenal flow of nitrogen (*Figure 9.5*).

Experiments on the effect of intra-abomasal infusion of protein on milk yield and protein yield in the dairy cow were summarised by Clark (1975). He concluded that, in cows fed to accepted standards, infusion of casein increased milk yield by up to 21 per cent and milk protein yield by up to 15 per cent; the responses were higher in animals yielding more than 20 kg milk day^{-1}. The efficiency of nitrogen utilisation must also be influenced by the proportion of amino acids in the total nitrogen absorbed from the small intestine and by their composition. With commercial production diets, the importance of these effects may be difficult to demonstrate as there is limited variation in the nucleic acid content and amino acid composition of the duodenal digesta. Distinct responses in wool growth to abomasal infusions of methionine or cystine in sheep have been observed (Reis and Schinckel, 1963). Nitrogen retention in growing lambs has also been improved by abomasal infusions of methionine, methionine and

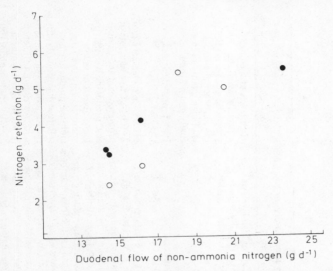

Figure 9.5 The relationship between the nitrogen retention (g d⁻¹) and the duodenal flow of non-ammonia nitrogen (g d⁻¹) in sheep receiving natural diets containing various protein supplements (○) (Hume, 1974) or semi-purified diets (●) (Hume, 1970b) providing about 650 g d⁻¹ of digestible dry matter

lysine, and methionine, lysine and threonine; but the basal diet was purified and contained little protein and almost all the protein entering the duodenum must have been of microbial origin (Nimrick *et al.*, 1970). These conditions would rarely apply with natural diets but theoretical calculations indicate that methionine and possibly threonine are the acids most likely to be limiting for growth (Hutton and Annison, 1972; Armstrong, 1973; Armstrong and Annison, 1973).

Various approaches have been used to identify the amino acids most limiting for milk protein synthesis (Brown, 1969; Mepham, 1971; Clark, 1975). The uptake of individual amino acids by the udder, calculated by using the arterio-venous difference technique, compared with their output in milk protein indicates that methionine, threonine, lysine, histidine and phenylalanine are the acids for which the proportional uptake is highest, methionine and lysine being particularly high. There is some supporting evidence from experiments in which methionine and lysine have been given as intravenous or abomasal infusions to lactating cows (Fisher, 1972; Schwab and Satter, 1974), but the diets used in these studies were low in crude protein and in some instances the proportion of non-protein nitrogen was high. In contrast to the generally beneficial effects of abomasal infusions of casein on milk yield, responses to the infusion of single amino acids or simple amino acid mixtures have been variable and inconsistent.

Manipulation of the diet and its influences on rumen fermentation and animal performance

The partition of dietary energy and nitrogen between the various products of digestion has been considered so far in terms of individual products. The various

Table 9.3 CHARACTERISTICS OF THE DIGESTION OF VARIOUS TYPES OF DIET

	All forage, or a very high proportion of forage		Mixed cereal and forage, or all cereal		
Type of diet and conditions of feeding	Forage of low or moderate quality	Forage of high quality, especially at high levels of feeding	Moderate or occasionally high levels of feeding	Moderate or high levels of feeding, especially when the forage is of high quality	High levels of feeding, especially when the proportion of forage is low, or when the forage is of high quality or in a finely ground form
Type of rumen fermentation	High acetic acid (>68% C_2)	Acetic acid (64–68% C_2)	Butyric acid (>18% C_4)	Propionic acid (25–33% C_3)	High propionic acid (>33% C_3)
Fermentation characteristics	pH 6.3–7.0; clearance rate 5–12 h⁻¹. High proportion of fibre digesters, e.g. *Bacteroides succinogenes*, *Ruminococcus albus*, *Ruminococcus flavefaciens*, and methanogenic bacteria are abundant. High rates of methane production and cellulose digestion. Efficiency of bacterial cell synthesis high and constant at about 19–23 g crude protein/100 g organic matter apparently digested. Hydrogenation of dietary polyunsaturated acids virtually complete.		pH 5.7–6.8; clearance rate 5–10 h⁻¹. Variable bacterial population but contains *Bacteroides*, *Selenomonads* and *Butyrivibrios* and in some instances a large number of ciliate protozoa. High rates of methane production and cellulose digestion. Extensive hydrogenation of polyunsaturated fatty acids. Variable efficiency of bacterial cell synthesis, from as low as 5 g to a maximum of about 20 g crude protein/100 g organic matter apparently digested.	pH 5.1–6.6; clearance rate 2–7 h⁻¹. Variable bacterial population, similar to that for butyric acid fermentation but often with larger numbers of propionic acid producing organisms and Lactobacilli. Numbers of protozoa and *Butyrivibrios* are low. Low rates of methane production and cellulose digestion. Partial hydrogenation of polyunsaturated fatty acids. Efficiency of bacterial cell synthesis about 13–20 g crude protein/100 g organic matter apparently digested.	pH 5.1–5.9; clearance rate 2–6 h⁻¹. Large numbers of propionic acid and lactic acid producing bacteria; protozoa absent or in low numbers. Very low rates of methane production and cellulose digestion. Hydrogenation of polyunsaturated acids restricted. Efficiency of bacterial cell synthesis 13–20 g crude protein/100 g organic matter apparently digested.

| *Substrates absorbed* | Short-chain fatty acids account for a large part of total energy absorbed, and the proportion of acetic acid in the fatty acids is high, more especially when the quality of the forage is low. Very small proportion of energy absorbed is in the form of sugars. | Proportion of total energy absorbed as short-chain fatty acids may be high, depending on efficiency of microbial synthesis. Proportion of acetic acid is variable but lower than for diets high in forage. Only a small proportion of absorbed fatty acids taken up from caecum. Absorption of sugar in small intestine low but is higher than for diets high in forage, and varies with type of dietary starch. | Proportion of energy absorbed as short-chain fatty acids varies with the efficiency of microbial synthesis but is often lower than for butyric acid fermentations and the proportion of acetic acid is lower. Significant amounts of sugar obtained from the small intestine, the quantity varying with the type of dietary starch. | Proportion of energy absorbed as short-chain fatty acids varies with the efficiency of microbial synthesis but may be less than for other types of fermentation, and the proportion of acetic acid is lower. Absorption of sugars in the small intestine varies with the type of dietary starch. |

processes are, however, highly integrated and a systematic approach to the manipulation of diet for the improvement of animal performance demands a knowledge of the inter-relationships between the various paths of digestion, the composition of the mixture of absorbed products and the utilisation of energy and nitrogen for specific synthetic purposes. Detailed knowledge is not yet available but broadly, the efficiency of utilisation of both energy and nitrogen tends to increase with an increase in the proportion of the absorbed products taken up from the small intestine.

Broad generalisations about digestion in the rumen are more difficult to make. Account needs to be taken of the stoichiometric relationships in the formation of methane and short-chain fatty acids (Hungate, 1966) and of any change in the efficiency of microbial cell synthesis or in the degree of ruminal digestion of fibrous carbohydrates, in addition to consequential effects on tissue metabolism. The information is not available to allow a systematic analysis of these relationships but empirically, an attempt has been made (*Table 9.3*) to summarise some of the characteristic aspects of the digestion of particular types of diet and, where gross variability in fermentation pattern has been observed, the digestive features associated with a fermentation of a particular type. In the absence of a more satisfactory method, fermentation types have been classified on the basis of the molar proportion of one or other of the short-chain fatty acids. The classifications are not precise, but represent the boundaries of the wide spectrum of fermentation patterns that can occur.

The complexity of the inter-relationships is such, however, that it is not possible to distinguish clearly effects on animal performance attributable to a change in rumen fermentation *per se* from those due to differences in diet composition and amount, in digestion in the abomasum and intestine or in animal metabolism. There is also the further complication that the effect of a single dietary characteristic may be profoundly modified by other features of the diet. Thus, it is difficult to define, in terms of underlying principles, the conditions under which there is scope for manipulation of rumen fermentation or the prospect of an animal response, and a more empirical approach has to be adopted. A review has therefore been made of the various modifications of diet, from those involving a change in the amount or composition of a major component to those concerned solely with a trace addition, which have been demonstrated to affect the fermentation pattern; and an attempt has been made to assess where the change in fermentation is important to any observed production response.

Level of feeding

An increase in feeding level is normally associated with some reduction of organic matter digestibility in the rumen and in the proportion of energy lost as methane. There is also a tendency for the proportion of butyric acid or propionic acid in the ruminal mixture of short-chain fatty acids to increase, at the expense of acetic acid. The net effect of these changes on the overall efficiency of energy utilisation is small and varies with diet. In cattle receiving a pelleted barley (85 per cent barley, 15 per cent protein-mineral-vitamin supplement) diet, however, a change from restricted feeding three times a day (at approximately 75 per cent of the calculated *ad libitum* intake) to *ad libitum* feeding has been shown to result in a major change of fermentation pattern (Eadie and Mann, 1970). On restricted feeding a high rumen ciliate population is established, and this is associated with a pH generally above 6.0 and a low ratio of propionate to butyrate in rumen liquor. In contrast, with *ad libitum* feeding the pH is generally lower, there is a virtual disappearance of ciliate protozoa and a high ratio of propionate to butyrate in rumen liquor. The production consequences of these differences in fermentation have not been assessed critically. With young lambs receiving a dried grass concentrate (2:1) diet, ciliate-free and faunated animals showed no substantial difference in performance but differences in rumen fermentation were also slight (Eadie and Gill, 1971).

Alteration of the ratio of forage to concentrate

With an increase in the ratio of concentrate to forage, there is a trend towards a decrease in ruminal pH, in the ratio of acetate to other short-chain fatty acids and in the proportion of energy lost as methane. The extent and the detail of fermentation changes are highly dependent on the proportion of concentrate in the diet and on the physical and chemical characteristics of both forage and concentrate components (see below). Within the normal range of diets, any fall in acetate may be compensated for by an increase in butyrate or in propionate or both, but with diets lacking the physical quality of fibrousness, especially if they contain a high proportion of readily soluble carbohydrate, there can be a dramatic switch of fermentation pattern. The new pattern is characterised (Rook, 1975) by a low pH, a reduction in the numbers of cellulolytic and fibre-digesting bacteria, large numbers of lactic-acid- and propionic-acid-producing bacteria and in some instances a virtual disappearance of the ciliate protozoa. There is a substantial fall in acetate and a rise in the ratio of propionate to butyrate in rumen liquor, a reduced hydrogenation of dietary unsaturated acids, an increased ruminal synthesis of lipid and an increased flow of soluble carbohydrate to the intestine. Associated with this change of fermentation pattern are well-documented production responses.

In the milking cow (Storry, 1970; Rook, 1975), milk-fat content and yield are depressed by up to 60 per cent, and the proportion of saturated fatty acids in milk-fat is decreased and that of unsaturated fatty acids, including polyunsaturated fatty acids, increased. At the same time there is an increased deposition of body fat and an increase of up to 0.5 percentage units in milk-protein content. Dietary supplements of sodium bicarbonate, calcium carbonate, calcium hydroxide, magnesium oxide, bentonite, vermiculite and milk whey have all been shown to prevent or reverse the change of fermentation pattern and the depression in milk-fat secretion.

In sheep and goats, but not in cattle or red deer, a 'very high-propionate' fermentation induced by diets containing about 90 per cent rolled barley produces an unusually soft subcutaneous adipose tissue characterised by a high proportion of odd-numbered, straight-chain fatty acids and branched-chain fatty acids (up to 15 per cent of the total fatty acids) (Garton, 1975). Offering the barley whole decreases the proportion of propionate in the ruminal mixture of short-chain fatty acids and increases that of acetate and results in a firmer subcutaneous fat (Ørskov, Fraser and Gordon, 1974); the efficiency of utilisation of the grain and the apparent digestibilities of dry and organic matter are unaffected (Fraser and Ørskov, 1974).

Alteration of physical form

FORAGES

Processing of forages (Osbourn, Beever and Thomson, 1976) can involve heat treatment and alteration of particle size. Heat may cause the formation of enzyme-resistant linkages between the carbonyl groups of reducing sugars and amino groups of the protein fraction. There is a reduction in the solubility of protein which may increase both the dietary protein escaping degradation in the rumen and the microbial protein synthesized in the rumen, and thus increase the flow of protein to the small intestine; the composition of the amino acids absorbed has been found not to be altered significantly, though there tend to be lower proportions of lysine, tyrosine and phenylalanine with ground, pelleted diets. Alteration of particle size may lead to a more rapid passage of material from the rumen with a consequent increase in the flow of cellulose, hemicellulose and energy to the small intestine and an increased disappearance of these materials from the large intestine. The net effect of these changes on the overall digestibility of cell walls is less in legumes than in grasses. Ruminal production of short-chain fatty acids is depressed, and there are reports of a reduction in the ratio of acetate to propionate in rumen liquor but this does not always occur.

When dried herbage (grasses or legumes) is the sole diet of sheep, chopping or grinding and pelleting increases net energy, the effect being negligible with highly digestible immature herbage but increasing with maturity, as the digestibility decreases. When ground and pelleted forages are offered to lactating cows as a component of diets containing long forage and concentrates, the grinding depresses digestibility and methane loss and there is a distinct effect on metabolizability. The efficiency of use of metabolizable energy may however be increased with little overall effect on net energy. These production effects have been explained in terms of two main consequences of processing, one a reduction in digestibility, the other an alteration in the balance of nutrients absorbed such that their efficiency of utilisation for fattening is increased, although it has been emphasized that the possible effect with mature forages on the energy cost of eating and gut aerobic metabolism should not be ignored.

CEREAL GRAINS

The digestibility in the ruminant of the starch of cereal grains is high (of the order of 99 per cent) but there is considerable variation in the site of this digestion. The proportion of starch digestion occurring in the reticulorumen may vary from 40 per cent to more than 90 per cent, depending on the cereal source and variety, the animal species, the proportion of cereal grain in the diet and the degree of processing (Armstrong, 1972, 1974; Waldo, 1973). Starch which escapes digestion in the reticulorumen, and this includes starch of microbial origin, is further digested in the small intestine, normally to an extent of 70 per cent or more although there appears to be a limit to the quantitative capacity for starch digestion in the intestine, and the remainder is largely fermented in the large intestine. There is a wide variety of processing methods but they have the common objective of increasing the exposure of starch grains and their susceptibility to enzyme degradation. The effect on ruminal fermentation of increasing the proportion of cereal grains in the diet has already been discussed, and increasing the extent of starch digestion in the reticulorumen, whether by altering the cereal source or through processing, may be expected to produce comparable changes; in addition, there may be a depression in the digestibility of the forage component of the diet and an improvement in microbial protein synthesis. In diets containing a high proportion of cereal grains, processing of the cereal increases the probability of a 'very high propionate' type of fermentation.

The effects of a 'very high propionate' type of fermentation on production in lactating cows and growing sheep have already been outlined. The recorded effects on growth in steers and lambs of processing cereal grains included in diets containing about 75 per cent of cereals are variable and differ according to the type of cereal. Heat processing of barley appears to improve performance in steers but this may be largely the result of an improved voluntary intake. Whole dry shelled maize, or cracked maize, tends to give better performance than ground or ground and pelleted maize which appear to depress feed intake; steam-processed maize may offer a slight benefit but better results might be obtained from a steam-cracked maize.

MODIFICATION OF DIETARY PROTEIN

The solubility of dietary protein influences the extent to which it escapes degradation in the rumen, and therefore the flow and composition of protein entering the small intestine and the availability of nitrogen for microbial protein synthesis (Ferguson, 1975; Barry, 1976). The differences between protein sources in the solubility of their protein offer some scope for manipulation of nitrogen metabolism in the rumen but several processing treatments (heat, tannin, formaldehyde, etc.) have been used to increase the proportion of dietary protein which is not degraded in the rumen (Chalupa, 1975). The most favourable processing conditions have been shown to give net increases in the flow of amino acids to the small intestine and in their absorption, although responses differ between different amino acids. The most marked production responses have been in wool growth, for which the sulphur amino acids are the first limiting ones, to formaldehyde-treated casein; the responses are poorer and more variable with protected concentrates and herbage, herbage being a poor source of sulphur amino acids. Treatment of herbage with formaldehyde prior to ensilage, however, has given improved intake and performance (including nitrogen utilisation) in sheep, growing cattle and lactating cows, and improvements in milk yield have been reported in cattle receiving maize silage following formaldehyde treatment of rapeseed and soya bean meals offered at $1-1.5$ kg day^{-1} (Verité and Journet, 1977). Various techniques have been devised for the encapsulation of amino acids, and 'protected' supplements of D-L methionine have improved performance of growing lambs but have been without effect on milk production in lactating cows. Attention is presently being given to the possible use of amino acid analogues as a means of increasing the flow to the intestine of specific amino acids.

Closure of the oesophageal groove (Ørskov, 1972) has been used to allow part of the food to bypass the rumen, and in lambs improvements in growth rate and efficiency of feed conversion have resulted but the method is not yet practical.

MODIFICATION OF DIETARY FAT

Though the modification of lipid in the rumen is restricted to hydrolysis and hydrogenation, dietary oils and fats themselves may inhibit fermentation, with consequent effects on the extent of digestion in the rumen, methane loss and composition of fermentation products, and this limits the extent of incorporation of fats in ruminant diets. The extent of the changes is affected both by the manner of incorporation of the fat in the diet (e.g. 'free' versus unextracted meal) and the composition, especially the degree of unsaturation, and the effects on digestibility may be partially offset by the addition of calcium salts (Davidson and Woods, 1963). The dietary incorporation of highly unsaturated oils, for example soya bean oil but more especially marine oils such as cod liver oil, may, particularly with high concentrate diets, induce a 'very high propionate' type of fermentation and in milking cows cause a sharp depression in milk-fat content. With the fish oils, which contain C_{20} and C_{22} polyunsaturated fatty acids, in addition to the depression in milk-fat content due to a change of fermentation, there may be a direct inhibition of uptake of fatty acids by the mammary gland (Brumby *et al.*, 1969). These effects of unsaturated oils are more pronounced when they are included free rather than as a component of unextracted meal or cracked seed (Steele, Noble and Moore, 1971), or, when free, offered in a single feed rather than several feeds a day (Moore, Hoffman and Berry, 1945).

Through attention to the form and type of inclusion, in recent years it has proved possible to achieve much higher rates of inclusion of fats and oils into proprietary concentrate cubes and thus achieve a higher energy density than was once thought possible. The most recent development has been the micro-encapsulation of fat in a layer of formaldehyde-treated protein (Scott *et al.*, 1970) which is resistant to the action of rumen micro-organisms but is rapidly digested in the abomasum and intestine. The feeding of 'protected' safflower oil has been used to raise the content of polyunsaturated fatty acids in milk fat. Preliminary investigation of the use of a formaldehyde-treated mixture of crushed soya beans and tallow as a supplementary feed for dairy cows in early lactation has demonstrated improvements in milk and milk-fat yield at rates of supplementation of up to 1.7 kg day^{-1} (Bines, Storry and Brumby, 1975).

Dietary supplements

The most important factor controlling microbial activity in the reticulorumen is the supply of energy but under some dietary conditions the supply of nitrogen, sulphur or other growth factors may be limiting.

NITROGEN

When nitrogen is limiting, microbial activity may be stimulated by a supplement of protein or of non-protein nitrogen, the most effective supplement being one that gives a sustained and even release of amino acid and/or ammonia nitrogen. Distinct increases in organic matter digestion and microbial protein synthesis within the rumen have been obtained when cereal straws, and other coarse forages low in nitrogen, have been supplemented with a nitrogen source, and there have been associated improvements in voluntary food intake and live-weight gain. The justification for the use of non-protein nitrogen as a component of production rations is more equivocal and for success requires selection of a basal diet which results in low rumen ammonia levels and high concentrations of energy-yielding components. Production benefits from non-protein nitrogen supplementation have been obtained with fattening cattle but the evidence for benefits in lactating cows is less certain.

SULPHUR

The addition of sulphur as sulphate or cystine to diets adequate in nitrogen but low in sulphur offered to sheep has been shown to increase the synthesis of microbial protein in the rumen and to improve live-weight gain, wool production and nitrogen retention (Hume and Bird, 1970; Bird and Hume, 1971).

HIGHER VOLATILE FATTY ACIDS

With virtually protein-free diets containing an adequate amount of non-protein nitrogen, the addition of a mixture of higher volatile fatty acids increases rumen microbial protein production (Hume, 1970a); and Hemsley and Moir (1963) have observed an increased voluntary intake by sheep of a milled, oaten hay diet when the diet was supplemented with a mixture of isobutyric, isovaleric and n-valeric acids.

Dietary additives

METHANE INHIBITORS

A wide range of compounds (e.g. halogenated hydrocarbons and their derivatives and both saturated and unsaturated lipids) depress methane production within the rumen when included in the diet (Clapperton, 1977). In association, there is usually an increase in the proportion of propionate and a depression in that of acetate in the rumen mixture of short-chain fatty acids, and the total concentration of acids may be depressed. Only a partial suppression of methane production is obtained with lipids and, because of the high energy content of the supplements, it is difficult to identify any production response attributable specifically to inhibition. Polyhalogenated compounds initially produce a more complete inhibition but there is frequently a partial recovery through adaptation of rumen micro-organisms. Appetite may be depressed but of the several trials now reported some have demonstrated improvements in efficiency of feed conversion. With lactating goats, milk-fat content has been depressed and that of milk-protein content increased, without any evident effect on milk yield (Clapperton and Basmaeil, 1977).

MONENSIN

When introduced into diets monensin, a coccidiostat derived from *Streptomyces cinnamonensis*, causes inappetance but there is then a recovery of appetite and with this a change of fermentation associated with a reduction in methane production. Improved live-weight gain and efficiency of feed conversion have been demonstrated with steers with a wide variety of diets (Dinius, Simpson and Marsh, 1976).

SULPHITE

The inclusion of sodium sulphite in a forage-concentrate (1:2) diet offered to lactating cows has depressed significantly the proportion of acetate and increased that of propionate and butyrate in the rumen mixture of short-chain fatty acids without effect on the total concentration. There were no significant effects on milk yield or composition but the design of the trial and the number of animals used did not allow critical evaluation (Alhassan, Krabill and Satter, 1969).

NITRATE

Salts containing nitrate, an electron acceptor, when added to high concentrate, milk-fat depressing diets, induce a marked increase in the proportion of acetate with corresponding decreases in the proportions of propionate and especially butyrate in the rumen mixture of short-chain fatty acids. In a single experiment with milking cows there was a tendency for milk yield to be depressed and for milk-fat content to be increased but these effects were not significant (Farra and Satter, 1971).

Feed combinations

When a mixture of foods is offered as a single diet, the digestion of each individual food within the rumen is modified by the presence of the others, giving rise to what are known as 'associative' effects. For example, increasing the amount of starch-rich concentrates depresses the digestion of cellulose in forage components. Associative effects on voluntary food intake have been demonstrated when silage and pellets prepared from the same crop of perennial ryegrass (Wilkins, 1970) and when silage and lucerne pellets (Wilkins, Osbourn and Taylor, 1970) have been fed in combination and these probably arise in part from effects within the rumen. The voluntary intake of high digestibility silage by lactating cows is depressed less by a supplement of groundnut cake than by one of barley (Castle and Watson, 1977), and the explanation may be that the protein supplement does not depress silage digestion within the rumen, as does barley.

pH and clearance rate

Though, from the above consideration of empirically induced changes in fermentation it is not possible to discern any single underlying mechanism, there is nevertheless a degree of consistency between some of the observed effects that suggests certain common mechanisms. The availability of hydrogen, as reflected in methane production and the proportion of propionate in the short-chain fatty acids, may often be a crucial factor but though there have been several attempts to relate fermentation conditions to the Eh of rumen liquor, there has been little success. There has also been a suggestion that low pH favours the formation of propionate but this is not supported by the results of Satter and Esdale (1968). A negative relationship between the molar percentage of propionic acid and the clearance rate of rumen liquor has, however, been established for sheep given mixed hay and concentrate diets, and it has proved possible to manipulate fermentation through the addition of buffers when increases in clearance rate were associated with increased microbial protein synthesis (Harrison et al., 1975; Hodgson and Thomas, 1975; Hodgson, Thomas and Wilson, 1976). This relationship though does not appear to have general validity even for concentrate diets. With forage diets, for which there is greatest scope for improved efficiency, clearance rate is difficult to alter, and where this has been achieved there has been no associated change in fermentation pattern.

Conclusions

The aspects of rumen fermentation which are most readily manipulated in a controlled way are nitrogen and lipid metabolism. There are now several technical processes for the modification of feeds or supplements such that ruminal degradation of these dietary components is reduced; these appear to be commercially feasible even though they may have application only in selected and well-defined production situations. The prospects for achieving production benefits from a more general manipulation, aimed at modifying the whole pattern of rumen fermentation, are less certain. With diets which fail to meet the nutrient requirements of rumen micro-organisms, fermentation may be stimulated by an appropriate supplement and production benefits obtained. More generally, however, though extremes of fermentation pattern have been identified which are associated with differences in overall efficiency and in metabolism, the scope for exploitation may be restricted.

In many instances, observed changes in fermentation are linked to a distinct change of diet and these variations do not themselves offer the possibility of independent manipulation. Nevertheless, even for diets characteristically associated with stable fermentation patterns techniques have been devised to alter the relationship between diet composition and fermentation pattern and to give associated production benefits. Examples are dietary additives for the inhibition of methane production or the alteration of clearance rate, and the processing of dietary constituents. Before widespread practical adoption can be recommended, a fuller description is required of the dietary and production situations under which reproducible effects on fermentation pattern and animal performance are to be expected. In addition there are a few well-documented dietary and production situations in which major variations in fermentation pattern can occur without significant alteration of diet composition. These have been shown to have important production consequences and it has proved possible to manipulate fermentation by dietary means such that an undesirable production trait is prevented, or a desirable one promoted. One example is the depression in milk-fat content which occurs in association with a 'very high propionate' fermentation in cows receiving diets low in fibre, which may be offset by the dietary addition of a variety of additives. Another is the depression of the voluntary intake of dried grass by lambs when offered a supplement of barley, which is considerably lessened when the barley is offered whole instead of pelleted (Ørskov and Fraser, 1975). The need now is to examine ways of exploiting such situations more fully and to identify other situations which offer similar possibilities.

References

Abe, M., Shibui, H., Iriki, T. and Kumeno, F. (1973). *Br. J. Nutr.*, **29**, 197

Alhassan, W.S., Krabill, L.F. and Satter, L.D. (1969). *J. Dairy Sci.*, **52**, 376

Armstrong, D.G. (1972). *Cereal Processing and Digestion*, p. 9. US Feed Grains Council

Armstrong, D.G. (1973). General meeting of the European Grassland Federation 5th, Uppsala, 12–15 June

Armstrong, D.G. (1974). *Cereal Supply and Utilisation*, p. 21. US Feed Grains Council

Armstrong, D.G. and Annison, E.F. (1973). *Proc. Nutr. Soc.*, **32**, 107

Armstrong, D.G. and Beever, D.E. (1969). *Proc. Nutr. Soc.*, **28**, 121

Armstrong, D.G. and Blaxter, K.L. (1957). *Br. J. Nutr.*, **11**, 413

Armstrong, D.G. and Blaxter, K.L. (1965). In *Energy Metabolism*, p. 59. Ed. K.L. Blaxter. London; Academic Press

Barry, T.N. (1976). *Proc. Nutr. Soc.*, **35**, 221

Beever, D.E., Thomson, D.J. and Cammell, S.B. (1976). *J. Agric. Sci.*, **86**, 443

Beever, D.E., Coelho da Silva, J.F., Prescott, J.H.D. and Armstrong, D.G. (1972). *Br. J. Nutr.*, **28**, 347

Beever, D.E., Thomson, D.J., Pfeffer, E. and Armstrong, D.G. (1971). *Br. J. Nutr.*, **26**, 123

Bines, J.A., Storry, J.E. and Brumby, P.E. (1975). *Proc. Nutr. Soc.*, **34**, 108A

Bird, P.R. and Hume, I.D. (1971). *Aust. J. agric. Res.*, **22**, 443

Blaxter, K.L. (1962). In *The Energy Metabolism of Ruminants*, p. 217. London; Hutchinson

Broster, W.H. (1972). In *Hanbuch der Tierernahrung*, Vol. 2, p. 292. Eds. W. Lenkeit, K. Brierem and E. Craseman. Hamburg; Paul Parey

Brown, R.E. (1969). In *University of Nottingham Nutrition Conference for Feed Manufacturers – 3*, p. 23. Eds. H. Swan and D. Lewis. London; J. & A. Churchill
Brumby, P.E., Tuckley, B., Hall, A.J., Storry, J.E., Sutton, J.D. and Johnson, V.W. (1969). *Rep. natn. Inst. Res. Dairy.*, 1968, p. 89
Bull, L.S., Reid, J.T. and Johnson, D.E. (1970). *J. Nutr.*, **100**, 262
Castle, M.E. and Watson, J.N. (1977). *J. Br. Grassld. Soc.*, **31**, 191
Chalupa, W. (1975). *J. Dairy Sci.*, **58**, 1198
Chamberlain, D.G. and Thomas, P.C. (1975). Unpublished data
Chamberlain, D.G., Thomas, P.C. and Wilson, A.G. (1976). *J. Sci. Fd Agric.*, **27**, 231
Clapperton, J.L. (1977). *Anim. Prod.*, **24**, 169
Clapperton, J.L. and Basmaeil, S. (1977). In *Energy Metabolism of Farm Animals*, p. 73. Ed. M. Vermorel. Clermont-Ferrand; de Bussac
Clapperton, J.L. and Blaxter, K.L. (1965). *Br. J. Nutr.*, **19**, 511
Clark, J.H. (1975). *J. Dairy Sci.*, **58**, 1178
Cuthbertson, D.P. and Chalmers, M.I. (1959). *Biochem. J.*, **46**, XVII
Davidson, K.L. and Woods, W. (1963). *J. Anim. Sci.*, **22**, 27
Dinius, D.A., Simpson, M.E. and Marsh, P.B. (1976). *J. Anim. Sci.*, **42**, 229
Eadie, J.M. and Mann, S.O. (1970). In *Physiology of Digestion and Metabolism in the Ruminant*, p. 335. Ed. A.T. Phillipson. Newcastle-upon-Tyne; Oriel Press
Eadie, J.M. and Gill, J.C. (1971). *Br. J. Nutr.*, **26**, 155
Eadie, J.M., Hyldgaard-Jensen, J., Mann, S.O., Reid, R.S. and Whitelaw, F.G. (1970). *Br. J. Nutr.*, **24**, 157
Farra, P.A. and Satter, L.D. (1971). *J. Dairy Sci.*, **54**, 1018
Ferguson, K.A. (1975). In *Digestion and Metabolism in the Ruminant*, p. 448. Eds. I.W. McDonald and A.C.I. Warner. Armidale; University of New England Publishing Unit
Fisher, L.J. (1972). *Can. J. Anim. Sci.*, **52**, 377
Fraser, C. and Ørskov, E.R. (1974). *Anim. Prod.*, **18**, 75
Garton, G.A. (1975). *Ann. Rpt. Rowett Res. Inst.*, **31**, 124
Hagemeister, H., Kaufmann, W. and Pfeffer, E. (1976). In *Protein Metabolism and Nutrition*, p. 425. Eds. D.J.A. Cole, K.N. Boorman, P.J. Buttery, D. Lewis, R.J. Neale and H. Swan. London; Butterworths
Harrison, D.G., Beever, D.E., Thomson, D.J. and Osbourn, D.F. (1973). *J. Agric. Sci.*, **81**, 391
Harrison, D.G., Beever, D.E., Thomson, D.J. and Osbourn, D.F. (1975). *J. Agric. Sci.*, **85**, 93
Harrison, D.G., Beever, D.E., Thomson, D.J. and Osbourn, D.F. (1976). *J. Sci. Fd. Agric.*, **27**, 617
Hemsley, J.A. and Moir, R.J. (1963). *Aust. J. agric. Res.*, **14**, 509
Hersberger, T.V. and Hartsook, E.W. (1970). *J. Anim. Sci.*, **30**, 257
Hodgson, J.C. and Thomas, P.C. (1975). *Br. J. Nutr.*, **33**, 447
Hodgson, J.C., Thomas, P.C. and Wilson, Agnes C. (1976). *J. agric. Sci., Camb.*, **87**, 297
Hogan, J.P. and Weston, R.H. (1969). *Aust. J. agric. Res.*, **20**, 347
Hogan, J.P. and Weston, R.H. (1971). *Aust. J. agric. Res.*, **22**, 951
Holter, J.B., Heald, C.W. and Colovos, N.F. (1970). *J. Dairy Sci.*, **53**, 1241

182   Manipulation of rumen fermentation

Houpt, T.R. (1968). *Aust. J. Vet. Res.*, **29**, 411
Hovell, F.D. De B., Greenhalgh, J.F.D. and Wainman, F.W. (1976). *Br. J. Nutr.*, **35**, 343
Hume, I.D. (1970a). *Aust. J. agric. Res.*, **21**, 297
Hume, I.D. (1970b). *Aust. J. agric. Res.*, **21**, 305
Hume, I.D. (1974). *Aust. J. agric. Res.*, **25**, 155
Hume, I.D. and Bird, P.R. (1970). *Aust. J. agric. Res.*, **21**, 315
Hume, I.D. and Purser, D.B. (1974). *Aust. J. agric. Res.*, **26**, 199
Hungate, R.E. (1966). *The Rumen and its Microbes*, p. 266 and p. 307. London; Academic Press
Hutton, K. and Annison, E.F. (1972). *Proc. Nutr. Soc.*, **31**, 151
Ishaque, M., Thomas, P.C. and Rook, J.A.F. (1971). *Nature* (New Biology), **231**, 253
Jackson, P., Rook, J.A.F. and Towers, K.G. (1971). *J. Dairy Res.*, **38**, 33
Johnson, D.E. (1972). *J. Nutr.*, **102**, 1093
Kennedy, P.M., Christopherson, R.J. and Milligan, J.P. (1976). *Br. J. Nutr.*, **36**, 231
Kitchen, D.I. (1974). *The Effect of the Inclusion of Volatile Fatty Acids in the Diets of Dairy Cows*. PhD Thesis, University of Leeds
Lawrence, P.R. and Thomas, P.C. (1972). *Animal Prod.*, **17**, 209
Leibholz, J. and Hartmann, D.E. (1972). *Aust. J. agric. Res.*, **23**, 1059
Leng, R.A. (1970). In *Physiology of Digestion and Metabolism in the Ruminant*, p. 406. Ed. A.T. Phillipson. Newcastle-upon-Tyne; Oriel Press
Leng, R.A. and Brett, D.J. (1966). *Br. J. Nutr.*, **20**, 541
Lindsay, J.R. and Hogan, J.P. (1972). *Aust. J. agric. Res.*, **23**, 321
MacRae, J.C. and Armstrong, D.G. (1969). *Br. J. Nutr.*, **23**, 377
Marston, H.R. (1948). *Biochem. J.*, **42**, 564
McMeniman, N.P., Ben-Ghedalia, D. and Armstrong, D.G. (1976). In *Protein Metabolism and Nutrition*, p. 217. Eds. D.J.A. Cole, K.N. Boorman, P.J. Buttery, D. Lewis, R.J. Neale and H. Swan. London; Butterworths
Menke, K.H. and Ehrensvaard, U. (1974). *Energy Metabolism in Farm Animals*, p. 91. Eds. K.W. Menke, H.J. Lantzsch and J.R. Reichl. Stuttgart; Universitat Hohenheim Do Kumentation-sstelle
Mepham, T.B. (1971). In *Lactation*, p. 297. Ed. I.R. Falconer. London;Butterworths
Moore, L.A., Hoffman, G.T. and Berry, M.H. (1945). *J. Dairy Sci.*, **28**, 161
Nimrick, K., Hatfield, E.E., Kaminski, J. and Owens, F.N. (1970). *J. Nutr.*, **100**, 1293
Nolan, J.V. (1976). In *Digestion and Metabolism in the Ruminant*, p. 416. Eds. I.W. McDonald and A.C.I. Warner. Armidale; The University of New England Publishing Unit
Ørskov, E.R. (1972). 2nd World Congress of Animal Feeding. 1. General Reports. Madrid. p. 627
Ørskov, E.R. and Allen, D.M. (1966a). *Br. J. Nutr.*, **20**, 295
Ørskov, E.R. and Allen, D.M. (1966b). *Br. J. Nutr.*, **20**, 509
Ørskov, E.R. and Allen, D.M. (1966c). *Br. J. Nutr.*, **20**, 519
Ørskov, E.R. and Fraser, C. (1975). *Br. J. Nutr.*, **34**, 493
Ørskov, E.R., Fraser, C. and Corse, E.L. (1970). *Br. J. Nutr.*, **24**, 803
Ørskov, E.R., Fraser, C. and Gordon, J.G. (1974). *Br. J. Nutr.*, **32**, 59

Ørskov, E.R., Fraser, C. and McDonald, I. (1972). *Br. J. Nutr.*, **27**, 491
Ørskov, E.R., Hovell, F.D. DeB. and Allen, D.M. (1966). *Br. J. Nutr.*, **20**, 307
Ørskov, E.R., Flatt, W.P., Moe, P.W. and Munson, A.W. (1969). *Br. J. Nutr.*, **23**, 443
Osbourn, D.F., Beever, D.E. and Thomson, D.J. (1976). *Proc. Nutr. Soc.*, **35**, 191
Poole, D.A. and Allen, D.M. (1970). *Br. J. Nutr.*, **24**, 695
Pullar, J.D. and Webster, A.J.F. (1974). *Br. J. Nutr.*, **31**, 377
Purser, D.B. and Buechler, S.M. (1966). *J. Dairy Sci.*, **49**, 81
Reis, P.J. and Schinckel, P.G. (1963). *Aust. J. Biol. Sci.*, **16**, 218
Robb, J. and Reid, J.T. (1972). *Br. J. Nutr.*, **28**, 249
Rook, J.A.F. (1975). In *Principles of Cattle Production*, p. 221. Eds. H. Swan and W.H. Broster. London; Butterworths
Rook, J.A.F. and Balch, C.C. (1961). *Br. J. Nutr.*, **15**, 361
Rook, J.A.F., Balch, C.C. and Johnson, V.W. (1965). *Br. J. Nutr.*, **19**, 93
Satter, L.D. and Esdale, W.J. (1968). *Appl. Microbiol.*, **16**, 680
Schwab, C.G. and Satter, L.D. (1974). *J. Dairy Sci.*, **57**, 632
Scott, T.W., Cook, L.J., Ferguson, K.A., McDonald, I.W., Buchanan, R.A. and Loftus-Hills, G. (1970). *Aust. J. Sci.*, **32**, 291
Smith, R.H. (1969). *J. Dairy Res.*, **36**, 313
Steele, W., Noble, R.C. and Moore, J.H. (1971). *J. Dairy Res.*, **38**, 43
Storry, J.E. (1970). *J. Dairy Res.*, **37**, 139
Sutton, J.D. (1968). *Br. J. Nutr.*, **22**, 689
Sutton, J.D. (1969). *Br. J. Nutr.*, **23**, 567
Sutton, J.D. and Johnson, V.W. (1969). *J. agric. Sci., Camb.*, **73**, 445
Thomas, P.C. (1973). *Proc. Nutr. Soc.*, **32**, 85
Thomas, P.C. and Clapperton, J.L. (1972). *Proc. Nutr. Soc.*, **31**, 165
Tyrell, H.F., Reynolds, P.J. and Moe, P.W. (1976). In *Energy Metabolism of Farm Animals*, p. 57. Ed. M. Vermorel. Clermont-Ferrand; de Bussac
Ulyatt, M.J. and MacRae, J.C. (1974). *J. agric. Sci., Camb.*, **82**, 295
Ulyatt, M.J., MacRae, J.C., Clarke, R.T.J. and Pearce, P.D. (1975). *J. agric. Sci., Camb.*, **84**, 453
Verité, R. and Journet, M. (1977). *Annls Zootech.*, **26**, 183
Waldo, D.R. (1973). *J. Anim. Sci.*, **37**, 1062
Watson, M.J., Savage, G.P. and Armstrong, D.G. (1972). *Proc. Nutr. Soc.*, **31**, 98A
Webster, A.J.F., Osuji, P.O., White, F. and Ingram, J.F. (1975). *Br. J. Nutr.*, **34**, 125
Weller, R.A. and Pilgrim, A.F. (1974). *Br. J. Nutr.*, **32**, 341
Weston, R.H. and Hogan, J.P. (1968). *Aust. J. agric. Res.*, **19**, 963
Weston, R.H. and Hogan, J.P. (1971). *Aust. J. agric. Res.*, **22**, 139
Whitelaw, F.G., Hyldgaard-Jensen, J., Reid, R.S. and Kay, M.G. (1970). *Br. J. Nutr.*, **24**, 179
Wilkins, R.J. (1970). *J. Br. Grassl. Soc.*, **25**, 125
Wilkins, R.J., Osbourn, D.F. and Tayler, J.C. (1970). *J. Br. Grassl. Soc.*, **25**, 37

10

PROTEIN QUANTITY AND QUALITY FOR THE UK DAIRY COW

W.H. BROSTER
J.D. OLDHAM
National Institute for Research in Dairying, Reading

Introduction

The general philosophy of judging an allowance of protein for a dairy cow is based on converting her output of nitrogen, as controlled by her size and her milk output, to dietary supply in proportion to efficiency of utilisation. The traditional approach has been feeding experiments from which are judged the particular amounts of protein above which no further improvement in yield is obtained. This is then declared to be the required rate of feeding. Supplementary evidence from nitrogen balance trials has been obtained in some experiments and has provided estimates of digestible protein and of biological value, i.e. efficiency of utilisation of digested protein. Efficiency of utilisation has hitherto been based on digestibility as the first stage and then efficiency of utilisation of digested protein as the second stage. The digestible fraction of dietary nitrogenous compounds has been variously described as digestible crude protein, digestible true protein, protein equivalent. All these units and biological value itself have been undermined as knowledge of utilisation of dietary protein expands, encompassing gradually the appreciation of the use of non-protein nitrogen (NPN). Evidence is now sufficiently strong in this area that attempts can be made to formulate protein requirements from efficiencies of the various stages of nitrogen metabolism. In this paper two questions are therefore posed: 'What does the cow do with the protein supply — how is output affected?' and 'How efficient is metabolism of protein?'. Both questions seek information leading to statements of amounts of protein to feed. Feeding trials dominate the first question; metabolism studies are providing the key answers to the second. For both approaches the major factor emerging from recent research is the role of energy supply in protein utilisation. This will be highlighted in this review.

Perspective in assessing protein requirements

Almost universally the experimental approach adopted has been to assess protein utilisation over short periods and at energy intakes equal to requirements. This is a logical but limited starting point. Forced on the research worker to a considerable extent by shortage of experimental facilities it precludes assessment of a number of long-term issues: adaptation to a diet (Jackson, 1974); early lactation mobilisation of protein as well as fat from the body in the establishment of peak yield (Paquay, de Baere and Lousse, 1972); later recouping of such body losses; effect of protein on fertility and general health (Broster, 1972; Hewitt, 1975); effect of protein intake on persistency of milk yield (Thomas, 1971; Broster and Bines, 1974). All these long-term considerations have been seriously neglected. Requirements of protein for pregnancy (*Table 10.1*) have been documented (Jakobsen, 1957, quoted by Agricultural Research Council (ARC), 1965). It is necessary to recall these long-term issues to maintain perspective in considering protein requirements for an animal from which long-term as well as current high output is sought.

Two further issues allied to protein requirements may also be conveniently dealt with here. Firstly it is generally acknowledged that nitrogen intake can affect consumption of forages (Balch and Campling, 1962). The level of protein consumption at which this occurs to an appreciable

Table 10.1 PROTEIN REQUIREMENT OF COWS DURING PREGNANCY (45 kg CALF) (JAKOBSEN, 1957, INTERPRETED BY ARC, 1965)

Months of pregnancy	N retained (g per day)	Available protein (g per day)
5–6	1.7	15
7	5.1	45
8	12.0	110
9	29.0	260

Table 10.2 RESPONSES TO ADDITIONAL GROUNDNUT CAKE IN THE CONCENTRATES FED TO DAIRY COWS RECEIVING A BASAL RATION OF SILAGE (MURDOCH, 1962)

Treatment	A	B	C	D	s.e. mean
Silage intake* (kg per day)	36.55	36.18	39.91	41.09	±0.86
Concentrates (kg per day)	5.58	5.58	5.58	5.58	–
% groundnut in concentrates	0	8	16	25	–
Milk yield (kg per day)	15.75	16.57	17.34	17.25	±0.03
SNF (%)	8.90	8.84	8.87	8.78	±0.05
Non-protein N in milk (mg N per 100 ml milk)	19.3	21.5	22.6	25.5	–

*Silage of 11% digestible crude protein in the dry matter

Table 10.3 THE EFFECT OF LEVEL OF INTAKE ON APPARENT DIGESTIBILITY OF PROTEIN (%) IN THREE ISOCALORIC DIETS (BROSTER *ET AL.*, 1973–4)

Diet (% concentrates:% hay)		60:40	75:25	90:10
Digestible energy intake	3.0	73.38	74.60	75.28
(Multiples of maintenance)	3.8	72.67	74.27	75.76
	4.3	72.45	76.39	76.90

extent, less than 10% of the dry matter, is below that reasonably anticipated in diets for lactating cows. However Ørskov *et al.* (1971) observed responses to additional protein in lambs up to 16–20% protein in the dry matter; Broster, Tuck and Balch (1964) reported appreciable effects from groundnut meal on hay intake of heifers in late pregnancy — a lactation phase when intake may be critically low; and Murdoch (1962) reported beneficial effects on silage intake and hence on milk yield of additional protein in the concentrates given to lactating cows (*Table 10.2*). Indeed the role of protein in consumption and utilisation of forage is not adequately understood (Campling, 1964; Campling and Murdoch, 1966; Tagari *et al.*, 1965, 1971; Griffiths, Spillane and Bath, 1973; T. Smith, 1976).

Secondly Moe, Reid and Tyrrell (1965) and Wagner and Loosli (1967) have observed large falls in N digestibility to occur as intake of maize-based rations increases. Wiktorsson (1971) and Broster *et al.* (1973–4) (*Table 10.3*) (*see also* Broster *et al.* (1971–2)) have not found this with diets based on grass, hay or silage. No firm conclusions can be made on digestibility of nitrogen in this regard.

Feeding experiments on protein requirements

PROTEIN AND ENERGY INTERRELATIONSHIPS

Generally experiments have included energy intakes equal to nominal requirements with variation in protein supply (Broster, 1972). This simple situation belies the complexities of the problem that the use made of protein is markedly dependent on the energy supply. The evidence on this is meagre for dairy cows though it is more plentiful for growing cattle and for sheep (Broster, 1972, 1973).

Elliott, Reed and Topps (1964) described the relationship between protein and energy with a quadratic equation. Balch (1967) modified this, retaining its general curvilinear nature (*Figure 10.1*). Black and Griffiths (1975) derived linear functions for the two phases of the response curve to protein intake: for a low intake range with protein limiting growth; and for a higher range of intake with protein no longer limiting growth. The equation by Elliott, Reed and Topps (1964) is of the general form y (growth) $= b_1 C + b_2 P + b_3 P^2 + b_4 CP + k$ [where C is energy intake, P is protein intake, $b_1 \ldots _4, k$ are constants]. This includes an additive and a multiplicative beneficial effect from each nutrient. Since b_4 is universally negative the effects of high protein intake are detrimental. Output from a given level of protein intake is

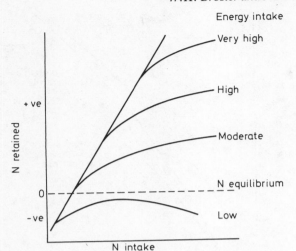

Figure 10.1 Diagrammatic model of the relationship between intake of nitrogen and nitrogen retained in heifers receiving various amounts of dietary energy (after Balch, 1967)

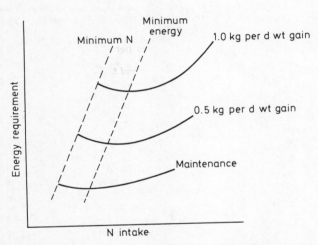

Figure 10.2 Diagrammatic representation of the amounts of digestible protein and digestible energy required for various rates of growth in young cattle (based on Stobo and Roy, 1973)

dependent on energy supply; and, vice versa, amount of protein to sustain a particular output depends on energy supply. These requirements can be set out by a reconstruction of the above relationship (Broster, 1973) (*Figure 10.2*) as for milk N output by Robinson and Forbes (1970). Minimum intakes of protein and energy can be distinguished. They do not, it must be pointed out, occur together: minimum protein supply requires more than minimum energy supply.

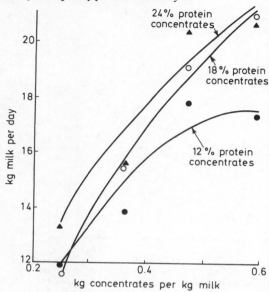

Figure 10.3 Effect of rate of concentrates feeding and % crude protein in the concentrates on milk yield (kg per day) of cows (Gordon and Forbes, 1973, unpublished results)

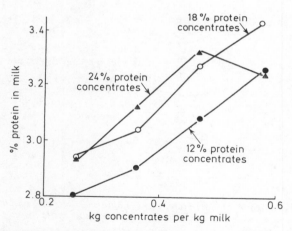

Figure 10.4 Effect of rate of concentrates feeding and % crude protein in the concentrates on milk protein % of cows (Gordon and Forbes, 1973, unpublished results)

Evidence from studies including independent variation of energy and protein within experiments is quite inadequate to construct a corresponding model for dairy cows. The few experiments reported (*see* Broster, 1972) confirm that energy intake does influence the milk output supported by a given amount of protein.

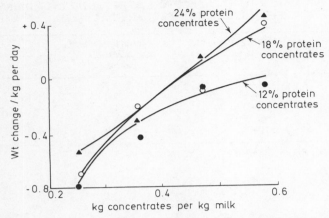

Figure 10.5 Effect of rate of concentrates feeding and % crude protein in the concentrates on live weight change (kg per day) of cows (Gordon and Forbes, 1973, unpublished results)

More recently Gordon and Forbes (1973), quoted by Bines and Broster (1974), have produced the most comprehensive experiment on the issue. It is used here to illustrate the relationships involved. In a randomised block experiment with 72 cows, using a 7 week experimental period, four rates of concentrates feeding were arranged factorially with three levels of protein intake. Concentrates varied from 0.2 to 0.6 kg per kg milk and, for each level, concentrates of 12, 18 and 24% crude protein were used. Curvilinear responses to each nutrient were obtained. *Figures 10.3, 10.4* and *10.5* give the results for milk yield, milk protein content and live weight change. It is immediately clear that, in general, 12% crude protein is insufficient and 24% excessive; also that there is a response relationship between milk output and inputs of energy and protein. At low levels of concentrates levels 18% or 24% protein contents were not as beneficial compared with 12% as at high rates of concentrates consumption. The effect of increasing energy supply was greater than that of increasing protein. Live weight changes will be dealt with on p. 206.

OPTIMAL RATIO OF PROTEIN TO ENERGY IN THE DIET

Paquay *et al.* (1973) have estimated optimal dietary ratios of metabolisable energy to protein (*Table 10.4*). Too wide a ratio reduces milk yield; too narrow a ratio is not beneficial. The optimal ratio of protein to energy was judged to fall with increasing time from calving.

The ARC (1965) pointed out that for their estimates of protein requirements, increasing metabolisable energy (ME) density in the diet must be accompanied by increased protein contents. These must increase at a greater rate than the energy density because of greater efficiency of utilisation of ME in diets of high energy concentration.

Table 10.4 OPTIMAL PROTEIN-ENERGY RATIOS IN THE DIETS OF DAIRY COWS ACCORDING TO STAGE OF LACTATION (PAQUAY *ET AL.*, 1973)

Months of lactation	Optimal ratio of g digestible N per MJ ME
1–3	2.2
4–5*	2.4
6–7	1.7
8–9*	1.7
10+	1.3

*Few values (authors' comment)

REQUIREMENTS VERSUS RESPONSES

Taking then the limited case of cows adequately fed for energy Broster (1972) estimated from the results of 16 experiments the nature of the response curve to variation in protein intake. Over the lower range of intakes the response to additional protein was 0.44±0.058 kg milk per 0.1 kg additional digestible crude protein intake. At high levels of intake the response was 0.06±0.002 kg milk per 0.1 kg additional digestible crude protein intake. Thus at high levels of intake the response is so small that the point of inflexion in the curve can be regarded as the requirement. The predicted requirement was 58.5±1.82 g digestible crude protein per kg milk with confidence limits ($P = 0.05$) of 52.3–60.0 g per kg milk. The unit of intake – digestible crude protein – is challenged later in this chapter (Miller, 1973b quoted by Bines and Broster, 1974).

Some specific examples of the effects of underfeeding protein will draw out the significance of the response concept. A reduction of intake from 100% to 60–70% standards (Woodman, 1957) caused the following falls in milk yield: 1.4 kg in 10.4 kg (Rowland, 1946); 0.9 kg in 11.3 kg (Breirem, 1949); 2.7 kg in 18.1 kg (Rook and Line, 1962). At 80% standards (Woodman, 1957), falls in milk yield of 0.7 kg in 20.4 kg (Frens and Dijkstra, 1959); 0.9–1.8 kg in 18.1 kg (Rook and Line, 1962); 0.6 kg in 18.1 kg (Broster *et al.*, 1969); 0.5 kg in 12.2 kg (Broster *et al.*, 1960) were reported. These falls represent changes in output with change in input and they are as important as the concept of a requirement. The latter is a rigid, oversimplified version of food utilisation. The concept of responses permits the pinpointing of particular combinations of nutrient inputs for a given animal to support a given level of performance.

For comparison the change in milk output with change in energy intake is 0.1 kg milk per MJ ME for a cow yielding 20 kg at ARC (1965) rates of feeding (Broster, 1974).

MILK COMPOSITION

Figure 10.4 shows the unpublished data of Gordon and Forbes (1973).
Level of energy in the diet affects protein content of the milk; so does
protein content up to 18% protein in the concentrates but not beyond.
Quoting extensive studies by Rook and Line (1961), Balch (1972)
plotted the relationship between energy intake and milk solids-not-fat
content shown in *Figure 10.6*. The effect was due almost wholly to an
increase in protein content, increases occurring in all the major milk
proteins, casein, β-lactoglobulin and α-lactalbumin. Though Gordon and
Forbes showed some effect of protein intake at low levels of consumption
on protein content of the milk, in general protein intakes around normal
levels have little effect on protein content though extra may increase
NPN in the milk (Rook, 1961). Thus in practice it is energy supply
rather than protein supply which is of major interest in milk protein
content.

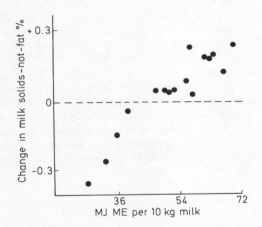

Figure 10.6 Effect of level of energy intake on milk solids-not-fat content (after Balch, 1972)

FACTORIAL ESTIMATES OF PROTEIN REQUIREMENTS

The ARC (1965) used the summation of the nitrogen requirements for
various body functions and output pathways as a measure of net N
requirements. These in turn were converted into dietary N by application
of various factors estimating rates of utilisation. In general these latter
values presented minimal requirements. That they undercut some traditional
estimates has been noted (Bines and Broster, 1974). They do represent,
as the authors comment, estimates of minimal requirements *without* safety
margins. As such they are not necessarily directly comparable with values
for present feeding standards which are allied to energy intakes equal to
requirements and which may include safety margins.

VARIATION IN ESTIMATES OF REQUIREMENTS

Safety margins apart, not all experimental results can be reconciled to the above estimates of protein requirements. Evidence by Drori and Folman (1970) is a notable exception. They found that 125% of the protein level in the milk was sufficient to sustain high yields over whole lactations. Huber (1975) quoted various pieces of evidence that fluctuate in estimates of protein requirements between 12.8 and 17% crude protein and he concluded that 15% is sufficient in early lactation – catering in part for low food consumption at this time – and 12% later in lactation. This draws out the distinction between requirements at different stages of the lactation, building up to the long-term issues referred to earlier.

There is the basic question of optimum percentage protein in the diet for cows of differing yield level. In their experiment, Cuthbert, Thicket and Wilson (1973) used four levels of crude protein in the dry matter (10, 12, 14 and 16%). A family of response curves was obtained for cows of different milk yield capacities. Greater responses were obtained from the higher yielding cows (greater than 20 kg milk yield per day), for which it was concluded 60 g digestible crude protein per kg milk was the required rate of feeding. Less was required for lower yielders. In general inadequate evidence is available on the higher yielding cow that now forms the national herd. Cuthbert, Thicket and Wilson's (1973) figure does not exceed the mean value from published data (Broster, 1972) and *Table 10.8* (p. 209). In these the 19:1 confidence limits were 52–60 g digestible crude protein per kg milk. Van Es' (1972) figure of 0.3 kg digestible crude protein per 500 kg live weight for maintenance has been accepted for this particular calculation. The variation in size of response to change in protein intake was notably small. Even so reference to the classical experiment by Frederiksen *et al.* (1931) (*Figure 10.7*) shows the variation in response

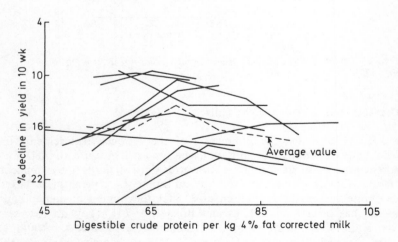

Figure 10.7 Graphical representation of responses in milk production to variation in protein supply (Frederiksen et al., 1931)

that occurs, even within a trial. Local managerial and biological variation is partly the cause of this but also differences of interpretation of units (digestible crude protein, digestible true protein, protein equivalent), of the use of non-protein nitrogen, and of the efficiency of utilisation of absorbed nitrogenous compounds.

Not least of the causative factors has been the inadequate appreciation of the part in protein metabolism played by the energy supply in the rumen and in the body (Oldham, 1973). It is therefore timely and proper to bring into the analysis of the problem the increasing volume of evidence regarding metabolism of protein in the cow, to provide a correction to misapplication of half knowledge and to provide an alternative and more basically orientated approach to estimation of protein requirements.

Efficiency of metabolism of protein as a guide to requirements

As with energy utilisation (Blaxter, 1967) so with protein, a series of coefficients of efficiency of utilisation at the various key stages of metabolism can provide, when integrated, an estimate of protein requirements. Several workers (e.g. Miller, 1973a; Ørskov, 1976; Satter and Roffler, 1975) have reasoned that sufficient evidence now exists to justify consolidation of the approach into tabulations of amounts of protein to feed. The merits of this line of attack are several: its scientific basis is obvious; it draws protein quality directly into the system; it forms a cross-check on feeding trial estimates of requirements; and it assists understanding of the variation in results encountered there. As with the metabolisable energy system it is capable of absorbing new information into the logic of the approach; the basic pattern caters for all classes of ruminants. This section summarises the approach, indicates the present state of knowledge, and provides an estimate of protein requirements for lactation based on it.

Response to increases in protein input has been shown to depend on energy supply. This indicates an interaction between protein and energy which determines the manner in which protein will be used. Protein requirements, quantity and quality, must therefore be stated in relation to defined energy inputs. This provides a point of reference in studying the transformations which occur to food protein and NPN during fermentation in the rumen, digestion in the abomasum and intestines and utilisation in the host body.

The important questions are: What is the quantitative role of rumen microbes in determining the fate of ingested nitrogen? What happens to protein which is absorbed from the gastrointestinal (GI) tract and can its fate be manipulated by changing the quality of protein absorbed or the type of food offered? How accurately can the value of NPN in feeds be predicted? The reliability of the answers to these questions determines the usefulness, in practice, of an approach based on metabolic considerations.

The ARC Committee to study nutrient requirements of ruminants has been deeply concerned since 1973 with an assessment of protein requirements based on metabolic considerations, and will publish the results of their deliberations shortly (Blaxter, 1976). Kaufmann and Hagemeister

(1975) in W. Germany and Burroughs, Nelson and Mertens (1975) and Satter and Roffler (1975) in the United States have suggested practical approaches. What follows is our assessment of the situation in relation to the UK dairy cow.

RUMEN MICROBIAL GROWTH AND ENERGY SUPPLY

The rumen contains bacteria and protozoa in proportions which depend on a host of factors, many of which are interdependent, for example, source of dietary carbohydrate and rumen pH. It is usually tacitly assumed that the energy cost of rumen microbial growth is a direct reflection of the energy cost of bacterial growth and most published estimates relate only to bacteria. It will, similarly, be assumed here that measurements for bacteria can be applied to the entire rumen population and the term 'energy cost of microbial growth' will be used for all measurements. It must, however, be borne in mind that the presence of a large protozoal population may impose an extra energy burden on the rumen. As protozoa rely to a large extent on bacteria for their protein supply, protozoal protein production includes an extra energy cost for resynthesis of protein. If protozoa merely sequester in the rumen and make only a minor contribution to microbial protein flowing from the rumen, as suggested by Weller and Pilgrim (1974), then a further level of energy inefficiency may be involved.

The relationship between bacterial growth and energy supply is complex (Stouthamer and Bettenhaussen, 1973). It is likely that the most important variable which may affect microbial growth yield in the rumen is the dilution rate of rumen fluid (Harrison *et al.,* 1975). No doubt other variables play a part in the broad range of values found for the energy cost of rumen microbial growth. Many of these values are drawn together in *Table 10.5*. We have chosen to relate microbial N production to the amount of organic matter which is apparently digested in the rumen (rumen ADOM). This differs from the amount of organic matter truly digested (rumen TDOM) by the amount of OM which is re-incorporated into microbial biomass (*Figure 10.8*). Although rumen TDOM is the better measure of total energy made available from the fermentation rumen ADOM represents the excess energy which is required to resynthesise degraded food OM into microbial OM. Microbial growth can therefore be related to rumen ADOM (A $\propto$ B in *Figure 10.8*). In addition rumen ADOM is the quantity which is actually measured whereas rumen TDOM is derived from this by making allowance for microbial OM from a knowledge of microbial protein supply from the rumen. This is a hazardous procedure as microbial OM composition is quite variable (McAllan and Smith, 1974; Czerkawski, 1975).

The mean of the values in *Table 10.5* indicates that 32 g microbial N are synthesised per kg rumen ADOM. This value will be used to cover all situations but we are aware that it is not a biological constant and is associated with a degree of variability. It is a difficult value to use in practice as it does not relate to a readily identifiable fraction in food. It

Table 10.5 THE RELATIONSHIP BETWEEN MICROBIAL N YIELD AND THE APPARENT DIGESTION OF ORGANIC MATTER IN THE RUMEN (RUMEN ADOM). FOR EACH SOURCE THE RANGE OF VALUES SHOWN REFERS TO ALL EXPERIMENTAL DIETS USED IN THAT EXPERIMENT

Source	*g Microbial N per kg ADOM (rumen)*	*Ration constituents*
DAIRY COWS		
Hagemeister and Pfeffer (1973)	32—47	Hay + barley, concentrates
Hagemeister and Kaufmann (1974)	20—35	Hay + barley, concentrates
SHEEP		
Hume (1970a, b)	23—33	Purified diets
Hogan and Weston (1970)	22—32	Clover or grasses
Hogan and Weston (1971)	32—55	Alkali-treated straw
Lindsay and Hogan (1972)	37—61	Lucerne hay or dried clover
Leibholz (1972)	11—21	Various
Ørskov, Fraser and McDonald (1972)	29—35	Barley + urea
Miller (1973a)	34—40	No details
Hume and Purser (1975)	28—26	Clovers
Sutton *et al.* (1975)	27—38	Hay + barley, concentrates
Overall mean	32	

is possible, though, to predict microbial N yield from the energy content of the food. Miller (1973a, b) related microbial N production to metabolisable energy (ME) intake. This is consistent with the ARC (1965) approach to defining energy allowances and will also be adopted here. There is generally a strong relationship between digestible organic matter (DOM) intake and rumen ADOM (*Figure 10.9*). Most rations conform to one pattern, the major exception being ground and pelleted forage diets. Apart from these, rumen ADOM represents 65% of DOM (*Figure 10.9*). It should be noted that Tamminga (1975) has recently reported values for dairy cows falling in the range 47—54% for the proportion of digestible organic matter apparently digested in the rumen. Nevertheless the consensus value of 65% will be used here. If DOM has an energy content of 18.5 MJ kg^{-1} and ME is 82% of DE (Blaxter, 1967) then microbial N production is:

$$\frac{32 \times 0.65}{18.5 \times 0.82} = 1.371 \text{ g microbial N per MJ ME}$$

This defines the maximum quantity of microbial nitrogen which can be synthesised for a fixed ME intake. The quantity and quality of food nitrogen needed to supply this amount of N is governed by:

(1) The efficiency of conversion of food N to microbial N.
(2) The degradation of food N in the rumen.

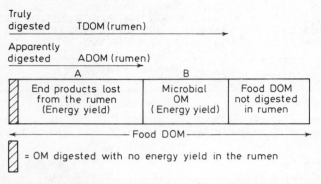

Figure 10.8 The partition of digested organic matter showing the relationship between true (TDOM) or apparent (ADOM) digestion of organic matter in the rumen. See text for further explanation.

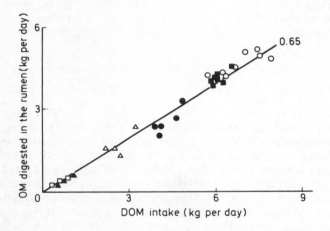

Figure 10.9 The proportion of food digestible organic matter (DOM intake) which is apparently digested in the rumen. ○ Klooster and Rogers (1969); ● Pfeffer, Kaufmann and Dirksen (1972); ▲ Beever et al. (1972); △ McGilliard (1961); □ Nicholson and Sutton (1969); ■ Calculated from Hagemeister and Kaufmann (1974). The line at 0.65 digestion in the rumen is shown

There is a shortage of information on both points. Studies with ^{15}N in sheep show that a large part (35–78%) of bacterial N is derived from ammonia, but the efficiency of capture of rumen ammonia into microbial protein is diet-dependent (Pilgrim *et al.*, 1970; Mathison and Milligan, 1971; Nolan and Leng, 1972): 80–85% of rumen ammonia may be incorporated into microbial protein with highly fermentable diets (fresh lucerne, rolled barley), but only 45–55% with hays. The efficiency of capture of ammonia is therefore high when energy supplies are adequate. As maximum microbial protein yield is achieved at low ammonia concentrations (Satter and Slyter, 1974; Buttery, 1976) inevitable losses of rumen ammonia by rumen fluid outflow or by absorption should be small when the correct balance between fermented OM and N is achieved. When recycled urea-nitrogen is taken into account the apparent efficiency of capture of ammonia from food N approaches 100%. This refers to ammonia only. The microbial N which is not derived from ammonia may include amino acids or peptides of food origin which have been directly incoporated into microbial protein. These are probably incoporated with high efficiency as the free amino acid content of rumen fluid is low (Mangan, 1972). Consequently we have assumed that degraded food N is converted to microbial N with an apparent efficiency of 100%.

There is insufficient information to justify the use of individual degradability values for each food and an umbrella value is an undesirably broad generalisation. We have chosen to place foods in groups according to their degradation characteristics (*Table 10.6*). The experimental basis for these tentative estimates is unsatisfactory — greater definition is urgently required.

The above information makes it possible to determine, at a given ME intake, the amount of food protein needed to maximise microbial N production or the quantity of urea which can be used to replace food protein. In isolation, however, it reveals nothing of the animal's requirement for protein. To gain knowledge of this it is necessary to examine the course of digestion and utilisation of protein after it leaves the rumen.

QUANTITATIVE PROTEIN SUPPLY TO THE RUMINANT

Protein N represents 72–88% of microbial N (Weller, 1957; Purser and Buechler, 1966; McAllan and Smith, 1972; Burris *et al.,* 1974; Smith and McAllan, 1974). A median value of 80% is adopted here. Microbial protein N yield is thus $0.80 \times 1.371 = 1.097$ g N per MJ ME intake. This predicts the microbial protein N supply to the absorptive area of the gut. The protein mixture which enters the duodenum normally consists of at least 50% microbial protein. Other proteins presented for digestion and absorption derive from food protein not degraded in the rumen, and endogenous secretions. The proportion of protein N absorbed between the proximal duodenum and the terminal ileum is not influenced greatly by the ratio

Table 10.6 THE PROPORTION OF FOOD PROTEIN DEGRADED IN THE RUMEN (COMPILED BY DR. R.H. SMITH (NIRD))

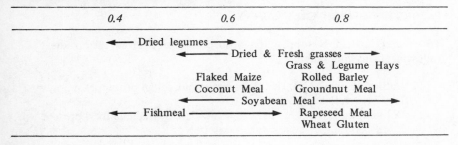

Table 10.7 THE APPARENT ABSORPTION OF PROTEIN N* FROM THE SMALL INTESTINES OF RUMINANTS. FOR EACH SOURCE THE RANGE OF VALUES SHOWN REFERS TO ALL EXPERIMENTAL DIETS USED IN THAT EXPERIMENT

Source	*Apparent absorption coefficient*	*Ration constituents*
CATTLE		
Klooster and Rogers (1969)	0.61–0.71	Semi-purified concentrates
Sharma, Ingalls and Parker (1974)	0.65–0.72	Hay + semi-purified concentrates and grass
Watson, Savage and Armstrong (1972)	0.52–0.69	Dried grass + concentrates
Tamminga (1975)	0.69–0.77	Dried grass or grass silages
SHEEP		
Clarke, Ellinger and Phillipson (1966)	0.45–0.76	Hay + maize and soya supplements
Ørskov *et al.* (1971)	0.51–0.71	Rolled barley + urea or fishmeal
Coelho da Silva *et al.* (1972a)	0.67–0.79	Dried grass, chopped or pelleted
Coelho da Silva *et al.* (1972b)	0.66–0.71	Lucerne, chopped, cobbed, or pelleted
MacRae *et al.* (1972)	0.62–0.64	Dried grass + protein supplements
Ørskov, Fraser and McDonald (1972)	0.64–0.68	Rolled barley + urea
Hogan (1973)	0.61	Clover
Ørskov and Fraser (1973)	0.31–0.81	Barley + soyabean meal
MacRae and Ulyatt (1974)	0.65–0.75	Grasses
Ørskov *et al.* (1974)	0.61–0.69	Barley + fishmeal and urea

*Where possible values refer to uptake of amino acid N between the proximal duodenum and terminal ileum but where necessary values for uptake of non-ammonia N or total N are included

of microbial:undegraded food protein even when the food protein is of a type which is highly digestible in non-ruminant species. Available data variously refer to the disappearance of non-ammonia N, amino acid N or total N in the small intestine. Much of this information is drawn together in *Table 10.7*. From this it is apparent that most situations are adequately described by allowing a value of 0.7 for the proportion of abomasal or duodenal N absorbed in the small intestine. There is at present no justification for using separate values for microbial and food protein.

PREDICTION OF PROTEIN N SUPPLY

To predict protein N supply and absorption for a given ration the following steps are taken:

(1) Define ME intake (I). Hence maximum microbial protein N supply = $1.097 \times I = MP$.
(2) Define food protein N intake and calculate degradable food protein N (DP) and undegradable food protein N (FP).

(3) If DP $\geqslant$ microbial N calculated as MP/0.8 (to account for protein N content of microbial total N) then microbial protein N production is maximal. If theoretical microbial N > DP the difference in N is the quantity of urea N which should be added to the ration to maximise MP.
(4) Total protein N supply to duodenum = MP + FP.
(5) Absorbed protein N = 0.7 (MP + FP).

These calculations allow prediction of protein supply to the tissues. The response of the tissues to this protein input is then vitally important in determining protein quantity and quality requirements.

THE UTILISATION OF ABSORBED PROTEIN

Protein which has been absorbed from the gut is used to maintain body tissues and to synthesise new body protein and milk. The efficiency with which these processes are achieved is dependent on the quantity and amino acid composition of the protein and on the supply of energy.

The definition of efficiency used here is the proportion of absorbed protein which is deposited in body protein and milk. It is strictly an input/output relationship and is clearly related to the old established term, biological value (BV). In fact, the efficiency of utilisation of protein made available for absorption is BV in the truest sense; but it is the BV of protein which leaves the abomasum not the BV of food protein, and to use the same term here would introduce a considerable degree of confusion. The intervention of rumen microbial fermentation renders BV, as defined by the ARC (1965), redundant for ruminants. The same can be said for digestible crude protein (DCP). The value of apparently digested protein depends on the conversion of protein digested in the rumen to microbial protein. DCP on its own does not give a clear indication of the processes concerned with crude protein digestion. An alternative to BV is required which relates to the protein which is presented for absorption. The most useful term is the efficiency of utilisation of absorbed protein.

The efficiency of utilisation of protein for milk production is the main concern here but the efficiency of utilisation of protein for body maintenance must not be forgotten. The net utilisation of absorbed protein contains components for both maintenance and milk production. In considering the utilisation of absorbed protein we are really considering the response to a factor which limits the usefulness of the protein. The limiting factor may be an individual amino acid, a group of amino acids or some other factor such as the content of α-amino nitrogen. Success in identifying the limiting factor for milk production has been very limited. Clark (1975) has reviewed much of the recent work in which milking cows have been supplemented, post-ruminally, with amino acids, glucose or casein hydrolysate. Repeated efforts to define a first limiting amino acid for milk production have proved inconsistent. Methionine or phenyl-alanine may be the most likely choices but Clark (1975) noted that the greatest response in milk production has been produced by duodenal supplementation with casein. Increases of 10–15% in milk protein yield have been achieved. The active factor in casein remains unidentified. The amino acid composition of casein is ideally suited to boost milk production but it is unlikely that duodenally supplemented protein will reach the udder with its amino acid composition unchanged. Differential digestibilities of individual amino acids in the small intestine (Clarke, Ellinger and Phillipson, 1966; Coelho da Silva *et al.*, 1972a, b) and differential use of amino acids for gluconeogenesis will inevitably alter the amino acid composition of supplementary protein which reaches the udder (Black *et al.*, 1968).

The involvement of amino acids in gluconeogenesis may be important in determining the efficiency with which absorbed protein is used. As Clark (1975) suggests, increases in milk protein yield following post-ruminal supplementation with glucose may be the result of sparing amino acids otherwise required for gluconeogenesis. Evans *et al.* (1975) fed high or low roughage rations to milking cows and observed an increased milk protein yield and increased plasma glucose utilisation rate with cows on the low roughage rations. They suggested that insulin may have had a mediating influence, being stimulated by an increase in glucose supply and itself stimulating protein synthesis and inhibiting gluconeogenesis from amino acids. The net result, that increasing glucose supply rate allowed increased milk protein output, is important. The source of increased glucose supply may be twofold, either arising from increased rumen propionate production or increased duodenal starch passage with high concentrate diets. Sutton (1976) found the available data on rumen volatile fatty acids (VFA) production in cows inconclusive. High concentrate diets (8–13% hay) may produce greater amounts of propionate (mmol per kg digestible dry matter intake) than low concentrate diets (35–55% hay) but there are too few reliable measurements to define the situation properly. On the other hand up to 300–400 g starch can be digested daily in the small intestine of cattle (Sutton, 1976), a significant part of the daily requirement for glucose, which has been estimated by Armstrong and Prescott (1971) to be 1494 g per day for a 590 kg cow producing 20 kg milk per day. Manipulation of the carbohydrate component of the diet may therefore be a means of influencing amino acid utilisation in the body provided that, by increasing glucose supply to the tissues, amino acids are indeed released from gluconeogenic requirements to milk protein production. This would only apply to glucogenic amino acids, thus influencing the composition of amino acids available for milk synthesis as well as the total quantities of amino acids.

The information is not available which would allow these concepts to be incorporated into a description of the efficiency with which absorbed protein is utilised. It is apparent, though, that the 'quality' of absorbed protein may be important in determining responses in milk protein output and that there may be important interactions between absorbed carbohydrate and protein which determine, to some extent, the routes of utilisation of absorbed protein (i.e. gluconeogenesis or milk protein). There will also be an interaction between absorbed energy and protein which may be expected to comply with the diminishing returns law.

In each of these areas there is a woeful lack of data. While there is a considerable body of evidence to describe the course of protein digestion up to the point at which protein is absorbed from the gut of the ruminant, the course of its subsequent utilisation remains impossible to quantify at present. Purser (1970) noted this most powerfully and we can but call again for an increased research effort in this area. For our present purpose, that of defining protein allowances for lactation, it is nevertheless vital that we describe the efficiency of utilisation of absorbed protein. To do this we have chosen a range of values, from 65% to 85%, to compare the estimates of required protein allowances which derive from these with published estimates for minimum required protein allowances. This approach is less than ideal and due care is required in interpreting the results. We emphasise that the comparison is not a means for predicting the correct efficiency of utilisation by comparison with published schemes but is merely an investigative tool to demonstrate the effect which varying efficiencies may have on estimates of requirements.

Maintenance

A value of 59 g CP per day may be used for the daily endogenous urinary N excretion (EUN) of a 500 kg cow (Roy, 1975) but EUN is only part of the protein requirement which is usually termed the maintenance requirement. The other component to be considered is truly endogenous, or metabolic, faecal nitrogen.

Losses of nitrogen from gut wall detritus and endogenous secretions have been described as metabolic faecal nitrogen and assessed as proportional to dry matter intake (ARC, 1965). The quantity involved is assessed indirectly by extrapolation of regressions of faecal N on N intake or by direct measures of faecal N output on low N diets. Such losses form a further demand for dietary N for replacement. The factorial estimation of requirements allows for this, e.g. the adjustment of available protein to digestible crude protein for maintenance of a 500 kg cow is about 80 g added to 115 g for maintenance (ARC, 1965). An approach based on metabolic efficiency of protein utilisation requires cognizance also of these losses, ideally measured as the actual amount of N lost from the gut rather than as empirical estimates of metabolic faecal N (MFN). Such information is not available. Therefore estimates have been made here. Apparent MFN contains a component which is microbial in origin (Mason, 1969). Therefore ARC (1965) may overestimate MFN. The fraction of endogenous N appearing in the faeces will be related to urea recycled to the gut, also to cell fragments from gut tissue, and to endogenous secretion not reabsorbed. Information is lacking on quantitative aspects of these three components. In the absence of definitive evidence an estimate of MFN based on supply of endogenous N arising from turnover of gut protein would fall broadly within the range 25–45 g d^{-1} for a 500 kg cow. Here a value of 35 g d^{-1} has been used in calculations.

Calculation of protein requirements

Total protein requirements were calculated as follows. ARC (1965) estimates of ME requirements and DM intakes for a 500 kg cow were used for different levels of yield of milk of 3.35% protein content. These were added to estimated maintenance requirements based on the above discussions. *Figure 10.10* and *Figure 10.11* show estimates of protein requirements with and without endogenous faecal N (EFN).

To compile these figures total requirement for duodenal protein supply was calculated for the chosen efficiencies of utilisation of absorbed protein and compared with potential microbial protein supply at the required ME intake. Where necessary, due allowance was made for undegraded food protein which was required and, by reference to DM intake, the required ration CP % calculated. The procedure is clarified by an example – a cow producing 20 kg milk per day at 80% efficiency of utilisation of absorbed protein.

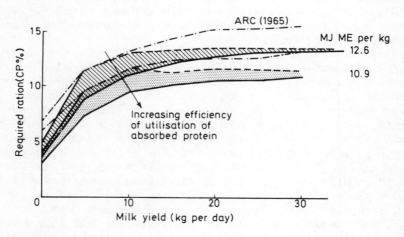

Figure 10.10 Predicted requirements for protein, as % CP in food DM, in relation to milk yield. Requirement was assumed to be milk protein output + EUN. Calulations were made for rations of two M/D values (10.9 and 12.6 MJ ME per kg) and for different efficiencies of utilisation of absorbed protein. The ARC (1965) recommended allowances are shown for both M/D values for comparison (–·—·–). For further explanation see text

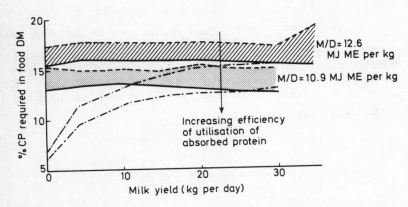

Figure 10.11 Predicted requirements for protein, as % CP in food DM, in relation to milk yield. Requirement was assumed to be milk protein output + EUN + truly endogenous faecal N (at 35 g N per day). Calculations were made for rations of two M/D values (10.9 and 12.6 MJ ME per kg) and for different efficiencies of utilisation of absorbed protein. The ARC (1965) recommended allowances are shown for both M/D values for comparison (–·–·–). For further explanation see text

Protein content of milk = 0.0335 × 20 kg = 670 g

Maintenance protein requirement = 59 g (excluding EFN; this would be 278 g if EFN of 35 g N per day were included)

Total protein output = 729 g per day

At 80% efficiency of utilisation of absorbed protein:

Absorbed protein requirement $= \dfrac{729}{0.8} = 911$ g

This is derived from duodenal protein which is 70% absorbed:

Duodenal protein required $= \dfrac{911}{0.7} = 1302$ g

From ARC (1965), ME requirement for 20 kg milk yield = 156 MJ per day and DM intake for a ration containing 10.9 MJ per kg = 14.3 kg per day

Maximum microbial protein yield = 6.25 × 1.097 (*see* p. 197)

= 6.86 g protein per MJ ME intake

For this ration (156 MJ ME intake) maximum microbial protein yield = 156 × 6.86 = 1070 g per day

This is less than the requirement for duodenal protein (1302 g per day) so the difference (1302 − 1070 = 232 g) must come from undegraded food protein. For this example, taking an overall value of 0.6 for the degradability of food protein in the rumen, to supply 232 g food protein to the duodenum $\frac{232}{0.4}$ = 580 g food protein must be fed. Note that the degraded food protein (580 × 0.6 = 348 g) is insufficient to maximise microbial protein production so that urea could profitably be used as a supplement to make up the deficit. As microbial protein is only 80% of microbial N the amount of degraded food CP to maximise microbial protein = $\frac{1070}{0.8}$ = 1338 g food CP.

Total food CP requirement is made up of:

Degraded food CP (including urea supplement) = 1338 g
                                                                                      +
Undegraded food CP   =   232 g
Total food CP required   = 1570 g

Therefore 1570 g CP is required in 14.3 kg DM. Required CP % = $\frac{1570}{143}$ = 11%

The results of many such calculations are gathered together in *Figures 10.10* and *10.11*.

The requirements are given as % CP required in DM when DM intake is defined by the ARC (1965). Calculations have been made for rations with two different ME concentrations (M/D) of 10.9 or 12.6 MJ kg^{-1} (2.6 or 3.0 Mcal per kg) and for a range of values for efficiency of utilisation of absorbed protein, from 65 to 85%. The figures show only those values for which the rumen requirement for protein (1.097 g microbial protein per MJ ME) is met but not exceeded, i.e. where there is no wastage of degraded protein in the rumen. The protein requirement is thus met by maximum microbial protein supply plus undegraded food protein supply.

VARIATION IN PREDICTED PROTEIN REQUIREMENTS

Required ration CP % is dependent on the energy concentration of the diet. This is simply because, to meet ME requirements, diets of high ME concentration require lower DM intakes; thus to meet a fixed CP requirement the protein concentration of the diet must rise. If absorbed protein is used with high efficiency, required dietary CP % is reduced. The notched lines in *Figures 10.10* and *10.11* indicate the upper limit to CP % above which, to meet duodenal needs for protein, protein starts to be wasted in the rumen. This happens particularly with highly degradable diets (*see Table 10.6*) and at low efficiencies of utilisation of absorbed protein. The calculations indicate that, dependent on the energy concentration of the diet, and for a required level of milk output, there is a level of ration CP % above which degraded protein is lost from the rumen. When the maintenance requirement is equated with EUN (*Figure 10.10*) the limiting value for ration CP % is 11.5% (M/D = 10.9 MJ kg⁻¹) or 13.3% (M/D = 12.6 MJ kg⁻¹) for milk yields in excess of 10 kg per day. If EFN is taken into account for the maintenance component (*Figure 10.11*) these levels rise to about 15% (M/D = 10.9) and 17.5% (M/D = 12.6) and are constant for all levels of production.

It is of importance to consider the response of cows to incremental changes in diet CP %. Below a limiting value responses are partly a function of increased microbial protein production and partly a function of undegraded food protein reaching the duodenum (0.8 unit increase in

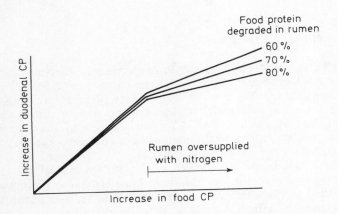

Figure 10.12 The response in duodenal protein supply to increases in food protein supply when the rumen is undersupplied or oversupplied with nitrogen. Response curves are shown for foods of rumen degradability 60, 70 and 80%

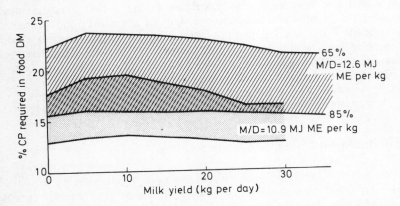

Figure 10.13 Predicted requirements for protein when the efficiency of utilisation of absorbed protein ranges from 65 to 85%. See also Figure 10.11 and text

microbial protein per unit degraded food protein + response to undegraded food protein). Above the limiting value the response is due to undegraded food protein alone. The difference in responses is shown in *Figure 10.12*.
When the limiting CP is exceeded the greatest response is achieved with proteins which are relatively resistant to rumen degradation.

To give an impression of the effect which wastage of protein in the rumen can have on predicted CP requirements *Figure 10.13* shows the range of CP % required for a ration of 60% rumen degradability for the two adopted M/D values. The upper and lower bounds of the estimates refer to 65% and 85% efficiencies of utilisation of absorbed protein. In this figure a requirement for EFN has been assumed. The range is broad, but tends to narrow for high yields − this probably reflects changing ME or DM requirements (ARC, 1965).

UREA AS A PROTEIN REPLACER

Figure 10.13 demonstrates quite clearly the importance of selecting ration components to balance the needs of the rumen, and of the host, in relation to energy input. There is, in this context, the need to consider, not only the possible oversupply of degraded nitrogen to the rumen, but also the situation in which less food protein is degraded than the rumen microbes can utilise. In this circumstance the use of urea can be contemplated (*see* p. 204).

Below the CP % in the dry matter which limits microbial protein production urea may be used to maximise microbial protein production. The proportion of CP which can be fed as urea is again dependent on M/D (on account of effects on DM intake), on the efficiency of retention of absorbed protein − at higher efficiencies microbial protein represents a greater proportion of requirement so more urea can be used − and, of course, on food protein degradability. The calculations from which *Figure 10.11* was derived have been used to provide *Figure 10.14* as an example. The inclusion rate of urea N was calculated as the deficit between maximum microbial N production and the supply of degraded food protein N in the rumen. From our calculations there may be scope for urea feeding even for high milk yields but this will depend on the variables described. We cannot make a simple advisory statement on the role of urea but, from *Figure 10.14,* a rule of thumb may be that no more than 20% of food CP should be fed as urea. It could be considerably less under some circumstances.

Protein intake and change of body reserves

Attention has by and large been riveted on milk production to the exclusion of other aspects of dairy cow performance. The experiments by Gordon and Forbes (1973) (*Figure 10.5*) revealed little effect on live weight gain from variation in protein intake at low energy intakes but an effect at high energy intakes, i.e. the same responses as occurred in milk

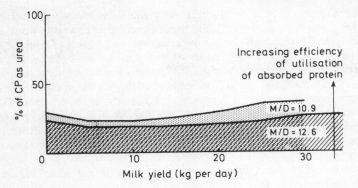

Figure 10.14 The proportion of food CP which can be fed as urea for various milk yields, for foods of different ME concentration (M/D) and for different efficiencies of utilisation of absorbed protein. It was assumed that food protein degradability in the rumen = 60%.

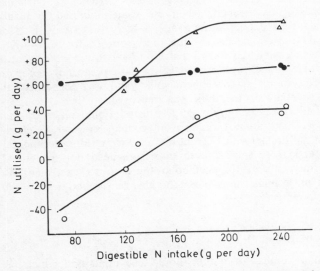

Figure 10.15 The response in dairy cows to digestible nitrogen in the diet (after Balch and Campling, 1961). ○ body nitrogen exchange; ● milk nitrogen excretion; ▲ total nitrogen output

yield. There was a major beneficial effect from higher energy intakes on live weight gain. Balch and Campling (1961) plotted milk nitrogen secretion and body nitrogen retention at various intakes of apparently digestible nitrogen, showing the response to extra nitrogen occurs mainly in body nitrogen retention (*Figure 10.15*). Paquay, de Baere and Lousse (1972) estimated 15 kg protein as the likely lower limit of protein that can be lost from the body, and a recovery period extending over 6 months or more after underfeeding.

The significance of the relationship of protein intake to body changes lies in the long-term nature of milk production. The cow functions in a recurring cycle of gestation–lactation–gestation and so on. Lenkeit (1972) stressed this issue from a long series of experiments on protein utilisation and Broster (1974) stressed it from the point of view of total plane of nutrition. Reid, Moe and Tyrrell (1966) pointed out the possibly erroneous conclusions from short-term trials in which changes of body protein reserves could mask effects of level of protein feeding on milk production. This is especially true in early lactation, a period notoriously difficult to investigate but critical to the success of long-term performance (Broster, 1974).

All this indicates two issues about which there is not adequate information at present: (1) the amount of labile body reserves of the cow; (2) the long-term as opposed to the short-term effects of variation in protein intake.

Huber (1975) made the point that the cow yielding 34 kg milk in early lactation and consuming 21 kg food, needs 15.3% crude protein. This intake provides 21 MJ net energy below NRC (1971) standards. If protein is 20% of tissue energy then the 1 kg mobilised to furnish 21 MJ is equivalent to 0.2 kg protein and a body loss of 30 g N per day, reducing crude protein needed in the diet from 15.3% to 14.4%. For first calf cows Broster, Tuck and Balch (1964) found no advantage from 1.0 kg digestible crude protein per day in late pregnancy compared with 0.7 kg per day so far as subsequent milk yield was concerned, though solids-not-fat content of the milk was improved.

It is implied from the results of Drori and Folman (1970) that cumulative adverse effects do not occur from protein shortage. Such a result was apparent in Broster's (1972) survey of long-term experiments. Thus traumatic effects from small protein shortages need not be looked for.

Future refinements of the metabolic approach to assessment of protein requirements must make allowances for changes in bodyweight during the lactation cycle.

General discussion

In conclusion a number of points should be emphasised which pertain to:

(1) The results of the described approach to defining protein requirements and
(2) The future development of the approach.

Our approach has been to describe the requirement as the sum of milk protein output plus an allowance for maintenance (EUN plus truly endogenous faecal N). Some estimates are brought together in *Table 10.8*. At high milk yields the results of our calculations agree quite well with published estimates. Estimates are particularly high for maintenance and low milk yields, and are generally higher than ARC (1965) figures. This could mean that we are underestimating microbial protein production for these ME intakes. These calculations suggest that undegraded food protein

Table 10.8 REQUIRED CP % IN DRY MATTER IN RELATION TO MILK YIELD FOR RATIONS OF TWO M/D VALUES (MJ ME kg^{-1}) AND FOR TWO EFFICIENCIES OF UTILISATION OF ABSORBED PROTEIN OF 60% DEGRADABILITY IN THE RUMEN

| | *Milk yield* (kg per day) | | | |
| | 0 | 10 | 20 | 30 |
		CP%		
M/D = 10.88				
0.85 Efficiency	13.0	13.6	13.0	12.6
0.75 Efficiency	14.5	15.1	14.5	14.0
ARC (1965)	5.9	11.4	12.6	12.9
Miller (1973b)	11.3	13.3	14.4	14.5
Broster (1972)	7.1	11.9	15.8	15.7
M/D = 12.55				
0.85 Efficiency	15.5	15.9	15.8	15.3
0.75 Efficiency	17.3	17.7	17.6	17.1
ARC (1965)	6.6	13.0	14.9	15.3

may be required even at maintenance, which is contrary to much of current thinking (Broster and Bines, 1974; Ørskov, 1976). It may also suggest that maintenance should be treated differently from production requirements — if ARC (1965) estimates are correct, then agreement with our approach is reached at an efficiency of utilisation of absorbed protein of > 100%. What this means is not clear. Elliott and Topps (1963) however achieved stability of live weight with diets containing 6.5% CP in DM. Their evidence, and that of others, is incontrovertible.

In all our calculations it has been assumed that microbial protein production can be maximised in relation to defined ME intake by judicial choice of dietary nitrogen components. Choice of feedstuffs is influenced by economic as well as nutritional considerations. It should be simple to apply least cost ration formulation to balance a ration for microbial protein production and undegraded food protein supply.

The importance of energy intake in predicting protein requirements has been stressed and there is also the effect of the ME concentration in the diet. There is a lot of information about protein—energy interactions within the rumen but very little on possible interactions at tissue level. For this we have been forced to take account of any imbalance between absorbed protein and energy supplies within the term 'efficiency of utilisation of absorbed protein'. This is unsatisfactory and future sophistication of the approach will depend on increased knowledge of factors which affect the utilisation of protein within the body. Part of this knowledge must be a description of the maintenance process. Can maintenance be treated in the same way as milk production and how should it be quantitatively described? It is logical that both EUN and endogenous faecal N should be treated as functions of the body rather than of the food. Good estimates of endogenous faecal N are urgently required.

A major strength of considering protein supply as microbial protein plus undegraded food protein is that the place of urea as a feeding supplement can be accurately defined. When degraded food protein supply in the rumen is known urea can be fed to maximise microbial protein production in relation to energy supply. But, at present, degradability characteristics of foods are few and poorly defined. This is another major area where much more information is needed to improve the accuracy of descriptions of requirements. Such information would also lead to better understanding of responses to increased protein inputs — it should be possible to predict a response either in the rumen and in the body, or in the body alone.

A revision of terms is necessary to avoid the inaccuracies of conventional descriptions of protein requirements. Digestible crude protein is meaningless in the present description of protein requirements. It should be abandoned. Protein allowances are described as g CP per day, but as ME and DM intake will always be defined, requirements can be expressed as CP % in DM. Biological value should be replaced by a term which relates to duodenal protein supply or by a value for the digestibility of duodenal protein and an 'efficiency of utilisation of absorbed protein'. Metabolic faecal nitrogen should be replaced by a term for truly endogenous faecal N and related to body size.

The suggested metabolic scheme for predicting protein requirements is robust because it is based on sound descriptive principles. It is resilient because new knowledge can readily be absorbed into its structure without destroying it. Feeding trials, by measuring inputs and outputs, can take the problem of protein requirements only so far, and, notably, variation in results between experiments cannot be analysed in depth. The metabolic approach is an incisive tool for predicting optimal amounts of protein for the dairy cow. The framework is established and greater precision will be achieved as knowledge grows. Adoption of the approach into practice can now be sought.

Acknowledgements

We wish to thank Drs Gordon and Forbes for permission to quote unpublished experimental results; and we should like to thank many colleagues at this Institute and elsewhere, especially Dr. J.H.B. Roy and Dr. R.H. Smith for helpful discussions. We are grateful to the ARC Committee on Nutrient Requirements of Ruminants for permission to participate in some of their discussions on protein utilisation, which have clarified our thinking and influenced the approach made in this paper.

References

Agricultural Research Council (1965). *The Nutrient Requirements of Farm Livestock, No. 2, Ruminants.* London; HMSO

Armstrong, D.G. and Prescott, J.H.D. (1971). In *Lactation*, pp.349—377. Ed. by I.R. Falconer. London; Butterworths

Balch, C.C. (1967). *Wld Rev. Anim. Prod.*, 3, 84

Balch, C.C. (1972). In *Handbuch der Tierernährung*, Vol. 2, pp.259—291. Ed. by W. Lenkeit, K. Breirem and E. Crasemann. Hamburg; Paul Parey

Balch, C.C. and Campling, R.C. (1961). *J. Dairy Res.*, 28, 157

Balch, C.C. and Campling, R.C. (1962). *Nutr. Abstr. Rev.*, 32, 669

Beever, D.E., Coelho da Silva, J.F., Prescott, J.H.D. and Armstrong, D.G. (1972). *Br. J. Nutr.*, 28, 347

Bines, J.A. and Broster, W.H. (1974). *Proc. Br. Soc. Anim. Prod.*, 3, 51

Black, J.L. and Griffiths, D.A. (1975). *Br. J. Nutr.*, 33, 399

Black, A.L., Egan, A.R, Anand, R.S. and Chapman, T.E. (1968). In *Isotope Studies on the Nitrogen Chain*, p.247. Vienna; IAEA

Blaxter, K.L. (1967). *The Energy Metabolism of Ruminants* (2nd edn.). London; Hutchinson

Blaxter, K.L. (1976). Personal communication

Breirem, K. (1949). *Proc. XII Int. Dairy Congr.*, 1, 28

Broster, W.H. (1972). In *Handbuch der Tierernährung*, Vol. 2, pp.292—322. Ed. by W. Lenkeit, K. Breirem and E. Crasemann. Hamburg; Paul Parey

Broster, W.H. (1973). *Proc. Nutr. Soc.*, 32, 115

Broster, W.H. (1974). *Bienn. Rev. natn. Inst. Res. Dairy*, 14

Broster, W.H. and Bines, J.A. (1974). *Proc. Br. Soc. Anim. Prod.*, 3, 59

Broster, W.H., Tuck, V.J. and Balch, C.C. (1964). *J. agric. Sci., Camb.*, 63, 51

Broster, W.H., Balch, C.C., Bartlett, S. and Campling, R.C. (1960). *J. agric. Sci., Camb.*, 55, 197

Broster, W.H., Tuck, V.J., Smith, T. and Johnson, V.W. (1969). *J. agric. Sci., Camb.*, 72, 13

Broster, W.H., Sutton, J.D., Bines, J.A., Corse, D.A., Johnson, V.W., Smith, T. and Jones, P.A. (1971—2). *Rep. natn. Inst. Res. Dairy*, 1971—2, p.74

Broster, W.H., Sutton, J.D., Bines, J.A., Corse, D.A., Johnson, V.W., Smith, T., Siviter, J.W., Napper, D.J. and Broster, V.J. (1973—4). *Rep. natn. Inst. Res. Dairy*, 1973—4, p.67

Burris, W.R., Boling, J.A., Bradley, N.W. and Ludwick, R.L. (1974). *J. Anim. Sci.*, 39, 818

Burroughs, W., Nelson, D.K. and Mertens, D.R. (1975). *J. Dairy Sci.*, 58, 611

Buttery, P.J. (1976). In *Principles of Cattle Production*, pp. 145—168. Ed. by H. Swan and W.H. Broster. London; Butterworths

Campling, R.C. (1964). *Proc. Nutr. Soc.*, 23, 80

Campling, R.C. and Murdoch, J.C. (1966). *J. Dairy Res.*, 33, 1

Clark, J.H. (1975). *J. Dairy Sci.*, 58, 1178

Clarke, E.M.W., Ellinger, G.M. and Phillipson, A.T. (1966). *Proc. R. Soc.* Series B 166, 63

Coelho da Silva, J.F., Seeley, R.C., Thomson, D.J., Beever, D.E. and Armstrong, D.G. (1972a). *Br. J. Nutr.*, 28, 43

Coelho da Silva, J.F., Seeley, R.C., Beever, D.E., Prescott, J.H.D. and Armstrong, D.G. (1972b). *Br. J. Nutr.*, **28**, 357

Cuthbert, N.H., Thickett, W.S. and Wilson, P.N. (1973). *Proc. Br. Soc. Anim. Prod.*, **2**, 70

Czerkawski, J.W. (1975). *Proc. Nutr. Soc.*, **34**, 62A

Drori, D. and Folman, Y. (1970). *Proc. 18th Int. Dairy Congr.*, p.84

Elliott, R.C. and Topps, J.H. (1963). *Br. J. Nutr.*, **17**, 549

Elliott, R.C., Reed, W.D.C. and Topps, J.H. (1964). *Br. J. Nutr.*, **18**, 519

Evans, E., Buchanan-Smith, J.G., MacLeod, G.K. and Stone, J.B. (1975). *J. Dairy Sci.*, **58**, 672

Frederiksen, L., Østergaard, P.S., Eskedal, H.W. and Steensberg, V. (1931). 136 *Beretn. Forsøgslab.*

Frens, A.M. and Dijkstra, N.D. (1959). *Versl. landbouwk. Onderz.*, Wageningen, 65.9

Gordon, F.J. and Forbes, T.J. (1973). Unpublished

Griffiths, T.W., Spillane, T.A. and Bath, I.H. (1973). *J. agric. Sci., Camb.*, **80**, 75

Hagemeister, H. and Kaufmann, W. (1974). *Kieler Milchw. Forschungsb.*, **26**, 199

Hagemeister, H. and Pfeffer, E. (1973). *Z. Tierphysiol. Tierernährg. Futtermittelk.*, **31**, 275

Harrison, D.G., Beever, D.E., Thomson, D.J. and Osbourn, D.F. (1975). *J. agric. Sci., Camb.*, **85**, 93

Hewitt, C. (1975). *Svensk Veterinärtidning*, **16**, 663

Hogan, J.P. (1973). *Aust. J. agric. Res.*, **24**, 587

Hogan, J.P. and Weston, R.H. (1970). In *Physiology of Digestion and Metabolism in the Ruminant*, pp.474–485. Ed. by A.T. Phillipson. Newcastle upon Tyne; Oriel Press

Hogan, J.P. and Weston, R.H. (1971). *Aust. J. agric. Res.*, **22**, 951

Huber, J.T. (1975). *J. Anim. Sci.*, **41**, 954

Hume, I.D. (1970a). *Aust. J. agric. Res.*, **21**, 297

Hume, I.D. (1970b). *Aust. J. agric. Res.*, **21**, 305

Hume, I.D. and Purser, D.B. (1975). *Aust. J. agric. Res.*, **26**, 199

Jackson, P. (1974). *Proc. 8th Nutr. Conf. Feed Mfrs.*, University of Nottingham, pp.123–142. Ed. by H. Swan and D. Lewis. London; Butterworths

Jakobsen, P.E. (1957). 299 *Beretn. Forsøgslab.*

Kaufmann, W. and Hagemeister, H. (1975). *Übers. Tierernährg.*, **3**, 33

Klooster, A. Th. van't and Rogers, P.A.M. (1969). *Meded. LandbHoogesch. Wageningen.*, **69–11**, 3

Leibholz, J. (1972). *Aust. J. agric. Res.*, **23**, 1073

Lenkeit, W. (1972). In *Festskrift Til Knut Breirem*, pp.123–140. Ed. by L.S. Spildo, T. Homb and H. Hvidsten. Gjovik; Mariendals Boktrykkeri As

Lindsay, J.R. and Hogan, J.P. (1972). *Aust. J. agric. Res.*, **23**, 321

MacRae, J.C. and Ulyatt, M.J. (1974). *J. agric. Sci., Camb.*, **82**, 309

MacRae, J.C., Ulyatt, M.J., Pearce, P.D. and Hendtlass, J. (1972). *Br. J. Nutr.*, **27**, 39

McAllan, A.B. and Smith, R.H. (1972). *Proc. Nutr. Soc.*, **31**, 24A

McAllan, A.B. and Smith, R.H. (1974). *Br. J. Nutr.*, **31**, 77

McGilliard, A.D. (1961). 'Re-entrant duodenal fistula techniques: application to the study of digestion and passage in the bovine alimentary tract.' Ph.D. thesis. Michigan State University

Mangan, J.L. (1972). *Br. J. Nutr.*, **27**, 261

Mason, V.C. (1969). *J. agric. Sci., Camb.*, **73**, 99

Mathison, G.W. and Milligan, L.P. (1971). *Br. J. Nutr.*, **25**, 351

Miller, E.L. (1973a). *Proc. Nutr. Soc.*, **32**, 79

Miller, E.L. (1973b). Quoted by Bines and Broster (1974)

Moe, P.W., Reid, J.T. and Tyrrell, H.F. (1965). *J. Dairy Sci.*, **48**, 1053

Murdoch, J.C. (1962). *J. Br. Grassld Soc.*, **17**, 268

National Research Council (1971). *Recommended Dietary Allowances.* (7th edn.). Washington, DC; Natl. Acad. Sci.

Nicholson, J.W.G. and Sutton, J.D. (1969). *Br. J. Nutr.*, **23**, 585

Nolan, J.V. and Leng, R.A. (1972). *Br. J. Nutr.*, **27**, 177

Oldham, J.D. (1973). 'Dietary carbohydrate and nitrogen interactions in the rumen.' PhD Thesis, University of Nottingham

Ørskov, E.R. (1976). In *Protein Metabolism and Nutrition*, pp.457–476. Ed. by D.J.A. Cole, K.N. Boorman, P.J. Buttery, D. Lewis, R.J. Neale and H. Swan. London; Butterworths

Ørskov, E.R. and Fraser, C. (1973). *Proc. Nutr. Soc.*, **32**, 68A

Ørskov, E.R., Fraser, C. and McDonald, I. (1971). *Br. J. Nutr.*, **25**, 243

Ørskov, E.R., Fraser, C. and McDonald, I. (1972). *Br. J. Nutr.*, **27**, 491

Ørskov, E.R., Fraser, C., McDonald, I. and Smart, R.I. (1974). *Br. J. Nutr.*, **31**, 89

Ørskov, E.R., McDonald, I., Fraser, C. and Corse, E.L. (1971). *J. agric. Sci., Camb.*, **77**, 351

Paquay, R., de Baere, R. and Lousse, A. (1972). *Br. J. Nutr.*, **27**, 27

Paquay, R., Godeau, J.M., de Baere, R. and Lousse, A. (1973). *J. Dairy Res.*, **40**, 329

Pfeffer, E., Kaufmann, W. and Dirksen, G. (1972). *Z. Tierphysiol. Tierarnähr. Futtermittelk.*, Suppl 1, 22

Pilgrim, A.F., Gray, F.V., Weller, R.A. and Belling, C.B. (1970). *Br. J. Nutr.*, **24**, 589

Purser, D.B. (1970). *Fedn. Proc. Fedn. Am. Socs. exp. Biol.*, **29**, 51

Purser, D.B. and Buechler, S.M. (1966). *J. Dairy Sci.*, **49**, 81

Reid, J.T., Moe, P.W. and Tyrrell, H.F. (1966). *J. Dairy Sci.*, **49**, 215

Robinson, J.J. and Forbes, F.J. (1970). *Anim. Prod.*, **12**, 601

Rook, J.A.F. (1961). *Dairy Sci. Abstr.*, **23**, 251 and 303

Rook, J.A.F. and Line, C. (1961). *Br. J. Nutr.*, **15**, 109

Rook, J.A.F. and Line, C. (1962). *Proc. XVI Int. Dairy Congr.*, **1:1**, 57

Rowland, S.J. (1946). *Dairy Ind.*, **11**, 656

Roy, J.H.B. (1975). Personal communication

Satter, L.D. and Roffler, R.E. (1975). *J. Dairy Sci.*, **58**, 1219

Satter, L.D. and Slyter, L.L. (1974). *Br. J. Nutr.*, **32**, 199

Sharma, H.R., Ingalls, J.R. and Parker, R.J. (1974). *Can. J. Anim. Sci.*, **54**, 305

Smith, R.H. and McAllan, A.B. (1974). *Br. J. Nutr.*, **31**, 27

Smith, T. (1976). Unpublished

Stobo, I.J.F. and Roy, J.H.B. (1973). *Br. J. Nutr.,* **30,** 113

Stouthamer, A.H. and Bettenhausen, C. (1973). *Biochimica et Biophysica Acta,* **301,** 53

Sutton, J.D. (1976). In *Principles of Cattle Production,* pp.121–143. Ed. by H. Swan and W.H. Broster. London; Butterworths

Sutton, J.D., Smith, R.H., McAllan, A.B., Storry, J.E. and Corse, D.A. (1975). *J. agric. Sci., Camb.,* **84,** 317

Tagari, H., Krol, O. and Bondi, A. (1965). *Nature,* **206,** 37

Tagari, H., Ben Gedalya, D., Shevach, Y. and Bondi, A. (1971). *J. agric. Sci., Camb.,* **77,** 413

Tamminga, S. (1975). *Neth. J. agric. Sci.,* **23,** 89

Thomas, J.W. (1971). *J. Dairy Sci.,* **54,** 1629

Van Es, A.J.H. (1972). In *Handbuch der Tierernährung,* Vol. 2, pp.2–54 Ed. by W. Lenkeit, K. Breirem and E. Crasemann. Hamburg; Paul Parey

Wagner, D.C. and Loosli, J.K. (1967). *Mem. Cornell Agric. Exp. Stn.* No. 400

Watson, M.J., Savage, G.P. and Armstrong, D.G. (1972). *Proc. Nutr. Soc.,* **31,** 98A

Weller, R.A. (1957). *Aust. J. biol. Sci.,* **10,** 384

Weller, R.A. and Pilgrim, A.F. (1974). *Br. J. Nutr.,* **32,** 341

Wiktorsson, H. (1971). *J. Dairy Sci.,* **54,** 374

Woodman, H.E. (1957). *Bull. Minist. Agric. Fish. Fd* (14th edn.). No. 48. London; HMSO

11

THE APPLICATION OF NON-PROTEIN NITROGEN, PROTECTED PROTEINS AND RUMEN FERMENTATION CONTROL IN UK FEEDING SYSTEMS

D.A. CORSE
BP Nutrition (UK) Ltd, Cheshire

In contrast to the uniformity of the poultry industry, and to some degree also the pig industry, systems of ruminant livestock production in the United Kingdom are markedly heterogenous. They are characterised by units of quite different sizes, controlled by managers of very different abilities and stocked by animals of mixed breeds and types. The production season is usually spent in changing environmental conditions because, for about half of the year pasture is grazed whilst for the remainder most animals are housed. As a consequence, the feeds available are highly diverse both in type and composition, and they are dispensed with a degree of accuracy ranging from computer controlled to *ad libitum* service.

These comments are not derisory. They are presented to illustrate the range of situations with which advisors are faced when decisions are required on the value of a particular dietary supplement or the efficacy of a feed additive. In some situations a response can only be gauged at best in vague, qualitative terms. On the other hand, there are particular production systems or, in some cases, individual highly sophisticated production units, where a quantitative response can be predicted and an economic return suggested with reasonable accuracy. The structure of the dairy and beef cattle industries was described in some detail by Craven and Kilkenny (1976).

Not only is the industry in which research findings are applied a variable one but the research data themselves are assimilated in conditions which cannot always be related to the industry. By way of example, very many of the reports published on feeding urea to dairy cows are based on trials in the USA in which a substantial part of the daily ration is maize silage. It is questionable whether these data can be used as a basis for advisory work in the United Kingdom where grass silage, which usually contains a higher level of a more soluble protein than maize silage, is used because in some cases, its contribution of non-protein nitrogen can be substantial. Indeed, much of the work in recent years on nitrogen metabolism in the rumen has been conducted using *in vitro* systems and the gap between such trials and practice in the field remains a wide one. Methane inhibitors have been tested in feed lot conditions in the United States and, in the absence of any report on trials in systems of intensive or semi-intensive beef production in the United Kingdom, a practical recommendation cannot be made. In this case, of course, no product is yet licensed for use, despite research activity spanning a decade.

It is against this background, on the one hand of a diverse industry and on the other of reports which are not always relevant to that industry, that an attempt is made in this chapter to assess the application of the principles presented in the earlier chapters. In several of these the information provided covers advances which have been made in recent years, and much of it is basic in nature. For this reason, and because of the long time gap which frequently occurs between the inception of an idea and its ultimate application, the practical acceptance of various aspects must be speculative rather than actual. Speculation, however, is not the theme of the present chapter. The purpose, rather, is twofold. First, in light of current research, there is a need to examine whether various recommendations, for example on the utilisation of non-protein nitrogen, require to be updated, and, secondly, to select those developments which appear to have immediate application in livestock production systems.

For convenience the chapter is divided into two sections. The first considers supplementary nutrients including urea, slow release non-protein nitrogen compounds, Starea, protected proteins, protected amino acids and protected fats. In the second section on the manipulation of rumen fermentation attention is given to additives including methane inhibitors, monensin and bicarbonate. Reference is made finally to manipulation of dietary ingredients.

Supplementary nutrients

NON-PROTEIN NITROGEN

Urea

Non-protein nitrogen, almost exclusively as urea, is currently supplied in a range of ruminant diets in the United Kingdom. It is included in some compound feedingstuffs for dairy and beef cattle, it is added on the farm by some home-mixing farmers and mobile mixers, and it is supplied in liquid feeds and feed blocks.

Despite the voluminous scientific literature on non-protein nitrogen supplementation, recommendations in practice are relatively unrefined and are made on a generalised basis. For example, part of the advice from the East of Scotland College of Agriculture is as follows: 'Suckler cows, store cattle over 4 months, finishing cattle (if necessary), barley beef over 4 months, finishing lambs — maximum urea in concentrate 2½ per cent. Dairy cows giving under 4 gallons day^{-1} — maximum urea in concentrate 1¼ per cent. Dairy cows giving over 4 gallons day^{-1} — preferably none (but if necessary ¾ per cent).'

Differing views are held by most advisors (Andrews, 1974) as to whether urea should be fed when grass silage is the main roughage. Attention is usually given to ensuring an adequate supply of vitamins, minerals (including sulphur) and trace elements, and the necessity of providing a readily available source of energy from carbohydrates is not neglected. Whenever possible, adaptation to feeds containing non-protein nitrogen is practised by gradual addition of the feed or supplement to the ration although, especially in parlour-fed dairy herds, this is not always possible. The 'little and often' principle of feeding is frequently preached but, again, with twice-a-day feeding in the parlour, is then ignored.

With a few exceptions little attention is paid to individual systems of production in which urea is fed. For example, despite evidence on the undesirability of feeding urea to cows in early lactation (Satter and Roffler, 1975), the inflexibility of parlour feeding does not often allow feeds with and without added urea to be fed to different groups of animals in a herd. Also, liquid feeds are offered to herds whether they be fed hay twice daily or grass silage *ad libitum*. Yet, it is possible in the latter situation for more NPN to be provided from the roughage than from the supplement.

The situation in practice then is that as many as possible of the rules for efficient utilisation of urea are adhered to. There are many systems in the United Kingdom, for feeding dairy cows in particular, which do not allow all of the basic requirements to be met. This, together with the sometimes biased, adverse publicity, is a reason why the usage of non-protein nitrogen has never reached the anticipated level in this country or in Europe generally. Rutherford (1974) suggested that in Europe the usage of urea was about one-tenth of the potential that could be used. Moreover, Jackson (1974) stated that in Europe, with an equivalent cattle population, the use of urea was a fraction of that used in the USA but some 8 million tons of oil seed protein were imported, equivalent to 1.2 million tons of urea.

However, estimates like the foregoing, calculated from statistics of cattle populations and tonnages of manufactured feeds, are not necessarily valid. They ignore the differences in production systems in the various countries. Thus, whilst undoubtedly there is a potential for greater use of urea in the United Kingdom, it is unlikely that it will replace the proportion of vegetable proteins that it has in the United States.

In the United States, substantial numbers of beef cattle are finished in enormous feed lots on predominantly cereal-based diets. In the dairy industry many cows are fed maize silage, virtually *ad libitum*, and often with close admixture of the forage and concentrate components. These production systems are fundamentally better suited to supplementation with urea. Even so, there is now a changing climate of opinion on the use of non-protein nitrogen indicating that excessive supplementation is probably being practised with the consequence that non-protein nitrogen is being used wastefully. Satter and Roffler (1975) stated that the demand for supplements where 15 to 40 per cent of the nitrogen was of a non-protein nitrogen origin should diminish greatly. A report commissioned by the National Research Council (1976) concluded that it was apparent that the old guidelines — urea up to (*a*) one-third of the dietary nitrogen, (*b*) one per cent of the total diet dry matter and (*c*) three per cent of the grain mixture — needed major modifications.

Conclusions such as those above are the result of basic research which in recent years has concentrated on quantitative aspects of digestion in ruminants, and has added greatly to an understanding both of the extent to which different dietary proteins are degraded in the rumen and also the rate of microbial protein synthesis. Nonetheless, information is still lacking on the protein requirements of ruminants especially for the high yielding dairy cow in early lactation. An integrated approach to this problem, by examining the nitrogen needs not only of the host animal but also of the rumen micro-organisms, together with their contribution to the protein supply to the host, has already been attempted and should prove fruitful. The metabolizable protein system, first suggested by Burroughs *et al.* (1972), and simplified by Satter and Roffler (1975), is encouraging.

A similar approach was proposed by Broster and Oldham (1976). This should permit more accurate recommendations, not only on non-protein nitrogen supplementation, but also on the extent to which protein protection may be beneficial in different production situations and various feeding systems. Satter and Roffler (1975), in particular, have outlined a scheme whereby it should be possible to put together feeding systems for ruminants to meet the requirements for metabolizable energy and metabolizable protein and to fit non-protein nitrogen supplementation into the system. Such a scheme would point to the use of high protein rations based on vegetable proteins for cows in early lactation, and lower protein rations containing a high proportion of non-protein nitrogen for cows beyond peak.

At this stage, however, such information is not ready for application in the immediate future. Indeed, any short-term change in attitude to non-protein nitrogen usage in the United Kingdom will be influenced more by economic considerations than by application of basic knowledge in current feeding programmes. What does behove advisors is to use the information that is becoming available, firstly, to update and improve recommendations on the use of non-protein nitrogen and, secondly, to be aware of changes that are occurring in feeding systems and to attempt to fit non-protein nitrogen more effectively into them.

With regard to updating recommendations, generalisations must no longer be used but rather full attention paid to individual production systems in combination with forage analyses. Is it justifiable to feed urea in a compound, or to use a liquid-urea feed, without first knowing whether the crude protein in silage is 10 per cent or 18 per cent of the dry matter, or whether the volatile nitrogen in the silage represents 5 per cent or 30 per cent of the total nitrogen?

A recent report in the farming press (*Livestock Farming*, 1976) indicated that urea can be used in dairy feeds at up to 2.9 per cent inclusion without harmful effects. However, the compound feed was fed four times daily and the basic ration was composed of straw and lucerne cobs. Even then, milk production was lower in the non-protein nitrogen supplemented group compared with control cows fed vegetable proteins. Not all farmers feed compounds four times daily and straw and lucerne cobs form the basic roughage on a minority of farms. In line with the conclusion of the National Research Council (1976), generalised recommendations cannot be made; more attention must be given to the constituents of the ration and to the particular feeding system employed.

With regard to changes that are occurring in feeding systems, three developments are relevant. These are the increasing move toward the grouping of cows in a herd, the tendency to feed cows outside the parlour, either by electronically controlled feed dispensers or by more frequent feeding in troughs, and the development of systems of complete feeding. The division of herds into lactation groups and feeding outside the parlour raises the possibility of providing different compound feeds to match more closely the nutritional requirements of the cow. Evidence that the protein requirements of the high yielding cow in early lactation are currently underestimated is controversial and inconclusive. What is certain is that many current feeding systems are a compromise; too little protein may be provided in early lactation and too much protein is frequently provided at other stages.

Possibilities of feeding concentrates of varying protein content have been stifled by the inflexibility of parlour feeding. Group feeding outside the parlour removes this problem and a case can be made for providing two compounds, along the lines suggested by Satter and Roffler (1975), and alluded to earlier in this chapter. A high protein concentrate in early lactation would contain no non-protein nitrogen. Urea could be added in the final two-thirds of lactation, provided that attention was paid to the type and chemical composition of the roughage. Practical difficulties, however, still exist not the least of which is the transport cost incurred in delivering different feeds especially with the increase in bulk deliveries of compounded feedingstuffs.

The development of complete feeding systems (Owen, Miller and Bridge, 1971; Owen, 1975) in the United Kingdom allows greater flexibility to be built into feeding programmes. Since the principal roughage likely to be used is silage or haylage, and because the success of the system is highly dependent upon the quality of the roughage, it is imperative that the chemical composition of this component, as well as that of the others in the ration, is known. Potentially, the use of non-protein nitrogen, without prior knowledge of the analysis of the ration, could be more harmful to milk production than in conventional feeding systems. On the other hand, complete feeding systems allow the principles suggested in the metabolizable protein approach of Satter and Roffler (1975) to be applied with the greatest accuracy and to define situations where urea can be included beneficially and economically.

Slow release non-protein nitrogen compounds

The use of slow release non-protein nitrogen compounds in feeds has been discussed by various authors (Jackson, 1974; Fonnesbeck, Kearl and Harris, 1975; National Research Council, 1976). Products which have been considered include biuret, triuret, cyanuric acid and isobutylidene-diurea. The slow release properties have been confirmed in numerous studies and, although this is an advantage in terms of providing a pattern of ammonia release more consistent with rates of fermentation of soluble carbohydrates, they suffer a disadvantage in that rumen micro-organisms require a longer period of adaptation.

In agreement with most authors, and particularly in light of the evidence of Satter and Roffler (see Chapter 3, p. 28) on optimal concentrations of ammonia for maximal microbial protein synthesis in *in vitro* conditions, it is concluded that there are few economic benefits in the use of slow release NPN compounds. Safety aspects are important in situations where control over food intake is not readily possible, for example in the provision of feed blocks containing urea. The scope in conventional dairy and beef production systems is more limited.

Starea

The use of Starea, a product manufactured by combining cereal grains and urea in a cooker-extruder, was reviewed by Bartley and Deyoe (1975), who suggested that maximal amounts of microbial protein are synthesized as a result of energy and ammonia being released at similar rates in the rumen. Annison (1974) stated that the product had excellent *in vitro* characteristics but questioned whether these were reflected in improved production in practical feeding systems. The review by Bartley and Deyoe (1975) confirmed that, in feeding trials, performance of beef cattle and dairy cows fed Starea was almost always superior to that when equivalent amounts of nitrogen were provided as urea. Performance was marginally lower in some trials in which Starea was compared to conventional vegetable proteins such as soya bean meal and cotton seed cake.

Other advantages claimed for Starea over urea is that danger of toxicity is markedly reduced, feeds containing Starea are more palatable, a shorter period of adaptation is required and pelleting or cubing is improved. These benefits result principally from the close dispersion of urea in the gelatinised cereal during the extrusion process.

Protected proteins and protected amino acids

Earlier comments on the lack of sufficient information with regard to protein requirements of ruminants, and especially requirements for individual amino acids, are also pertinent to this section. Limiting amino acids for different classes of ruminant stock are not clearly defined and, indeed, it has been suggested that supplementation of ruminant diets with free amino acids cannot be justified (Swan, 1971). Whilst there is good evidence that milk production can be stimulated markedly when proteins or amino acids are infused into the abomasum of dairy cows (Clark, 1975), data to suggest that rumen bypass by protected proteins is beneficial in practice are very limited. An exception is in the area of wool growth in sheep but, although this may have some relevance in UK feeding systems, the findings are more applicable to intensive wool production in Australia where the observations were made initially.

The concept of protected proteins in the United Kingdom is likely to progress on two fronts: firstly, the protection of protein in roughages, mainly by formalin and organic acids in silage, and to a lesser degree by heat treatment of artificially dried roughage; and secondly, in the protection of vegetable proteins, more probably by chemical means than by heat. At this stage there are too many unknowns to allow early application in practice. Advantages of improved productive performance and economic return remain to be proven under field conditions and problems of over-protection are a distinct possibility.

When this technology is developed and, at the same time knowledge of amino acid requirements is advanced, attention could turn not only to protected amino acids but also to rumen bypass of individual amino acids. It is quite conceivable that a degree of protection of proteins in roughages could be aimed at, such that the amino acid requirements of ruminants could then be met from concentrates of a lower protein content than at present but containing protected amino acids. American trials with methionine hydroxy analogue, for example, have shown that the crude protein content of the ration can be reduced from 15.5 to 12.5 per cent without any effect on milk production (Chandler *et al.,* 1976). There are no reports in the literature of the use of methionine hydroxy analogue in UK feeding situations but examination is warranted in light of the potential savings of imported proteins.

Protected fats

Although developed originally to manipulate the fatty acid content of milk and depot fats for human health reasons (Scott *et al.*, 1970), the main advantage of lipid protection lies in the possibility of providing high energy foods to the dairy cow. Whilst preliminary information is encouraging, in that high levels of fat can be ingested (Bines, Storry and Brumby, 1975), data from field trials are still lacking. American experiments suggest that, in *ad libitum* feeding regimes, whilst the intake of fat was increased by protection, the amount of total energy consumed was no greater than for non-supplemented controls (Smith, 1976). Nonetheless, in agreement with findings of Bines and his colleagues, Smith demonstrated that milk fat production was enhanced when protected lipids were fed.

Manipulation of rumen fermentation

ADDITIVES

Monensin

A number of trials has been reported from the United States indicating that monensin, the coccidiostat derived from *Streptomyces cinnamonensis*, when added to rumen contents *in vitro* or *in vivo*, enhances the molar proportion of propionic acid and decreases that of acetic acid. In several feeding trials with beef cattle the intake of food was somewhat reduced when rations containing the additive were compared with unsupplemented controls, but, because live weight gain was unchanged, efficiency of utilisation of the ration was improved. The product has proved commercially viable in US feed lots and it is estimated that about 80 per cent of animals finished in these conditions are fed monensin.

Trial data are now available from a range of UK beef production systems. *Table 11.1* describes the types of rations and levels of monensin that have been examined. In *Table 11.2*, preliminary results demonstrating effects on daily gain daily feed intake and feed conversion ratio are presented.

In general, the extent of depression in feed intake was not so great as in the American trials. With the exception of Trial 4, there was a tendency for average daily live weight gain to improve when monensin was fed and the response was statistically significant in Trial 5. The net effect was an improved feed conversion ratio, in agreement with earlier data. The effect was greatest in Trial 5, and was statistically significant, under conditions of roughage feeding where the molar proportion of acetic acid in the rumen would be expected to be greater from the control ration. Pooled analysis of the data showed statistically significant improvements in average daily live weight gain and food conversion efficiency of 6.7 per cent and 9.4 per cent respectively at 30 ppm. There was an overall reduction in feed intake of 2.7 per cent, but this was not statistically significant.

Table 11.1 TYPES OF RATIONS AND LEVELS OF ADDITION OF MONENSIN IN BEEF RATIONS [1]

Trial no.	Initial weight (kg)	Final weight (kg)	Average trial duration (days)	Treatments monensin[2] (ppm/kg)	Rationing system	Ration description
1	288	406	93	0, 10, 30	*Ad libitum*	Pelleted concentrate 78% barley
2	169	403	188	0, 10, 30	*Ad libitum*	Pelleted concentrate 82.5/87.5% barley
3	285	403	93	0, 30	*Ad libitum*	Pelleted concentrate 78% barley
4	346	467	112	0, 30	*Ad libitum*	Meal 67% barley, 18.5% ground straw
5	281	385	123	0, 125, 250	Restricted	Hay/concentrate/turnips

[1] These unpublished data presented by kind permission of Elanco Products Limited, Wimbledon

[2] Trials 1–4, ppm monensin/kg food; Trial 5, mg monensin per animal

Table 11.2 EFFECTS OF MONENSIN IN BEEF RATIONS ON ANIMAL PERFORMANCE[1]

Trial no.	Average daily live weight gain (kg head^{-1} day^{-1}) Monensin dose (ppm)			Average daily feed intake (kg DM head^{1} day^{1}) Monensin dose (ppm)			Average feed conversion ratio (kg DMI/kg grain) Monensin dose (ppm)		
	0	10	30	0	10	30	0	10	30
1	1.127[a]	1.199[a]	1.249[a]	7.68[a]	7.05[a]	7.49[a]	6.85[a]	5.91[a]	6.00[a]
2	1.202[a]	1.274[a]	1.252[a]	6.42[a]	6.52[a]	6.19[a]	5.35[a]	5.12[ab]	4.94[b]
3	1.243[a]	–	1.340[a]	6.69[a]	–	6.57[a]	5.40[a]	–	4.91[a]
4	1.233[2]	–	1.170	9.18	–	8.13	7.44	–	6.95
5	0.775[a]	–	0.914[b,3]	6.16[a]	–	6.24[b]	7.99[a]	–	6.87[b]

[1] These unpublished data presented by kind permission of Elanco Products Limited, Wimbledon

[2] Statistical analysis – only 1 replicate per treatment

[3] 125/168/250 mg dose equivalent to an average of 22 ppm monensin in the ration

[a,b] Within each parameter and trial, means with same superscript do not differ significantly ($P > 0.05$)

Methane inhibitors

Since the early observation of Czerkawski, Blaxter and Wainman (1966) that the addition of saturated and unsaturated fatty acids to the diet of sheep reduces the amount of methane produced in the rumen, various components have been examined and many shown to have the same effect. The change is generally accompanied by a reduction in the proportion of acetic acid and an increase in that of propionic acid.

Despite a decade of research, however, only one feeding trial has been reported in the UK and that with lactating goats (Clapperton and Basmaeil, 1977). In the United States, Trei *et al.* (1971) showed that when trichloroacetamide was added to the diet of lambs, live weight gain was unchanged but food intake was slightly reduced, thus resulting in an improvement in food conversion efficiency. Trei, Scott and Parish (1972) showed that the rate of increase in live weight in lambs was significantly increased when $1-2$ g day^{-1} of a hemiacetal compound of starch and chloral hydrate was incorporated into the food. In each of these trials there was a suggestion that the effect of the additive was greatest at the start of the experiment and gradually diminished with time.

It is clear at this stage that sufficient data are not available to permit a decision to be made on possible benefits from using methane inhibitors in UK feeding systems. A fall-off in performance, possibly due to an adaptation of rumen micro-organisms, is not desirable and remains to be confirmed in feeding trials. An increase in the proportion of ruminal propionic acid, depending on the degree of change from a predominantly acetate type fermentation, could cause an undesirable depression in the milk fat content of dairy animals. In the Hannah trial with lactating goats (Clapperton and Basmaeil, 1977) milk fat content was decreased and milk protein increased, with no effect on milk yield. Work is also required to examine the carry-over of residues into milk and meat. In the absence of further information, it is concluded that supplementation of dairy rations with methane inhibitors could result in a depression in milk fat content. This, together with the likely depression in food intake, especially in early lactation, is most undesirable. The potential use of methane inhibitors, therefore, would appear to be in beef cattle feeding systems. Even then, possible diminution in performance with time remains to be examined before the use of these products can be recommended.

Buffers

Intensification of ruminant production systems has been accompanied by an increase in concentrate feeding and/or by the feeding of more finely ground, pelleted feeds. The physiological effects, both in the rumen and in the animal, have been widely examined and have stimulated a considerable research interest into the use of buffers to counteract certain of the less desirable effects such as acidosis and depressed milk fat content.

The use of buffers in ruminant feeds was reviewed recently (Diven, 1975a, b), although many of the data pertain to conditions in the United States where relatively higher levels of grain feeding are practised rather than to the United Kingdom feeding systems. Buffers can depress food consumption by dairy and beef cattle but the effect is dependent upon the ingredients of the ration, their physical form and the feeding regime. For reasons that are not understood, buffers frequently depress the intake of lucerne-based feeds, especially when small amounts of lucerne hay are fed with *ad libitum* concentrates. On the other hand, the intake of silage-based rations is often increased when buffers are included, as also is that of pelleted feeds.

In many, although not all, studies, depressions in milk fat content, resulting from the feeding of high levels of concentrates, were overcome or partially rectified when buffers were included in the concentrates. No effect was noted on milk protein content, or that of solids not-fat, and milk yield was unaffected. In most cases the change in milk composition was reflected also in an alteration of rumen fermentation pattern. A decrease in the proportion of propionic acid in the rumen was accompanied by a corresponding increase in that of acetic acid and occasionally also that of butyric acid.

Suggestions that buffers can cause kidney lesions in steers (Nicholson and Cunningham, 1961) have not been confirmed in many studies and, in subsequent trials by the same authors, kidney lesions occurred in control as well as buffer-fed groups. Possible links with urinary calculi are equally inconclusive as are suggestions that buffers reduce the incidence of rumen parakeratosis in high-grain fed animals.

From a review of the literature, together with the present author's experience in field conditions, it is concluded that, in certain circumstances, buffers can be included beneficially in UK feeding systems. The tendency towards more finely chopped grass before ensiling appears to lead to digestive upsets and food refusal, although this may be associated with pH of the silage, as well as to depressions in milk fat production. In these circumstances it is recommended that adverse effects can be overcome by the provision of between 250 and 350 g day^{-1} of sodium bicarbonate buffer to adult lactating cows. Benefits in beef production systems are less well defined in the UK situation.

DIETARY MANIPULATION

During the past 35 years many investigations have been carried out on factors affecting rumen fermentation. Particular attention has been paid to effects on proportions of volatile fatty acids produced in the rumen and to effects on animal production such as milk yield and composition, and rate of live weight gain. Many review articles have been prepared on aspects of feed processing, such as grinding, of ration composition including roughage to concentrate ratios, and on level and frequency of feeding. A summary, in terms of broad categories of types of fermentation pattern resulting from various dietary manipulations, has been presented in Chapter 9.

Superimposed upon the basic factor, namely influence of diet, Sutton (1976) proposed three other factors, each operating at a different level, which modify the response to the feed. As a primary factor he considered the rumen microbial population but concluded that, because of the complexity of interactions among different bacteria, it is not possible to establish clearly a direct relationship between species of micro-organisms and pattern of production of volatile fatty acids. An exception cited was the work of Whitelaw *et al.* (1972) in which, by restricting the level of feeding of barley to defaunated steers and introducing protozoa into the rumen, the pattern of fermentation was switched from high-propionate to high-butyrate production. Such manipulation, however, appears to have little significance in practical systems of production.

The secondary factor proposed was that of rumen environment. This he described as the result of the interaction between the basal factor (the diet) and the primary factor (the microbial population). He cited parameters, including osmotic pressure, pH and turnover rate, which influence fermentation. Again, although factors such as pH have been related to volatile fatty acid (VFA) proportions, the tenuous nature of the association and the complexity of interaction leaves little scope to aim at a particular environmental factor, or combination of factors, that will beneficially affect performance. Rather, the aim should be to prevent detrimental changes in the rumen environment such as a sudden drop in pH resulting from the rapid fermentation of soluble carbohydrates and culminating in off-feed acidosis.

The tertiary factors considered by Sutton (1976), i.e. feed additives which are used to modify normal interactions within the rumen, were discussed earlier in this chapter. Two types of additive, monensin and methane inhibitors, were mentioned, both of which alter the basal type of fermentation pattern and lead to improved animal performance. Data from trials in which a range of basal diets were fed indicated that additives can be effective in different dietary situations although, from basic principles, a greater response should be anticipated when predominantly high roughage rations are fed. The second group of products, namely buffers, indicated that these can sometimes be used in practical feeding systems to alleviate the problems resulting from undesirable patterns of fermentation, produced themselves from particular diets such as high proportions of concentrates.

There does not seem to be much scope for manipulation of the composition of the ration under current or even future feeding systems to produce a well-defined, optimal pattern of fermentation which will substantially benefit animal performance, whether such manipulation be by alteration of the proportion of ingredients or their composition, by processing dietary ingredients or by including additives. An exception is the high-propionate fermentation in high-grain, barley beef systems and even then the production benefit is the result, only in part, of the more efficient utilisation of propionic acid. The whole area of cereal feeding was extensively reviewed by Armstrong (1972), and although he cited examples of improved animal performance through various methods of processing grain, a common finding was that animals receiving high proportions of cereal show a great variability in the molar proportions of individual volatile fatty acids within treatment. When lower proportions of grain were fed, different processes of treatment of the grain prior to feeding were able to induce considerable differences in VFA proportions in rumen liquor. Nonetheless, there is no good evidence that a particular pattern of fermentation can be established which could be said to produce an optimal return in terms of animal performance.

One positive example which should be cited is the effect of high levels of flaked maize in narrowing the acetate/propionate ratio in the rumen and thereby reducing the synthesis of milk fat. This is not a desirable effect, at least not under current systems of payment. In all cases it appears that a knowledge of rumen physiology, as affected by manipulation of dietary composition, can be used more beneficially to prevent undesirable traits rather than to suggest particular types of fermentation which might optmise productive performance. Manipulation of basal fermentation by additives appears to have more potential than control of particular types of fermentation by diet composition. In practice it appears that greater advances could be made by improving feeding systems, for example in replacing the inflexibility of twice-a-day parlour feeding of dairy cows, than in attempting to establish unique patterns of fermentation. It must be emphasised that this refers only to dietary composition as it affects type of fermentation. Manipulation by protection of individual nutrients and rumen bypass was considered earlier and different conclusions were reached.

Summary

Although during the last three or four decades a wealth of knowledge has accumulated on ruminant nutrition and rumen physiology, much of the information, particularly in the latter area, has been qualitative rather than quantitative.

This is especially true in the field of protein digestion, microbial protein synthesis and the extent to which dietary protein escapes degradation in the rumen. However, it is true also for the extent of energy absorbed from the rumen and the degree to which this contributes to overall energy·metabolism in the animal.

The development of new research techniques, including the use of surgically modified animals and *in vitro* techniques, has done much to rectify these gaps in an understanding of ruminant nutrition. However, it must be stated that, at present, many of the developments in basic research have not yet been applied in field trials in order to evaluate the practical potential of the work.

It has not been the intention of this chapter to adopt a negative attitude to the more basic work. At the same time it would be imprudent to make sweeping recommendations on their practical application in UK feeding situations. Such principles must be tested in practical field trials before their potential application can be adequately assessed. Further, the application of any principle must be considered against the highly diverse nature of ruminant livestock systems in the UK, and in many situations it may be essential to look more carefully at individual production systems or even individual production units.

References

Andrews, R.J. (1974). In *University of Nottingham Nutrition Conference for Feed Manufacturers — 8*, p. 146. Eds. H. Swan and D. Lewis. London; Butterworths

Annison, E.F. (1974). In *University of Nottingham Nutrition Conference for Feed Manufacturers — 8*, p. 157. Eds. H. Swan and D. Lewis. London; Butterworths

Armstrong, D.G. (1972). In *Cereal Processing and Digestion*, p. 9. US Feed Grains Council

Bartley, E.E. and Deyoe, C.W. (1975). *Feedstuffs*, 47, 42

Bines, J.A., Storry, J.E. and Brumby, P.E. (1975). *Proc. Nutr. Soc.*, 34, 108A

Broster, W. and Oldham, J. (1976). In *Nutrition and the Climatic Environment*, p. 123. Eds. W. Haresign, H. Swan and D. Lewis. London; Butterworths

Burroughs, W., Jacobson, N.L., Trenkle, A.H. and Vetter, R.L. (1972). Iowa State Univ., Coop. Ext. Serv. Leaflet, EC–7771. Ames

Chandler, P.T., Brown, C.A., Johnston, R.P., MacLeod, G.K., McCarthy, R.D., Moss, B.R., Rakes, A.H. and Satter, L.D. (1976). *J. Dairy Sci.*, 59, 1897

Clapperton, J.L. and Basmaeil, S. (1977). In *Energy Metabolism of Farm Animals*, p. 73. Ed. M. Vermorel. Clermont-Ferrand; de Bussac

Clark, J.H. (1975). *J. Dairy Sci.*, 58, 1178

Craven, J.A. and Kilkenny, J.B. (1976). In *Principles of Cattle Production*, p. 1. Eds. H. Swan and W. Broster. London; Butterworths

Czerkawski, J.W., Blaxter, K.L. and Wainman, F.W. (1966). *Br. J. Nutr.*, 20, 485

Diven, R.H. (1975a). *Feedstuffs*, 47, 31, 21

Diven, R.H. (1975b). *Feedstuffs*, 47, 32, 23

East of Scotland College of Agriculture (1973). Advisory Leaflet No. 74

Fonnesbeck, P.V., Kearl, L.C. and Harris, L.E. (1975). *J. Anim. Sci.*, 40, 1150

Jackson, P. (1974). In *University of Nottingham Nutrition Conference for Feed Manufacturers — 8*, p. 142. Eds. H. Swan and D. Lewis. London; Butterworths

Livestock Farming (1976). 13, No. 9, 42

National Research Council (1976). *Urea and Other Non-protein Nitrogen Compounds in Animal Nutrition.* Washington, D.C.; National Academy of Sciences

Nicholson, J.W.G. and Cunningham, H.M. (1961). *Can. J. Anim. Sci.,* **41**, 134

Owen, J.B. (1975). In *Simplified Feeding for Milk and Beef*, p. 9. US Feed Grains Council

Owen, J.B., Miller, E.L. and Bridge, P.S. (1971). *J. Agric. Sci., Camb.,* **77**, 195

Rutherford, B. McC. (1974). In *University of Nottingham Nutrition Conference for Feed Manufacturers – 8*, p. 21. Eds. H. Swan and D. Lewis. London; Butterworths

Satter, L.D. and Roffler, R.E. (1975). *J. Dairy Sci.,* **58**, 1219

Scott, T.W., Cook, L.J., Ferguson, K.A., McDonald, I.W., Buchanan, R.A. and Loftus-Hills, G. (1970). *Aust. J. Sci.,* **32**, 291

Smith, N.E. (1976). Programme 71st Annual Meeting, American Dairy Sci. Assoc., Abstr. 24, p. 68

Swan, H. (1971). In *University of Nottingham Nutrition Conference for Feed Manufacturers – 5*, p. 126. Eds. H. Swan and D. Lewis. Edinburgh; Churchill Livingstone

Sutton, J.D. (1976). In *Principles of Cattle Nutrition*, p. 121. Eds. H. Swan and W. Broster. London; Butterworths

Trei, J.E., Parish, R.C., Singh, Y.K. and Scott, G.C. (1971). *J. Dairy Sci.,* **54**, 536

Trei, J.E., Scott, G.C. and Parish, R.G. (1972). *J. Anim. Sci.,* **34**, 510

Whitelaw, F.G., Eadie, J.M., Mann, S.O. and Reid, R.S. (1972). *Br. J. Nutr.,* **27**, 425

12

THE CONTRIBUTION OF UNDEGRADED PROTEIN TO THE PROTEIN REQUIREMENTS OF DAIRY COWS

P.N. WILSON
BOCM SILCOCK, Basing View, Basingstoke, Hampshire
P.J. STRACHAN
Unilever Laboratory, Colworth House, Sharnbrook, Bedfordshire

Introduction

THE SHORTCOMINGS OF EXISTING SCHEMES FOR CALCULATING PROTEIN REQUIREMENTS

The expression of protein requirements for ruminants, and the nutrient content of feedstuffs to satisfy these requirements, in terms of crude protein (CP) or digestible crude protein (DCP), have been used in the field for many years. However, they have been regarded as inadequate and unsatisfactory for a long time. Neither of these parameters recognize the close relationship between nitrogen requirements and either total energy intake or energy density of the ration fed. Even more pertinent, neither system gives an adequate description of the identity of dietary nitrogen, nor the role of rumen microbes in its metabolism to amino acids, ammonia or other non-amino acid nitrogen.

In an attempt to improve on the CP and DCP systems, an alternative approach based on available protein (AP) was proposed (Agricultural Research Council, 1965). The AP system still did not consider protein:energy inter-relationships, nor the large contribution made by undigested microbial protein to faecal nitrogen loss.

The AP system can be further criticized for the use of biological values to describe dietary proteins which are not relevant to the ruminant. This is because the composition, and hence biological value, of the ingested protein is changed by rumen degradation and subsequent incorporation into microbial protein. For these reasons, the AP system was not adopted by the animal feed trade, nor by the advisory services serving dairy farmers.

PROPOSALS FOR A NEW SYSTEM

In order to overcome these severe limitations, a fundamental scheme for evaluating ruminant feeds as sources of nitrogen and amino acids was proposed by Miller (1973). This skeleton scheme identified the importance of considering metabolic implications, including the fermentable energy contribution in the rumen and the proportions of dietary nitrogen, either degraded or escaping

228

degradation in the rumen. This approach identified areas in which research effort was required in order to introduce a new system, and was elaborated by Broster and Oldham (1977) who made suggestions for the practical feeding management of the UK dairy herd. This second publication emphasized the lack of knowledge about the protein degradability characteristics of ruminant feeds.

These authors classified a small number of raw materials and three types of forage into groups, to describe qualitatively the proportion of dietary protein degraded in the rumen. However, they stressed that the experimental basis for the classification was unsatisfactory and they called for a greater definition of the protein characteristics of ruminant feeds.

The metabolic approach was also adopted by the Agricultural Research Council (ARC) protein subgroup of the working party on nutrient requirements of ruminants, whose proposals for a new method for calculation of the nitrogen requirement for ruminants were first published in 1977 (Roy *et al.*, 1977). The proposals are described in full in the second edition of *The Nutrient Requirement of Farm Livestock* (Agricultural Research Council, 1980). However, the ARC generously gave permission for the chapter dealing with protein to be made available to the British Veterinary Association, the Agricultural Development and Advisory Service and the United Kingdom Agricultural Supply Trade Association before the publication of this new edition.

The new ARC system recognizes that dietary crude protein must be thought of in terms of rumen-degradable protein (RDP) and undegradable protein (UDP), and estimates the requirements for these at the specific energy input and density in the diet necessary for a particular level of production. The estimates are based on an approximation of the amino acid nitrogen absorbed from the small intestine (supplied in the form of undegraded dietary protein, microbial protein or endogenous secretion) and its efficiency of utilization for maintenance and production. The efficiency of each metabolic nitrogen conversion is obtained from mean values derived from published metabolic studies.

ADOPTION OF THE NEW APPROACH

BOCM SILCOCK recognized that the new system, as described by Roy *et al.* (1977), was a marked improvement on existing methods used in practice, in spite of the fact that it was based on a static model developed from average values, taken from data which were often variable and sometimes limited in number.

Bearing in mind the nutritional benefits which resulted from adoption of the ME system 'on farm', and the fact that DCP had been shown by BOCM SILCOCK (Cuthbert, Thickett and Wilson, 1973), among others (*see* Broster and Oldham, 1977), to describe inadequately the requirement of the dairy cow, the decision was taken to implement the new system as soon as possible. This decision was taken on the basis of a cost:benefit study. The cost was that the system would require a large expenditure by Unilever Research Laboratories on estimates of basic rumen degradability values. There was also the risk of introducing a model in which certain of the assumptions made were still the subject of debate (e.g. the yield of microbial protein). The perceived benefit was that the farmer would be able to allocate his total protein feeds more cost-effectively than previously, and could save as much as 2 per cent crude protein on his purchases of branded dairy compound feed. This would decrease the cost of bought-in feed to a large number of dairy farmers, because the level of protein is a major price-determining factor.

The results of critical feeding experiments showing the production benefits of the proposed new system to the UK dairy farmer are not yet available. Such experiments need to be carried out on as wide a basis as possible, using different breeds of cows and different systems of feeding, including 'traditional' feeding to yield, complete feeding and flat-rate feeding systems. However, so far, research and development facilities have been preoccupied with obtaining the data on which to base the system, rather than providing comprehensive evidence that the system works in practice. A great deal of empirical evidence is available, both in the UK and the USA, (e.g. Roffler and Satter, 1975; Miller *et al.*, 1977) but there is a need to carry out objective studies on this aspect of the work in the near future.

The implementation of the total system 'on farm' requires the ability to formulate compound diets on a degradability basis, and a method for balancing the energy and degradable and undegradable protein, supplied by on-farm feeds, with the energy and protein provided by compound feeds, in order to meet the total calculated requirements.

Table 12.1 AN ILLUSTRATION OF THE EFFECT OF A CHANGE IN DEGRAD-ABILITY OF THE CONCENTRATE FEED ON RDP AND UDP SUPPLY IN THE DAIRY COW. (600 kg COW GIVING 30 kg MILK/DAY OF 3.5 PER CENT BUTTERFAT AND 8.7 PER CENT SOLIDS NOT FAT, WITH NO INCREASE OR DECREASE IN LIVEWEIGHT)

	RDP (g/d)	*UDP* (g/d)
Requirements	1644	680
Supplied: (kg/d as fed)		
Ration 1　　37 silage	1114	230
2 barley	158	24
5 ensiled brewers grains	158	68
6.5 16% CP compound, 65% degradability	665	358
Total	2095	680
Surplus/deficit	+451	–
Ration 2　　37 silage	1114	230
2 barley	158	24
5 ensiled brewers grains	158	68
6.5 16% CP compound, 75% degradability	767	256
Total	2197	578
Surplus/deficit	+553	−102[†]

† The deficit of about 100 g UDP is theoretically equivalent to the protein requirement for approximately 2 kg milk.

Table 12.1 illustrates the importance of the degradability of the compound feed in a typical ration. A 10 per cent increase in the degradability of the compound feed from 65 to 75 per cent would change the degradability of the whole ration by approximately 3 per cent and would decrease the undegradable protein supply by about 100 g/d, being the protein required for about 2 kg milk. Furthermore, in early lactation, when the compound feed makes a relatively greater contribution to the total ration, the degradability of the compound ration will have a greater influence on the total supply of degradable and undegradable protein.

Clearly, certain milk production systems are sensitive to the level of dietary protein degradability. The ARC have recognized this fact, and their suggested approach is to rank feeds into classes A, B, C and D to cover the degradability ranges 0.71–0.90, 0.51–0.70, 0.31–0.50 and < 0.31 respectively, and to assign to the first three classes the mean degradability values of 0.80, 0.60 and 0.40 respectively. However, in a situation where many raw materials contribute to a compound ration, the use of these ranges may result in large discrepancies. In addition, the recommended practice of assigning untested raw materials to class A may grossly overestimate degradability, thus reducing the effectiveness of the system in practice.

It was felt that, by waiting until standard tables of degradability were published, an unnecessary delay of many years in implementing the new system would result. Even when these tables become available, it will not be certain that they will cover the appropriate raw materials for the animal feed trade, or the particular buying pattern and specific sources of supply of raw materials applicable to a single company.

Unilever Research Laboratory, Colworth House, has provided BOCM SILCOCK with a large resource in terms of raw material expertise (e.g. Robb, 1976). In addition, workers at Colworth House have studied various aspects of protein metabolism in the ruminant for over a decade (e.g. Annison, 1972; Hutton and Annison, 1972; Mercer and Annison, 1976).

In parallel with these basic studies, carried out under laboratory conditions, BOCM SILCOCK conducted a significant amount of development work at Barhill Development Farm on the protein responses of dairy cows (Cuthbert, Thickett and Wilson, 1973). These latter studies showed that responses in milk yield could be obtained from diets containing more DCP than was theoretically required, and indicated that DCP by itself was an insufficient measurement of protein requirement.

For these reasons it was decided, in 1977, to undertake a programme of degradability evaluation of individual raw materials, in order to enable the Company to build up a degradability data base to be used in least-cost formulation of cattle compound feeds. It was also decided to develop a practical rationing scheme to meet the protein requirements of milking cows, and possibly other classes of ruminants, along the lines of the system proposed by Broster and Oldham (1977), and by Roy *et al.* (1977), and therefore in conformity with the new Protein System suggested by the ARC Protein Working Party (Agricultural Research Council, 1980).

The problem of providing a data bank on protein degradability of raw materials

DEGRADABILITY MEASUREMENTS

Over the past 20 years, a considerable amount of international research effort has been put into the investigation of methods for measuring protein degradation in the rumen, and a number of values are available in the literature. Technical difficulties, including identification and measurement of dietary protein reaching the duodenum, and an inadequate documentation of the feedstuffs and their processing history, have contributed to discrepancies in some of the degradability values reported. For instance, the variation in reported values for soya and fish meals is shown in *Table 12.2*.

Table 12.2 VARIATION IN REPORTED PROTEIN DEGRADABILITY VALUES MEASURED *IN VIVO* FOR SOYA BEAN MEAL AND FISH MEALS

Raw material	Proportion of protein degraded in the rumen	Animal	Author
Soya bean meal	0.39	Sheep	Hume (1974)
Soya bean meal	0.43	Sheep	Ling and Buttery (1978)
Soya bean meal	0.55	Sheep	Miller (1973)
Soya bean meal	0.74	Cow	Brett *et al.* (1979)
Fish meal	0.29	Sheep	Hume (1974)
White fish meal	0.38	Sheep	Ling and Buttery (1978)
Peruvian fish meal	0.31	Sheep	Miller (1973)
Fish meal	0.67	Cow	Hagemeister and Kaufmann (1974)
Fish meal (a)	0.22		
(b)	0.30	Sheep	Mehrez, Ørskov and Obstevdt
(c)	0.38		(1980)
(d)	0.51		

In order to implement the system 'on farm', a large-scale study of the degradability of all raw materials, compounds and on-farm feeds was required. The approach chosen was not designed to replace the in-depth metabolic studies on small numbers of raw materials that were continuing at Universities and Research Institutes, but to complement such studies. Not only had different raw materials to be considered, but within raw material variation due to differences of plant variety, season, source, harvesting, storage and processing conditions had to be examined.

The same problems apply to this aspect of protein evaluation as to the energy evaluation of large numbers of feeds (Morgan and Barber, 1980). A method for assessing degradability was required to:

(1) give estimated values as close as possible to that likely to be observed under practical feeding situations;
(2) have sufficient sensitivity to distinguish quantitatively between raw materials;
(3) have sufficient replication over a long time-scale to allow a continuous comparison of raw materials;
(4) assess the large numbers of raw materials on offer to the trade.

AVAILABLE METHODS

In vivo

Several techniques have been developed in an attempt to measure dietary protein degradability *in vivo*. Most of these methods measure the proportion of protein reaching the duodenum which is microbial in origin, and, by difference, the proportion of undegraded dietary protein. The methods currently used have been summarized by Buttery (1977). Although these techniques are beset with difficulties, the values obtained using the RNA and ^{35}S methods on the same feeds and animals have shown a close relationship (Ling and Buttery, 1978). A disadvantage of the *in vivo* methodology is that a single value is placed on each raw material, which applies to the feeding situation of the actual experiment. This does not provide information on the rate of degradation, or allow for any adjustment of rumen retention time, which may differ in other feeding regimes. In spite of uncertainties as to whether the values obtained by these methods are absolute, they have provided a great deal of information about the rumen metabolism of protein. However, they are unsuitable for the assessment of large numbers of ingredients used in the manufacture of compound feeds.

In vitro

In vitro methods, such as the measurement of ammonia and α-amino nitrogen release on incubation with rumen inoculum, appeared to be attractive on the basis of handling large numbers of samples. However, they have been found to be unsatisfactory for determining rates of degradation, because of poor replication and variation in microbial assimilation of ammonia resulting from differences in energy content of feeds. Furthermore, the rates of degradation do not correlate with *in vivo* observations.

These limitations appear to have been overcome by an increased sophistication in methodology such as the 'Rusitec' technique (Czerkawski and Breckenridge, 1977), but these comparatively complex procedures progressively detract from the ability to handle large numbers of samples, which is the attraction of *in vitro* methodology.

Solubility

The observed relationship between protein 'digestion' and solubility in buffer (Henderickx and Martin, 1963) suggested that protein solubility might be used as a simple method for ranking feeds in terms of degradability. Workers in the USA have been studying the possibility of formulating rations on such a solubility basis. Although some of the results have been conflicting (Hawkins and Strength, 1977), several workers have observed significant differences in milk production with cows fed on a protein solubility basis (Braud, 1976; Majdoub, Lane and Aitchison, 1978).

A simple nitrogen-solubility measurement describes only the fraction of total nitrogen immediately available for bacterial degradation, and will not describe the degradation of nitrogen not immediately soluble. However, solubility measurements corrected by a fixed factor for each raw material, which is derived by a comparison of solubility with degradability at six hours *in vitro*, has been suggested as a routine procedure for protein evaluation of feedstuffs by the French PDI System (Institut National de la Recherche Agronomique, 1978).

In situ

The principle of the *in situ* technique was first used to assess the digestibility of leaves placed in a perforated brass capsule and fed to sheep (Reaumur, 1752). In the current method, feeds contained in porous polyester bags are suspended in the rumen of surgically modified ruminants. This method has been used with varying success throughout this century, but the possibility of applying this method to the determination of protein degradability values to be used in the proposed ARC system was first identified by Ørskov and Mehrez (1977) and has been used by several research workers (Mathers, Horton and Miller, 1977; Mohamed and Smith, 1977).

The attraction of the method lies in the ability to follow sequentially the rate of protein degradation. It also allows the use of animals fed on commercial rations and, although it still requires the use of surgically modified animals, larger numbers of raw materials can be processed than with traditional *in vivo* methods.

A further advantage is the ability to study the nutritive value of feed residues after rumen incubation in order to estimate the qualitative contribution of undegradable protein to the duodenum (Mathers *et al.*, 1979).

Errors can arise from this method if inadequate consideration is given to the possible loss of undersized particles from the bag, the particle size of feed placed in the bag, or the diets fed to the experimental animals. The *in situ* method describes and ranks feeds in order of degradation rate and potential. However, there exists some uncertainty as to the incubation period most relevant to determine protein degradation in the dairy cow. Several ways of selecting the appropriate incubation time are possible. Mathers, Horton and Miller (1977) found an incubation of 4—6 h gave the best prediction of *in vivo* degradability for the feed studied. Ørskov and Mehrez (1977) suggested determining the extent of degradation when 90 per cent of digestible DM had disappeared from the bag. A third possible approach is to calculate a rate constant of disappearance from a logarithmic plot of the proportion of nitrogen remaining in the residue (Mohamed and Smith, 1977).

A recent approach (Ørskov and McDonald, 1979) has been the mathematical combination of *in situ* and rumen retention time measurements on the same feed. Measurements of this type, made throughout lactation in dairy cows fed commercial rations, not only show the greatest possibility of describing protein degradation under practical feeding situations, but must also give a better understanding of the energy contribution of feeds to the dairy cow. Correlation of the *in situ* methodology is required, not just with traditional *in vivo* methods, but with production trials in the field.

CHOICE OF METHODOLOGY

In selecting an approach to determine protein degradability a decision had to be made, as with the ARC system itself, as to which of the available methods would make a positive contribution to the practical implementation of the new Protein System.

Experience gained with the available methods indicated the *in situ* technique as the most suitable for routine measurement, without the disadvantage of using an *in vitro* determination. Initial difficulties were encountered with this method in relation to precision of measurement and replication, especially in the period up to 12 hours of incubation, as noted by other workers (Mehrez and Ørskov, 1977). Further study showed that this problem was due to variables not previously controlled. The development of a technique which does control most of these variables has resulted in an acceptable level of precision and repeatability (Strachan, P., In preparation). The high precision thus obtained is clearly illustrated in *Table 12.3*.

Table 12.3 THE ESTIMATED VARIANCE COMPONENTS FOR DRY MATTER AND NITROGEN DISAPPEARANCE *IN SITU*. (FACTORIAL:— 4 COWS, 4 PERIODS, 4 RAW MATERIALS IN A LATIN SQUARE DESIGN)

| *Source of variation* | *Variance components* | | | |
| | *DM disappearance* (%) | | *N disappearance* (%) | |
	0—48 h[a]	*12—48 h*[b]	*0—48 h*[a]	*12—48 h*[b]
Between animals	1.24	0.45	1.95	0.43
Between periods	0.63	0.49	2.02	0.66
Between bags	1.45	0.05	2.91	0.02
Residual	4.60	1.28	7.55	2.11

a Data included from six sequential observations.
b Data included from three sequential observations.

In the Unilever experimental design for routine assessment of feeds, dairy cows are used which are fed on rations as close to UK practice as possible. A dairy compound, containing 209 g crude protein/kg DM and a metabolizable energy of 13.6 MJ/kg DM formulated to contain the major protein raw materials used by the compound trade, is fed with good quality hay in equal quantities. One-third of the daily allowance of compound is fed at 08.00, 16.00 and 22.00 h and half the daily allowance of hay is fed at 08.30 and 16.30 h.

Particular attention is paid to sample preparation, with the particle size of raw materials going into the bags similar to that of raw materials formulated into commercial compound diets. Particle size studies using a Quantimet Image Analyser are also run in parallel to degradability studies, in order to investigate the influence of particle size on degradation. Rumen parameters, such as pH and ammonia-nitrogen concentrations, are routinely measured during *in situ* determinations and these, together with the use of an appropriate standard raw material, provide a between-assay control.

Figure 12.1 illustrates in simple terms the main features of the technique described. The raw material is weighed into a porous polyester bag which is introduced into the rumen of a cow. The bags are weighted to maintain them below the surface of the digesta and up to 30 bags can be introduced at any one time. Bags are withdrawn after timed intervals, washed, dried and weighed and the nitrogen content of the residuum is estimated. This allows loss of DM and N to be plotted against time and thus the degradability at any specified time to be calculated. To date, retention times have been derived from a survey of the literature (Mathers, Horton and Miller, 1977; Ørskov and Mehrez, 1977). However, the method of incorporation of rumen retention time measurements (Ørskov and McDonald, 1979) using dairy cows fed a practical ration is being

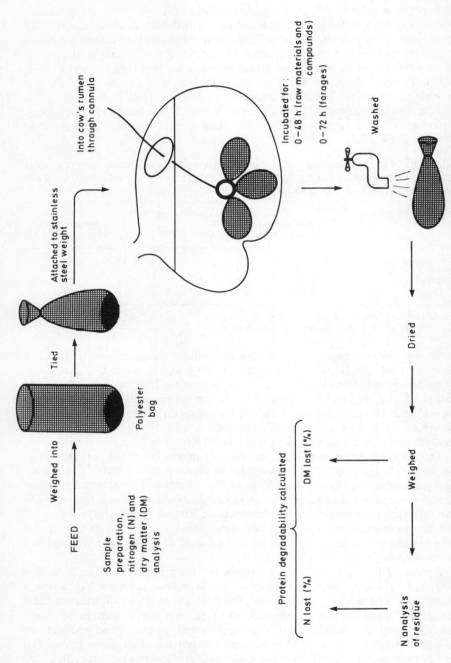

Figure 12.1 In situ technique for the determination of protein degradability

adopted at Colworth. Because all *in situ* investigations at Colworth have covered incubation times from 9 to 48 h for raw materials and compound diets, and from 0 to 72 h for forages, additional information such as rumen retention time at different production states can be incorporated when available.

Information about the nitrogen solubility of raw materials has been built up in parallel with degradability studies, and work has also been progressing with *in vitro* investigations. In our opinion, however, neither of these methods is as yet capable of taking the place of the *in situ* technique.

RESULTS AND OBSERVATIONS

The *in situ* technique described in this chapter has been running on a routine basis since 1977, and a high degree of precision and good replication have been achieved over this period.

The investigation of large numbers of samples of a raw material taken from a wide range of sources has shown that the degradability of some raw materials can vary considerably, but by careful documentation of origin and history of the materials it is possible to attribute many of these variables to processing history.

Failure to document raw material history, and the absence of a standard method of reporting in the past, have meant that the results of much relevant research cannot be fully utilized because of uncertainties about the identity of the materials studied. The possible variation between raw materials examined contributes to the wide range of degradability values quoted by different workers for any one raw material determined *in vivo*. For example, we have found that the rate of degradation of samples of an oilseed meal obtained from different sources can vary widely, as indicated in *Figure 12.2*. These differences have been largely related to manufacturing source. This variation between samples of a raw material is particularly important for the by-products of the

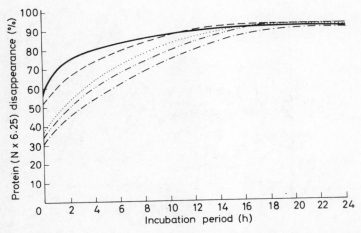

Figure 12.2   Variation in rate of protein degradation from samples of an oilseed meal obtained from five different commercial sources. Degradation determined in situ.

distillery, brewery and wet milling industries and again can be related to quantifiable production parameters. Similar findings have been obtained by Mehrez, Ørskov and Obstevdt (1980) with fish meals differing in processing technique.

A knowledge of the degradability characteristics of both the raw materials, compound diets produced therefrom, and the processing parameters used in our compound mills, has allowed the formulation of compound feeds on a degradability basis.

ON-FARM FEEDS

In order to get the new ARC Protein System working 'on farm' it is necessary to assign degradability values not only to the compound portion of the ration, but also to the forage and other 'on-farm' feeds. Extensive studies on the degradability of silage, hay, grass and other 'on-farm' feeds have been made, again using the principle of obtaining as much of the history of the feeds as possible (such as variety, stage of harvest, and methods of conservation). The aim in these studies has been to cover a wide range of home-grown feeds used on UK farms.

It would be possible to assign these feeds to broad classes of degradability, but again it was felt to be more satisfactory if a more precise estimate could be made

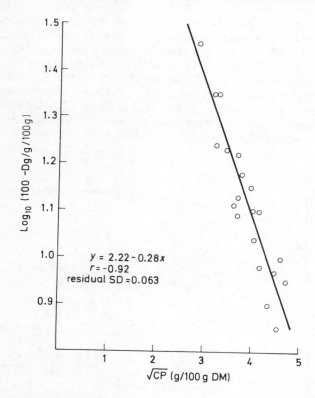

Figure 12.3 Correlation between protein degradability (Dg/g/100 g) of silages measured in situ and their crude protein (CP) content (g/100 g dry matter)

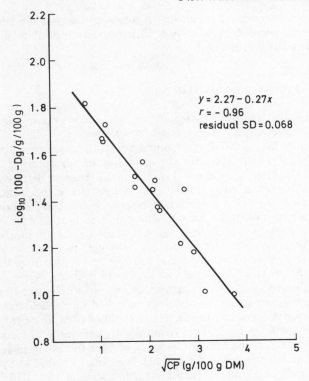

Figure 12.4 Correlation between protein degradability (Dg/g/100g) of hays measured in situ *and their crude protein (CP) content (g/100 g dry matter)*

of a farmer's own feeds. By a parallel study of degradability with the chemical parameters of nitrogen solubility, total nitrogen and detergent fibre analyses, we have derived predictive equations for the degradability of silage and hay, and these equations are set out below:

Silage: $y = 2.22 - 0.28x$ (12.1)
$(r = -0.92;$ residual SD $= 0.063)$

Hay: $y = 2.27 - 0.27x$ (12.2)
$(r = -0.96;$ residual SD $= 0.068)$

Where $x = \sqrt{\% \, CP}$ in DM and $y = \log_{10} (100 - \text{degradability} \%)$

These equations have been derived from the data illustrated in *Figures 12.3* and *12.4*. It must be stressed that these equations are current 'best estimates' and are relevant to typical forages used on farm, which have not been subjected to abnormal chemical or heat treatment. Further work at the Grassland Research Institute and Drayton EHF with forages of this type will be expected to produce an approved 'Standard System' approach to assessing the degradability of forages in due course. It was our opinion that a predictive method for the two forages most widely used in the UK was better than assigning a simple average degradability of 0.8 as suggested by the ARC (1980), as we have found that both silages and hays vary widely in degradability. We believe that the method described is an improvement on current methods of assessing the 'protein value' of on-farm forages and the predictive equations can be quickly modified as new research results become available.

QUALITY OF UNDEGRADED PROTEIN (UDP)

The knowledge that some proteinaceous raw materials are poorly digested in the ruminant, a classic example being dried coffee residues (Robb, 1976), has led to concern that not all UDP is absorbed with the same efficiency from the intestinal tract. A single figure for the efficiency of absorption is assigned by the ARC (1980). This figure is based on the mean apparent digestibility from a series of experiments in which few, if any, of the diets included raw materials, such as processed by-products, which may be poorly absorbed from the intestine. This lower rate of absorption may be due either to heat damage or naturally occurring constituents which may provide some degree of protection from digestion throughout the tract. Therefore, although some allowance is made in the new ARC system for indigestible nitrogen leaving the rumen, this could be an underestimate and a further allowance should be made.

We have observed a close correlation between acid detergent fibre nitrogen (ADF-N) content (using the methodology proposed by Pichard and Van Soest, 1977) and nitrogen remaining in the *in situ* residues after prolonged incubation in the rumen for most feeds. For chemically treated feeds, the correlation is observed only after rumen incubation followed by a further incubation in acid pepsin. The ADF-N content of feeds has been used by BOCM SILCOCK to estimate the indigestible undegradable protein fraction (IUP). IUP is routinely subtracted from the UDP fraction to give a new estimate of the potentially absorbable undegraded feed protein entering the duodenum, the 'digestible undegradable protein' fraction (DUP).

Within BOCM SILCOCK, the use of DUP has superseded UDP for constituent feedstuffs, because of the belief that this improves the estimation of absorbable protein reaching the duodenum. It is a first attempt to take into consideration the quality of undegraded protein leaving the rumen and must be followed by more refinements to take the system further by describing the flow of protein to the duodenum in terms of biologically available amino acids. Further work in this and other areas is progressing at Colworth, as well as in many other Research Institutes and University Departments. However, to avoid confusion in the field and to maintain as closely as possible the terminology employed in the new ARC system, BOCM SILCOCK issue field reports in terms of UDP and not DUP.

The system in practice

When data on the degradability values of our raw materials and prediction equations for on-farm feeds became available, it was possible to replace the DCP figures with new RDP/UDP values in the BOCM SILCOCK computerized least-cost formulation of dairy cow diets. In the autumn of 1978, once the full implications of the re-evaluation of all raw materials had been assessed, we were able, using a computerized BOCM SILCOCK rationing method known as

Dietplan, to advise farmers on the most economic way to feed their cows. This advice was based on the ME System proposed in *Technical Bulletin 33* (MAFF, DAFS and DANI, 1975) and our own version of the proposed new ARC system for protein with due allowance for essential micronutrients.

CALCULATION OF REQUIREMENTS IN PRACTICE

Perhaps the best way to illustrate how the new system is applied in the field is to give an example of how a suggested feeding regime may be derived for a 575 kg cow in early lactation yielding either 20, 30 or 40 kg milk/d. For the purposes of this example we have assumed that the composition of the milk is 4.0 per cent butterfat (BF) and 8.8 per cent solids not fat (SNF). As is normally the case in early lactation, there is the added complication of body weight loss which, for the purposes of this simple example, we have considered to be a constant 0.25 kg/d at each milk yield level.

ENERGY REQUIREMENTS

Because energy is the prime determinant of milk yield, it follows that the first step is to assess the ME required to meet the maintenance and differing production requirements of the cow. The values used for the differing yields are illustrated in *Table 12.4*, which shows that using MAFF, DAFS and DANI (1975)

Table 12.4 DEMONSTRATION OF CALCULATIONS FOR DETERMINING ME, RDP, UDP[a] REQUIREMENTS OF 575 kg COW IN EARLY LACTATION, LOSING 0.25 kg LIVEWEIGHT/D, PRODUCING MILK OF 4.0% BF and 8.8% SNF.

ME, RDP and UDP requirements	Milk yield (kg/d)		
	20	30	40
Metabolizable energy (ME) for:			
Maintenance (MJ/d)	61.0	61.0	61.0
Production (MJ/d)	105.4	158.1	210.8
ME supplied by weight loss (MJ/d)	7.0	7.0	7.0
∴ Total ME requirement (MJ/d)	159.4	212.1	264.8
Tissue protein requirement (TP) for:			
Maintenance (g/d)	73	73	73
Production (g/d)	662	993	1324
Contribution from weight loss (g/d)	28	28	28
∴ Total TP requirement (g/d)	707	1038	1369
∴ RDP required in ration (equation 6.4 (g/d))	1243.3	1654.4	2065.4
TMP (equation 6.5) (g/d)	526.0	699.9	873.8
∴ Deficiency of TP requirement (g/d)	181.0	338.1	495.2
∴ UDP required (equation 6.6) (g/d)[a]	354.1	657.0	959.8

[a] BOCMS employ DUP and not UDP values to formulate diets but, to maintain uniformity, DUP data are transformed back to UDP values when conducting feeding calculations in the field. For a description of Equations 12.4, 12.5 and 12.6 *see* p. 243.

recommendations, the maintenance requirement of a 575 kg cow is 61 MJ/d and that a further 105.4, 158.1 or 210.8 MJ/d are required to meet the 20, 30 or 40 kg milk yield/d. The total daily energy requirement derived by summation of the requirements for maintenance and milk yield is reduced, in each case, by 7 MJ when due allowance is made for the 0.25 kg/d weight loss.

PROTEIN REQUIREMENTS

Using the new protein system, ration calculations for protein requirements are based on an assessment of the tissue protein (TP) requirements for maintenance and production.

The requirement for maintenance is re-assessed by the ARC (1980) to the extent that the protein loss in hair and scurf of a 575 kg cow is estimated to be 13 g/d (as in ARC, 1965) but the endogenous urinary protein loss is 60 g/d (cf. ARC (1965) value of 77.5 g/d). The TP requirement for maintenance in our example is thus 73 g/d.

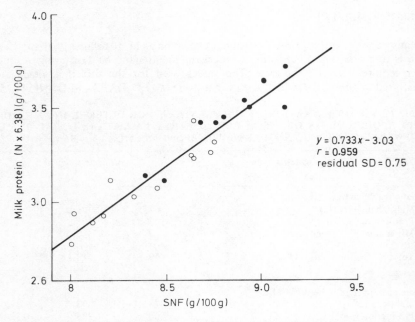

Figure 12.5 The relationship between the protein (N × 6.38) and solids not fat (SNF) content of milk. Data from ○ *Gordon and* ● *Wohlt and Clark (1978)*

The next step is to calculate the TP requirement of the desired level of milk production. In the factorial approach this value may be calculated as the product of milk yield and the protein concentration in that yield, the latter value being an assumed content of 30 g protein/kg milk. However, the protein content of the milk is closely correlated with the SNF fraction (*see Figure 12.5*) and in addition a factor of 6.38 rather than 6.25 (as used by the ARC working party) is more appropriate for the conversion of milk N to milk protein (Davies, 1936).

Consequently, the Dietplan model uses a variable factor for milk protein composition which is dependent on the SNF content. The actual regression equation used in Dietplan is:

$$\text{Milk protein (g/kg)} = 0.653 \text{ SNF (g/kg)} - 24.4 \qquad (12.3)$$

Figure 12.5, using data from two sources only (Gordon 1977; Wohlt and Clarke, 1978) illustrates this regression, although the best fit regression equation for these limited data is non-significantly different to that presented above and used in Dietplan.

In our example in *Table 12.4*, SNF has been assumed to be constant at the differing yields. Thus the requirement for production is the product of yield and a value of 33.1 g protein/kg milk.

The total TP requirement is therefore taken as the sum of TP (maintenance) and TP (production). However, TP is also affected by gain or loss in weight. The ARC (1980) estimate that, for ration calculations, 1 kg loss of body weight/d can make a contribution of 112 g of protein to the TP requirement. Similarly, they estimate that when cows are gaining weight (e.g. in late lactation) a further 150 g of TP is required for every kg of weight gain. These factors are also built into the Dietplan model so that farmers may alter their rations accordingly over the lactation cycle, making due allowances for estimated change in cow weight.

In the above example, the apparent total TP requirement is therefore reduced by 28 g/d to compensate for the 0.25 kg/d weight loss. The net TP requirements for the three milk yields are therefore as shown in *Table 12.4*.

The next stage is to calculate how the net TP requirement may be met from RDP and UDP. The ARC (1980) propose the use of three equations to determine these values:

$$\text{RDP (g/d)} = 7.8 \times \text{ME requirement (MJ/d)} \qquad (12.4)$$

$$\text{TMP (g/d)} = 3.3 \times \text{ME requirement (MJ/d)} \qquad (12.5)$$
(where TMP = the TP supplied from microbial protein syntheses alone)

$$\text{UDP (g/d)} = (1.91 \times \text{TP}) - (6.25 \times \text{ME requirement (MJ/d)}) \qquad (12.6)$$

The corresponding values from these three equations for the three milk yields are shown in *Table 12.4*. As can be seen, the energy supply for the three milk yields cannot support a microbial protein yield sufficient to meet the TP requirement: therefore, UDP must be fed to overcome the deficiency in each case. *Table 12.4* demonstrates that, as the milk yield increases, so the proportion of UDP required in the total protein (UDP + RDP) rises from 22 per cent for 20 kg milk yield to 32 per cent at 40 kg milk yield.

BALANCING REQUIREMENTS WITH DIETARY SUPPLY

If we consider a cow yielding 30 kg milk/d, *Table 12.5* demonstrates how a practical ration may be used to meet these requirements, described in terms of ME, RDP and UDP and compared with DCP.

Table 12.5 DEMONSTRATIONS OF HOW A PRACTICAL RATION MAY MEET THE PROTEIN AND ENERGY REQUIREMENTS OF A 575 kg COW IN EARLY LACTATION, YIELDING 30 kg OF MILK/D of 4.0 PER CENT BF AND 8.8 PER CENT SNF, AND LOSING 0.25 kg LIVEWEIGHT/D.

Type of ration	kg fed/d	DM intake (kg/day)	ME intake (MJ/day)	RDP intake (g/day)	UDP intake (g/day)	DCP intake (g/day)
Ration 1						
Silage	25.0	7.0	69.0	791	140	812
14% CP Compound A[a]	13.0	11.15	142.7	1310	460	1361
Totals	38.0	18.15	211.7	2101	600	2173
Required	–	18.11	212.1	1654	657	2020
Surplus	–	0.04	0.4	447	−57	+53
Ration 2						
Silage	25.0	7.00	69.0	791	140	812
16% CP Compound B[b]	13.0	11.15	142.7	1445	517	1617
Totals	38.0	18.15	211.7	2236	657	2429
Required	–	18.11	212.1	1654	657	2020
Surplus	–	0.04	0.4	582	nil	+409
Ration 3						
Silage	25.0	7.00	69.0	791	140	812
14% CP Compound C[c]	13.0	11.15	142.7	1239	517	1361
Totals	38.0	18.15	211.7	2030	657	2173
Required	–	18.11	212.1	165.4	657	2020
Surplus	–	0.04	0.4	376	nil	+53

[a] 14% CP dairy Compound A of 72% degradability does not meet requirements for UDP.
[b] 16% CP dairy Compound B of 72% degradability meets requirements.
[c] 14% CP dairy Compound C of 68% degradability also meets requirements.
DCP requirements are met for all diets.

If we assume that the available feeds consist of grass silage and either a 14 per cent or a 16 per cent CP compound, and if the degradabilities of both the silage and the compounds are known, then an appropriate feeding regime can be calculated.

Table 12.5 gives details of the total ration formulation, using three alternative compounds. In Ration 1, compound A (72 per cent degradability) satisfies ME and DCP. The RDP is grossly over-supplied but, in spite of the more than adequate provision of DCP, the ration is short of 57 g of UDP.

Ration 2 shows how this shortfall of UDP can be made good by substitution of the 14 per cent CP compound by a 16 per cent CP compound of the same degradability (72 per cent) as the former. The DCP excess is increased from 53 g to 409 g and the RDP excess is increased from 447 g to 582 g but, in this instance, the requirement for UDP is met.

Ration 3 illustrates how an alternative solution can be obtained by the use of a 14 per cent CP compound of lower degradability (68 per cent instead of 72 per cent). The excess of DCP and of RDP is reduced, but the UDP supply still meets requirement.

It would normally be less expensive to purchase the 14 per cent CP compound C than the 16 per cent compound B, so Ration 3 should give better value for money, and might be expected to produce a saving of £2–£5/tonne, according to the raw materials used.

Discussion

The Foreword to *Technical Bulletin 33* (MAFF, DAFS and DANI, 1975) states, 'This is the first Bulletin to provide guidelines for the practical implementation of the modified ME system in the UK. Obviously research on all aspects of this topic continues. The present system is flexible and may be easily adjusted, when necessary, to include new data emerging from research. Further amendments to the Bulletin will probably be needed during the next few years. The adoption of a policy of periodic review and revision will also meet another request, made at the joint conference, for a continued close liaison and exchange of ideas and information between advisers and research workers.' Identical remarks and qualifications apply both to the *in situ* methodology and to the practical feeding system for protein described in this chapter.

Clearly, a lot more work requires to be done on various aspects of the proposed new ARC Protein system, but as in the analogy with the ME system, the framework suggested allows for easy substitution of new data as further studies provide improved information. For example, as the ARC (1980) system indicates, amino acid requirements can be readily incorporated as an adjunct to the UDP and RDP values when definitive data become available.

The scientific basis of the new ARC system is beyond dispute. Therefore, debate should properly be pursued on the values used and the assumptions made in the proposed system (ARC, 1980). There is also need for refinement and continued updating of the data bank. These will be more productive areas for future work than prolonged discussion on whether the outdated DCP system ought to be retained or the previously suggested AP system (ARC, 1965) should be put into practice. Lastly, it is of paramount importance that any system designed for widespread use in the field, by advisers and farmers, is well understood and based on as few assumptions as possible. Although more complicated models may be scientifically more acceptable, there is a danger that such models may be ill used or misused due to lack of understanding by the personnel involved with their implementation. There is a need to differentiate between refining research knowledge, on the one hand, and improving practical feeding advice to the farmer as speedily as possible, on the other.

There was a delay of over a decade between the first publication of the principles underlying the ME system (Blaxter, 1962) and their practical implementation (MAFF, DAFS and DANI, 1975). It is to be hoped that there will be a much shorter interval between the publication of the proposed new protein system (ARC, 1980) and the development of an agreed replacement for the outdated and discredited DCP system, and we regard the initiative reported in this chapter as a step in this direction.

Acknowledgements

The authors wish to thank many of their colleagues who have assisted them with the preparation of this paper, especially T.D.A. Brigstocke, P.E.M. Cowdy, N.H. Cuthbert, P.J. Evans, D.G. Filmer, I.L. Johnson, M.A. Lindeman and A. Penman.

References

AGRICULTURAL RESEARCH COUNCIL (ARC) (1965). *The Nutrient Requirement of Farm Livestock, No. 2. Ruminants.* London; HMSO

AGRICULTURAL RESEARCH COUNCIL (ARC) (1980). *The Nutrient Requirement of Ruminant Livestock.* Farnham Royal, Slough; CAB

ANNISON, E.F. (1972). In *Proceedings of the 6th Conference for Feed Manufacturers*, p.2. Eds H. Swan and D. Lewis. Edinburgh and London; Churchill Livingstone

BLAXTER, K.L. (1962). *The Energy Metabolism of Ruminants.* London; Hutchinson

BRAUD, D.G. (1976). *Feed Management*, 27 (11), 10

BRETT, P.A., ALMOND, M., HARRISON, D.G., ROWLINSON, P., ROOKE, J. and ARMSTRONG, D.G. (1979). *Proc. Nutr. Soc.*, 38, 148A

BROSTER, W.H. and OLDHAM, J.D. (1977). In *Nutrition in the Climatic Environment*, p. 123. Eds W. Haresign, H. Swan and D. Lewis. London; Butterworths

BUTTERY, P.J. (1977). In *Recent Advances in Animal Nutrition*, p. 8. Eds W. Haresign and D. Lewis. London; Butterworths

CUTHBERT, N.H., THICKETT, W.S. and WILSON, P.N. (1973). *Proc. BSAP. 1973. New Series*, 2, 70 (Abstr)

CZERKAWSKI, J.W. and BRECKENRIDGE, G. (1977). *Br. J. Nutr.*, 38, 371

DAVIES, W.L. (1936). *The Chemistry of Milk.* London; Chapman Hall

GORDON, F.J. (1977). *Anim. Prod.*, 25, 181

HAGEMEISTER, H. and KAUFMANN, W. (1974). *Kieler Milchwirtsch Forschungster.*, 26, 199

HAWKINS, G.E. and STRENGTH, D.R. (1977). *J. Dairy Sci.*, 60, (Suppl. 157 (abstr.))

HENDERICKX, B. and MARTIN, J. (1963). *C.r. Rech. Inst. Encour. Rech. scient. Ind. Agric.*, 31, 110

HUME, I.D. (1974). *Aust. J. agric. Res.*, 25, 155

HUTTON, K. and ANNISON, E.F. (1972). *Proc. Nutr. Soc.*, 31, 151

INSTITUT NATIONAL DE LA RECHERCHE AGRONOMIQUE (INRA) (1978). In *Alimentat des Ruminants*, p. 89. Versailles, France; INRA Publications

LING, J.R. and BUTTERY, P.J. (1978). *Br. J. Nutr.*, 39, 165

MAFF, DAFFS and DANI (1975). *Technical Bulletin 33.* London; HMSO

MAJDOUB, A., LANE, G.T. and AITCHISON, T.E. (1978). *J. Dairy Sci.*, 61, 59

MATHERS, J.C. and MILLER, E.L. (1977). *Proc. Nutr. Soc.*, 36, 7A

MATHERS, J.C., HORTON, C.M. and MILLER, E.L. (1977). *Proc. Nutr. Soc.*, 36, 37A

MATHERS, J.C., THOMAS, R.J., GRAY, N.A.M. and JOHNSON, I.L. (1979). *Proc. Nutr. Soc.*, 38, 122A

MEHREZ, A.Z. and ØRSKOV, E.R. (1977). *J. agric. Sci.*, 88, 645

MEHREZ, A.Z. and ØRSKOV, E.R. (1978). *Br. J. Nutr.*, 40, 337

MEHREZ, A.Z., ØRSKOV, E.R. and OBSTEVDT, J. (1980). *J. Anim. Sci.*, 50, 737

MERCER, J.R. and ANNISON, E.F. (1976). In *Protein Metabolism and Nutrition*, p. 397. Eds D.J.A. Cole, K.N. Boorman, P.J. Buttery, D. Lewis, R.J. Neale and H. Swan. London; Butterworths

MILLER, E.L. (1973). *Proc. Nutr. Soc., 32,* 79

MILLER, E.L. (1977). In *International Association of Fish Meal Manufacturers 4th European Symposium on the use of Fish Meal in Animal Feeding,* p. 51.

MILLER, E.L., BALCH, C.C., ØRSKOV, E.R., ROY, J.H.B. and SMITH. R.H. (1977). In *Proc. 2nd Int. Symp. on Protein Metabolism and Nutrition,* p. 137. Wageningen, The Netherlands; Centre for Agricultural Publishing and Documentation

MOHAMED, O.E. and SMITH, R.H. (1977). *Proc. Nutr. Soc., 36,* 152A

MORGAN, D.E. and BARBER, W.P. (1980). In *Recent Advances in Animal Nutrition – 1979,* pp. 93–106. Eds W. Haresign and D. Lewis. London; Butterworths

ØRSKOV, E.R. and MEHREZ, A.Z. (1977). *Proc. Nutr., Soc., 36,* 78A

ØRSKOV, E.R. and McDONALD, I. (1979). *J. agric. Sci., 92,* 499

PICHARD, G. and VAN SOEST, P.J. (1977). In *Proc. Cornell Nutr., Conf.,* 91

REAUMUR, R.E.F. (1752). *Mem. Acad. Sci. (Paris).,* cited by R.E. Hungate (1966) In *The Rumen and its Microbes,* p. 461. London; Academic Press

ROBB, J. (1976). In *Feed Energy Sources for Livestock,* p. 13. Eds H. Swan and D. Lewis. London; Butterworths

ROFFLER, R.E. and SATTER, L.D. (1975). *J. Dairy Sci., 58,* 1889

ROY, J.H.B., BALCH, C.C., MILLER, E.L., ØRSKOV, E.R. and SMITH, R.H. (1977). In *Proc. 2nd Int. Symp. on Protein Metabolism and Nutrition,* p. 126. Wageningen, The Netherlands; Centre for Agricultural Publishing and Documentation

WOHLT, J.E. and CLARKE, J.H. (1978). *J. Dairy Sci., 61,* 902

13

CALCIUM REQUIREMENTS IN RELATION TO MILK FEVER

D.W. PICKARD
Department of Animal Physiology and Nutrition,
University of Leeds

Milk fever must have been a considerable problem to dairy farmers for many years. In 1819, Knowlson gave a precise description of the symptoms and was aware of the effect of age and yield on the incidence of the disease, which must have been prevalent in those days in order to warrant the comment 'It is a heavy disorder, and kills many.'

The relationship between milk fever and hypocalcaemia was established by Little and Wright (1925) and Dryerre and Greig (1928) and it is now generally accepted that parturient hypocalcaemia results from the rapid withdrawal of calcium from the blood by the udder at the start of lactation. When the hypocalcaemia becomes severe (usually less than 2.5 mEq l^{-1}) cows show symptoms of milk fever.

The influence of diet on the incidence of milk fever has been the subject of much research and considerable controversy has surrounded the subject of 'steaming up' in relation to milk fever. In the discussion which followed the paper of Dryerre and Greig (1928) it appears that a majority of the participants believed that feeding concentrates before calving resulted in a greater incidence of milk fever. The final word rested with Professor Dryerre who, referring to the divergent views, said that there were 'concentrates and concentrates. Unless one knows exactly the composition of these, the amount and frequency of administration and the weight and condition of the animals, it would be unwise to venture any opinion as to their efficacy.' It now appears that it is the composition of such rations, particularly the content of calcium and phosphorus, and the amount consumed before calving, which governs their effect on the incidence of milk fever. Milk fever commonly occurs where large amounts of dairy rations are fed to dry cows in the last weeks before calving. It can also occur on farms where no supplementary feed is offered prior to calving. These two situations may provide very different intakes of calcium and phosphorus but both produce a similar result — that is, a high incidence of milk fever. This apparent anomaly can be explained in the light of evidence which has recently emerged on the ability of animals to adapt to changes in their intake of calcium.

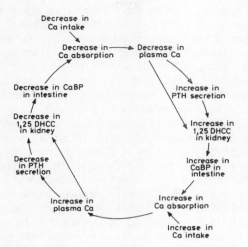

Figure 13.1 Calcium adaptation

When an animal is fed a diet containing a greater amount of calcium than it requires, the proportion of the dietary calcium which is actually absorbed declines. Conversely, an animal adapts to a decrease in the amount of calcium in its diet by absorbing more of it. Calcium adaptation (*Figure 13.1*) has been recognised for some time in rats (Ellis and Mitchell, 1933), cattle (Comar *et al.*, 1953) and humans (Malm, 1963). It is the mechanism whereby an animal adapts to a change in calcium intake which has recently been elucidated.

When an animal such as a pig, or a chick, is fed on a diet low in calcium, changes take place in the metabolism of vitamin D, such that more 1,25 dihydroxycholecalciferol (1,25 DHCC) is formed in the kidney (Boyle, Gray and DeLuca, 1971) from 25 hydroxycholecalciferol, produced in the liver from vitamin D itself. The low calcium diet also results in an increase in the levels of circulating parathyroid hormone (PTH) and the evidence to support the theory that PTH also stimulates 1,25 DHCC production is considerable (Tanaka and DeLuca, 1973). The active metabolite of vitamin D under normal circumstances is 1,25 DHCC (Lawson *et al.*, 1971) and this stimulates the formation of a specific calcium-binding protein in the small intestinal mucosa (Corradino, 1973). This specific calcium-binding protein is involved in the active transport of calcium across the intestinal mucosa (Wasserman and Taylor, 1963), and enables the adapted animal to absorb a greater proportion of its dietary intake of calcium.

When the intake of calcium is increased these mechanisms of adaptation operate in reverse; the secretion of PTH declines and the kidney, instead of producing 1,25 DHCC, produces the 24,25 dihydroxy metabolite of vitamin D. In the absence of 1,25 DHCC the amount of calcium-binding protein in the intestinal mucosa declines and the absorption of calcium is reduced. It must be noted that since calcium adaptation involves changes in the intestinal mucosa, it takes days rather than hours for an animal to adapt to a change in its calcium intake. Animals are also able to adapt to changes in their requirement for calcium; when this increases (as at the beginning of lactation) the animal adapts by absorbing a greater proportion of its dietary intake. It appears that animals attempt to keep the amount of calcium actually absorbed very close to their requirement for calcium irrespective of the amount present in the diet.

Cows which are fed large amounts of dairy rations in the weeks before calving are receiving more calcium than they require because dairy rations contain sufficient calcium to meet the requirements of lactating animals. They adapt to this excess of dietary calcium by absorbing less of it. Since it takes several days for the intestine to change in response to a change in the demand for calcium, the intestine is unable to absorb sufficient calcium to meet the increased demand when calcium is withdrawn from the blood by the udder to produce milk in the day or two before calving. This rapid withdrawal of calcium by the udder results in milk fever. Over-feeding calcium in the dry period also has a detrimental effect on the cow's ability to mobilise calcium from her bones to maintain blood calcium above the danger level at calving.

The calcium intake of cows which are given no supplementary feed before calving may be much closer to their actual requirement at this time and they would absorb a high proportion of the calcium which is eaten. These animals are likely to suffer from milk fever because there is insufficient calcium in the diet to meet the demands for extra calcium just before calving. If a cow produced 15 kg of milk in her udder on the day before calving, this would contain more than 20 g of calcium. Cows on grass with an estimated intake of 50 g of calcium per day would be unable to absorb sufficient calcium to supply the udder at this time. Younger cows may be able to mobilise calcium from their bones and so avoid milk fever, but the availability of calcium from the bones declines with advancing age and this makes older animals more susceptible to milk fever.

The method developed at Leeds for preventing milk fever relies on matching the intake of calcium and phosphorus to the requirement for these elements around parturition. Cows which need supplementary feeding before calving are given a ration low in calcium and phosphorus such as rolled barley or a cereal based compound without minerals, in addition to their normal diet of grass, hay or silage. Normal dairy rations are gradually substituted for the low calcium and phosphorus ration beginning seven days before calving such that cows are receiving a minimum of 4 kg dairy ration by the time they calve.

For animals which are given no supplementary rations before calving, milk fever may be prevented by introducing dairy rations two or three days before calving to coincide with the formation of milk in the udder. When the appetite of the cow is not able to cope with sufficient normal dairy ration, a special ration with a higher calcium and phosphorus content may be needed.

In general, the aim is for an intake of calcium of around 50 g per day and of phosphorus around 30 g per day during the dry period. The intake of both elements should be increased by 50 g per day by the day before calving (Pickard, 1975; Pickard *et al.*, 1975).

The requirement of the dairy cow for calcium in the last month of pregnancy is approximately 15 g per day (Agricultural Research Council, 1965) and using the ARC figure for the availability of calcium, which is 45%, an intake of something less than 40 g per day would be adequate for the cow at this time. The figure of 50 g quoted above is based on this ARC figure and on the fact that under farm conditions an intake of less than 50 g per day would be difficult to achieve (the average composition of herbage being 0.50% DM, and assuming a DM intake of 10 kg per day). It appears that although the figure of 50 g calcium per day is higher than the ARC recommendation, it is not much too high. This may be because the availability of calcium is not a constant 45%. As the ARC acknowledged, the availability of calcium falls as the intake increases.

Figure 13.2 shows that the availability of calcium falls in a linear manner as intake increases, but it appears more likely that the relationship is curvilinear, with the result that the net absorption of calcium might remain constant over a wide range of calcium intakes. There are at present insufficient data available to prove this point conclusively but it is suggested that it is only at intakes of calcium above 50 g per day that the suppression of parathyroid gland activity, the reduction in 1,25 DHCC production and the depressed efficiency of calcium absorption become severe enough to cause embarrassment to the cow, as she adapts to a situation where her net requirement for calcium has increased by a factor of 2 or 3 over a period of hours around the time of parturition.

Whilst the ARC were compelled, for the sake of simplicity in presenting tables of requirements, to take a figure of 45% for the availability of calcium, they were careful to draw attention to the fact that

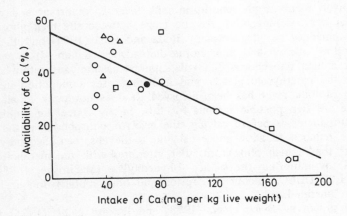

Figure 13.2 The relationship between calcium intake and its availability in cattle weighing 300–400 kg. ○ = *values for individual heifers and steers;* ● = *mean for Hereford cattle;* △ = *means for steers;* □ = *values for individual cows (ARC, 1965)*

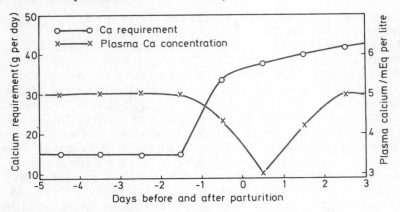

Figure 13.3 Diagram of changes in calcium requirement and in plasma calcium concentration at parturition

calcium availability does indeed fall as intake increases. This point is very important when dealing with the dry cow which has a low absolute requirement for calcium and a very high potential for its consumption.

Recent experience indicates that where dry cows are fed according to the ARC requirement for calcium, the incidence of milk fever is low. A refinement is necessary, however, because the calcium requirements of the cow increase *before* parturition, not afterwards. Milk is usually formed in the udder before calving and the fall in plasma calcium levels begins one or two days before calving.

Figure 13.3 illustrates in diagrammatic form the changes which take place in the level of calcium in the plasma, coincident with changes in the absolute requirement for calcium. It is therefore advisable to increase the intake of calcium before parturition.

The involvement of phosphorus in milk fever is important and will be dealt with next. Comparisons may be made between the high phosphorus diet recommended for dry cows by Boda and Cole (1954) and the relatively low calcium and phosphorus diet advocated here. It is certainly true that a high phosphorus diet will suppress calcium absorption and stimulate the parathyroid glands, and in many cases a reduction in the incidence of milk fever has been achieved. It does not work in all cases and there are two possible reasons for this. Firstly, since the requirement for calcium increases before calving, the level of phosphorus in the diet should be reduced to allow more calcium to be absorbed. Secondly, it is clear that a high phosphorus diet interferes with the metabolism of vitamin D by inhibiting the kidney 1-hydroxylase (MacIntyre, 1975). Without 1,25 DHCC, calcium absorption and bone mobilisation are likely to remain unstimulated.

It was shown by Black *et al.* (1973) and Pickard *et al.* (1975) that a fairly low calcium and phosphorus diet will allow the parathyroid glands to respond adequately to a fall in plasma calcium at parturition. In other words, there is no need for a high phosphorus diet in order to achieve active parathyroid glands.

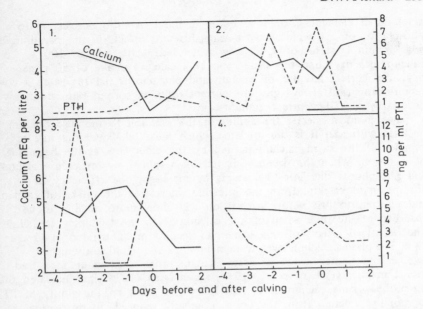

Figure 13.4 Plasma calcium and PTH levels in calving cows. 1. This cow was given a steaming-up ration which supplied an additional 20 g Ca and 15 g P from 4 to 5 weeks before calving. The PTH response was poor, despite the very low plasma calcium level. 2. This cow received no supplementary ration until the time indicated by the solid bar when 50 g Ca and 50 g P were supplied per day. There was a good PTH response which showed a clear inverse relationship with plasma calcium. 3. This cow was treated in a similar manner to No. 2 but the calcium and phosphorus supplement (50 g per day of each) was fed only for the time indicated by the solid bar. Failure to maintain calcium and phosphorus intake after calving resulted in a decline in the plasma calcium level. Again there was a good PTH response. 4. This cow was fed the supplementary 50 g Ca and P per day for 6 days before calving − calving date is not always easy to estimate. The parathyroid glands were still able to respond at calving, indicating that it takes several days for adaptation to the higher calcium intake to be completed

Figure 13.4 shows the results from four cows. This indicates that with an intake of calcium of approximately 50 g and phosphorus 30 g per day, the parathyroid glands do not appear to have been suppressed, and that by increasing the intake of calcium and phosphorus before calving it is possible to prevent the plasma calcium level from falling to the low levels which result in milk fever. Low phosphorus intakes are occasionally stated as the cause of milk fever but it appears that although phosphorus deficiency is not uncommon, the intake of calcium is often too high, and this may reduce the availability of the phosphorus. Much has been spoken of the importance of the calcium to phosphorus ratio in relation to milk fever. The work of Gardner in the last few years (Gardner, 1970; Gardner and Park, 1973) indicated that a ratio of 2.3:1 was optimal for the prevention of milk fever but Beitz, Burkhart and Jacobson (1974) could not agree with this conclusion. When referring to ratios, the actual amounts of elements should be borne in mind. A ratio of calcium to phosphorus of 2:1 would have a very different effect on the parathyroid and vitamin D status of a dry cow when fed at the rate of 100 g calcium per day than the same ratio at a calcium intake of 50 g per day. The correct amount of calcium and phosphorus fed to match a cow's requirements will always give the correct ratio. A correct ratio does not necessarily give the correct amounts.

Since in most species the ability of the skeleton to mobilise calcium declines with age, it is the intestine which must take over the role of supplier of the extra calcium needed by the older cow at the beginning of lactation. When the dry cow is fed on a fairly low intake of calcium and phosphorus, the intestine adapts by increasing the efficiency of absorption of calcium from the intestine. Increasing the intake of calcium and phosphorus just before parturition will allow more calcium to be absorbed at the time when plasma calcium levels are beginning to fall. The beneficial effects of this system of feeding are illustrated in *Figure 13.5*. The plasma calcium levels were maintained at a significantly higher level in the treated group of cows than in those steamed up in a traditional manner (Pickard *et al.*, 1975). Rasmussen (1973) has indicated that when the plasma calcium level falls below 2.5 mEq l^{-1} the ability of PTH to mobilise calcium from the bones is greatly reduced. By increasing the dietary intake just before calving it appears that it is possible to maintain the plasma calcium well above this dangerously low level. The importance of continuing to feed high levels of calcium after calving must be stressed. Most cases of milk fever occur within 48 hours of calving and every effort should be made to maintain the cow's appetite over this period.

Field trials have recently been carried out from Leeds in an attempt to put some of this theory into practice, and some results are now available.

Figure 13.6 includes results from the 24 farms that have returned results so far. A total of 216 cows was selected from these farms.

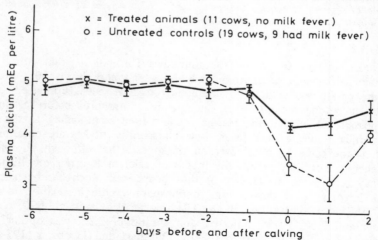

Figure 13.5 Comparison of plasma calcium levels in two groups of cows, one treated with Ca and P, the other untreated

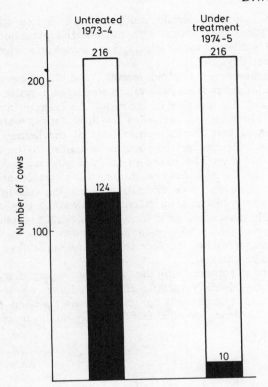

Figure 13.6 Effect of regulation of Ca and P intake on incidence of milk fever in farm trials

They were the high risk cases, either because they had had milk fever in 1973–74 or were considered by their owners to be very likely to go down this time. In fact, 124 of the cows had previously had milk fever but only 10 cases occurred in 1974–75. Seven of these 10 cases were on farms with a history of hypomagnesaemia and it is known that PTH action is impaired when the magnesium status is low (Estep *et al.,* 1969; Muldowny *et al.,* 1970). The hypomagnesaemia may have contributed to the partial failure of the treatment on these farms. On this point it should be noted that high magnesium intakes are also likely to cause trouble because of the known inhibitory effect of high levels of magnesium on the absorption of calcium from the intestine. Despite the fact that these results only allow a comparison to be made between different years, the data came in throughout the year, and indicate that the incidence of milk fever is related to the intake of calcium and phosphorus.

How was the intake of calcium and phosphorus controlled on these farms with a variety of feeding systems operating? In general, those steaming up were asked to avoid dairy rations and either feed rolled barley or a low calcium and phosphorus steaming-up ration, and to introduce dairy rations just before calving. Those not steaming up were asked to increase the intake of calcium and phosphorus before calving by introducing dairy rations or a special high calcium and phosphorus ration which supplied sufficient extra calcium and phosphorus when fed at the rate of 2 kg per day.

More results have been received recently, and there are very few reports of failures from farms where the steaming-up system of feeding has been followed. The practice of increasing the calcium intake just before calving without steaming up has failed on three farms, where it was subsequently found that the calcium content of the herbage was higher than average, and the content of phosphorus tended to be low. Manston (1967) found that when the intake of calcium was increased before calving, on an already high calcium intake, the incidence of milk fever increased. It is obviously more difficult to guess the calcium and phosphorus intake where steaming up is not practised and care should therefore be taken to assess the likely intake of calcium and phosphorus from the herbage of such farms. Where farmers are unwilling to substitute their high calcium grass with low calcium concentrates, milk fever must be controlled by other means.

In conclusion, it appears from this work that where dairy cows are fed levels of minerals, especially calcium and phosphorus, which are as close as possible to their requirements for these minerals around the time of parturition, the incidence of milk fever is likely to be much reduced.

Summary

It is believed that the two major causes of milk fever are:

(1) Overfeeding calcium and phosphorus by steaming up with dairy rations.
(2) Underfeeding calcium and phosphorus by failing to increase the intake of calcium and phosphorus just before calving when the requirement for these elements suddenly increases.

Milk fever may be prevented by:

(1) Avoiding steaming up with dairy rations and using a low calcium phosphorus ration instead.
(2) Increasing the calcium and phosphorus intake by 50 g per day for each element, beginning 2–3 days before calving.

References

Agricultural Research Council (1965). *Nutrient Requirements of Farm Livestock, No. 2, Ruminants.* London; Agricultural Research Council

Beitz, D.C., Burkhart, D.J. and Jacobson, N.L. (1974). *J. Dairy Sci.,* **57**, 49

Black, H.E., Capen, C.C. and Arnaud, C.D. (1973). *Lab. Invest.,* **29**, 173

Boda, J.M. and Cole, H.H. (1954). *J. Dairy Sci.*, **37**, 360

Boyle, I.T., Gray, R.W. and DeLuca, H.F. (1971). *Proc. natn. Acad. Sci. USA*, **68**, 2131

Comar, C.L., Monroe, R.A., Visek, W.J. and Hansard, S.L. (1953). *J. Nutr.*, **50**, 459

Corradino, R.A. (1973). *Science*, **179**, 402

Dryerre, H. and Greig, R. (1928). *Vet. Rec.*, **8**, 721

Ellis, M. and Mitchell, H.H. (1933). *Am. J. Physiol.*, **104**, 1

Estep, H., Shaw, W.A., Wathington, C., Hobe, R., Holland, W. and Tucker, St. G. (1969). *J. clin. Endocrin.*, **29**, 842

Gardner, R.W. (1970). *J. Dairy Sci.*, **53**, 682

Gardner, R.W. and Park, R.L. (1973). *J. Dairy Sci.*, **56**, 385

Knowlson, J.C. (1819). *The Cattle Doctor*. London and Otley; Wm. Walker & Sons

Lawson, D.E.M., Fraser, D.R., Kodicek, E., Morris, H.R. and Williams, D.H. (1971). *Nature*, **230**, 228

Little, W.L. and Wright, N.C. (1925). *Br. J. exp. Path.*, **6**, 129

MacIntyre, I. (1975). In *Calcified Tissue*. Edited by S. Pors-Nielson and E. Hjørting Hansen. Copenhagen; FADC Publishing Co

Malm, O.J. (1963). In *The Transfer of Calcium and Strontium across Biological Membranes*. Edited by R. Wasserman. New York; Academic Press

Manston, R. (1967). *J. agric. Sci.*, **68**, 263

Muldowny, F.P., McKenna, T.J., Kyle, L.H., Freaney, R. and Swan, M. (1970). *New Engl. J. Med.*, **282**, 61

Pickard, D.W. (1975). *Br. vet. J.*, **131**, 744

Pickard, D.W., Care, A.D., Tomlinson, S. and O'Riordan, J.L.H. (1975). *J. Endocrin.*, **67**, 45P

Rasmussen, H. (1973). *Triangle*, **12**, 103

Tanaka, Y. and DeLuca, H.F. (1973). *Archs Biochem. Biophys.*, **154**, 566

Wasserman, R.H. and Taylor, A.N. (1963). *Nature*, **198**, 30

14

RECENT ADVANCES IN THE UNDERSTANDING OF CEREAL PROCESSING FOR RUMINANTS

E.R. ØRSKOV
Rowett Research Institute, Aberdeen

Processing of cereal grains plays a central role for many feed manufacturers in their trade with farmers and therefore a discussion of the topic at this time seems most appropriate, since recent developments may bring about some re-assessment of the industry's role as supplier of concentrated feeds for ruminants.

The processing of cereals in the past has been carried out for two main reasons, first, to cause an increase in the digestibility of the feed, and secondly, to help to provide a suitable package for the inclusion of other essential or non-essential ingredients in the diet. Pelleting also helps to provide a dust free, palatable material with minimum spillage and rejection by the animals. This chapter will attempt to discuss some recent findings relating both to sheep and cattle, but, as will be apparent when cereal processing is discussed, it is necessary to consider sheep and goats separately from cattle.

Processing of cereals for sheep

INTENSIVE CEREAL BASED DIETS

A line of research to study the effect of processing cereals for sheep became relevant after the successful development of an intensive lamb production system (Ørskov *et al.*, 1971). Although a high efficiency of food utilisation was observed, with growth rates of 400–500 g/d, it became apparent that the meat trade had severe reservations about the carcass meat produced. The fat was found to be too soft for easy handling of the meat, even at temperatures in cold storage. While it was first assumed that the soft consistency of the fat was due to a high content of unsaturated fatty acids, analysis of the fatty acid composition showed it to be normal. The softness was due to a very high proportion of odd-numbered, mono— and dimethyl—branched chain fatty acids, the latter having very low melting points (Duncan, Ørskov and Garton, 1971; *Table 14.1*).

The causes of the high content of the unusual fatty acids were found to originate from a very high production of propionic acid in the rumen, the absorption of which exceeded the capacity of the liver to metabolize it so that

Table 14.1 COMPONENT FATTY ACIDS OF TRIGLYCERIDES OF PERINEPHRIC AND SUBCUTANEOUS ADIPOSE TISSUE OF LAMBS FED ON BARLEY-RICH DIETS OR ON GRASS-CUBE DIETS (FROM DUNCAN, ØRSKOV and GARTON, 1971)

	14:0	16:0	16:1	18:0	18:1	18:2	n-acids with odd number of C atoms*	Branched-chain acids**
Barley-rich diets								
Lamb A								
perinephric	4	27	2	19	35	5	4	2
subcutaneous	2	23	1	10	42	5	6	9
Lamb B								
perinephric	4	26	2	21	37	4	3	3
subcutaneous	2	22	2	6	42	3	8	13
Lamb C								
perinephric	4	26	2	21	38	4	2	1
subcutaneous	4	23	2	6	39	5	–	13
Grass-cube diet								
Lamb D								
perinephric	2	19	2	36	30	3	3	2
subcutaneous	2	21	3	14	46	4	4	2
Lamb E								
perinephric	2	20	1	30	32	5	3	2
subcutaneous	3	22	4	9	47	5	3	1

* Mostly 15:0, 17:0 and 17:1
** Mostly monomethyl substituted 14:0, 15:0 and 16:0

propionic acid and its intermediary of metabolism, methylmalonic acid, were appearing in the peripheral circulation and participating in the synthesis of fat in the subcutaneous adipose tissue. This subject has been reviewed recently by Garton (1976).

Up to that time, diets for the early weaned lambs were essentially based on rolled grain which was subsequently pelleted (Ørskov *et al.*, 1971). The first attempt to reduce the proportion of propionic acid in the rumen by pelleting whole barley directly failed, but since food utilisation was, if anything, improved the further step was taken of avoiding processing altogether (Fraser and Ørskov, 1974). The essential features of this work are summarised in *Table 14.2*, where it can be seen that feeding of whole, as compared to processed, grain for lambs did not reduce food utilisation or digestibility. Whole grain diets increased the rumen pH and eliminated ruminitis (Ørskov, 1973), but more importantly it reduced the proportion of propionic acid to levels acceptable for normal metabolism and thereby eliminated the soft fat problem in the intensively fed lamb.

This development was followed-up by looking at the effect on voluntary intake of roughage by sheep when they were given supplements of whole or processed grain. It was thought that the higher rumen pH, caused by a more controlled rate of starch release from whole grains, might be expected to eliminate some of the problems associated with the inhibiting effect on cellulose digestion which occurs when ruminants given roughage based diets are supplemented with processed concentrate.

Table 14.2 THE EFFECT OF PROCESSING OF DIFFERENT CEREALS ON RUMEN pH AND PROPORTION OF ACETIC AND PROPIONIC ACID AND ON FOOD UTILISATION IN LAMBS (FROM ØRSKOV, FRASER AND GORDON, 1974; ØRSKOV, FRASER AND McHATTIE, 1974)

Cereal	Form	Rumen pH	Molar proportion of:		Liveweight gain (g/d)	Digestibility of organic matter (g/kg)	Food conversion (kg dry matter/ kg gain)
			Acetic acid	Propionic acid			
Barley	Whole loose	6.4	52.5	30.1	340	81.1	2.75
Barley	Ground pelleted	5.4	45.0	45.3	347	77.2	2.79
Maize	Whole loose	6.1	47.2	38.7	345	84.3	2.52
Maize	Ground pelleted	5.2	41.3	43.2	346	82.1	2.62
Oats	Whole loose	6.7	65.0	18.6	241	69.9	3.07
Oats	Ground pelleted	6.1	53.2	37.5	238	67.5	3.33
Wheat	Whole loose	5.9	52.3	32.2	303	82.7	2.97
Wheat	Ground pelleted	5.0	34.2	42.6	323	86.6	2.56
SE of mean		0.14	2.4	3.2	15	1.2	0.11

Table 14.3 THE EFFECT OF GIVING SUPPLEMENTS BASED ON WHOLE OR PELLETED BARLEY ON VOLUNTARY INTAKE OF DRIED GRASS AND ON TOTAL INTAKE OF DRY MATTER (DM) IN LAMBS (FROM ØRSKOV AND FRASER, 1975)

Supplement			Intake of dried grass (g DM/d)	Total daily intake (including supplement) (g DM/d)
Form	(g/kg$^{0.75}$)	(g DM/d)		
	0	0	991	991
Whole	25	310	790	1100
barley	50	616	642	1258
Pelleted	25	309	820	1129
barley	50	608	472	1080
SE of treatment differences			45	44

A summary of this work from Ørskov and Fraser (1975) is given in *Table 14.3*, where it can be seen that at low levels of supplementation the degree of processing did not appear to have an effect on the voluntary consumption of dried grass. On the other hand, at a higher level of grain supplementation the reduction in the intake of dried grass was much greater for processed rather than whole grain. In fact the increase from 25 to 50 g/kg$^{0.75}$ of pelleted barley did not have the effect of supplementation at all, but rather a complete substitution effect was noted since the intake of DM from grass was reduced to the same amount as the DM supplied by the pelleted supplement.

ADDITION OF UREA AND MINERALS TO WHOLE GRAIN

When it was first established that whole grains were preferable to processed grain for sheep, a pelleted supplement containing protein, minerals and vitamins was mixed with grain as a mastermix and was found to be excellent for feeding to early weaned lambs and lactating ewes. There are, however, several production systems in which protein supplementation is not required but where supplements of non-protein nitrogen (NPN) would be adequate. In most grains the nitrogen content is less than that required by the rumen microbes, and if the grain is offered without any nitrogen supplementation the intake will be low and digestion inefficient (Mehrez and Ørskov, 1978). Supplementing whole grain with urea was first found to be a great problem as the crystals of urea segregated from the grain. The addition of molasses to bind the crystals and the grain together was unsuccessful, but the problem was solved when it was observed that a solution of urea, 50–60% by weight in water (Ørskov, Smart and Mehrez, 1974), could be absorbed completely into the grain without recrystallisation. Later observations (Rowett Research Institute, 1974; Ørskov and Grubb, 1977) showed that not only urea but also essential minerals and even vitamins could be included and absorbed or adsorbed to the grain. Thus, at least for sheep, it was possible to produce a simple complete feed with no problems of segregation and where the urea was intimately and homogeneously mixed with the grain ensuring a more steady release of ammonia in the rumen than would be achieved by adding it as crystals. since urea absorbs so easily into the grain, up to at least 5% can be incorporated and it can then be used as a carrier for urea to support other dietary constituents where urea inclusion may be less convenient, e.g. with simultaneous feeding of roots or roughage low in nitrogen.

Processing of grain for cattle

While for sheep grains should be given in the whole form, there is plenty of evidence to show that when whole loose grains are fed to cattle the digestibility is low and can be improved considerably by processing (Nicholson, Gorrill and Burgess, 1971; MacLeod, Macdearmid and Kay, 1972; Nordin and Campling, 1976). It is interesting to note that the difference in this respect between sheep and goats on the one hand and cattle on the other appears to be due mainly to the size of the animals, or more precisely to the size of the reticulo-omasal orifice because calves can digest whole grain quite effectively (Nicholson, Gorrill and Burgess, 1971). In the case of smaller ruminants, the grains which have not been cracked during eating will be cracked during rumination because whole grains do not readily pass the orifice. However, for larger animals the size of the orifice does not apparently prevent whole grain from entering the abomasum and if they are not cracked during eating there is a likelihood that no digestion at all occurs since the affect of bacteria and digestive enzymes depends on breakage of the seedcoat.

From the discussion above it can be concluded that for cattle some processing of the cereal is required in order to avoid an unacceptable lowering of digestibility. The observations made with sheep, however, led one to believe that a method of processing which achieved no more than breaking the seedcoat would be most appropriate both for systems based on complete cereal feeding and for systems where cereal based concentrates were used to supplement roughage based diets.

To test this hypothesis several physical treatments of cereals were compared (Ørskov, Soliman and Macdearmid, 1978). A method which was used in the brewing industry involving heat treatment of the cereals to achieve an expansion of the grain just sufficient to cause a visible crack was also included. The digestibility of this material was found to be satisfactory and the rumen pH with complete cereal feeding was about pH 6.2. Another method was tried when it became apparent that only access to the grain was required, namely an attempt

Table 14.4 THE EFFECT OF METHOD OF CEREAL PROCESSING ON INTAKE OF DRY MATTER BY CATTLE AND ON THE RATIO OF HAY TO CONCENTRATE IN THE DIET CONSUMED (FROM ØRSKOV, SOLIMAN AND MACDEARMID, 1978)

Type of processing	Intake of hay (g DM/kg$^{0.75}$/d)	Total intake (g DM/kg$^{0.75}$/d)	Ratio of hay to concentrate
Whole	42.1	83.5	1.01
Alkali treated	43.0	80.4	1.15
Torrified	38.1	79.6	0.93
Crimped	35.1	76.6	0.84
Rolled	34.9	76.8	0.83
Ground	34.4	76.7	0.81
Ground and pelleted	30.5	70.9	0.75
SE	1.4	—	0.04

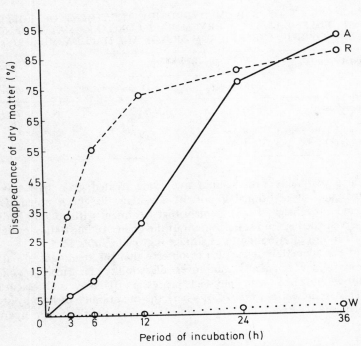

Figure 14.1 The disappearance of DM from barley incubated in nylon bags in the rumen of sheep. The barley was either incubated whole (W), rolled (R), or alkali treated (A) (From Ørskov, Soliman and Macdearmid, 1978)

to spray grain with concentrated sodium hydroxide. This is described by Ørskov and Greenhalgh (1977). The results obtained by feeding a restricted amount of supplementary grain on voluntary consumption of hay is given in *Table 14.4*. It can be seen that the observations obtained with sheep were essentially confirmed with cattle, and that they demonstrated that the slower release of starch interfered less with roughage fermentation and allowed a greater consumption of roughage.

The difference in release of dry matter per unit of time is demonstrated in *Figure 14.1* from Ørskov, Soliman and Macdearmid (1978), where the disappearance of substrate from nylon bags of whole, rolled and sodium hydroxide treated barley was compared.

Table 14.5 THE EFFECT OF SODIUM HYDROXIDE ADDITION AT 74 AND 84% DRY MATTER OF THE GRAIN ON COUNT OF BACTERIA AND FUNGAL PROPAGULES (FROM ØRSKOV, STEWART AND GREENHALGH, 1978)

Dry matter (%)	74	80	74	80
Sodium hydroxide concentration (g/kg)	Log viable bacteria/g		Log fungal propagule/g	
0	9.0	8.0	8.2	6.1
20	7.1	5.1	5.0	3.8
35	<2.6	<2.6	<2.6	<2.6

Table 14.6 EFFECT OF SODIUM HYDROXIDE TREATMENT OR ROLLING OF OATS ON DIGESTIBILITY OF DRY MATTER, ORGANIC MATTER AND ACID DETERGENT FIBRE BY STEERS (FROM ØRSKOV AND MACDEARMID, 1978)

Processing method	Digestibility (%)		Acid detergent fibre
	Dry matter	Organic matter	
Whole unprocessed	67.3	68.3	26.3
Rolled	68.1	69.1	16.0
Sodium hydroxide treated	78.8	79.0	37.7
SE of means (±)	2.1	2.1	2.3

Several experiments with sodium hydroxide treated grain have now been conducted and an additional important advantage has been noted (Ørskov, Stewart and Greenhalgh, 1978), namely that treatment with sodium hydroxide also preserved the high moisture content of the grain. An illustration of bacterial and fungal counts after 6 months of storage is given in *Table 14.5*.

It is of considerable interest also to observe that the treatment of oats with sodium hydroxide apparently improves digestibility in cattle beyond the digestibilities obtained with physical processing (Ørskov and Macdearmid, 1978). This is shown in *Table 14.6*, where the digestibility of oats by steers is given when the oats were fed whole, rolled or treated with sodium hydroxide.

TECHNIQUE OF TREATMENT WITH SODIUM HYDROXIDE

Concentration required

As could be expected the sodium hydroxide required to achieve an optimum digestibility varies with the type of grain used. About 3–3.5% by weight is required for barley, 4–4.5% for oats and about 2.5% for wheat. The optimum effect can be obtained when the sodium hydroxide solution contains 30–40% by weight of sodium hydroxide.

Application methods

There are several methods which can be used to apply the sodium hydroxide solution to the grain. In most experiments carried out at the Rowett Research Institute the sodium hydroxide was applied to batches of grain mixed in an Oswalt Feed Mixer trailer. It can also be applied in a continuous process as a spray similar to application of propionic acid, although not with the same equipment. This method is very rapid and may well be preferred.

Safety precautions

As with sodium hydroxide treatment of cereal straw, extreme precautions must be applied to avoid spillage and uncontrolled spraying or leakage of the solution when treating grains. The most appropriate is a method which completely avoids handling of the sodium hydroxide solution, i.e. from a stationary tank with an appropriate arrangement of valves as instructed by the suppliers of this material.

FLOW CHARACTERISTICS OF SODIUM HYDROXIDE TREATED GRAIN

Following treatment, the grain can form into a hard solid mass. For some farmers this will give problems in the subsequent handling. While the clumps will break in the mixer trailer the problem can be at least partly avoided if the treatment is carried out in the mixer trailer unit and mixing is continued for about 40 minutes. When the spray method is used the hard clumping can be avoided if the treated grain is moved to its destination approximately 3—6 hours after treatment.

STORAGE OF TREATED GRAIN

While observations suggest that the treated grain can be stored under cover from rain for many months, there is evidence that some residual sodium hydroxide can persist for 3—5 days before it has reacted completely with carbon dioxide to form carbonates and, therefore, it should not be fed until about one week after treatment.

STORAGE OF TREATED GRAIN WITH UREA AND MINERALS

In many feeding situations it is desirable to add urea to the grain. It was first considered that urea would not be stable with treated grain due to the alkaline conditions created. This was shown not to be the case as treated grain stored with urea for several months did not loose appreciable amounts of nitrogen (Ørskov, Stewart and Greenhalgh, 1978). The method used for the preparation of urea containing diets for sheep can be used. Urea and minerals, but obviously not the vitamins, can also be added with cold sodium hydroxide.

SODIUM HYDROXIDE TREATMENT AND RUMEN METABOLISM

Feeding of the sodium hydroxide treated grain to cattle maintains a rumen pH of about 6.0 with complete grain feeding as compared to an approximate pH of 5.2 with feeding of processed grain. This change in rumen pH results in a higher production of acetic acid and complete elimination of ruminitis.

The effect on rumen fermentation of feeding complete diets of sodium hydroxide treated or rolled barley or oats are given in *Table 14.7*.

The increases in acetic acid and the decreases in propionic acid proportion as a result of feeding alkali treated cereals to cattle are almost identical to the changes observed with feeding whole as opposed to pelleted cereals for sheep (*Table 14.2*). This decrease in propionic acid is less likely to cause metabolic problems, particularly since the lactic acid, normally associated with a very high propionic acid proportion, is also reduced. While no experiments have been conducted with dairy cows the results suggest that a higher proportion of

Table 14.7 THE EFFECT OF SODIUM HYDROXIDE TREATMENT ON GRAIN ON PROPORTIONS OF VOLATILE FATTY ACIDS IN THE RUMEN LIQUOR OF STEERS (FROM ØRSKOV AND MACDEARMID, 1979)

Treatment	Acetic acid	Propionic acid	Butyric acid
Rolled barley	46.2	40.7	8.0
Treated barley	51.3	34.9	10.2
Rolled oats	50.4	39.2	5.9
Treated oats	64.5	23.4	7.8

concentrate could be given before problems of low milk fat are encountered. The development discussed above obviously needs to be tested on a large scale before an all-out application can be advocated; so far the results look encouraging.

Conclusions

For sheep, grain processing is undesirable since there is little or no improvement in digestibility which can, for intensively fed lambs, lead to problems of carcass quality and ruminitis; when given as a supplement it can adversely affect roughage intake and digestion. For cattle, some processing of cereal grains is required, however, any processing in excess of that which is required to achieve a high digestibility is undesirable since, as for sheep, it accentuates problems of ruminitis and roughage utilisation. A new process involving the treatment of whole grain with a concentrated solution of sodium hydroxide looks promising since it ensures a high digestibility, a good intake of roughage, and its efficient utilisation, and it can preserve high moisture grain. Disadvantages lie in higher water intakes by the animals, more difficult flow characteristics of the grain and hazards in dealing with a dangerous liquid.

References

DUNCAN, W.R.H., ØRSKOV, E.R. and GARTON, G.A. (1971). *Proc. Nutr. Soc.*, **31**, 19A

FRASER, C. and ØRSKOV, E.R. (1974). *Anim. Prod.*, **18**, 175

GARTON, G.A. (1976). *Rep. Rowett Inst.*, **31**, 124

MACLEOD, N.A., MACDEARMID, A. and KAY, M. (1972). *Anim. Prod.*, **14**, 111

MEHREZ, A.Z. and ØRSKOV, E.R. (1978). *Br. J. Nutr.*, **40**, 337

NICHOLSON, J.W.G., GORRILL, A.D. and BURGESS, P.L. (1971). *Can. J. Anim. Sci.*, **51**, 697

NORDIN, M. and CAMPLING, R.C. (1976). *Anim. Prod.*, **23**, 305

ØRSKOV, E.R. (1973). *Res. vet. Sci.*, **14**, 110

ØRSKOV, E.R. and FRASER, C. (1975). *Br. J. Nutr.*, **34**, 493

ØRSKOV, E.R. and GREENHALGH, J.F.D. (1977). *J. agric. Sci., Camb.*, **89**, 253

ØRSKOV, E.R. and GRUBB, D.A. (1977). *Anim. Feed Sci., Technol.*, **2**, 307

ØRSKOV, E.R. and MACDEARMID, A. (1978). *Anim. Prod.*, **26**, 401

ØRSKOV, E.R., FRASER, C., GILL, J.C. and CORSE, E.L. (1971). *Anim. Prod.*, **13**, 485

ØRSKOV, E.R., FRASER, C. and GORDON, J.G. (1974). *Br. J. Nutr.*, **32**, 59

ØRSKOV, E.R., FRASER, C. and MCHATTIE, I. (1974). *Anim. Prod.*, **18**, 85

ØRSKOV, E.R., SMART, R.I. and MEHREZ, A.Z. (1974). *J. agric. Sci., Camb.*, **83**, 299

ØRSKOV, E.R., SOLIMAN, H.S. and MACDEARMID, A.   (1978). *J. agric. Sci., Camb.*, **90**, 611

ØRSKOV, E.R., STEWART, C. and GREENHALGH, J.F.D. (1978). *J. agric. Sci., Camb.* In press

ROWETT RESEARCH INSTITUTE (1974). *Ann. Rep.*, **30**, 67

15

THE NUTRITIVE VALUE OF SILAGES

R.J. WILKINS
Grassland Research Institute, Berkshire

The production of silage in the UK has doubled in the last five years and now exceeds 13 million tonnes annually. Despite this increase in silage making, hay remains the dominant conserved forage. Much progress has been made in reducing loss in silage-making. Systems to restrict the access of air into silos have been widely adopted (Ministry of Agriculture, Fisheries and Food, 1970; Raymond, Shepperson and Waltham, 1972) and fermentation quality has been improved by wilting crops prior to ensiling and by the use of chemical additives. The nutritive value of silage is, however, often disappointingly low and this limits the extent to which silage can contribute to feeding highly-productive ruminant animals.

This chapter considers the changes in composition that occur during ensiling, the effects of ensiling on nutritive value and, finally, analytical schemes for the evaluation of silage quality.

Changes in composition during ensiling

Ensiling is basically an anaerobic fermentation process. Water-soluble carbohydrates (WSC) in the crop are fermented by homolactic bacteria to give lactic acid, by heterolactic bacteria to give lactic and acetic acids, mannitol, ethanol and carbon dioxide and by yeasts to give lactic acid, ethanol and carbon dioxide (McDonald and Whittenbury, 1967; Woolford, 1973). Non-volatile organic acids (McDonald and Whittenbury, 1967) and structural carbohydrates (Küntzel and Zimmer, 1972) also make some contribution to fermentation. If the decline in pH resulting from this fermentation is sufficient, the growth of clostridia is prevented because they are more sensitive than lactic acid bacteria and yeasts to low pH (Wieringa, 1958). If clostridia proliferate a secondary fermentation takes place in which lactic acid is degraded to acetic acid, butyric acid and carbon dioxide and extensive deamination and decarboxylation of amino acids take place (McDonald and Whittenbury, 1967).

Proteolysis starts soon after the crop is cut and, even in well-preserved silages, protein nitrogen is normally less than 50% of total nitrogen. Plant enzymes appear to be largely responsible for decrease in true protein content in well-preserved silages (Bousset *et al.,* 1972). Simple nitrogenous compounds — the amines and ammonia — are normally present in large quantities only in silages which have undergone a clostridial fermentation (McDonald, Watson and Whittenbury, 1966).

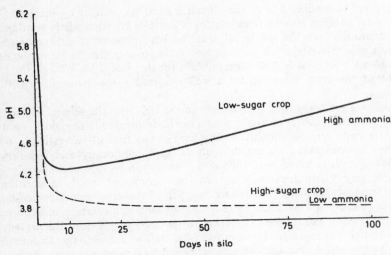

Figure 15.1 Typical changes in pH during the fermentation of crops of low and high sugar content

Changes in pH with time in the silo for well-preserved and badly-preserved silages are shown in *Figure 15.1*. These changes in composition commonly result in the gross energy of silage being higher than that of the crop before it is ensiled (Waldo *et al.*, 1965; Waldo *et al.*, 1969; Alderman, Collins and Dougall, 1971; Reever *et al.*, 1971; McDonald, Henderson and Ralton, 1973). The gross energy values of some grass and silage constituents are given in *Table 15.1*. The values for butyrate and ethanol are particularly high, whereas those for lactate and acetate are lower than for glucose and fructose. McDonald *et al.* (1973) reported that the mean gross energy of six silages was 9.3% higher than that of the grasses before they were ensiled and that the increase ranged from 3.4% to 14.7%.

Much research has been directed towards the elaboration of methods for the prevention of clostridial fermentation. Grass varieties with high contents of WSC have been bred at the Welsh Plant Breeding Station (Breese and Davies, 1970 and 1972) with the object, in part, of producing materials which are less likely to undergo a clostridial fermentation. In the Dorset Wedge system of filling bunker silos, in which the silo is sealed when filling is not in progress, heating through respiration is restricted and thus more WSC are available for fermentation and lactic acid production (Raymond *et al.*, 1972). Other approaches are to wilt

Table 15.1 GROSS ENERGY VALUES (kJ/g) OF SOME GRASS AND SILAGE CONSTITUENTS (McDONALD, HENDERSON AND RALTON, 1973)

Grass		Silage		Constituents common to grass and silage	
Glucose	15.64	Lactate	15.16	Crude fibre	17.45
Fructose	15.70	Acetate	14.60	Protein	24.60
		Butyrate	24.93	Ether extract	38.53
		Ethanol	29.80		

crops prior to ensiling and to use chemical additives. Wilting by increasing the dry matter content reduces fermentation. Clostridia are particularly restricted in dry conditions with the net result that the WSC content (% DM) required to produce a stable silage which does not undergo a clostridial fermentation is reduced with increase in DM content. As a rough guide 2.5% WSC in the fresh weight of the crop is needed for a well-preserved silage to be made without additives.

Additives are being used increasingly in the UK. Here the general approach is to add material, such as molasses, which can be fermented in the silo to produce acid or to add an acid directly to the crop at the time of harvesting or when ensiling. Viscous materials are difficult to apply uniformly and free-flowing liquids — generally based on formic acid — which can be applied uniformly with a simple gravity-drip applicator are now most commonly used. Application of formic acid at 2.3 ℓ/ton will reduce the pH of the crop entering the silo to 4.2–4.6 (Wilson and Wilkins, 1973a). Subsequent fermentation of crop components to acids will reduce pH further to the level required for the prevention of clostridial fermentation. Preservation is, therefore, achieved by the combined effect of the added acid and the acid generated by fermentation. Additives with specific effects against clostridia have been sought. Sodium nitrite and nisin are effective against some clostridia, but unfortunately some of the clostridia in silage are quite tolerant to these two chemicals (Woolford, 1973 and unpublished data). There has recently been a renewed interest in completely preventing fermentation in the silo. Formalin may be used for this purpose and silages made with 7–9 ℓ/ton of formalin contain only low concentrations of fermentation acids and low levels of soluble nitrogen (Wilkins, Wilson and Woolford, 1974).

The effect of ensiling on nutritive value

In view of the large changes in chemical composition which occur during ensiling it is not surprising that the nutritive value of silage differs in several respects from that of fresh or dried forages. The effects of ensiling on digestibility and metabolisable energy, the efficiency of utilisation of digested nutrients, and voluntary intake are discussed in this section.

DIGESTIBILITY AND METABOLISABLE ENERGY

It is well established that when crops are ensiled in well-sealed silos the digestibility of dry matter and of organic matter in the ensilage is very similar to that in the crop before silage. Crops studied have included perennial grasses and legumes (Harris and Raymond, 1963; Demarquilly, 1973; Dulphy and Demarquilly, 1973) and maize (Harris, 1965). Some increase in the concentration of structural carbohydrates usually occurs during ensiling, but this is compensated for by a small increase in the digestibility of crude fibre in the silage (Jackson and Anderson, 1968; Dermarquilly, 1973). Chopping into small particles prior to ensiling had no effect on digestibility in experiments of Harris and Raymond (1963) and Dulphy and Demarquilly (1973). Wilting generally results in a small reduction in digestibility (Harris, Raymond and Wilson, 1966; Alder, McLeod and Gibbs, 1969). Formic acid may increase digestibility slightly (Castle, 1972; Wilson and Wilkins, 1973b), but formalin may reduce organic matter digestibility by 2-4 units and crude protein digestibility by a larger amount (Wilkins, Wilson and Cook, 1976).

In view of the relatively high gross energy of silage, it might be expected that ensiling would result in an increase in metabolisable energy (ME). However, in eight comparisons between fresh grass and ensiled grass ME was 10.45 ± 0.13 kJ/g for grass and 10.41 ± 0.29 kJ/g for silage (*Table 15.2*). In these experiments

Table 15.2 THE METABOLISABLE ENERGY OF FRESH GRASS AND SILAGE

Reference	Grass	Silage
	(kJ/g)	
Jackson and Anderson (1968)	10.49	10.32
	10.87	9.99
McDonald, Henderson and MacGregor (1968)	10.45	10.74
	10.03	10.49
Jackson and Anderson (1970)	10.53	11.29
	10.53	11.33
Jackson (1971)	9.95	8.95
	10.62	10.07
Mean (± S.E.)	10.45 ± 0.13	10.41 ± 0.29

intake of energy and loss of energy in faeces and urine were measured directly, but loss of energy in methane was estimated. Further experiments are required, particularly with silages of high gross energy content.

This evidence that ensiling has little effect on either the digestibility or metabolisability of forages enables farmers to use existing information on crop development and change in digestibility (Green, Corrall and Terry, 1971) in planning their silage-making programmes.

EFFICIENCY OF UTILISATION OF METABOLISABLE ENERGY

Very little calorimetric work has been carried out with silage. Van Es and Nijkamp (1969a and b) have reported experiments with both lactating and non-lactating cattle in which the efficiency with which ME was used for negative and positive energy balance was similar for rations with or without silage (*Table 15.3*). When hay and silage similar in digestibility were fed to non-lactating cattle the efficiency of utilisation for positive balance was 54% for silage and 51% for hay (van Es and Nijkamp, 1969a). Recently van der Honing *et al.* (1973) and Ekern and Sundstøl (1974) found no differences between silages and hays made from the same crops in the efficiency of utilisation of ME. The silages in these experiments contained 23-60% DM; mostly in the upper part of this range. In a single experiment with a wet silage of low fermentation quality, referred to by Blaxter (1964), the efficiency of utilisation of ME for negative balance was 61.4% compared with an expected value of 69.7%. There is clearly a need for more information on silages with high moisture content.

Table 15.3 EFFICIENCY OF UTILISATION OF METABOLISABLE ENERGY BY NON-LACTATING NON-PREGNANT COWS (VAN ES AND NIJKAMP, 1969a)

	Efficiency of utilisation of ME (%)	
	Rations with silage	*Rations without silage*
For negative balance	81.1 ± 2.9	76.6 ± 5.1
For positive balance	52.4 ± 2.9	54.9 ± 1.8

Feed conversion efficiencies on diets containing silage have been compared with those for other diets in numerous experiments. In reviewing these experiments Wernli (1972) concluded that when differences in intake and digestibility were allowed for there was no consistent difference in feed conversion efficiency between silage and hay. Saue and Breirem (1969) have, however, clear evidence of higher milk yields with well-preserved formic-acid silage than with hay; they suggested that the silage might have a chemical effect on stimulating milk secretion.

NITROGEN UTILISATION

The nitrogenous constituents in silage are often used with low efficiency. Several authors have reported lower nitrogen retention in ruminants fed silage compared with the same crop fed after freezing or drying (Waldo *et al.*, 1965; Fatianoff *et al.*, 1966; Durand, Zelter and Tisserand, 1968; Forbes and Irwin, 1968; Thomson, 1968). Wilted silages (Fatianoff *et al.*, 1966; Durand *et al.*, 1968) and silages made with formic acid (Waldo *et al.*, 1969; Wilkins, unpublished data) have tended to give higher levels of nitrogen retention than have unwilted silages made without additives.

Levels of ammonia in the rumen are characteristically high with silage diets (Fatianoff *et al.*, 1966; Schmekel, 1967; Durand *et al.*, 1968; Ciszuk and Eriksson, 1973) leading to high nitrogen losses in urine. Supplementation of silage with cereals reduces ammonia in the rumen (Durand *et al.*, 1968; Wernli, 1972) and results in a large improvement in nitrogen retention (Thomson, 1968; Griffiths, 1969; Griffiths and Spillane, 1970; Griffiths, Spillane and Bath, 1971); the addition of readily-available carbohydrate presumably leads to more efficient utilisation of silage non-protein nitrogen for microbial proteo-synthesis in the rumen (Conrad and Hibbs, 1968). Supplementation with oil-cakes also results in improved nitrogen retention (Griffiths and Spillane, 1970; Griffiths *et al.*, 1971).

The situation is very different when formaldehyde is added at ensiling. Ammonia in the rumen is reduced as the amount of formaldehyde is increased (Brown and Valentine, 1972; Lampila *et al.*, unpublished data). Silage made with formalin at 9.2 ℓ/ton fresh crop was found by Wilkins, Wilson and Cook (1976) to give rumen ammonia nitrogen values less than 8 mg/100 ml. Beever, Thomson and Harrison (1976) reported that the quantity of amino acids entering the small intestine was higher with formalin-treated silage than with silage made without additive. This increase was brought about by the formalin preventing much of the forage protein from being digested in the rumen. The digestibility of the protein in the small intestine was, however, also reduced. Clearly there is potential to manipulate the pattern of digestion of nitrogen by the addition of formaldehyde at ensiling, but the circumstances in which this treatment will result in a net improvement in the value of the nitrogenous constituents in silage are not yet defined.

INTAKE OF SILAGE

Many experiments have shown the voluntary intake of silage to be lower than that of fresh or dried feeds from the same crop. The results of Demarquilly (1973) illustrate this point well. He found that the intake of 87 silages by sheep was on average 33% lower than that of the fresh grasses and legumes from which the silages were made; the reduction in intake varied from 1% to 64%.

Effect of fermentation in the silo

There is now evidence that silage intake may be depressed either by products of clostridial fermentation or by high concentrations of free acids in silage.

Wilkins *et al.* (1971), in a study of 70 grass and legume silages, found close negative correlations between intake and the concentrations of ammonia (% total nitrogen), and acetic acid (% DM) in the silage and positive correlations between intake and lactic acid (% total acids) and Flieg Index (Zimmer, 1966). Demarquilly (1973) found significant negative correlations between intake and the contents of acetic acid and total volatile fatty acids in silage. Silages which have undergone a clostridial fermentation are characterised by high contents of ammonia, acetic acid and total volatile fatty acids and by low contents of lactic acid. There are close correlations between these parameters (Wilkins *et al.*, 1971) and they may be thought of as alternative measures of fermentation quality. When the use of an additive prevents a clostridial fermentation, increase in intake will result (Saue and Breirem, 1969; Waldo *et al.*, 1969; Wilson and Wilkins, 1973b). Successive increments of formic acid resulted in progressive increase in the intake by sheep of silages made from cocksfoot and lucerne in the work of Wilson and Wilkins (1973b).

The reason for the depression in intake with poorly-preserved silage is not established. Most attention has been paid to amines because of the known pharmacological effects of amines and the presence of amines, particularly histamine and tryptamine, in silages of this type (Wrenn *et al.*, 1963; Neumark, Bondi and Volcani, 1964). Neumark and Tadmor (1968) have found that the pattern of feed consumption is altered by infusion of histamine in association with acids, but intra-ruminal infusion of histamine has not affected intake (McDonald, Macpherson and Watt, 1963).

High concentration of free acids can also restrict silage intake. Partial neutralisation with sodium bicarbonate before feeding has increased the intake of well-preserved grass and maize silages (McLeod, Wilkins and Raymond, 1970; Thomas and Wilkinson, 1973) and intake of silage is reduced by addition of lactic acid (McLeod *et al.*, 1970). Free acids appear to have ruminal or metabolic effects, because infusions into the rumen of formic acid, lactic acid (Wilkins and Valdemoro, 1973) and acetic acid (Hutchinson and Wilkins, 1971) have all depressed voluntary intake. Thomas (1973) found that the partial neutralisation of maize silage resulted in increased blood pH and attributed the increase in intake to a reduction in acid-base stress. There is need for similar experiments with grass silage. There is also evidence for acidity affecting intake in studies with silages which have undergone different fermentations. In the work of Wilkins *et al.* (1971), although pH was not significantly related with intake in a simple regression, when pH was considered as a second variate in addition to a measurement of fermentation quality substantially more variation in intake was accounted for. Intake increased with reduction in total acid content in work by Ettala (1971) with cows and Brown and Radcliffe (1972) with sheep.

Effect of restricting fermentation

Two approaches to restricting fermentation in the silo have been pursued — wilting prior to ensiling and the use of additives to sterilise or partially sterilise the crop at ensiling.

The extent of fermentation is progressively restricted with increase in dry matter content of the ensiled crop (McDonald and Whittenbury, 1967). When materials ranging in dry matter content from 20 to 80% are preserved in anaerobic conditions the complete spectrum in composition from that of a normal silage to that of a hay is encompassed. Intake generally increases with increase in dry-matter content but in the studies of Wilkins *et al.* (1971) and Demarquilly (1973) the correlation coefficients relating intake with dry matter content were not as high as those in which intake was related to measurements of fermentation quality. Silage with a high dry matter content is widely used in the Netherlands, Federal Germany and some other European countries, but the production of such silage increases the weather-sensitivity of silage making and may also require high capital investment in tower silos.

The AIV method was the first approach to the use of chemicals to prevent fermentation and proteolysis in the silo (Virtanen, 1933). Sodium metabisulphite has also been used with this objective (Bratzler, Cowan and Swift, 1956), but fermentation was not consistently prevented in either of these methods and the chemicals used resulted in metabolic stress in ruminant animals and reduced intake (Woodward and Shepherd, 1942; Devuyst *et al.,* 1967). The development of successful applicators for adding liquids uniformly to crops at ensiling (Naerland, 1968) now makes it much more feasible to prevent fermentation in the silo. Wilkins, Wilson and Woolford (1974) reported that the addition of formalin (35% w/w HCHO) at 7-9 ℓ/ton resulted in silages with very low contents of fermentation acids. In some experiments formalin-treated silages have been consumed in greater quantities than silages made without additives, but this has not always occurred (Wilkins, Wilson and Cook, 1976). Where treatment with formalin has decreased intake, digestion rates in the rumen have been reduced, apparently by a direct effect of formalin on the rumen microbiota. More consistent effects on intake have been obtained by the use of a mixture of formalin and formic acid as an additive. Here, such mixtures suppress fermentation in the silo with a lower level of formaldehydes (Wilkins, Wilson and Woolford, 1974).

Effect of particle length

Chopping prior to ensiling has both indirect and direct effects on intake. Murdoch (1965) reported that cattle consumed larger quantities of silage made from flail-cut material than from material cut and ensiled without chopping or laceration. More recently, Dulphy and Demarquilly (1973) found that silages made from precision-chopped forages were, on average, of higher fermentation quality than those made with a flail-harvester. Voluntary intake was increased in line with the improvement in fermentation quality, but there was also an increase in intake when silage made with a flail-harvester was chopped directly before feeding. Eating behaviour was affected by the length of the particles fed; sheep given the chopped silage had fewer meals, but the silage was consumed more rapidly than was the silage with longer particles. Clearly, physical as well as chemical factors may affect silage intake.

Effect of the crop

The intake of silage is not closely related to its digestibility (Wilkins *et al.*, 1971; Demarquilly, 1973). This is in contrast to the close positive relationships between intake and digestibility for fresh and dried forages (Balch and Campling, 1962). This appears to result, at least in part, from a confounding of digestibility and fermentation quality, because fermentation quality is often poor in young crops that are high in digestibility. In a recent experiment, however, perennial ryegrass was cut on three occasions during first growth and ensiled at similar DM contents (18-20%) (Wilkins and Tetlow, unpublished data). All silages were well preserved and contained similar quantities of volatile fatty acids and ammonia. In this situation voluntary intake increased by 18% with increase in *in vivo* 'D' value from 65 to 70%.

The intake of well-preserved legume silages tends to be higher than that of grass silages of similar digestibility (Wilkins, Wilson and Cook, 1976). This is in line with the higher intake of legumes than grasses when fed fresh or after dehydration (van Soest, 1965; Osbourn, 1967).

Effect of other feeds

Feeding of supplements generally reduces differences in intake between forages. Starch-based concentrates reduce the intake of silage less than that of hay (Murdoch, 1964; Campling and Murdoch, 1966; Osbourn, 1967). Experiments with sheep at the Grassland Research Institute have shown that substitution rate (change in DM intake of silage/unit of supplement DM fed) is positively correlated with the voluntary intake of the silage when fed alone (*Figure 15.2*). Silage intake will drop rapidly when concentrates are fed if the intake of the silage is high when it is fed alone.

Different supplements have different effects on silage intake. Several experiments have shown silage intake to be higher when the silage is fed with supplements of dried grass pellets than with barley or a mixture of barley and a protein feed (Tayler, 1970; Wernli and Wilkins, 1971; Tayler and Aston, 1973). This appears to result from the conditions in the rumen being more suitable for the

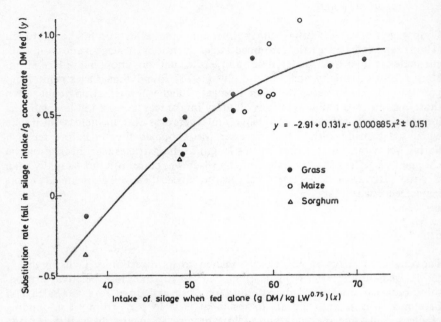

Figure 15.2 Substitution rates when sheep are fed silage without supplement or with a barley-based concentrate at 17-25 g DM/kg LW$^{0.75}$. Data from experiments at Grassland Research Institute

digestion and onward passage of silage when dried grass rather than barley is fed as a supplement (Wernli, 1972). There is need for further experiments in which different types of feed are compared as supplements for silage.

When choosing the appropriate supplement for a silage, consideration must be given not only to the characteristics of the possible supplements, but also to the potential intake of the silage and its gross nutritional characteristics (contents of nitrogen and energy).

Silage evaluation

In this section the prediction of the nutritive value of silage is considered from the viewpoint of, particularly, the feedstuff adviser. Digestible and metabolisable energy, the efficiency with which metabolisable energy is utilised, nitrogen content and the efficiency with which the nitrogen fraction is utilised are clearly important, as is, in many situations, the level of voluntary intake. The evaluation of silage is made difficult not only by biological variation in relationships between chemical measurements and nutritive characteristics, but also by difficulties in sampling and analysis which result from the unstable nature of silage and its variable content of volatile components.

DIGESTIBILITY AND METABOLISABLE ENERGY

The normal approach has been to predict digestibility from a measurement of fibre content or *in vitro* digestibility and then to assume ME to be a constant proportion of the digested energy.

The correlation between the contents of either crude fibre (CF) or modified acid detergent fibre and *in vivo* digestibility is not as close with silage as with other classes of feed. Alderman *et al.* (1971) reported a correlation coefficient of -0.42 between CF and *in vivo* digestible organic matter in the dry matter (DOMD) compared with -0.53 for the correlation between MADF and DOMD. The correlations were lower when these parameters were related to digested energy content, but higher when related to starch equivalent. In this study analyses were carried out on oven-dried material and no allowance was made for volatile components lost during oven drying. This procedure is common in analytical laboratories although the volatiles may be as much as 20% of the silage dry matter (Wilson, Tilley and Steemers, 1964). It is not clear to what extent these relationships were affected by this factor. Toluene distillation (Dewar and McDonald, 1961) is normally used in research laboratories for determining the true dry matter content of silages. The difference between dry matter determined by toluene distillation and by oven-drying appears to be correlated with both dry-matter content and fermentation quality; the content of volatiles being partiularly high in wet silages with low fermentation quality. The exact relationships have, however, not been calculated. On logical grounds some adjustment to values determined on oven-dried silage should clearly be made.

In vitro digestion techniques based on the method of Tilley and Terry (1963) have been widely adopted in research laboratories for predicting the *in vivo* digestibility of fresh and dried forages. Alderman *et al.* (1971) found that the *in vitro* DOMD of oven-dried silages was related to *in vivo* DOMD more closely than were measurements of fibre content. The relationship was best when the silage had been dried at 100°C for 6 h. Brown and Radcliffe (1971) reported that the accuracy of prediction of *in vivo* dry matter digestibility (DMD) from a determination of *in vitro* DMD on oven-dried silage was much improved when the volatile components lost during oven-drying were considered and assumed to be completely digestible. An alternative approach has been followed by Alexander and McGowan (1969) who find good prediction of *in vivo* DMD from *in vitro* digestibility determined on a homogenate of fresh silage and water. Although the digestibility and starch equivalent of silages is predicted from *in vitro* digestibility in some of the Agricultural Development and Advisory Service regions in England, *in vitro* digestion techniques have disadvantages in the length of time required for completion of the assay, difficulty in standardising the method and the need for a source of rumen liquor. In many laboratories these disadvantages preclude the use of the method.

The digestibility of fresh and dried forages can be predicted with reasonable accuracy from the solubility with cellulase enzyme (Jones and Hayward, 1973) and from summative equations based on van Soest's method of fractionation (van Soest, 1964; Terry *et al.,* 1974). There is a strong case for examining the suitability of these methods for use with silages.

The analytical approaches that have been so far discussed make no direct allowance for variation in the gross energy content of silages. Bomb calorimetry is unlikely to be used in routine analyses. Determinations made on silages often have substantial analytical error owing to both sampling difficulties and problems in achieving complete combustion. Alderman *et al.* (1971) found significant correlations between gross energy and a number of the Weende components in silage. Gross energy was positively correlated with crude protein and ether extract and negatively correlated with nitrogen-free extract. Ethanol, butyric acid and protein are the components in silage with highest gross energy contents and measurement of these components should increase the precision with which the digestible energy of silage can be predicted.

The assumption that digestible energy is a constant proportion of metabolisable energy appears from the experiments reviewed earlier to be unlikely to introduce major errors.

PROTEIN VALUE

In assessing the protein value of silage decisions have to be made on the method of preparing the sample for analysis and on the value to be ascribed to the non-protein nitrogen contained in silage. *Table 15.4* gives nitrogen contents determined by a Kjeldahl method on a range of silages analysed fresh, after oven-drying (100°C for 16 h) or after freeze-drying. Considerable quantities of

Table 15.4 THE EFFECT OF SAMPLE PREPARATION ON THE NITROGEN CONTENT OF SILAGE (BARNES, WILSON AND COOK, UNPUBLISHED DATA)

		Nitrogen (% of dry matter)		
Silage	*pH*	*Fresh*[1]	*Oven-dried*[2]	*Freeze-dried* [3]
1	4.2	2.25	1.99	2.13
2	5.4	2.16	2.16	1.99
3	3.6	2.24	2.19	2.15
4	5.6	3.43	2.64	2.62
5	5.2	3.04	2.05	1.88
Mean:		2.62	2.21	2.15

All silages were made from ryegrass and had dry matter content of 16–20%. Silage 3 was made with formic acid added at ensiling and silage 4 with formalin added at ensiling; other silages were made without additives.

[1] Dry matter determined by toluene distillation

[2] Expressed as a percentage of the oven-dried material

[3] Values have been adjusted for the moisture in the freeze-dried material determined by the Fischer method.

nitrogen are lost when silages are prepared by both oven-drying and freeze-drying. This applies particularly to badly preserved silages with high pH. At the Grassland Research Institute, macro-Kjeldahl digestions are carried out on fresh silages which have been chopped in a bowl-chopper.

The depressed efficiency with which the nitrogenous compounds in silage may be utilised, is associated with large quantities of non-protein and particularly volatile, nitrogen in silage. The volatile nitrogen is mainly ammonia and this can be determined rapidly using a specific-ion electrode. The quantity of volatile nitrogen is particularly important when non-protein nitrogen is being considered as an ingredient in supplements to be fed with silage.

INTAKE

Fermentation quality is responsible for much of the variation in the intake of silages currently produced on farms. The pH value can be measured easily, but the relationship between pH and fermentation quality is complicated by the high pH of both badly-preserved silages which have undergone a clostridial fermentation and well-preserved silages in which little fermentation has taken place. The contents of either ammonia or of total volatile fatty acids are much more satisfactory indices of fermentation quality and both are related to intake. The volatile acids may be analysed rapidly by gas-liquid chromatography and ammonia by specific-ion electrode. Ammonia would probably not be suitable for intake prediction when additives containing ammonia (Bruce, 1972) or hexamethylene-tetramine (Hellberg, 1967) are used.

To allow for the restriction to intake which occurs in silages with high concentrations of acids, anticipated levels of intake should be reduced when pH is particularly low. Absolute levels of intake will, of course, vary with the physiological condition of the animal being fed and the quantity of supplementary feeds given.

SCHEME OF ANALYSIS

It may be concluded that the nutritive characteristics of silage can be predicted by a simple analytical scheme involving determination of (i) dry matter by oven-drying (ii) CF (or MADF) in dried silage (iii) pH and nitrogen in fresh silage and (iv) ammonia in an acid extract of the silage. Volatiles in the silage would be predicted from oven dry-matter content and ammonia content and other analyses adjusted to allow for the loss of volatiles during oven drying. This scheme has not yet, however, been tested in practice.

Summary

The composition of the crop has a major effect on the nutritive value of silage. Changes in the silo reduce nutritive value largely through bringing about reduction in voluntary intake and in the efficiency with which the nitrogen fraction is utilised. Intakes are particularly low with silages of low fermentation quality. These silages are characterised by high contents of volatile fatty acids and ammonia. High total concentrations of acids in silage also restrict intake, but at a higher level than when the silage is badly-preserved. Research is being directed to preventing fermentation and protein breakdown in the silo in order to produce silages with higher nutritive value. A simple scheme for the analysis of silage is suggested.

References

ALDER, F.E., McLEOD, D.St.L. and GIBBS, B.G. (1969). *J. Br. Grassld Soc.*, **24**, 199–206

ALDERMAN, G., COLLINS, F.C. and DOUGALL, H.W. (1971). *J. Br. Grassld Soc.*, **26**, 109–11

280   *The nutritive value of silages*

ALEXANDER, R.H. and McGOWAN, M. (1969). *J. Br. Grassld Soc.*, 24, 195–8

BALCH, C.C. and CAMPLING, R.C. (1962). *Nutr. Abstr. Revs.*, 32, 669–86

BEEVER, D.E., THOMSON, D.J. and HARRISON, D.G. (1976). 'Energy and Protein Transformations in the Rumen and the Absorption of Nutrients by Sheep Fed Forage Diets.' *Proc. 12th Int. Grassld Congr., Moscow 1974*, 3, 56–62

BEEVER, D.E., THOMSON, D.J., PFEFFER, E. and ARMSTRONG, D.G. (1971). *Br. J. Nutr.*, 26, 123–34

BLAXTER, K.L. (1964). *Proc. Nutr. Soc.*, 23, 62–71

BOUSSET, J., BOUSSET-FATIANOFF, N., GOUET, Ph. and CONTREPOIS, M. (1972). *Ann. Biol. Anim. Bioch. Biophys.*, 12, 453–77

BRATZLER, J.N., COWAN, R.J. and SWIFT, R.W. (1956). *J. Anim. Sci.*, 15, 163–76

BREESE, E.L. and DAVIES, W.E. (1970). 'Herbage Plant Breeding,' *Welsh Plant Breeding Station Jubilee Rep. 1919–1969*, 11–47

BREESE, E.L. and DAVIES, W.E. (1972). 'Herbage Breeding,' *Rep. Welsh Plant Breeding Station, 1971*, 15–25

BROWN, D.C. and RADCLIFFE, J.C. (1971). *Aust. J. agric. Res.*, 22, 787–96

BROWN, D.C. and RADCLIFFE, J.C. (1972). *Aust. J. agric. Sci.*, 23, 25–33

BROWN, D.C. and VALENTINE, S.C. (1972). *Aust. J. agric. Res.*, 23, 1093–100

BRUCE, D.T. (1972). *Maize Bull.*, No. 42, 3–4

CAMPLING, R.C. and MURDOCH, J. (1966). *J. Dairy Res.*, 33, 1–11

CASTLE, M.E. (1972). *Scot. Agric.*, 51, 302–4

CISZUK, P. and ERIKSSON, S. (1973). *Swedish J. agric. Res.*, 3, 13–20

CONRAD, H.R. and HIBBS, J.W. (1968). *J. Dairy Sci.*, 51, 276–85

DEMARQUILLY, C. (1973). *Ann. Zootech.*, 22, 1–35

DEVUYST, A., ARNOUD, R., VANBELLE, M., VERVACK, W., AUSLOOS, M. and MOREELS, A. (1967). *Agricultura Louvain*, 15, 107–17

DEWAR, W.A. and McDONALD, P. (1961). *J. Sci. Fd Agric.*, 12, 790–5

DULPHY, J.P. and DEMARQUILLY, C. (1973). *Ann. Zootech.*, 22, 199–217

DURAND, M., ZELTER, S.Z. and TISSERAND, J.L. (1968). *Ann. Biol. Anim. Bioch. Biophys.*, 8, 45–67

EKERN, A. and SUNDSTØL, F. (1974). 'Energy Utilization of Hay and Silage by Sheep', *Proc. 6th Symp. Energy Metabolism, Stuttgart, EAAP.* pp. 221–4

ETTALA, E. (1971). Thesis, Helsinki University

FATIANOFF, N., DURAND, M., TISSERAND, J.L. and ZELTER, S.Z. (1966). 'Comparative Effects of Wilting and of Sodium Metabisulphite on Quality and Nutritive Value of Alfalfa Silage', *Proc. 10th Int. Grassld Congr., Helsinki*, pp. 551–5

FORBES, T.J. and IRWIN, J.H.D. (1968). *J. Br. Grassld Soc.*, 23, 299–305

GREEN, J.O., CORRALL, A.J. and TERRY, R.A. (1971). 'Grass Species and Varieties. Relationships between Stage of Growth, Yield and Forage Quality', *Tech. Rep. 8, Grassld Res. Inst.*

GRIFFITHS, T.W. (1969). *Anim. Prod.*, 11, 286

GRIFFITHS, T.W. and SPILLANE, T.A. (1970). *Anim. Prod.*, 12, 359–60

GRIFFITHS, T.W., SPILLANE, T.A. and BATH, I.H. (1971). *Anim. Prod.*, 13, 386

HARRIS, C.E. (1965). *Expl Agric.*, 1, 121–3

HARRIS, C.E. and RAYMOND, W.F. (1963). *J. Br. Grassld Soc.*, 18, 204–12

HARRIS, C.E., RAYMOND, W.F. and WILSON, R.F. (1966). 'The Voluntary Intake of Silage', *Proc. 10th Inst. Grassld Congr., Helsinki*, pp. 564–7

HELLBERG, A. (1967). *J. Br. Grassld Soc.*, 22, 289–97

HUTCHINSON, K.J. and WILKINS, R.J. (1971). *J. agric. Sci., Camb.*, 77, 539–43

JACKSON, N. (1971). *J. Sci. Fd Agric.*, 22, 419–23

JACKSON, N. and ANDERSON, B.K. (1968). *J. Sci. Fd Agric.*, **19**, 1–4

JACKSON, N. and ANDERSON, B.K. (1970). *J. Sci. Fd Agric.*, **21**, 453–7

JONES, D.I.H. and HAYWARD, M.V. (1973). *J. Sci. Fd Agric.*, **24**, 1419–26

KÜNTZEL, U. and ZIMMER, E. (1972). 'Untersuchungen über Vorkommen, Veränderung und Verbrauch von Kohlenhydraten bei der Silierung', *LandbForsch-Völkenrode*, No. 13, 88 pp

McDONALD, P., HENDERSON, A.R. and MacGREGOR, A.W. (1968). *J. Sci. Fd Agric.*, **19**, 125–32

McDONALD, P., HENDERSON, A.R. and RALTON, I. (1973). *J. Sci. Fd Agric.*, **24**, 827–34

McDONALD, P., MACPHERSON, H.T. and WATT, J.A. (1963). *J. Br. Grassld Soc.*, **18**, 230–2

McDONALD, P., WATSON, S.J. and WHITTENBURY, R. (1966). *Z. Tierphysiol. Tierernähr. Futtermittelk.*, **21**, 103–10

McDONALD, P. and WHITTENBURY, R. (1967). *Br. Grassld Soc. Occ. Symp.*, **3**, pp. 76–84

McLEOD, D.S., WILKINS, R.J. and RAYMOND, W.F. (1970). *J. agric. Sci., Camb.*, **75**, 311–9

MINISTRY OF AGRICULTURE, FISHERIES AND FOOD (1970). 'Silage,' *Bull. 37, Min. Agric. Fish. Fd.* London; H.M.S.O.

MURDOCH, J.C. (1964). *J. Br. Grassld Soc.*, **19**, 316–20

MURDOCH, J.C. (1965). *J. Br. Grassld Soc.*, **20**, 54–8

NAERLAND, G.O. (1968). 'Utvikling av LTI-Syreutstyr,' *Forsøksmelding nr. 14, Landbruksteknisk Institutt, Vollebekk*

NEUMARK, H., BONDI, A. and VOLCANI, R. (1964). *J. Sci. Fd Agric.*, **15**, 487–92

NEUMARK, H. and TADMOR, A. (1968). *J. agric. Sci., Camb.*, **71**, 267–70

OSBOURN, D.F. (1967). *Br. Grassld Soc. Occ. Symp.*, **3**, pp. 20–28

RAYMOND, W.F., SHEPPERSON, G. and WALTHAM, R. (1972). *Forage conservation and feeding.* Ipswich; Farming Press Ltd.

SAUE, O. and BREIREM, K. (1969). 'Comparison of Formic Acid Silage with other Silages and Dried Grassland Products in Feeding Experiments,' *Proc. 3rd Gen. Meeting European Grassld Fed., Braunschweig*, pp. 282–4

SCHMEKEL, J. (1967). *LantbrHogsk. Annlr*, **33**, 767–83

TAYLER, J.C. (1970). *J. Br. Grassld Soc.*, **25**, 180–90

TAYLER, J.C. and ASTON, K. (1973). *Grass. J. Br. Assn Gr. Crop Driers*, No. 6, 3–8

TERRY, R.A., OSBOURN, D.F., CAMMELL, S.B. and FENLON, J.S. (1974). 'In Vitro Digestibility and the Estimation of Energy in Herbage,' *Proc. 5th Gen. Meet. European Grassld Fed., Uppsala 1973*, pp. 19–25

THOMAS, C. (1973). 'The Utilization of Maize Silage for Beef Production.' Ph.D. thesis, University of Reading

THOMAS, C. and WILKINSON, J.M. (1973). 'Nitrogen and Acidity as Factors Influencing the Voluntary Intake of Maize Silage', *Proc. Br. Soc. Anim. Prod., 1973*, pp. 67–8

THOMSON, D.J. (1968). *Anim. Prod.*, **10**, 240

TILLEY, J.M.A. and TERRY, R.A. (1963). *J. Br. Grassld Soc.*, **18**, 105–11

VAN DER HONING, Y., VAN ES, A.J.H., NIJKAMP, H.J. and TERLUIN, R. (1973). *Z. Tierphysiol. Tierernähr. Futtermittelk.*, **31**, 149–58

VAN ES, A.J.H. and NIJKAMP, H.J. (1969a). 'Energy, Carbon and Nitrogen Balance Experiments with Non-Lactating, Non-Pregnant Cows,' in *Energy Metabolism of Farm Animals*. Ed. K.L. Blaxter, J. Kielanowski and G. Thorbek. Newcastle-upon-Tyne; Oriel Press Ltd., pp. 203–7

VAN ES, A.J.H. and NIJKAMP, H.J. (1969b). 'Energy, Carbon and Nitrogen Balance Experiments with Lactating Cows,' in *Energy Metabolism of Farm Animals*. Ed. K.L. Blaxter, J. Kielanowski, and G. Thorbek. Newcastle-upon-Tyne; Oriel Press Ltd., pp. 209–12

VAN SOEST, P.J. (1964). *J. Anim. Sci.*, **23**, 838–45

VAN SOEST, P.J. (1965). *J. Anim. Sci.*, **24**, 834–43

VIRTANEN, A.I. (1933). *Emp. J. Exp. Agric.*, **1**, 143–55

WALDO, D.R., MILLER, R.W., OKAMOTO, M. and MOORE, L.A. (1965). *J. Dairy Sci.*, **48**, 910–6

WALDO, D.R., SMITH, L.W., MILLER, R.W. and MOORE, L.A. (1969). *J. Dairy Sci.*, **52**, 1609–16

WERNLI, C.G. (1972). 'Nutritional Studies on Feed Supplements for Grass Silage.' Ph.D. thesis, University of Reading

WERNLI, C.G. and WILKINS, R.J. (1971). *Anim. Prod.*, **13**, 397

WIERINGA, G.W. (1958). *Neth. J. agric. Sci.*, **6**, 204–10

WILKINS, R.J., HUTCHINSON, K.H., WILSON, R.F. and HARRIS, C.E. (1971). *J. agric. Sci., Camb.*, **77**, 531–7

WILKINS, R.J. and VALDEMORO, M.D. (1973). 'Silage as a Sole Feed,' *A. Rep. Grassld Res Inst. 1972*, pp. 77–8

WILKINS, R.J., WILSON, R.F. and COOK, J.E. (1976). 'Restriction of Fermentation during Ensilage: the Nutritive Value of Silages Made with the Addition of Formaldehyde, *Proc. 12th Inst. Grassld Congr., Moscow 1974*, **3**, 674–690

WILKINS, R.J., WILSON, R.F. and WOOLFORD, M.K. (1974). 'The effect of Form—aldehyde on the Silage Fermentation,' *Proc. 5th Gen. Meet. European Grassld Fed., Uppsala Växtodling 29, 1973*, pp. 197–201

WILSON, R.F., TILLEY, J.M.A. and STEEMERS, M.A. (1964). *J. Sci. Fd Agric.*, **15**, 197–200

WILSON, R.F. and WILKINS, R.J. (1973a). *J. agric. Sci., Camb.*, **81**, 117–24

WILSON, R.F. and WILKINS, R.J. (1973b). *J. agric. Sci., Camb.*, **80**, 225–31

WOODWARD, T.E. and SHEPHERD, J.B. (1942). *J. Dairy Sci.*, **25**, 517–23

WOOLFORD, M.K. (1973). *'In Vitro* Techniques in Microbiological Studies of the Ensiling Process.' Ph.D. thesis, University of Edinburgh

WRENN, T.R., BITMAN, J., CECIL, H.C. and GILLIAM, D.R. (1973). *J. Dairy Sci.*, **46**, 1243–5

ZIMMER, E. (1966). *Wirtschaftseigene Futter*, **12**, 229–303

16

FEED INPUT–MILK OUTPUT RELATIONSHIPS IN THE AUTUMN-CALVING DAIRY COW

H. SWAN
University of Nottingham School of Agriculture

The autumn-calving dairy cow presents a particular challenge to the dairy farmer. Such cows calve from September through to December when the growth of herbage is at a minimum level and ground conditions are unfavourable for grazing throughout most of North-West Europe. From calving until the following spring, food has to be provided to meet the nutrient requirements of the lactating dairy cow. This includes the first hundred days of lactation, when a complex interaction of nutrient intake and body reserves is exploited by a mammary system having a high priority for circulating metabolites.

The autumn-calving dairy cow is offered a diet based on one of two conserved forages: mixed grass hay or ryegrass silage. The nutritive value and production of these two forage sources is shown in *Table 16.1*. Silage dry matter is characterized by a higher 'D' value (digestibility of organic matter in the dry matter, DOMD) than hay (63 compared with 60). Although numerically small, this difference could be critical in terms of voluntary food intake. The level of voluntary food intake is affected by the rate of passage of digesta through the gut. Rate of passage is affected by rate of digestion and there is evidence that a value of 60–65 D falls within the critical range (Montgomery and Baumgardt, 1965). Dry matter intake of forage may be seriously impaired if the value falls below 65.

Silage contributes 40 per cent more crude protein from dry matter consumed than does hay. Since 1960, the contribution made by silage has increased from 13 per cent of total dry matter fed as forage, to 44 per cent in 1978. In the same period the contribution to crude protein supply has risen from 17 per cent to 54 per cent.

The forage component of the diet is generally considered to be inadequate to sustain the levels of milk yield required for a profitable dairy enterprise. Thus, forages are supplemented with foods supplying energy or protein or, more commonly, energy and protein. Forage should generally contribute a minimum of 30 per cent of the total dry matter offered (Broster, Sutton and Bines, 1979).

Traditionally, supplementary foods rich in protein have been prescribed for the commercial dairy cow. The publication of *Technical Bulletin 33* (MAFF, DAFS and DANI, 1975) stimulated an awareness of the importance of food intake and metabolizable energy supply, but the outline publication of the ARC proposals for meeting the protein requirement of ruminant livestock has re-focused attention on protein (Roy *et al.*, 1977).

Table 16.1 PRODUCTION AND AVERAGE COMPOSITION OF SILAGES AND HAYS MADE IN ENGLAND AND WALES 1960–1978

Production and composition		Period					
		1960	1970/73[b]	1975	1976	1977	1978
Production							
Silage (tonne × 10³)		3751	7541	9488	10222	13498	15382
Hay (tonne × 10³)		6478	7098	5722	6048	6892	6450
Nutritional value							
Silage	Dry matter (g/kg)	218	182	286	268	279	277
	D value		61	63	63	64	63
	Crude protein (g/kg in DM)	128	140	147	144	143	144
Hay[a]	Dry matter (g/kg)	850	850	850	850	850	850
	D value	57	57	62	60	61	59
	Crude protein (g/kg in DM)	92	99	100	102	101	96
Yield of nutrients (tonne × 10³)							
Silage	Dry matter	818	1372	2714	2739	3766	4261
	Digestible organic matter		837	1710	1726	2410	2684
	Crude protein	105	192	399	394	539	614
Hay	Dry matter	5506	6033	4864	5141	5858	5483
	Digestible organic matter	3138	3439	3016	3085	3573	3235
	Crude protein	507	597	486	524	592	526
Silage as % of Total							
	Dry matter	13	19	36	35	39	44
	Digestible organic matter		20	36	36	40	45
	Crude protein	17	24	45	43	48	54

DM = Dry Matter; a = Hay dry matter assumed to be 850 g/kg; b = 4-year average 1970–73
Sources: ADAS Science Arm Annual Reports (1975–78); Ministry of Agriculture, Fisheries and Food (1979); National Economic Development Office (1974)

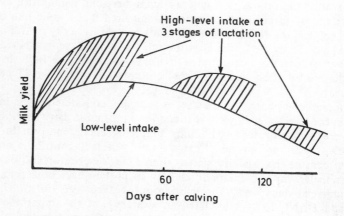

Figure 16.1 Decline in response to extra food as lactation advances (after Broster, Broster and Smith, 1969)

Response in milk yield to variable energy input

The nature of the response of the cow to variation in energy input has been studied and reviewed by many groups of research workers throughout the world (Blaxter, 1966; Moe and Tyrell, 1974; Broster, 1976; Van Es, 1976; Wiktowsson, 1979).

The nature of the response to energy is elegantly shown in the results of experiments published by Broster and his colleagues (Broster, Broster and Smith, 1969). *Figure 16.1* demonstrates the changing nature of the response to food energy as lactation advances. In the early stages of lactation the response to a fixed allowance of extra food is marked. The magnitude of this response declines as lactation advances. In early lactation, metabolites for the synthesis of milk are taken from body reserves, while in mid and late lactation, nutrients are stored as body reserves.

This relationship is confirmed in calorimetric studies conducted by Flatt and his colleagues (1969). *Table 16.2* shows the partition of food energy input with

Table 16.2 ENERGY BALANCE OF HIGH-YIELDING COWS WITH STAGE OF LACTATION (AFTER FLATT *ET AL.*, 1969)

Energy balance	Lactation stage			Significance	SEM (N = 72)
	Early	*Mid*	*Late*		
Days *post partum*	57	167	284		
Gross energy (MJ)	223	244	235	NS	± 9.78
Faeces energy (MJ)	58	67	65	NS	± 3.34
Heat production (MJ)	97	100	98	NS	± 2.42
Total energy balance (MJ)	49	56	49	NS	± 4.34
Milk energy (MJ)	78	51	29	**	± 3.05
Body tissue energy (MJ)	−29	+5	+21	**	± 5.22
Crude protein of ration (g/kg)	200	198	187	NS	± 2.10

stage of lactation. The input of gross energy (223–244 MJ) was digested with similar efficiency throughout lactation (73–75 per cent). Energy balance was very similar at all stages of lactation (20.8–22.7 per cent of gross energy intake). Milk energy output varied with stage of lactation from 78 MJ at day 57, through 51 MJ at day 167, to 29 MJ at day 284. Body tissue energy was used for milk synthesis in early lactation, while the energy balance was diverted towards body tissue in mid and late lactation. In this experiment, the relationship between energy balance and metabolizable energy input was linear with a slope of 0.66; the relationship explained some 96 per cent of the total variance (*Figure 16.2*).

The fixed intake of gross energy for all cows at all stages of lactation allows a very clear view of the nature of response of Holstein cows to an energy input. There was variation between cows and stage of lactation in the partition of food energy between milk production and body reserves. The efficiency with which metabolizable energy was used for milk production and body gain was comparable during lactation. There are two major practical points arising from these data, previously pointed out by Moe and his colleagues:

(1) body reserves mobilized in early lactation should be replenished in mid and late lactation rather than in the dry period;

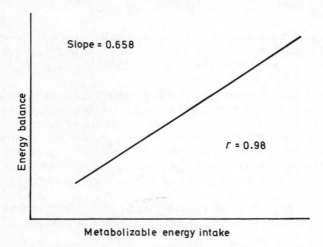

Figure 16.2   Relationship between energy balance and metabolizable energy intake (after Flatt et al., *1969)*

(2)   there should be positive selection in a dairy herd for those cows using energy balance for milk production rather than the accretion of body tissue.

The high crude protein concentration of the experimental rations in this experiment has been focused upon by many commentators (*Table 16.3*). These are indeed high (187–200 g/kg dry matter) but before too many relationships are spun between concentration of crude protein and the conversion of energy

Table 16.3 INPUT/OUTPUT DATA FOR HOLSTEIN COWS WITH STAGE OF LACTATION (AFTER FLATT *ET AL.*, 1969)

Input/output	Lactation stage			Significance	SEM (N = 72)
	Early	Mid	Late		
Days *post partum*	57	167	284		
Daily production of milk (kg)	29.4	19.5	10.6	**	± 0.92
Milk energy (MJ/kg)	2.63	2.60	2.64	NS	± 0.06
Body weight (kg)	589	592	638	**	± 8.99
Dry matter intake (kg/day)	12.0	13.2	12.8	NS	± 0.53
Crude protein content of ration (g/kg)	200	198	187	NS	± 2.10
Metabolizable energy intake (MJ/day)	146	155	147	NS	± 6.52
Digestibility of gross energy (%)	74.8	73.1	72.5	*	± 0.62

into milk, attention must be drawn to the low level of dry matter intakes set for the experiment. Although a level of 12 kg dry matter intake is reasonable for the early stage of lactation, food consumption in excess of 20 kg dry matter could be expected for Holstein cows from day 50 of lactation onwards. The high level of crude protein in early lactation may have affected the extent of body tissue mobilization.

Response in milk yield to variable protein input

Response to protein input has been reviewed by Broster (1972) and by Broster and Oldham (1977). The latter review approaches the subject from a physiological viewpoint and poses two questions: 'What does the cow do with protein supply — how is output affected?', and 'How efficient is the metabolism of protein?'. It is not the purpose of this chapter to re-interpret the data reviewed previously but to concentrate on recent studies where protein has been fed in variable quantities. A major effect of protein concentration may be on digestion. If dietary protein is severely limited, then organic matter digestion will be impaired and voluntary food intake reduced. This could occur if the concentration of crude protein in the dry matter fell substantially below 125 g crude protein per kg dry matter.

In early lactation, food intake fails to meet the nutrient requirement of the lactating cow, the balance of metabolites necessary for milk synthesis being taken from labile body tissue. Ørskov, Grubb and Kay (1977) examined the response of four Friesian dairy cows, in the first weeks of lactation, to infusions of either casein or glucose given to each cow. Casein or glucose were infused through an abomasal fistula over a 12-day infusion period; measurements were taken for the last five days of this period (*Table 16.4*). Food intake was restricted to 8–9 kg dry matter per day, thus ensuring that the cows were in a state of negative energy balance. Replacement of glucose in the infusate by casein significantly increased milk yield (kg/day), milk fat (g/kg) and milk protein yield (g/day). The calculated negative energy balance was doubled from −20.5 MJ/day to −41 MJ/day in moving from an infusion of 750 g glucose/day to 750 g casein/day. The only weakness of the study is that a digestion trial was not conducted. It has to be assumed that the infused glucose was digested as effectively as the casein. In one previous study, when glucose was infused into lactating cows, faecal energy was increased by an amount equal to 48 per cent of that infused, whereas milk energy increased by only 16 per cent of that infused (Tyrell *et al.*, 1972). If it is assumed that both infusates were digested to an equal extent, the conclusion to be drawn from this experiment is unequivocal. For the cow in negative energy balance, an increased supply of amino acids stimulates the synthesis of all milk constituents, fat, protein and lactose, and increases the contribution of labile body tissue to milk synthesis. Thus, such cows lose further weight. This implies that, when a cow is in negative energy balance in early lactation, amino acids are limiting the process of milk synthesis.

Amino acids, whether from dietary sources or from the catabolism of body proteins, are an important source of glucose. Of the 20 amino acids occurring in protein, 18 are wholly or partly glucogenic. When the diet lacks carbohydrate but provides protein, the glucose necessary to maintain glucose-dependent systems can be formed from the amino acids in the dietary or infused protein. Thus, no matter whether the fate of the mix of amino acids is to provide glucose or to supply essential amino acids for direct incorporation into milk, protein stimulates milk synthesis in early lactation.

Where attempts have been made to maximize voluntary food intake in early lactation in high-yielding cows, the effect of dietary protein level has not been pronounced (Clay *et al.*, 1979). Forty-eight cows were fed three grain mixtures in a three-period experiment (*Table 16.5*). From days 15 to 56 of lactation cows were fed either Treatment 1 (in which protein up to 130 g CP (crude protein)/kg

288

Table 16.4 EFFECT OF CASEIN AND GLUCOSE INFUSION INTO THE ABOMASUM ON MILK YIELD, MILK AND BLOOD COMPOSITION, CALCULATED ENERGY BALANCE AND RECOVERY OF INFUSED NITROGEN IN MILK (AFTER ØRSKOV, GRUBB AND KAY, 1977)

Casein (g/d)	Glucose (g/d)	Food intake (kg DM/d)	Milk yield (kg/d)	Milk fat (g/kg)	Fat-corrected milk (kg/d)	Milk protein (g/kg)	Protein yield (g/d)	Milk solids (g/kg)	Blood free fatty acids (mg/ℓ)	Calculated energy balance (MJ/d)
0	750	8.7	16.8	48.2	18.9	25.2	423.3	128.5	0.347	−20.5
250	500	8.6	19.8	49.8	22.7	28.4	566.3	132.7	0.516	−30.5
500	250	8.8	21.6	51.0	25.2	29.6	644.4	134.2	0.606	−38.6
750	0	8.9	21.4	54.8	26.1	31.5	675.6	139.8	0.701	−41.0
SE of means		–	0.8	1.2	–	5.6	37.5	2.0	0.115	–

Table 16.5 MILK PRODUCTION RESPONSE TO EITHER PLANT PROTEIN OR NON-PROTEIN NITROGEN (AFTER CLAY *ET AL.*, 1979)

Treatment		Dry matter intake (kg)	Actual milk yield (kg)	Adjusted milk yield (kg)	Fat (%)	Milk protein (%)
(1)	130 g CP/kg dm from soya bean meal	18.7	34.4	34.2	3.73	2.91
(2)	160 CP/kg dm: 130 g/kg from soya bean meal; 30 g/kg from urea	18.8	34.6	34.8	3.67	2.90
(3)	160 g CP/kg dm, all from soya bean meal	18.0	35.7	35.7	3.71	2.92
Error mean square		2.7	5.0	2.7	0.38	0.44

dry matter was all supplied from soya bean meal), Treatment 2 (in which the crude protein level was raised to 160 g CP/kg dry matter through the addition of 30 g CP/kg from urea), or Treatment 3 (in which the 160 g CP/kg dry matter was all supplied from soya bean meal). In addition to the concentrate mix, cows were fed 3.2 kg alfalfa hay daily. Concentrate and corn silage were offered *ad libitum* in the ratio of 1 kg grain to 2.5 kg corn silage. Milk yields were adjusted by covariance analysis using milk yield during the first 14 days of lactation when all animals were fed Treatment 1. There was no significant response to increasing the concentration of protein above 130 g/kg in the dry matter. Neither milk yield nor composition was affected at this level of food intake and milk yield.

From a scientific viewpoint this is, of course, a short-term experiment and it is possible that an effect would have emerged if the treatment had been continued for longer. On the other hand, from a practical standpoint, the first eight weeks of lactation is the period during which a response to increased protein concentration would be expected and might be predicted from the results of the several infusion studies reviewed by Clark (1975).

Milk production averaged 35 kg/day at a milk fat concentration of 37 g/kg milk when the cows were consuming 18.3 kg dry matter. The differences between this experiment and that of Ørskov, Grubb and Kay (1977) were:

(1) food intake was more than twice as high in the experiment conducted by Clay *et al.* (1979) (18.3 as opposed to 8.8 kg/day);

(2) the additional protein was fed in the experiment of Clay *et al.* (1979), and infused in the experiment of Ørskov, Grubb and Kay (1977);

(3) the cows used by Ørskov, Grubb and Kay (1977) were in a greater state of negative energy balance than those used by Clay *et al.* (1979).

All of these factors would have influenced the results. It is likely, however, that food intake would be more influential than the other factors. The low protein concentration (130 g CP/kg dry matter) was designed to provide ammonia concentrations in the rumen adequate to meet microbial requirements (Satter and Roffler, 1977). The lack of response of the mammary system to increasing the concentration of dietary protein means that, either the dietary protein did not reach the mammary system as amino acid, or the amino acid requirement was met either by the products of digestion or by a combination of digestion products and body reserves.

The work of Virtanen (1966) made a considerable impact when he demon-strated the extent to which NPN (non-protein nitrogen) fed as urea in a semi-purified diet based on wood cellulose could support milk production. *Figure 16.3* shows the lactation curve of an Ayrshire heifer, Lila. Lila produced almost

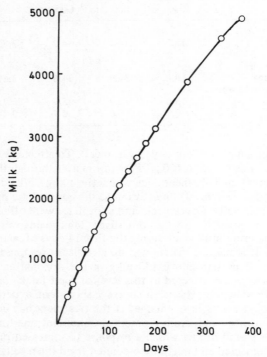

Figure 16.3   Cumulative milk yield of a cow fed a semipurified diet and NPN (after Virtanen, 1966)

5000 kg of milk in her first lactation in a period of less than 400 days. During the lactation of another heifer, Jairu, the following balance was carried out. Milk production was measured over a 77-day period from 1 July until 15 September, 1965. The cow weighed 445 kg on 30 June and then lost weight but had regained that weight by 31 August. During that 77-day period, milk production reached 865 kg at an average composition of 51 g/kg milk fat, 38 g/kg milk protein and 48 g/kg lactose. The heifer ate 670 kg of organic matter of which 10 kg was fat. The metabolizable energy supplied by these raw materials can be estimated, as shown in *Table 16.6*. The estimated supply is within 10 per cent of the estimated requirements and thus credence can be given to these data. The overall crude protein concentration of the diet was 157 g/kg dry matter, and dry matter con-sumption averaged 11 kg dry matter/day. Was food intake determining milk response in this experiment? Is the ability of the microflora to provide protein limited more by the type of protein or by the severe restriction imposed by the level of food supply? What is the maximum contribution of microbial protein at high levels of dry matter intake? Is the supply of microbial protein adequate to meet the amino acid contribution necessary to achieve the highest level of milk yield? Evidence from the experiment of Clay *et al.* 1978 seems to indicate that a concentration of 130 g crude protein/kg dry matter is adequate.

In the early weeks of lactation, the mammary system may draw on metabolites obtained from body tissue. The role of energy-yielding metabolites drawn from adipose tissue is well recognized in practical dairy farming by the term 'Milking off the back'. There is controversy, however, over the role of tissue protein in supplying amino acids to the mammary gland. High-yielding cows would benefit from protein reserves for the supplementation of dietary protein for milk production during early lactation. Some authors have suggested that the breakdown of muscle protein to provide amino acids for the production of milk protein is a mechanism of normal metabolic adaptation. The debate over the extent of the contribution of microbial protein and tissue protein to the amino acid requirement of the mammary system in early lactation, will continue. It is not the purpose of this chapter to either clarify or cloud that debate, but to review the evidence of input—output responses in the available experimental data.

Table 16.6 METABOLIZABLE ENERGY (ME): SUPPLY AND REQUIREMENTS (AFTER VIRTANEN, 1966)

Raw material	Weight fed (kg)	Estimated gross energy (MJ/kg)	Estimated apparent digestibility (%)	Estimated metabolizable energy (MJ/kg)	Estimated total ME (MJ)
Starch	343	18	90	13	4459
Cellulose	165	18	60	9	1485
Sugar	152	18	90	13	1976
Fat	10	36	90	26	260
Total	670				8190
Maintenance requirements of 445 kg/cow for 77 days					3757 MJ ME
864 kg milk at 51 g/kg SNF (solids not fat)					5186 MJ ME
Total requirements					8943

A reduction in dietary protein supply to 75 per cent of the recommended standard showed no significant depression of milk yield up to 14 weeks *post partum* (Treacher *et al.*, 1976). Milk yield (14—98 days) for the low-protein group was 2409 kg compared with 2496 kg for those fed 100 per cent of the recommended protein standard.

Experiments carried out here at the University of Nottingham School of Agriculture may also be considered. Thirty Friesian dairy cows have been used in two complete lactation experiments to investigate the response of the lactating dairy cow to variations in dietary protein supply. In both experiments, cows were offered diets based on hay and sugar beet pulp (30 per cent of the total dry matter offered) supplemented with a barley grain mix of variable protein content or type. A dry matter intake of 16 kg was achieved by the 40th day of lactation. Dry matter intake was not significantly different between treatments.

In the first complete lactation experiment, the cows were allocated to one of three treatments (*Figure 16.4*). Cows were fed either a barley grain mix containing 140 g crude protein/kg dry matter, the supplementary nitrogen required being supplied by urea, or a barley grain mix in which the crude protein concentration was raised from 140 to 180 g CP/kg dry matter by the addition of soya bean meal. These two diets were offered to two of the groups of cows throughout the whole lactation period. A third group of cows was offered the high concentration of crude protein (180 g CP/kg dry matter) in early lactation but was transferred to the lower concentration of crude protein (140 g CP/kg dry matter) at approximately 100 days of lactation. Analysis of the data indicates little effect on milk yield of raising the crude protein above the lower level of 140 g crude protein/kg dry matter in the overall diet.

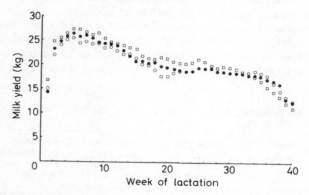

Figure 16.4 Response to changes in concentration of dietary crude protein in dairy cattle.
○ = *140 g CP/kg dm in grain mix;* □ = *180 g CP/kg dm in grain mix;* ● = *Changeover diet from 180 to 140 g/CP/dm at 14 weeks*

Soya bean meal was used to raise the level of crude protein to 160 g/kg dry matter of the total ration. It may be argued that this source of protein was readily degraded in the rumen and that the additional protein merely added to the ammonia pool in the rumen. In order to examine this the experiment was repeated. All cows were fed the same diet in which crude protein was raised from 130 to 160 g/kg by the addition of urea, soya bean meal or fish meal. Urea was also used to raise all three diets to 130 g crude protein/kg dry matter. At 160 g crude protein/kg dry matter the response of the urea-fed cows was limited by low food intake. There was no difference in milk yield between diets supplemented with either soya bean meal or fish meal. As fish meal is of low degradability, the conclusion must be that the protein levels used in this experiment exceeded the requirement for milk production. Milk production in both experiments averaged 6000 kg/cow by day 305 of lactation, a level well above the national average. Thus it is difficult to argue that a low level of production limited the response to dietary protein.

This chapter has reviewed the published evidence on the relationship between food intake and milk output in the dairy cow and leans heavily on the classical experiments of Broster and his colleagues (National Institute for Research in Dairying, Shinfield, Reading, England) and Flatt and his co-workers (United States Department of Agriculture, Bettsville, Maryland, USA). Their work indicates that food energy is partitioned towards milk in early lactation and progressively towards body tissue as lactation advances. The efficiency with which metabolizable energy is converted to net energy, either as milk or as body tissue, remains within the range 0.65–0.70 during lactation and is unaffected by food, cow or level of milk yield.

Whether or not there is a milk yield response to dietary protein depends on the type of protein and the nature of the energy balance in the cow. Cows in negative energy balance respond to an increase in protein supply by increasing the level and, depending on the stage of lactation, the secretion, of milk solids. If the cow is in zero or positive energy balance, the milk yield response from increasing crude protein concentration in the diet above 130 g CP/kg dry matter in the overall ration is small. The effect of protein type is also small.

If diets are based on hay, there is an obvious need for protein supplementation. The combination of grass silage and barley grain, however, would lead to a crude protein concentration meeting the minimum required. Is too much of our thinking based on hay diets? What milk yield could be sustained by a ryegrass silage/barley grain regime when the major nutritional effect was placed on maximizing dry matter intake and hence striving for zero or positive energy balance? The approach taken in meeting the nutrient requirement of the spring-calving cow may pay dividends if applied to the autumn-calving cow.

References

ADAS SCIENCE ARM REPORTS (1975–78). London; HMSO

BLAXTER, K.L. (1966). The feeding of dairy cows for optimal production. George Scott Robertson Memorial Lecture. *University of Belfast Bulletin No. 16*

BROSTER, W.H., BROSTER, V.J. and SMITH, T. (1969). Experiments on the nutrition of the dairy heifer. VIII. Effect on milk production of level of feeding at two stages of the lactation. *J. agric. Sci., Camb.*, 72, 229

BROSTER, W.H. (1972). In *Handbuch der Tierernahrung* Vol. 2, pp. 292–322. Eds W. Lenkeit, K. Breirem and E. Crasemann. Hamburg; Paul Parey

BROSTER, W.H. (1976). Plane of nutrition for the dairy cow. In *Principles of Cattle Production*, p. 271. Eds H. Swan and W.H. Broster. London; Butterworths

BROSTER, W.H. and OLDHAM, J.D. (1977). Protein quantity and quality for the UK dairy cow. In *Nutrition and the Climatic Environment*, pp. 123–153. Eds W. Haresign, H. Swan and D. Lewis. London; Butterworths

BROSTER, W.H., SUTTON, J.D. and BINES, J.A. (1979). Concentrate: forage ratios for high yielding dairy cows. In *Recent Advances in Animal Nutrition – 1978*, pp. 99–126. Eds W. Haresign and D. Lewis. London; Butterworths

CLARK, J.H. (1975). Lactational responses to postruminal administration of proteins and amino acids. *J. Dairy Sci.*, 58, 1178

CLAY, A.B., BUCKLEY, B.A., HASBULLAH, M. and SATTER, L.D. (1978). Milk production response to either plant protein or NPN. *J. Dairy Sci.*, 61, (Suppl. 1), 170

FLATT, W.P., MOE, P.W., MUNSON, A.W. and COOPER, T. (1969). Energy utilisation by high producing dairy cows. II. Summary of energy balance experiments with lactating Holstein cows. In *Energy Metabolism of Farm Animals*, p. 235. Eds K.L. Blaxter, J. Kielanowski and Greta Thorbek. Newcastle upon Tyne, England; Oriel Press

MAFF, DAFS and DANI (1975). *Technical Bulletin 33*. London; HMSO

MINISTRY OF AGRICULTURE, FISHERIES AND FOOD (1979). Agricultural Census – December returns. London; HMSO

MOE, P.W. and TYRRELL, H.F. (1974). Observations on the efficiency of utilisation of metabolisable energy for meat and milk production. In *Nutrition Conference for Feed Manufacturers*, 7, p. 27. Eds H. Swan and D. Lewis. London; Butterworths

MONTGOMERY, M.J. and BAUMGARDT, B.R. (1965). *J. Dairy Sci.*, **48**, 569–574

NATIONAL ECONOMIC DEVELOPMENT OFFICE (1974). *UK Farming and the Common Market, Grass and Grass Products.* London; NEDO

ØRSKOV, E.R., GRUBB, D.A. and KAY, R.N.B. (1977). Effect of postruminal glucose or protein supplementation on milk yield and composition in Friesian cows in early lactation and negative energy balance. *Br. J. Nutr.*, **38**, 397

ROY, J.H.B., BALCH, C.C., MILLER, E.L., ØRSKOV, E.R. and SMITH, R.H. (1977). Calculation of the N-requirement for ruminants from nitrogen metabolism studies. In *Proceedings of the 2nd International Symposium of Protein Metabolism and Nutrition*, pp. 126–129. Wageningen, The Netherlands; Centre for Agricultural Publishing and Documentation

SATTER, L.D. and ROFFLER, R.E. (1977). Influence of nitrogen and carbohydrate inputs on rumen fermentation. In *Recent Advances in Animal Nutrition – 1977*, pp. 25–49. Eds W. Haresign and D. Lewis. London; Butterworths

TREACHER, R.J., LITTLE, W., COLLIS, K.A. and STARK, A.J. (1976). The influence of dietary protein intake on milk production and blood composition of high yielding dairy cows. *J. Dairy Res.*, **43**, 357–369

TYRRELL, H.F., BOLT, D.J., MOE, P.W. and SWAN, H. (1972). Abomasal infusion of water, casein or glucose in Holstein cows. *J. Anim. Sci.*, **35**, 277 (abstr.)

VAN ES, A.J.H. (1976). Factors influencing the efficiency of energy utilisation by beef and dairy cattle. In *Principles of Cattle Production*, pp. 237–253. Eds H. Swan and W.H. Broster. London; Butterworths

VIRTANEN, A.I. (1966). Milk production of cows on protein free feed. *Science*, **153**, 1603–1614

WIKTOWSSON, H. (1970). General plane of nutrition for dairy cows. In *Feeding strategy for the high yielding dairy cow*, p. 148. Eds W.H. Broster and H. Swan. St. Albans; Crosby Lockwood Staples

17

FEED INPUT–MILK OUTPUT RELATIONSHIPS IN THE SPRING-CALVING DAIRY COW

F.J. GORDON[a]
Agricultural Research Institute of Northern Ireland, Hillsborough, Co. Down

The long-term viability of the dairy industry is dependent both upon the milk producer receiving sufficient return for his inputs of labour and capital, and the consumer being offered a product at a price which is realistic enough to ensure an adequate demand. This implies that the costs involved in milk production must not be excessive. As feed costs constitute the greatest portion of total costs involved in milk production, this in turn means making maximum use of the cheapest source of food. Under United Kingdom conditions this generally implies making the best use of grass. However, because of the seasonality of grass growth, the difference in the productive potential of fresh and conserved grass and the cyclic requirements of the lactating cow, it has often been argued that production systems which match the requirements of the animals to the growth curve for grass offer the greatest opportunities for reducing feed costs. This can be achieved when parturition coincides with the onset of grass growth in the spring. Delaying calving to this time will, however, result in low milk yields per cow, as Wood (1970) has demonstrated a progressive decline in yield per cow when calving was delayed after January. This was also confirmed by Gordon (1978), who reported a mean decline in lactation yield of 220 kg for each one-month delay in calving between January and April, and a similar decline of 180 kg/month has been reported by Cunningham (1972). For this reason it is a normal objective in spring-calving systems to commence calving during January in an effort to maximize yield per cow, although it must be remembered that early calving increases the requirement for supplementary feed (Evans, 1979) and the economic implications of this must be balanced against any increased production. When this effect is taken into consideration, the information available would suggest that there is little difference in profitability between January –March calving but, thereafter, a rapid decline occurs. There is, however, no doubt that as yields per cow increase, through improved breeding and management, later calving poses problems with regards to the conflict between achieving a high peak yield at pasture and efficient grass utilization.

[a] Also member of staff of the Department of Agriculture for Northern Ireland and the Queen's University, Belfast.

Response to changes in total feed input

Within a spring-calving system there are obviously a great number of periods during which variations in feed input could be effected. However, for the purposes of this chapter, the effects of variations in feed input during the period from calving until going to pasture only will be considered. The discussion will also be confined to situations where grass silage is offered *ad libitum*, because silage constitutes the major basal component of present-day dairy farming systems within the United Kingdom. For example McMurray *et al.* (1978) reported a survey which showed that 99 per cent of dairy herds in Northern Ireland used silage as the basal diet, although in England and Wales the proportion may be much lower.

During the post-calving indoor feeding period, variations in total feed input can be effected both through changes in the quality of the basal diet and the level of supplementation offered. Both of these aspects will be discussed.

CHANGE IN LEVEL OF SUPPLEMENTATION

The nutritional status of the dairy cow at any one stage of lactation may affect future as well as present performance (Broster, Broster and Smith, 1969); direct and residual responses will therefore be considered separately.

Direct response to level of supplementation

A large volume of research evidence has been accumulated in recent years on the effects of levels of concentrate supplementation on animal production. Unfortunately, little of this research has been specific to spring-calving cows receiving basal diets of grass silage *ad libitum*, with dry roughages, mainly given at fixed levels of input, being used in most experiments. The results from such trials cannot be transferred directly to the *ad libitum* silage situation. *Table 17.1* gives a summary of the information available in the literature on direct responses using spring-calving animals with *ad libitum* access to silage. The overall mean response obtained from these data, 0.78 kg milk per additional kg concentrates, is considerably below that normally achieved when the basal diet has consisted of restricted intakes of hay: Strickland (1975) and Johnston (1977) have reported mean direct responses of 1.47 and 1.35 kg milk per kg additional concentrates, respectively.

In the data presented in *Table 17.1* there is a considerable variation in the responses reported, ranging from 1.60 to 0.28 kg milk per additional kg concentrate. This variation could be attributed to a number of factors, the most important of which are the level of feeding relative to the milk yield of the animal and the quality of the basal silage. As level of feeding is increased, the response to additional feed declines (Blaxter, 1967) although the relationship between supplementation level and milk output has not been clearly defined with spring-calving cows. However, the data from four experiments carried out at Hillsborough (Gordon 1976, 1977; Steen and Gordon 1980a,b), in which animals of similar yield potential and with access to similar types of silage (mean D value 66) and offered differing levels of supplementation, have been

Table 17.1 DIRECT EFFECTS OF LEVEL OF CONCENTRATE SUPPLEMENTATION FOR SPRING-CALVING COWS WITH ACCESS TO GRASS SILAGE

Source	Concentrate intake (kg/d)	Milk yield (kg/d)	Response (kg milk/kg extra concentrate)
Gleeson (1969): cows	0	8.8	–
	9.1	18.6	1.07
heifers	0	6.5	–
	9.1	13.1	0.72
Gleeson (1970): cows	0	11.3	–
	4.8	15.6	0.9
heifers	0	9.2	–
	2.8	10.8	0.61
Gleeson (1972)	0	8.9	–
	3.6	12.4	0.97
Gleeson (1973)	1.8	12.4	–
	3.6	14.7	1.25
Gordon (1976)	7.1	22.7	–
	9.5	23.7	0.42
Gordon (1977)	3.7	21.6	–
	5.3	24.2	1.6
	7.0	25.0	0.47
Steen and Gordon (1980a)	3.8	21.4	–
	5.5	22.9	0.88
	7.2	24.0	0.65
Steen and Gordon (1980b)	7.5	26.3	–
	10.4	27.1	0.28
Butler (1976)	3.0	13.7	–
	5.5	16.0	0.92
	8.0	17.0	0.39
Evans (1979)	5	na	–
	10	na	0.64
	Mean 4.9		Mean 0.78

used to investigate this overall relationship. While there was a slight difference between experiments in the absolute levels of production achieved from similar levels of supplementation, the overall relationship was adequately described by a family of parallel curves differing only in their intercept value. The 'best fit' relationships within the data were found to be double logarithmic and the family of curves are described by equation 17.1:

$$y = a + 7.5 \log_e \log_e x \tag{17.1}$$

where y = mean milk yield/day (kg), x = concentrate input/day (kg fresh weight) and a is the intercept, being 17.6, 20.0, 19.0 and 20.9, for the data of Gordon (1976), Gordon (1977), Steen and Gordon (1980a) and Steen and Gordon (1980b) respectively. The mean relationship from these data is shown diagrammatically in *Figure 17.1*.

Using these relationships, the response to increments of concentrate input at any level of supplementation (within the range of 3.7–10.4 kg/day – the range of data used to derive the equations) can be calculated. The results from these

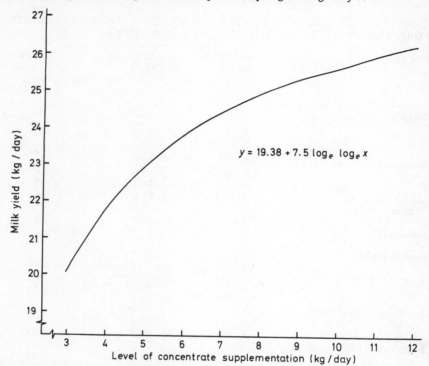

$$y = 19.38 + 7.5 \log_e \log_e x$$

Figure 17.1 The relationship between level of concentrate supplementation (kg/d) and milk yield (kg/d) during the period of feeding for spring-calving cows

calculations are shown in *Table 17.2* for a range of basal concentrate inputs. At the lower range of concentrate inputs the addition of 1 kg concentrates has a marked effect on milk output with, for example, an increase in concentrate input from 3 to 4 kg/day increasing yield by 1.8 kg/day. However, as the basal level of concentrate being given increases, the response to additional feed declines markedly with 1 kg of extra concentrates given above 7.0 kg/day increasing milk output by only 0.5 kg/day. At even higher levels of concentrate input, only very marginal increases in milk output are obtained.

Table 17.2 DIRECT RESPONSE IN MILK YIELD (kg/day) TO A CHANGE IN CONCENTRATE SUPPLEMENTATION (kg fresh wt/day)

Basal level of supplementation (kg/d)	*Direct response* (kg milk/day) *per kg additional concentrate*
3	1.8
4	1.1
5	0.8
6	0.6
7	0.5
8	0.4
9	0.4
10	0.3

These responses derived from equation 17.1 and shown in *Table 17.2* are in fairly close agreement with those shown in *Table 17.1* from the survey of the literature. The calculated mean response in *Table 17.1* was 0.78 kg milk per kg concentrates where the mean concentrate input over which the response was measured was 4.9 kg/day, while from equation 17.1 the calculated response this concentrate level is 0.97 kg milk/kg additional concentrate. It is also worth noting that the basal silages offered in the experiments used to derive equation 17.1 were not of exceptionally high quality, having a mean D value of 66. However, all these responses are considerably below those normally achieved when dry forages have been offered in fixed amounts. This can be accounted for by the marked effect of supplementation on forage intake, the net effect being that the increases in total nutrient intake with *ad libitum* silage are well below those obtained where fixed intakes of forage are used. For example, Steen and Gordon (1980a,b) reported decreases in silage dry matter intake of 1.1 and 1.2 kg/day when concentrate input was increased by 3.0 and 2.5 kg/day dry matter. When these effects are taken into consideration, and the responses calculated on a net intake basis, the responses obtained in the trials with *ad libitum* silage agree with other published data. For example, the mean response obtained by Steen and Gordon (1980a) was equivalent to 0.09 kg milk per MJ increase in ME intake, which is in line with those reported by Broster and Tuck (1967) and Broster, Broster and Smith (1969) on hay diets. Even at the highest level of supplementation in this series of trials (Steen and Gordon, 1980b) the response per MJ of ME increase, at 0.05 kg milk, was reasonably large even though the response per kg additional concentrate given was small.

The quality (as defined by digestibility) of the basal forage also has a considerable effect on the response in milk yield to additional concentrate supplementation. A summary of the data available is given in *Table 17.3*. The data of Gleeson (1970, 1972), from experiments in which low levels of supplementation were used, show little effect of silage type on the response, but with higher levels of supplementation a much smaller response to increased supplementation was obtained with the higher digestibility silage (Parker, 1976; Steen and Gordon, 1980b). It is also noteworthy that similar interactions between silage digestibility and response to increased supplementation have been obtained with growing beef animals (McIlmoyle, 1976, 1977).

Table 17.3 THE EFFECT OF SILAGE QUALITY ON THE RESPONSE FROM INCREASED SUPPLEMENTATION

Source	Silage quality	Supplementation (kg/day) Low	High	Response in milk yield (kg/kg concentrate)
[b] Gleeson (1970)	6 wk interval	0	2.7	1.32
	9 wk interval	0	2.7	1.05
[b] Gleeson (1972)	6 wk interval	0	3.6	0.90
	9 wk interval	0	3.6	1.04
	12 wk interval	0	3.6	1.00
[a] Parker (1976)	67 D	3.6	5.4	−0.02
	64 D	3.6	5.4	0.71
Steen and Gordon (1980b)	68 D	7.5	10.4	0.18
	64 D	7.5	10.4	0.48

[a] These data do not refer to spring-calving animals.
[b] Silage quality figures relate to interval between harvests

It is likely that this reduction in response with increased silage digestibility is due to two factors. First, the basal plane of nutrition will be higher with the higher digestibility silages; secondly, the rate at which additional concentrates replace forages increases markedly with increasing digestibility. For example, Steen and Gordon (1980b) reported decreases in forage intake of 0.52 and 0.36 kg DM per additional kg concentrates DM given for silages with D values of 68 and 64 respectively.

Residual and total lactation responses

It has been recognized for some time that the total lactation effects of any change in feed input may be widely different from those assessed as direct effects. Broster (1972a), in a review of the information on this topic, concluded that, when levels of input were changed during early lactation, the total lactation responses were likely to be 3–4 times the direct responses as a result of large residual effects. This has been adequately demonstrated when diets have been based on fixed intakes of dry forages. However, when silage is offered *ad libitum* during the period of adjusted feeding and animals are grazed at pasture during the residual period, as occurs with spring-calving animals, it would appear that residual effects are much smaller and in certain instances may even be negative. *Table 17.4* gives a summary of the information available on the ratio of residual

Table 17.4 RATIO OF RESIDUAL TO DIRECT EFFECTS FOR SPING-CALVING COWS WITH *AD LIBITUM* ACCESS TO GRASS SILAGE

Source	Ratio of residual/ direct response
Gleeson (1969): cows	1.01
heifers	0.39
	1.03
Gleeson (1970): cows	0.06
heifers	1.28
Gleeson (1973)	0.36
	0.40
Butler (1976)	0.33
	0.16
Gordon (1976)	−0.65
Evans (1979)	−0.93
Steen and Gordon (1980a)	0.54
	0.53
Steen and Gordon (1980b)	2.04
	−2.85
	Mean 0.25

to direct effects, with the overall mean residual effect being 0.25 times the direct effect. However, the data presented show a marked range in the magnitude of residual responses, with negative responses being recorded on several occasions and, on others, residual responses being as large as twice the magnitude of the direct responses. In general it would seem that, where levels of post-calving nutrition are very low, the residual effects are greatest and, as the level of feeding is increased, the residual effects become smaller and become negative when moderate to high levels of feeding have been used. This is more fully demonstrated in the results shown in *Table 17.5* which are taken from three experiments

Table 17.5 DIRECT AND RESIDUAL EFFECTS FROM EXPERIMENTS CARRIED OUT AT HILLSBOROUGH IN WHICH LEVELS OF CONCENTRATE SUPPLEMENTATION WERE VARIED DURING THE POST-CALVING INDOOR FEEDING PERIOD

Steen and Gordon (1980a)			
Mean concentrate input (kg/d)	3.8	5.5	7.2
Milk yield indoors (kg)	1732	1860	1959
Milk yield at pasture (kg)	2996	3064	3266
Total lactation (kg)	4727	4919	5224
Gordon (1976)			
Mean concentrate input (kg/d)	7.0	9.5	
Milk yield indoors (kg)	1971	2064	
Milk yield at pasture (kg)	2739	2679	
Total lactation (kg)	4934	4991	
Steen and Gordon (1980b)			
Mean concentrate input (kg/d)	7.2	10.5	
Milk yield indoors (kg)	1870	1924	
Milk yield at pasture (kg)	3470	3312	
Total lactation (kg)	5451	5366	

carried out at Hillsborough using similar types of animals. In both instances where level of supplementation was above 7.2 kg/day the residual response has been negative, indicating a detrimental effect of high-energy inputs via diets higher in concentrate content during early lactation. Butler (1976) also recorded a negative residual effect when using a supplementation level of 8.0 kg/day. While few other published results are available to substantiate this negative residual effect, it is important to note that few experiments have examined the higher concentrate range of the feeding scale. However, recent evidence by Chalmers and Leaver (1980) has also shown a negative residual effect from high levels of supplementation. The mechanism involved in such an effect is open to speculation, but it could be either an effect on pasture intake or the efficiency with which the harvested grass is utilized within the animal. To date, herbage intake studies at Hillsborough have not shown any effect of previous concentrate intake on herbage intake during the subsequent pasture period.

The direct and residual effects, when taken together, result in the total lactation response. In *Table 17.1* the mean direct response reported over all experiments reviewed was 0.78 kg milk/kg concentrates at a relatively low level of concentrate supplementation of 5.2 kg/day, while the data in *Table 17.4* gave a mean residual response of 0.25 times the direct response. Combining these data gives a total lactation response of 0.98 kg milk per kg additional concentrate given at a concentrate intake of 5.2 kg/day. This total lactation response is remarkably close to that of 0.99 kg milk/kg concentrates calculated from the three-year study of Evans (1979), for which separate direct and residual effects were not available. The total lactation data of Evans (1979) is given in *Table 17.6*. In this experiment the basal level of supplementation was 5.0 kg/day, which is close to the mean of the other studies.

Table 17.6 EFFECT OF TWO LEVELS OF CONCENTRATE SUPPLEMENTATION TO JANUARY–MARCH CALVING ANIMALS DURING A THREE-YEAR PERIOD (EVANS, 1979)

Year	Concentrate (kg/d)		Total lactation response (kg milk/kg concentrate)
	5.0	10.0	
1. Total concentrate (kg)	490	811	0.36
Lactation yield (kg)	4534	4651	
2. Total concentrate (kg)	786	985	1.64
Lactation yield (kg)	4546	4872	
3. Total concentrate (kg)	488	700	0.97
Lactation yield (kg)	4855	5061	
			Mean 0.99

However, the extent of the total lactation response will depend upon the level of supplementation being used, as it has been demonstrated that both the direct and residual effects depend on feeding level. To quantify this overall relationship the total lactation data from three trials carried out at Hillsborough have been examined. In these data the relationship between concentrate input and total lactation performance within each experiment was described by a series of parallel exponential curves differing only in their asymptotic value. The series of curves is described by equation 17.2:

$$y = a - 4605 (0.5566)^x \qquad (17.2)$$

where y = total lactation milk yield (kg/day), x = mean concentrate input (kg fresh weight/day), and a is the asymptotic value being 5032, 5206 and 5442 for the data of Gordon (1976), Steen and Gordon (1980a) and Steen and Gordon (1980b) respectively. The mean relationship for these data is shown diagrammatically in *Figure 17.2*.

Using these relationships the responses to increments of concentrate supplementation above any basal level of supplementation can be calculated. This total lactation response is demonstrated by the data shown in *Table 17.7*. These data show a marked decline in total lactation response as level of supplementation is increased, being 352 and 6 kg additional milk for an additional kg concentrate/day given above basal levels of 3 and 10 kg/day respectively. The magnitude of the responses obtained by this approach are remarkably similar to the response noted by Evans (1979) and shown in *Table 17.6*. In a three-year experiment, a mean total lactation response of 216 kg milk was recorded when concentrate input was increased from 5 to 10 kg/day, whereas using equation 17.2 (or a summation of the values in *Table 17.7*), the calculated response for the same increment is 233 kg. The similarity of these two values is a measure of the soundness of the data upon which they are based.

With spring-calving cows (January–March calving) and with a turnout date to pasture of mid-April, each 1 kg increase in concentrate input per day increases total lactation concentrate input by approximately 50–60 kg. At present prices of concentrates of 13.5 p/kg and milk of 11.5 p/kg it would require an additional milk yield of at least 60–70 kg in order to offset the additional concentrate cost.

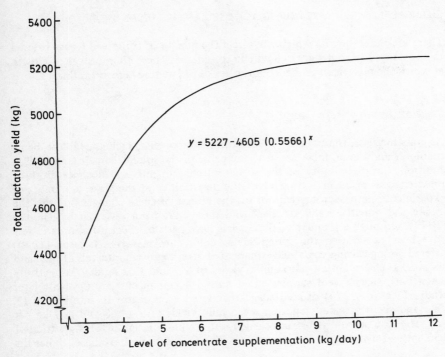

$$y = 5227 - 4605 \, (0.5566)^x$$

Figure 17.2 The relationship between level of concentrate supplementation (kg/d) during the post-calving indoor period and total lactation yield (kg) for spring-calving cows

This, however, does not take into account the slight reduction in silage intake at the higher concentrate input and, if this is considered, approximately 50 kg milk would offset the increased concentrate cost. From *Table 17.2* it can be seen that increments up to 7 kg concentrates will produce more than this additional amount of milk, and are therefore economic. Additional feed above 7.0 kg/day does not produce an economic return and, indeed, if the milk price:concentrate cost ratio declines further, the economic level of concentrate feeding will require to be reduced accordingly.

Table 17.7 RESPONSE IN TOTAL LACTATION YIELD (kg) TO A CHANGE IN DAILY INPUT OF CONCENTRATE (kg fresh wt/day)

Basal level of supplementation (kg/d)	*Response in total lactation yield (kg) to an additional kg of concentrates/day*
3	352
4	196
5	109
6	61
7	34
8	18
9	11
10	6

CHANGES IN THE QUALITY OF SILAGE USED AS THE BASAL DIET

There are many factors which will affect the quality of conserved forage offered to the dairy cow, but only two will be considered. These are the stage of growth at which the material is ensiled and the use of pre-wilting before ensiling.

Stage of growth at harvesting

As grass matures, the content of structural components, such as cellulose, hemi-celluloses and lignin, increases at the expense of the soluble constituents and, in addition, the digestibility of the structural components also declines. Both of these changes result in a lowering of the digestibility of the grass. A number of experiments have been carried out on the effects of these changes on both the intake and nutritive value of silage and these have been reviewed by Thomas (1979), although a number of these trials have been of short duration and few have been specific to the spring-calving dairy cow. However, Gleeson (1970) offered spring-calving cows silages harvested after regrowth intervals of nine and six weeks, and reported mean milk yields of 9.7 and 12.7 kg/day respectively when both silages were supplemented with 1.4 kg concentrates/day. In a later study, Gleeson (1972) offered silages harvested after regrowth intervals of 12, nine and six weeks and reported mean milk yields of 9.4, 9.8 and 12.7 kg per day. The results from two trials carried out at Hillsborough involving a total of 156 spring-calving cows are presented in *Table 17.8.* In both of these studies the

Table 17.8 THE EFFECT OF INTERVAL BETWEEN SILAGE HARVESTS ON THE PERFORMANCE OF SPRING-CALVING COWS AT HILLSBOROUGH

Steen and Gordon (1980b)			
Harvest interval (wk)	9		5
Silage D-value	64.2		68.2
Silage DM intake (kg/d)	8.5		9.4
Overall mean milk yield (kg/d)	25.0		27.5
Mean yield at end of winter (kg/d)	23.0		26.1
Gordon (1980a)			
Harvest interval (wk)	9	7	5
Silage D-value	61.7	69.9	72.6
Silage DM intake (kg/d)	8.1	10.0	10.7
Overall mean milk yield (kg/d)	26.3	28.2	28.9
Mean yield at end of winter (kg/d)	21.7	25.0	26.2

silages were offered *ad libitum* from one week *post partum* until going to pasture and all the results presented refer to unwilted silage. In the trial of Steen and Gordon (1980b) the animals received a mean concentrate input of 9.0 kg/day, while in that of Gordon (1980a) 7.6 kg/day was given. In both trials, reducing the interval between harvests increased silage digestibility, which resulted in an increase in the intake of the silage and also in milk yield. While the change from a nine- to five-week harvesting interval had a greater effect on silage digestibility in the trial reported by Gordon (1980a), the responses in milk yield were similar in both trials.

Using equation 17.1, relating mean milk yield to level of concentrate supplementation from data collected from similar animals, it is possible to calculate the additional concentrate supplementation required to produce similar responses to those achieved through improvements in forage quality. By this approach, and assuming the response to be measured above 5 kg concentrates/day due to the lower nutritive value (63 D) of the nine-week silages, it has been calculated that an additional 4.5 kg concentrates/day would be required with the lower digestibility silage to produce a similar milk yield to the material harvested after a five-week interval.

In both of the experiments discussed above, the residual effects during the pasture period were assessed and no residual effects of silage type on performance were obtained.

Wilting

Wilting of grass before ensiling has been widely used for many years to improve the preservation of silage. Reviews on the effect of wilting on both intake and production from dairy cows have recently been carried out by Steen (1978), Marsh (1979) and Thomas (1979). Steen (1978) reviewed the results from 11 experiments in which equal levels of supplementation were given between treatments, and reported a mean increase in silage dry matter intake due to wilting, of 23 per cent, with no increase in milk yield. However, only two of these experiments were specific to spring-calving animals. In one of these, Butler (1975) reported a mean increase in intake, due to wilting, of 55 per cent with no increase in milk yield, while in a second experiment the same author reported a significant increase in both intake and milk yield due to wilting. However, more recently Butler, Gleeson and Murphy (1978) have presented the results from four experiments, again using spring-calving cows, and showed that, while wilting consistently increased intake, it did not increase milk yield when formic acid was used to assist fermentation in direct ensiled material. Three studies have also been carried out at Hillsborough to examine the response to wilting

Table 17.9 THE EFFECTS OF WILTING BEFORE ENSILING ON THE INTAKE AND PRODUCTION FROM SPRING-CALVING COWS AT HILLSBOROUGH

Source	Intake and production	Unwilted	Wilted	
Steen and Gordon (1980b)	Silage DM content (%)	23.4	34.8	
	Silage DM intake (kg/d)	9.4	9.6	
	Mean milk yield (kg/d)	27.5	27.4	
	Yield at end of winter (kg/d)	26.1	24.7	
Gordon (1980a)	Silage DM content (%)	23.6	47.2	
	Silage DM intake (kg/d)	9.6	10.2	
	Mean milk yield (kg/d)	27.8	26.5	
	Yield at end of winter (kg/d)	24.8	22.8	
			Level 1	*Level 2*
Gordon (unpublished)	Silage DM content (%)	19.2	25.4	45.5
	Silage DM intake (kg/d)	9.1	9.4	9.7
	Mean milk yield (kg/d)	24.3	23.3	23.1
	Yield at end of winter (kg/d)	23.6	21.8	21.5

using spring-calving animals. In each of these experiments, all silages have received formic acid at ensiling and concentrates have been offered at equal levels across treatments. The results from these experiments are given in *Table 17.9*. In two of the experiments one level, and in one experiment two levels, of wilting were used. In two of these trials (Gordon (1980) and Gordon (unpublished)) mean milk output for the period from calving until going to pasture was significantly reduced when wilting was used. In all three experiments the performance at the end of the winter period, when the treatments would have produced their greatest effect, was markedly and significantly depressed on all wilted treatments.

While the mean difference taken over the total experiment was small, it is interesting to note that, using the relationship between concentrate input and milk yield given in equation 2.1, wilted silage on average would have required an additional input of approximately 2 kg concentrates per day to produce an equivalent milk yield to that achieved with the unwilted material. The magnitude of this requirement highlights the possible implications of wilting herbage for silage, particularly when the increased intake with the wilted silage is taken into consideration.

While there is, at present, a great deal of speculation about the possible explanation for the reduced efficiency of utilization of wilted material, no clear information is available. It is likely, however, that it is caused by the cumulative effects of a number of factors, which will involve both energy and protein effects.

Response to changes in protein intake

DIRECT EFFECTS OF PROTEIN

Broster (1972b) has reviewed the information available in the literature on the effect of level of digestible crude protein (DCP) intake on milk yield and reported that little additional response in yield is obtained at intakes of DCP above 56 g/kg milk. The information reviewed by Broster (1972b) was derived almost completely from experiments in which basal diets of dry forages had been used. Gordon (1977b) also calculated a similar level of protein requirement for cows on a basal diet of hay. However, in the context of spring-calving systems, winter diets are almost entirely based on grass silage. High-quality silages have high crude protein contents, which should provide adequate total protein intakes when using supplements of relatively low protein content. There are, however, indications from the work of Cuthbert, Thickett and Wilson (1973), using mainly autumn-calving animals, that the response to additional protein may not decline at the point where theoretically adequate protein is being supplied with basal diets of silage. This trend has also been noted in spring-calving animals by Butler (1973) and Butler and Gleeson (1973). Additional work on this subject has been carried out at Hillsborough to assess the response to supplementary protein with silage diets and, although the preliminary work in measuring direct effects has not been carried out solely with spring-calving animals, the experiments were carried out during early lactation and on animals offered basal diets of grass silage — a situation similar to that for the spring-calving cow.

In the first experiment (Gordon, 1979), pre-wilted grass silage containing 14.2 per cent crude protein and with a D value of 67 on a dry matter basis was offered *ad libitum* during the first 75 days of lactation. In addition, the animals received equal intakes of four supplementary concentrates with crude protein contents ranging from 9.5 to 20.9 per cent on a fresh weight basis. Although, in theory, adequate DCP was supplied with a supplement containing 13 per cent protein, the response in milk yield remained linear throughout the entire range examined. Furthermore, the magnitude of the response to protein, at 0.31 kg milk/day per percentage unit increase in the protein content of the supplement, was almost twice as great as that reported by Cuthbert, Thickett and Wilson (1973) and by Butler and Gleeson (1973). However, it was close to the response of 0.27 kg milk/day per unit increase in the protein percentage reported by Butler (1973). In fact, the size of these larger responses agree with those obtained with dry forage diets under conditions of extreme protein deficiency (Broster *et al.* 1960).

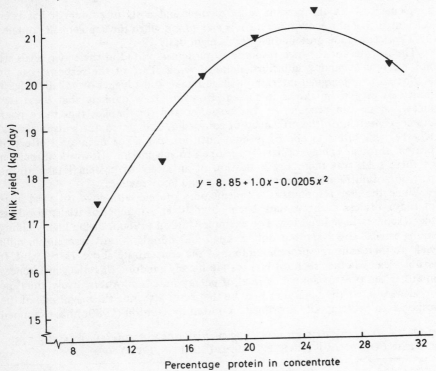

Figure 17.3   The relationship between protein content of the concentrate and milk yield for cows with access to grass silage.

In a further experiment, concentrates containing six levels of crude protein ranging from 10.3 to 30.3 per cent per kg fresh weight have been used in order to characterize the shape of the protein response curve, particularly at higher protein levels (Gordon and McMurray, 1979). The relationship developed is shown in *Figure 17.3* and is described by equation 17.3:

$$y = 8.85 + x - 0.0205x^2 \tag{17.3}$$

where y = milk yield (kg/day) and x = protein content of the supplement (percentage fresh weight basis). Using this relationship it is possible to calculate, not only the protein content which maximizes milk yield (24.4 per cent crude protein), but also the optimum economic protein content for any given set of protein feed costs and milk prices. In this situation the economic return is maximized at the point where the cost of an additional unit of protein in the concentrate is just offset by the return in terms of the additional milk produced. The response in milk yield obtained from an incremental increase in protein intake is given by equation 17.4:

$$\frac{dy}{dx} = 1.0 - 0.0409x \qquad (17.4)$$

where $\frac{dy}{dx}$ = increase in yield (kg) per unit increase in protein content (x) of the supplement. With the present value of milk and costs of protein it has been calculated that the economic return is maximized when the supplement contains 22.2 per cent crude protein on a fresh weight basis.

The reasons for the high response to protein reported in these two trials are not clear and require additional detailed work. Part of the response can be attributed to a marginal increase in silage intake and a higher overall diet digestibility as protein intake is increased. However, it is unlikely that these two factors alone can account for the response, and this implies that there is an effect of protein on the efficiency of conversion of digested nutrients into milk. Whether this effect is one of protein nutrition *per se*, or an indirect effect of protein through energy utilization, is open to speculation. However, in neither of these trials was there any indication of an effect of protein intake on the partition of nutrients between milk output and body reserves.

While the high responses to supplementary protein with cows on basal diets of silage, discussed above, have been obtained in a number of trials, in others the responses have been low. For example Gordon (1980b), using high-yielding spring-calving cows, showed only a small and non-significant response in milk yield to increasing the protein content of the concentrate above 13 per cent. It is not clear whether such differences are merely random, or reflect differences in either the type of animal or level of energy nutrition. Alternatively, the type of silage used as the basal diet may be the factor affecting the magnitude of the response to protein. An experiment reported by Gordon (1980c) has examined

Table 17.10 EFFECT OF SILAGE TYPE ON THE RESPONSE TO INCREASING THE PROTEIN CONTENT OF THE SUPPLEMENT (GORDON, 1980c)

Silage type	Percentage protein concentrate	Silage dry matter intake (kg/d)	Milk yield (kg/d)
High digestibility			
Unwilted	13	9.1	23.3
	21	9.4	23.9
Wilted	13	9.6	22.8
	21	9.4	25.0
Low digestibility			
Unwilted	13	8.2	21.0
	21	9.0	23.0

the effects both of wilting and of stage of growth at harvesting on the response in milk output to increasing the protein content of the supplement. In this experiment, three silage types were offered *ad libitum*, each supplemented with concentrates containing two levels of protein of 13 per cent and 21 per cent, on a fresh weight basis. The effects on feed intake and production are given in *Table 17.10*. While there was no significant interaction between silage type and protein level, there appeared to be marked differences in the response to increased protein between silage types. With the high-digestibility silages, the response to increased protein was low when the material was unwilted but high when wilted and, in the latter case, agreed with the responses reported by Gordon (1979) and Gordon and McMurray (1979). This response with the wilted silage was obtained even though total diet digestibility data indicated that, with this high-digestibility silage, the use of the lower protein supplement resulted in DCP intakes which were approximately 40 per cent above theoretical requirements. The response was also large with the low-digestibility silage, but this may reflect the fact that, due to the lower protein content of the low-digestibility silage, the use of the low-protein supplement resulted in a diet which was marginally deficient in DCP intake. However, this trial must be considered to be of a preliminary nature and there is a need for further production studies to clarify whether wilting of silage is the factor which causes the marked response to protein. This hypothesis is, however, supported by the fact that Beever (1979) has noted a reduction in the supply of amino acids to the ruminant when wilted rather than unwilted silage has been used.

Residual effects of protein

Little information is available on the extent of residual effects of level of protein in early lactation, particularly if this is limited to the spring-calving cow. However, the information available with autumn or mid-winter calving patterns would suggest that residual effects at pasture will not exist or may even be negative. Rijpkema (1977) has reported a mean direct effect of increasing protein intake from 86 to 104 per cent of requirements for the first 28 weeks of lactation, of 1.1 kg milk, while, in the subsequent period at pasture, a negative residual effect of 0.6 kg milk was obtained. A similar effect has been reported by Adamson, Newell and Castle (1979). Gordon (1977b) obtained no residual effects of increased protein levels during the first 75 days of lactation, even though very large direct effects were obtained, which agrees with the results of Jagusch (1971). On the other hand, Butler and Gleeson (1973) using spring-calving cows, reported residual effects at pasture which were positive and approximately 50 per cent of the direct effects. The information available from Hillsborough using spring-calving cows has, up to the present, shown no consistent residual effects from levels of protein feeding during early lactation.

Conclusion

The information reviewed on the relationship between concentrate input and milk output for spring-calving cows has shown that, when silage is offered *ad libitum*, direct responses decline rapidly with increasing level of supplementation.

Residual responses are also low and can even be negative when high levels of supplementation are used, with the overall consequence that under present economic conditions levels of supplementation above 7.0 kg/day cannot be justified. Improvements in the digestibility of the silage used can, however, produce very marked responses in milk yield, while prewilting of herbage before ensiling, although generally resulting in an increase in dry matter intake, does not improve milk output. Large responses to supplementary protein have also been reported in a number of experiments, but there is a need for further clarification of the whole question of protein responses with dairy cows receiving good quality silage.

References

ADAMSON, A.H., NEWELL, D.W. and CASTLE, M.E. (1979). *Grass and Forage Science*, **34**, 229–231

BEEVER, D.E. (1979). *Proc. European Grassland Federation Meeting*, Harrogate

BLAXTER, K.L. (1967). George Scott Robertson Memorial Lecture, Queen's University, Belfast, November 1966.

BROSTER, W.H. (1972a). *Dairy Sci. Abstr.*, **34**, 265

BROSTER, W.H. (1972b). In *Handbuch der Tierernährung*, Vol. 2, pp. 292–322. Eds W. Lenkeit, K. Breirem and E. Crasemann. Hamburg; Parey

BROSTER, W.H. and TUCK, V.J. (1967). *J. agric. Sci., Camb.*, **69**, 465

BROSTER, W.H., BALCH, C.C., BARTLETT, S. and CAMPLING, R.C. (1960). *J. agric. Sci., Camb.*, **55**, 197–202

BROSTER, W.H., BROSTER, V.J. and SMITH, T. (1969). *J. agric. Sci. Camb.*, **72**, 229

BUTLER, T.M. (1973). *Ir. Grassld. Anim. Prod. Assoc. J.*, **8**, 24

BUTLER, T.M. (1975). *An Foras Taluntais Anim. Prod. Res. Rep. 1975*, p. 102.

BUTLER, T.M. (1976). *Dairy Herd Management. An Foras Taluntais. Handb. Series No. 4*, p. 17

BUTLER, T.M. and GLEESON, P.A. (1973). *An Foras Taluntais, Anim. Prod. Res. Rept. 1973*, pp 98–99

BUTLER, T.M., GLEESON, P.A. and MURPHY, J.J. (1978). *Proc. European Association for Animal Production. Harrogate 1978*

CHALMERS, J.S. and LEAVER, J.D. (1980). *Anim. Prod. (Abstr.)*, **30**, 498

CUNNINGHAM, E.P. (1972). *Ir. J. agric. Res.*, **11**, 1

CUTHBERT, M.H., THICKETT, W.S. and WILSON, P.M. (1973). *Proc. Br. Soc. Anim. Prod. (New Series)*, **2**, 70 (Abstr.)

EVANS, B. (1979). Personal Communication

GLEESON, P.A. (1969). *Mimeograph Rep. Dairy Husbandry Seminar.* Moorepark Agric. Res. Sta., June 1969

GLEESON, P.A. (1970). In *Dairy Nutrition*, p. 85. Tech. publ. US Feed Grains Council, London

GLEESON, P.A. (1972). *Proc. An Foras Taluntais Dairying and Pig Conference, Fermoy, May 1972*, p. 55.

GLEESON, P.A. (1973). *Ir. Grassld. Anim. Prod. Assoc. J.*, **8**, 68

GORDON, F.J. (1976). *Anim. Prod.*, **22**, 175

GORDON, F.J. (1977a). *Anim. Prod.*, **25**, 175

GORDON, F.J. (1977b). In *Proc. 2nd Int. Symp. Protein Metabolism and Nutrition*, pp. 142–146

GORDON, F.J. (1978). *51st Ann. Rept of Res. Inst for N.I.*, p. 13

GORDON, F.J. (1979). *Anim. Prod.*, **28**, 183—189

GORDON, F.J. (1980a). *Anim. Prod.*, **31**, 35

GORDON, F.J. (1980b). *Anim. Prod.*, **30**, 23

GORDON, F.J. (1980c). *Anim. Prod.*, **30**, 29

GORDON, F.J. and McMURRAY (1979). *Anim. Prod.*, **29**, 283

JAGUSCH, K.T. (1971). *Town milk*, **29**, 21

JOHNSTON, C.L. (1977). *J. agric. Sci., Camb.*, **88**, 79

McILMOYLE, W.A. (1976). *Silage for Beef Production.* Occ. Publ. No. 2. Agric. Res. Inst. Nth. Ir.

McILMOYLE, W.A. (1977). Personal Communication

McMURRAY, C.H., McCAUGHEY, W.J., GOODALL, E. and UNSWORTH, E. (1978). Paper presented to Dept. of Agr. N.I. Advisory Staff, Greenmount.

MARSH, R. (1979). *Grass and Forage Science*, **34**, 1

PARKER, J.W.G. (1976). *Proc. Fourth Silage Conference, Grassland Research Institute Hurley 1976*

RIJPKEMA, Y.F. (1977). Personal communication

STEEN, R.W.J. (1978). PhD Thesis, Queen's University, Belfast

STEEN, R.W.J. and GORDON, F.J. (1980a). *Anim. Prod.*, **30**, 39

STEEN, R.W.J. and GORDON, F.J. (1980b). *Anim. Prod.*, **30**, 341

STRICKLAND, M.J. (1975). *Boxworth Experimental Husbandry Farm, Annual Report 1975*, p. 38

THOMAS, C. (1979). *ARC Seminar Strategies of Feeding Dairy Cows.* Harrogate

WOOD, P.D.P. (1970). *Anim. Prod.*, **12**, 253

18

COMPLETE-DIET FEEDING OF DAIRY COWS

J.B. OWEN
Department of Agriculture, University College of North Wales, Bangor

Introduction

Since 1975 there has been a rapid expansion in the use of complete-diet systems by dairy farmers in the UK.

A complete diet has been defined as 'an intimate mixture of processed ingredients presented in a form which precludes selection and which is designed to be the sole source of food' (Owen, 1971). It also implies a self-feeding system where the diet is on offer for most of the 24 hours in a day.

Complete diets used in practice have covered a wide range of basic feed ingredients, reflecting the normal constituents used in conventional, rationed, feeding (Owen, 1976). Most diets in the UK have been based on grass silage with a variety of cereal and protein feeds added, although there has been some limited use of straw-based, dry mixtures.

Complete-diet systems have been introduced with the aim of simplifying the feeding of high-yielding dairy cows so that labour is saved and the capital costs of building reduced, whilst maintaining tighter control of the cow's nutrition and facilitating the use of least-cost methods of formulation. The aim of the present chapter is to examine the biological and nutritional case for the adoption of a complete-diet system in relation to efficient food utilization from the dairy herd. It is also intended to examine some of the practical aspects of diet formulation including the strategy of changes in formulation over the lactation and the tactics of producing an efficient mix from the viewpoint of the cow and the herd manager.

Biological/nutritional considerations in the use of complete diets

SEPARATE V. MIXED INGREDIENTS

Many dairy-cow feeding systems in use today are based upon the self-feeding of grass silage (conserved in clamps or pits) together with the controlled feeding of concentrates, usually partly or entirely during milking. An apparently logical corollary of this trend would be to adopt a fully *ad-libitum* system where the concentrates are also given on a separate self-feeding basis. The evidence available on the performance of dairy cows on a free-choice system is not plentiful, particularly on a whole-lactation basis. Owen, Miller and Bridge (1968), using both hay and straw, showed that Friesian cows consumed only a very low amount of roughage when given free access to a barley-based concentrate. This resulted in progressively reduced butterfat content of the milk, erratic intake and little more milk as compared with cows given the same ingredients in a complete diet with 25% roughage included. Another potential drawback is the high variability between cows in the ratio of roughage to concentrates consumed. Studies using silage as the forage base have also demonstrated the progressive fall in silage intake with increasing allowance of concentrates (Campling and Murdoch, 1966). Recently, equipment has been developed which allows selective free choice of concentrates to high-yielding cows within a herd (Spahr, 1975; Broadbent, 1975). Evidence is available from several centres on feeding of concentrates *ad libitum* in early lactation. Some workers have found variable intake ('off-feed'), depressed fat content of the milk and inefficient use of concentrates. Bath, Gall and Ronning (1974) measured voluntary intake of alfalfa hay in Holstein–Friesians given 20%, 35%, 50%, 65% or 80% of their estimated net energy requirements as a concentrate mixture. Mean hay intake declined by 0.78 kg of dry matter (DM) per kilogram of concentrate DM consumed. The percentage of milk fat was consistently depressed in high-yielding cows offered 50% or more of their requirements as concentrates. Hijink (1976) found that feeding of unlimited concentrates, with roughage available, in the first three months after calving, resulted in health problems and inefficient use of concentrates. Wiktorsson (1973) also reported that cows fed concentrates *ad libitum* in the first part of lactation were frequently 'off-feed' and gave less milk than cows on controlled concentrate feeding; in this case there was no discernible difference in milk fat content. Shorter-term experiments of the Latin Square type are unlikely to be satisfactory in assessing the merits of self-feeding concentrates because of the relatively slow development of the obvious symptoms of inefficiency, such as lowered milk fat content. Even so, van der Merwe and McDonald (1973) found a depressed percentage of fat during 42-day treatment periods commencing two months after calving when a concentrate diet (containing 15% wheaten bran) was given as free choice, as compared with a complete diet and a conventional diet. Thomas, Emery and Brown (1974) investigated the effect of feeding concentrates *ad libitum* in the first 45 days of lactation as compared with restricted concentrate feeding during the same period, when both were followed by a variety of other treatments; in experiments over a period of four years, no differences in mean daily fat-corrected milk yields were found as a result of this type of feeding.

The classical Beltsville metabolism balance trials with high-yielding cows (Flatt *et al.*, 1969) have also clearly confirmed that at the higher levels of concentrate consumption the cow increasingly partitions her energy intake into body tissue without an increase in milk yield and with a lower milk energy content (*Table 18.1*).

From the viewpoint of early-lactation feeding particularly, two factors must be borne in mind: first, as shown in *Table 18.1,* the diet influences lactation through its effect on rumen fermentation and on the partition of energy between body gain and milk; secondly, if the forage concentration is increased

Table 18.1 BELTSVILLE BALANCE EXPERIMENTS

Stage of lactation	Alfalfa : concentrate ratio		
	60 : 40	*40 : 60*	*20 : 80*
Daily milk energy yield (Mcal)			
Early	22.42	19.02	14.37
Mid	12.58	13.01	9.32
Late	6.83	6.58	7.04
Body tissue gain (Mcal)			
Early	−10.13	−7.06	−3.46
Mid	0.08	1.61	1.83
Late	4.04	3.82	6.88

From Flatt *et al.* (1969)

beyond the point of maximum partition efficiency, the cow suffers from an energy deficit which, if too large, will suppress lactation, increase bodyweight loss and reduce fertility.

There is therefore little hard evidence of any advantage to a system which involves the self-feeding of concentrates over part or the whole of lactation and sufficient evidence to indicate that the practice can lead to inefficient use of concentrates, reduced fat content of the milk and health problems. A feeding system that is fully *ad libitum* should therefore be based on the complete-diet principle, although this concept does not rule out selective free access to a complete diet of high energy content that would be suitable as the sole diet, in addition to a standard medium-energy diet available to all cows within a herd.

AD-LIBITUM OR RESTRICTED FEEDING

There are obvious organizational advantages to self-feeding as opposed to a controlled feeding system, even when both are applied on a group basis. Competition can occur between cows at communal mealtimes on restricted feeding, usually necessitating sufficient feeding space so that all cows within a group can eat at the same time. There are also nutritional consequences to feeding *ad libitum*. Some of these stem from the changed pattern of food intake during the day and are discussed later in relation to the effect of frequency of feeding. There is also the observation that cows being fed complete diets *ad libitum* seem to eat more than cows on a conventional system, even though roughage intake on the conventional system may not be restricted. Some of this may be an effect of feeding as a group rather than individually. Coppock *et al.* (1972) noted that Guernsey cows on a diet composed of maize silage and concentrates (60 : 40 on a DM basis) consumed 7% more feed when group-fed as compared with individual feeding. Another reason for higher DM intake on feeding *ad libitum* appears to be that feeding standards do not adequately cater for the cow's actual intake. Bines, Napper and Johnson (1977) found that where all cows were individually fed, heifers achieved 10–20% higher DM intakes when fed *ad libitum* as compared with cows fed on a controlled high level. Yet another possible reason for higher DM intake by cows on a self-fed complete-diet system, as compared with cows given the same constituents on a traditional basis, lies in the extra processing of the diet that is usually involved. Complete diets processed through a mixer trailer are vigorously squeezed and end up as denser material than the original components (Owen, 1976). It is well established that more severe processing of the roughage component of the diet (as in grinding and pelleting) can markedly affect intake as shown later. However, the main feature of the effect of complete diets on intake and other aspects may lie in the frequency of feeding involved.

FREQUENCY OF FEEDING

Dearth of evidence is the hearth of controversy; this has been the case where theoretical expectations that frequent feeding can increase the efficiency of food use were not apparent in the few reports available as far as dairy cows are concerned. Burt and Dunton (1967), reviewing the evidence at the time of their paper, showed that experiments with non-lactating cattle and other species provided evidence that DM digestibility and nitrogen digestibility could be increased by frequent feeding, particularly on lower-quality feed. There was also evidence that frequent feeding could reduce the fluctuation in the concentration of volatile fatty acids and ammonia in rumen liquor, and that it resulted in slightly lower mean rumen pH values and an increase in the proportion of propionic acid. It was also noted that rumen protozoa counts increased.

However, the results of the few studies with cows up to 1967 and some others subsequently (Guglya, Gerb and Sokolov, 1975; Thomas and Kelly, 1976) showed little tangible evidence of the above expectations. However, Burt and Dunton (1967) pointed out the difficulty of experimentation in this field, where cows in the same building on different feeding frequency influence each others' behaviour; also, the studies mentioned above were not carried out with really high-yielding cows consuming large quantities of concentrates.

Several workers subsequently have noted effects on milk quality, DM intake and rumen fermentation due to more frequent feeding of dairy cows. O'Dell, King and Cook (1968) found that cows on pelleted, ground hay gave a higher milk fat content when fed four times rather than twice a day. Similar effects have been noted by other workers: Kaufmann *et al.* (1975) with complete diets and with conventional diets, Rohr and Daenicke (1973) with complete pelleted diets. An increase in DM intake is a common feature of some of the studies (Campbell and Merilan, 1961; Rohr and Daenicke, 1973). Actual increases in milk yield have more rarely been reported although increases in the yield of fat-corrected milk have been reported (Rohr and Daenicke, 1973). Several recent studies (reviewed by Kaufmann, 1976) have reported that for high-yielding cows higher frequency of feeding can allow higher intake of concentrates without incurring the same drop in rumen pH as on less frequent feeding. This tends to maintain the ratio of acetic to propionic acid near 3 : 1 and therefore prevents falls in butterfat content. The higher pH would also tend to favour cellulolytic activity and this could account for the higher intake, particularly of roughage, with increased frequency of feeding. Kaufmann's conclusions support the findings of Tremere, Merrill and Loosli (1968), who found that cows on a high level of feeding and liable to go 'off-feed' benefited from frequent feeding.

Other studies have shown that the use of complete diets, presumably through the effect of more frequent feeding on rumen ammonia concentration, has led to more efficient use of protein and higher milk yield (Kennet, 1974) and to more efficient use of non-protein nitrogen (Coppock, Peplowski and Lake, 1976).

It can therefore be concluded that the feeding of complete diets *ad libitum* is likely to prove beneficial in the feeding of high-yielding dairy cows through its effect on higher intakes (allowing therefore the possibility of a lower concentrate : forage ratio), preservation of milk quality and better utilization of nitrogen, quite apart from preventing the obvious hazard of acidosis from overeating of concentrates.

Efficiency of utilization in relation to the formulation of complete diets

So far some of the factors that provide a rationale for complete-diet feeding have been discussed. If the decision has been made to adopt the system, important questions arise relating to the optimum formulation of the diets and the strategy of changing such formulation according to the productive stage of the cows within the dairy herd.

The traditional concept of rationing the dairy cow has been strongly influenced by the obvious changes in milk output from one calving to the next. Observation of the lactation curve, allied with the notion of maintenance requirement as a constant, has naturally culminated in a feeding strategy designed to manipulate the concentrate : forage ratio so as to minimize the short-term negative energy balance of the cow. This has involved feeding the cow as an individual and the frequent adjustment of concentrate allowances according to milk production. This approach is well demonstrated in the Ministry of Agriculture Technical Bulletin 33 published in 1975. The complete-diet concept is radically different in that it is based on group rather than individual feeding and usually involves much fewer, if any, changes in diet formulation according to milk yield. In spite of the apparently logical basis of the traditional feeding concept and the fact that many of the principles have been derived from experimental data, sound evidence involving the whole of a lactation or longer, comparing such an approach with that embodied in the complete-diet concept, has only recently become available.

Experiments have been carried out on the flat-rate feeding of concentrates to groups of dairy cows as compared with detailed individual rationing. ADAS (1973) for example, at their Boxworth Farm, compared conventional individual feeding according to yield, including added 'lead' feeding in the first 6 weeks, with a flat-rate system applied to cows divided into three groups according to initial yield. Because of the experimental difficulty there was some difference in the amount of concentrates given on the two treatments. However, the results suggest that yield and efficiency were not improved by individual rationing at any level of cow potential. It is now common in farming practice to find individual feeding discontinued in favour of flat-rate feeding to cows grouped according to yield or stage of lactation.

A more profound question is that of how to optimize concentrate/forage distribution over the lactation for efficient production. Several interesting experiments have been done in this connection. Everson (1974) and Everson *et al.* (1976) compared two systems of complete-diet feeding: (a) a constant ratio of forage to grain DM of 60 : 40, and (b) a 50 : 50 ratio for 21 weeks, 65 : 35 for 23 weeks and 85 : 15 for 8 weeks. Over two years their results showed no advantage in milk yield or fat percentage for the more complicated distribution.

Harner (1972) at Illinois also found little effect from a more complicated sequence of complete-diet formulations compared with a medium energy ratio throughout. Rusoff, Branton and Evans (1976) concluded that where high-quality forage is available, a complete diet given *ad libitum* was preferable to a system of separate feeding of forage and concentrates according to feeding standards (including 'challenge' feeding of extra concentrates in early lactation).

A feature of some of these reports, such as that of Akinyele and Spahr (1975), is that whilst complicated systems of distributing concentrates over lactation give no differences in lactation milk yield, there is some evidence of a reduction in peak yield concomitant with an increase in persistency, when the same diet is fed throughout.

The experiments reported on the effect of differential distribution of concentrates during lactation on a conventional basis have given broadly similar results. There is little experimental justification, for instance, for the practice of 'lead' or 'challenge' feeding from the above studies and from those of Gordon (1977). An extensive series of apparently well designed trials in Denmark (Østergaard, 1977) has also shown little justification for distributing concentrates over the lactation according to yield as compared to one flat rate of feeding concentrates. Johnson (1977) found no benefit due to distribution for second-lactation cows but found a statistically significant effect for older cows.

In these experiments where the comparison was made, the actual level of concentrates or the concentrate : forage ratio was important in determining yield; usually the higher the concentrate level, the higher the yield. However, whilst yield is often higher there is a limit to the level that concentrate : forage ratio can rise without reducing the efficiency of energy conversion (Flatt *et al.*, 1969; Escano and Rusoff, 1973; Coppock, Noller and Wolfe, 1974).

The conclusion from an intensive search of the literature published in the 1970s is that the case for complicated methods of distributing concentrates over the lactation or of changing the concentrate : forage ratio in complete diets is not proven and that although increases in the level of concentrates given usually result in increased yield there seems no justification for reducing the concentrate : forage ratio below 60 : 40 where forage quality is good. Until further hard evidence is available, a complete-diet system based on a single concentrate : forage ratio for the whole lactation can be justified for the high-yielding herd on the grounds of efficiency and it is convenient and simple to use in practice.

The reason for this rather surprising conclusion may well lie in the way the voluntary intake and the milk yield of the well-fed cow vary over the lactation and interact with body energy reserves as shown in *Figure 18.1*. The voluntary intake of a high-energy diet over the lactation is similar to the curve shown in *Figure 18.2* with a relatively flat peak in mid-lactation after increasing from the lowest point at calving (Owen, 1976). Several authors, such as Bines, Napper and Johnson (1977), Bull, Baumgardt and Clancy (1976), Bines (1976), Conrad, Pratt and Hibbs (1964), Monteiro (1972) and Greenhalgh and Reid (1975) have shown that at the higher levels of energy concentration, dairy cows tend

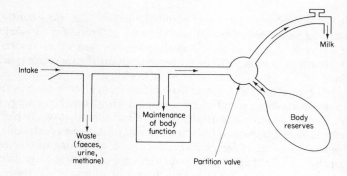

Figure 18.1 Model cow

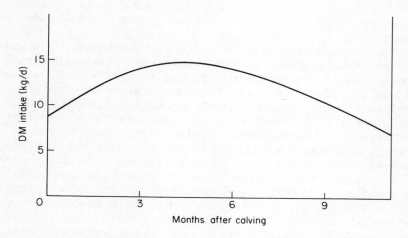

Figure 18.2 Pattern of dry-matter intake during lactation

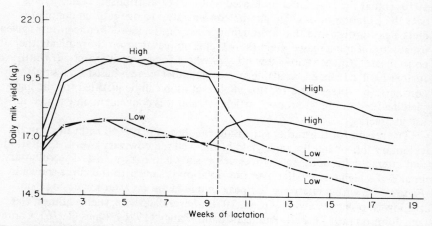

Figure 18.3 Daily milk yield during the course of lactation. Based on Broster, Broster and Smith (1969)

to eat broadly according to requirements and that energy intake does not increase with further increases in the concentrate : forage ratio. At this level of diet quality it would appear pointless to attempt to feed higher levels of concentrates in early lactation since this could result only in decreases in forage intake and only exacerbate the already substantial gap between energy input and output in the high-yielding cow. The milk production curve of the strictly rationed cow is very different from that of those on more generous levels of feeding. *Figure 18.3* shows the results of differential feeding levels at different stages of lactation (Broster, Broster and Smith, 1969) and the High–High treatment is similar to the approach adopted in high-yielding herds. This curve is much flatter than that under much lower feeding and corresponds more closely with the energy intake curve, although the unavoidable shortfall in early lactation is again evident.

It can be argued that current lactation curves may be the result of an abnormal distribution of feed during lactation rather than a rationale for such feeding. The finding that generous feeding in early lactation and high peak yield are desirable objectives when the cow is fed at restricted levels in mid- and late lactation (Broster, Broster and Smith, 1969) does not show that generous feeding throughout lactation is an inferior practice. When it is further taken into account that cows may benefit in their subsequent lactation(s) from good feeding in the current one (Broster and Johnson, 1977), it is less surprising to find little justification for the detailed manipulation of concentrate distribution in the lactation. In practice a standard feeding pattern for all lactating cows is very convenient with a separate diet given only to dry cows.

Formulation and preparation of complete diets

Having considered the principles and strategy of feeding complete diets the essentially practical questions on formulation and preparation now resolve into the following points:

(1) The appropriate concentrate : forage ratio.
(2) The optimum formulation of the concentrate
    (a) the optimum cereal components
    (b) the crude protein level
    (c) the source of protein supplement.
(3) The processing of the constituents and of the whole diet.
(4) Storage properties of complete diets.

CONCENTRATE : FORAGE RATIO

It has already been emphasized that economic formulation of complete diets is usually based on the use of high-quality forage and that where conserved forage (often grass or maize) is the base, the optimum concentrate : forage DM ratio is not likely to exceed 60 : 40. Even for high-yielding cows a 50 : 50 ratio is usually adequate. For example, a diet of 11.5 MJ/kg DM is considered suitable for high-yielding dairy cows on a grass silage basis; assuming a maize/barley-based concentrate of 13.0 MJ/kg DM the silage quality would need to be

10.0 MJ/kg DM to give a diet of the required energy concentration at a concentrate : forage DM ratio of 50 : 50. Economic considerations are also highly relevant including the relative costs of diet ingredients, particularly those of forage as compared with concentrates. In some cases the fact that land is limiting and other similar constraints may influence the optimum.

To state the optimum energy level for economic milk production with more precision, more data are required on a complete-diet system employing one energy level throughout lactation against a variety of background feeds, both forage and concentrate. The simplification of the system of feed allocation makes the task of development workers, in providing such information, much easier.

FORMULATION OF THE CONCENTRATE COMPONENT

Because of the complexity of interactions between dietary components in their effect on rumen micro-organisms and on the animal itself it still cannot be considered satisfactory to evaluate cereal components of the diet purely on the basis, say, of their metabolizable-energy (ME) content in relation to cost. It has been a belief long held by feed formulators that variety of sources provides some safeguard in this respect. Where cost per unit ME is not too disparate it is therefore wise to include more than one cereal source, such as a mixture of maize and barley, in complete diets for high-yielding dairy cows.

As regards protein level, several methods of expressing protein levels in ruminant diets have been suggested. For complete-diet formulation the simplest procedure is to take account of the crude-protein content of the dry matter of the diet and to use some judgement to ensure that the form of the nitrogen is adequate, particularly in terms of the degradability of the protein; it is important that the nitrogen and amino acid needs of the micro-organisms and the amino acid needs of the host cow are adequately met if efficient partition of energy into lactation is to be achieved (Ørskov and Grubb, 1977). Some recent reports relevant to the protein needs of the high-yielding cow are worth noting. Thomas (1975) suggested on theoretical grounds that 12.5% crude protein in the dry matter was sufficient for a cow giving 20 kg of milk per day. Treacher *et al.* (1976) could find no depressant effect when protein levels only 75% of those recommended by the Agricultural Research Council were given to cows from 8 weeks before to 14 weeks after calving. Horn *et al.* (1976), working with Holstein cows averaging 6370 kg 'mature equivalent' milk in 305 days, could show no benefit for exceeding 13.5% crude protein in the dry matter of complete diets (containing some soya bean protein). There seem to be few grounds at present therefore to recommend a higher level than 13.0% crude protein in the dry matter if protein quality is adequate. Adequacy of protein quality can be ensured where part of the protein supplement to a silage diet consists of dried grass, soya bean meal or fish meal (Castle and Watson, 1975; Horn *et al.*, 1976). These supplements ensure optimum micro-organism activity and also that some undegraded, good quality, protein reaches the cow's abomasum. More surprisingly, ground-nut cake, which is highly degraded in the rumen, also seems to be a useful supplement to silage (Castle and Watson, 1976). In spite of this, Virginia Polytechnic Institute recommendations for complete-diet formulation are substantially more generous (Murley and Collins, 1977).

FEED PROCESSING

The processing of the ingredients in a complete diet accomplishes several objectives. First, it ensures a uniformly mixed material which cannot be separated by the cow into its components and therefore eaten selectively. Few experimental results are available to establish the degree of processing required for this purpose. However, experience in the use of complete diets has given some guides.

For diets based on silage, precision chopping giving median particle lengths of 10–20 mm (Thomas, Kelly and Wait, 1976) ensures a uniform mix with cereals and other ingredients and this degree of chopping is needed to avoid too great a stress on a mixer trailer which uses opposing auger movement for its action (Whitton, 1975). Cereals and other concentrates normally need to be coarsely ground, crushed or rolled for maximum utilization. Dry roughages such as hay or straw can be coarsely ground through screens varying from 10 to 20 mm and will form part of the intimate mix whilst still retaining many of their 'roughage' properties. Feed processing has effects on intake and utilization quite apart from preventing selectivity (Murdoch, 1965; Owen, Miller and Bridge, 1971; Thomas, Kelly and Wait, 1976). To what extent auger mixer trailers provide a severe enough treatment in this respect is not known.

As regards accuracy of mixing, some of the mixing machinery now available enables the components of a mix to be weighed easily, employing the electronic load cell principle. It raises the question of how important accuracy of weighing is to the efficiency of the system. It would not be consistent with the reasoning behind the simple complete-diet system to insist, at great expense, on achieving very high levels of uniformity. However, consistent biases leading to a realized consumption very different from that planned are undesirable. Therefore regular calibration of the weights of roughage and other materials in relation to the handling machinery — fork lifts, silage grabs, etc. — would be necessary. Within the long-term accuracy required by most operators, fluctuations in the composition of individual mixes would be less important provided they do not exceed certain safety tolerance limits such as that for minimum roughage content of the mix.

STORAGE LIFE OF COMPLETE DIETS

Complete diets based on dry ingredients such as chopped hay and concentrates have the advantage for work organization that they can be stored after mixing for several days or even weeks. Provided sufficient storage capacity is available at the feeding area this can cut down the replenishment of the feeders or hoppers to the convenience of the personnel involved, whilst still allowing the cow constant access to high-quality feed.

Complete diets based on silage are obviously a different matter, and it was rather a surprise in our work at Aberdeen when it was observed that a mix based on silage, and containing wet distillers' grains in addition to the dry materials, could be stored for several days with no apparent deterioration (Allen, 1976). Further, more detailed observations (J.R. Davies, private communication) have confirmed that mixes consisting of (in terms of DM) 49–78% silage, 13–33% barley and a variety of other ingredients, such as maize and soya bean, showed little signs of outward deterioration for seven days during three winter months at mean monthly maximum temperatures of 8.1, 3.2 and 4.1 °C and mean minimum temperatures of 1.9, −1.0, −0.7 °C. Microbiological and chemical tests have confirmed that all the mixtures appeared to be stable and free from toxins for up to seven days. The silages used were well made with pH approximately 4.0; the mixed diets themselves were of pH 4.2–4.6 and remained stable over the seven days.

One of the reasons for this appears to be the mode of processing of the material (*see Figure 18.4*). The mixing process involves a compressing action of the augers so that air is expelled from the material and this, in conjunction

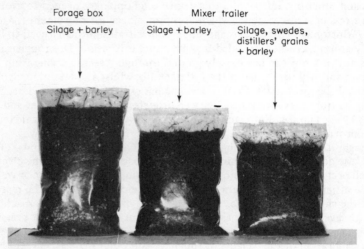

Figure 18.4 Effect of processing on diet. Note: each bag contains 1.36 kg

with the relatively stable pH level, seems to aid preservation. It is important now to check this finding over a range of ingredient types and diet formulations and under different environmental conditions. If it is possible to maintain the quality of complete diets for three to four days this opens up significant benefits for organizing work routines and in enabling machinery costs to be spread over several dairy units by contractor or co-operative-type activity.

References

ADAS (1973). Ministry of Agriculture, Fisheries and Food. Results of experiments at the EHF's (1972) No. 20 Pt. VIII, p. 20
AKINYELE, I.O. and SPAHR, S.L. (1975). *J. Dairy Sci.,* **58**, 917
ALLEN, P.N. (1976). Paper presented at a Dairy Farmers' Conference, Preston, 19 March 1976
BATH, D.L., GALL, G.A.E. and RONNING, M. (1974). *J. Dairy Sci.,* **57**, 198
BINES, J.A. (1976). *Livestk Prod. Sci.,* **3**, 115
BINES, J.A., NAPPER, D.J. and JOHNSON, V.W. (1977). *Proc. Nutr. Soc.,* **36**, 146A
BROADBENT, P.J. (1975). In *Simplified Feeding for Milk and Beef,* p. 95. London and Aberdeen; US Feed Grains Council and University of Aberdeen

BROSTER, W.H., BROSTER, V.J. and SMITH, T. (1969). *J. agric. Sci., Camb.*, **72**, 229

BROSTER, W.H. and JOHNSON, C.L. (1977). *ARC Res. Rev.*, **3**, 9

BULL, L.S., BAUMGARDT, B.R. and CLANCY, M. (1976). *J. Dairy Sci.*, **59**, 1078

BURT, A.W.A. and DUNTON, C.R. (1967). *Proc. Nutr. Soc.*, **26**, 181

CAMPBELL, J.R. and MERILAN, C.P. (1961). *J. Dairy Sci.*, **44**, 664

CAMPLING, R.C. and MURDOCH, J.R. (1966). *J. Dairy Res.*, **33**, 1

CASTLE, M.E. and WATSON, J.N. (1975). *J. Br. Grassld Soc.*, **30**, 217

CASTLE, M.E. and WATSON, J.N. (1976). *J. Br. Grassld Soc.*, **31**, 191

CONRAD, H.R., PRATT, A.D. and HIBBS, T.W. (1964). *J. Dairy Sci.*, **47**, 54

COPPOCK, C.E., NOLLER, C.H., CROWL, B.W., McLELLON, C.D. and RHYKERD, C.L. (1972). *J. Dairy Sci.*, **55**, 325

COPPOCK, C.E., NOLLER, C.H. and WOLFE, S.A. (1974). *J. Dairy Sci.*, **57**, 1371

COPPOCK, C.E., PEPLOWSKI, M.A. and LAKE, G.B. (1976). *J. Dairy Sci.*, **59**, 1152

ESCANO, J.R. and RUSOFF, L.L. (1973). *J. Dairy Sci.*, **56**, 1144

EVERSON, R.A. (1974). *Diss. Abstr. Int. B*, **35**, 7

EVERSON, R.A., JORGENSEN, N.A., CROWLEY, J.W., JENSEN, E.L. and BARRINGTON, G.P. (1976). *J. Dairy Sci.*, **59**, 1776

FLATT, W.P., MOE, P.W., MUNSON, A.W. and COOPER, T. (1969). In *Energy Metabolism of Farm Animals*, p. 235. Eds K.L. Blaxter, G. Thorbek and J. Kielanowski. EAAP Publication No. 12

GORDON, F.J. (1977). *Dairy Fmr, Ipswich*, **24**, 16

GREENHALGH, J.F.D. and REID, G.W. (1975). *Proc. Br. Soc. Anim. Prod.*, **4** (new series), 111

GUGLYA, V.G., GERB, E.I. and SOKOLOV, V.M. (1975). *Sib. Vestnik sel'sko-khoz. Nauki*, No. 5, 92, 131, 132

HARNER, J.P. (1972). *Diss. Abstr. Int. B*, **33**, 4

HIJINK, J.W.F. (1976). *Bedrijfsontwikkeling*, **7**, 95

HORN, H.H. VAN, OLALOKU, E.A., FLORES, J.R., MARSHALL, S.P. and BACHMAN, K.C. (1976). *J. Dairy Sci.*, **59**, 902

JOHNSON, C.L. (1977). *J. Agric. Sci.*, **88**, 79

KAUFMANN, W. (1976). *Livestk Prod. Sci.*, **3**, 103

KAUFMANN, W., ROHR, K., DAENICKE, R. and HAGEMEISTER, H. (1975). *Ber. Landw. Sonderheft*, **191**, 269

KENNET, W.S. (1974). *Diss. Abstr. Int. B*, **35**, 2523

VAN DER MERWE, F.J. and McDONALD, T. (1973). *S. Afr. J. Anim. Sci.*, **3**, 53

MINISTRY OF AGRICULTURE, FISHERIES AND FOOD, DEPARTMENT OF AGRICULTURE AND FISHERIES FOR SCOTLAND, DEPARTMENT OF AGRICULTURE FOR NORTHERN IRELAND (1975). 'Energy allowances and feeding systems for ruminants'. *Technical Bulletin 33*. London; HMSO

MONTEIRO, L.S. (1972). *Anim. Prod.*, **14**, 263

MURDOCH, J.C. (1965). *J. Br. Grassld Soc.*, **20**, 54

MURLEY, W.R. and COLLINS, W.H. (1977). *Hoard's Dairym.*, **122**, 79

O'DELL, G.D., KING, W.A. and COOK, W.C. (1968). *J. Dairy Sci.*, **51**, 50

ØRSKOV, E.R. and GRUBB, D.A. (1977). *Proc. Nutr. Soc.*, **36**, 56A

ØSTERGAARD, V. (1977). Unpublished paper, National Institute of Animal Science, Copenhagen

OWEN, J.B. (1971). *Agriculture, Lond.*, **78**, 331

OWEN, J.B. (1976). *Wld Anim. Rev.*, **20**, 36

OWEN, J.B., MILLER, E.L. and BRIDGE, P.S. (1968). *J. agric. Sci., Camb.*, **70**, 223

OWEN, J.B., MILLER, E.L. and BRIDGE, P.S. (1971). *J. agric. Sci., Camb.*, **77**, 195

ROHR, K. and DAENICKE, R. (1973). *LandbForsch-Völkenrode*, **23**, 133

RUSOFF, L.L., BRANTON, C. and EVANS, D.L. (1976). *La Agric.*, **19**, 10

SPAHR, S.L. (1975). In *Simplified Feeding for Milk and Beef*, p. 103. London and Aberdeen; US Feed Grains Council and University of Aberdeen

THOMAS, J.W., EMERY, R.S. and BROWN, L.D. (1974). *J. Dairy Sci.*, **57**, 463

THOMAS, P.C. (1975). *Wld Rev. Anim. Prod.*, **11**, 33

THOMAS, P.C. and KELLY, M.E. (1976). *J. Dairy Res.*, **43**, 1

THOMAS, P.C., KELLY, N.C. and WAIT, M.K. (1976). *J. Br. Grassld Soc.*, **31**, 19

TREACHER, R.J., LITTLE, W., COLLIS, K.A. and STARK, A.J. (1976). *J. Dairy Res.*, **43**, 357

TREMERE, A.W., MERRILL, W.G. and LOOSLI, J.K. (1968). *J. Dairy Sci.*, **51**, 1065

WHITTON, H.W. (1975). In *Simplified Feeding for Milk and Beef*, p. 71. London and Aberdeen; US Feed Grains Council and University of Aberdeen

WIKTORSSON, H. (1973). *Swed. J. agric. Res.*, **3**, 153

19

CONCENTRATE : FORAGE RATIOS FOR HIGH-YIELDING DAIRY COWS

W.H. BROSTER
J.D. SUTTON
J.A. BINES
National Institute for Research in Dairying, Reading

Introduction

Traditionally the ration for the dairy cow has been manipulated to encompass the demand for nutrients within her voluntary food intake limits (*see*, for example, Woodman, 1948). The system has had considerable success. In the past three decades, reviews of the ability of foods to supply energy include those of Blaxter (1949–50, 1956, 1962), Cooper (1955), Huffman (1959, 1961), Flatt *et al.* (1972), and, of the question of concentrate : forage ratios, those of Reid (1956), Van Soest (1963), Wagner and Loosli (1967), Ekern (1970), and Flatt and Moe (1971).

The earlier approach of summating the energy supplied by each ration constituent has been modified in the metabolizable-energy system (Blaxter, 1962; Agricultural Research Council, 1965; Min. Agric. Fish. Fd, 1975) to account for the composition of the diet and the plane of nutrition as factors influencing the use made of the energy supplied by the ration as a whole.

More recently there has been a move towards and much discussion of the several merits of complete feeding (Rakes, 1969; Owen, 1975, 1976; Allen, Prescott and Walker Love, 1977), group feeding, selector feeding, as systems of distribution which seek to reconcile on the one hand, managerial objectives such as ease of distribution and on the other, nutritional criteria of accuracy, appropriateness and adequacy of food allowance for each cow. These developments highlight such factors as voluntary constraints on food intake, variation in performance from animal to animal, frequency of feeding, and nutrition and health relationships. They equally influence least-cost ration formulation (Dent and Casey, 1967).

It is considered desirable in this chapter to continue the series of discussions in previous proceedings (Kay, 1969; Blaxter, 1974; Alderman *et al.*, 1974; Moe and Flatt, 1974) on the question of food utilization by ruminants, especially the dairy cow, with a further consideration of some aspects of concentrate : forage ratio of particular significance in feeding practice.

Whilst in general the literature on concentrates : forage ratio will be reviewed, in some respects that evidence is limited. Comprehensive long-term studies with a range of intakes of energy from a given diet formula together with equal energy intakes from various diets do not appear to exist in the literature. Some results, interim at this stage and subject to later revision, are drawn on from a large-scale experiment (Expt CH1) carried out at Reading. This included some 150 Friesian cows of three parities. The treatments consisted of a factorial arrangement of three diets (90 : 10; 75 : 25; and 60 : 40 proportions of concentrates to hay) and three levels of intake (approximately 75%, 100% of Min. Agric. Fish. Fd (1975) standards and *ad libitum*). Intakes were equalized in terms of digestible energy. Some short notes on the experiments have been published (Broster *et al.*, 1971–72, 1977; Bines, Napper and Johnson, 1977; Sutton *et al.*, 1977).

Food intake

Food intake by the lactating cow is determined by a number of factors related to the cow herself, to the feeds used and to certain aspects of management. These will be considered in turn and an attempt will be made to show their relative importance.

ANIMAL FACTORS

Size

Individual cows can vary from 250 kg to well over 700 kg. In general, the abdominal capacity will increase with size of cow, thereby increasing gut capacity and hence intake. This will be of greatest consequence when cows receive diets the intake of which is determined largely by physical limitations. Care should be taken, however, to differentiate between increases in weight due to greater overall size, and increases due to fattening without growth. During fattening, considerable amounts of fat are deposited within the abdominal cavity; these will effectively reduce rumen capacity and thereby food intake. Physiological inhibition of intake may also occur with increasing fatness (Bines, 1971).

Milk yield

Figure 19.1 (Broster and Alderman, 1977) shows the main trends in milk, live-weight and intake over the lactation. The increase in intake due to lactation varies according to the type of ration fed, but in general, changes of 30–40% are common. However, the relationship between the actual yield of milk and food intake is poor, partly at least owing to the influence of the lactation cycle on intake (*see below*).

A preliminary equation for heifers from Expt CH1 relating, for weeks 1–18, the food intake (I, kg/d) of the cow to size (W, kg), milk yield (M, kg/d), and to liveweight change (ΔW, kg/d) — the last factor, representing in effect time from calving, is $I = 0.160M + 2.450\Delta W + 0.0113W + 4.25$. The equation is the pooled one for three diets: 60 : 40, 75 : 25, 90 : 10 ratios of concentrates to hay in Expt CH1. The preliminary results for intakes and performance of first-calf cows receiving these diets *ad libitum* are shown in *Table 19.1*.

Lactation cycle

After parturition, milk yield rises rapidly to a maximum between days 35 and
50 of lactation; thereafter milk yield declines at a steady rate of about 2.5% per
week. Wood (1969) has described the shape of the lactation curve. In contrast,
the voluntary intake of the cow rises more slowly after parturition and the
maximum may not be reached until many weeks after maximum milk yield.
The rate of increase in intake and the time of peak intake are determined by the
composition of the ration (Ronning and Laben, 1966; Bines, Napper and
Johnson, 1977).

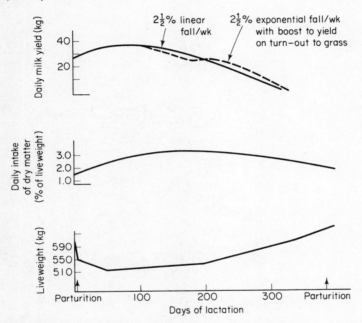

*Figure 19.1 Stylized curves of milk yield, liveweight change, and food intake of cows over
the lactation. From Broster and Alderman (1977)*

Table 19.1 SOME PRELIMINARY RESULTS IN INTAKES OF DRY MATTER (DM)
AND DIGESTIBLE ENERGY (DE), AND MILK YIELD AND LIVEWEIGHT CHANGE
(LWC) IN DAIRY HEIFERS GIVEN ACCESS *AD LIBITUM* TO DIETS CONTAINING
VARIOUS RATIOS OF CONCENTRATES : HAY

	Ratio of concentrates : hay		
	60 : 40	*75 : 25*	*90 : 10*
DM intake (kg/d)	13.7	13.2	13.7
DE intake (MJ/d)	171.0	171.1	183.6
Milk yield (kg/d)	18.7	22.1	22.2
LWC (kg/d)	−0.11	−0.01	+0.18

From Bines, Napper and Johnson (1977)

Figure 19.2 gives the curves of *ad-libitum* intake for weeks 1−18 of lactation for heifers and cows for the three diets used in Expt CH1. The slower rise to maximum for intake compared to milk yield is evident. Mean dry-matter (DM) consumption was similar for the three diets. The lag between the peaks of lactation and intake may also be greater in younger cows than in older animals (Bines, 1976a, b). During early lactation, the intake of energy from conventional rations is generally less than the animal's total capacity to utilize energy, so that the dairy cow is commonly seen to lose an appreciable amount of body-weight at this time and the potential milk yield may not be realized (Coppock, Noller and Wolfe, 1974).

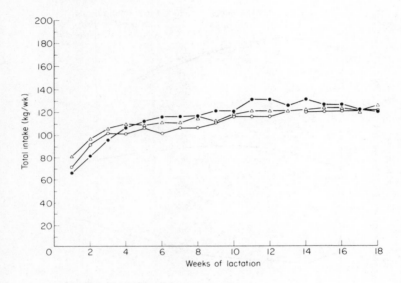

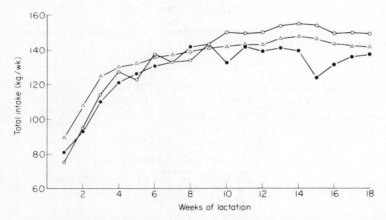

Figure 19.2 Preliminary results for intakes of air-dry food by heifers (above) and cows (below) over weeks 1−18 of lactation receiving ad-libitum diets containing (△) 60 : 40, (○) 75 : 25, (●) 90 : 10 proportions of concentrates to hay. See text for further details. From Bines, Napper and Johnson (1977)

After peak intake has been reached, appetite remains high for an extended period during which replacement of previously mobilized body tissue occurs, during the declining phase of lactation. Appetite does not fall markedly until lactation ceases, or the cow becomes fat or heavily pregnant.

Metabolic factors

If physical limitations to intake do not intervene, the cow will consume as much energy as she can utilize, not only for growth, maintenance and milk production, but also for the deposition of body fat. Only when there is no out-let for energy will the accumulation of products of digestion or associated phenomena inhibit further food intake. In the short term, temporary inhibition of intake may arise, for example from rapid fermentation in the rumen of a meal of starchy concentrate, but this will influence total daily intake only if time of access to food is severely limited (*see below*). Where maximum intakes are required, such inhibitions must be minimized. Accumulations of acetate in the rumen, and of propionate in or near the liver are probably the major factors concerned (Baile and Forbes, 1974).

FOOD FACTORS

Forage type and preparation

Intake of diets high in roughages is generally limited by physical factors. With very highly digestible spring grass, fresh or artificially dried, it is possible that the cow may come close to meeting her energy requirement fully. Then, intake will be controlled physiologically, as for concentrates. Otherwise, there is a general trend of increasing intake as the quality of the forage (measured in terms of digestibility) increases (Blaxter, Wainman and Wilson, 1961). This trend may be less apparent where silages are involved, their intake being less than that of dried material made from the same crop, and intake of silage may be further reduced where prehension is difficult, such as when self-feeding from a clamp is practised. Under these conditions intakes are unlikely to exceed 10 kg DM/d (W. Midlands ADAS Survey). The enhancing effect on intake of grinding roughages decreases as the quality of the roughage increases (Bines, 1976a).

When concentrates are added to a diet of poor-quality roughage, there may be a stimulation of roughage intake by low levels of supplementation, especially if the protein content of the forage is low and that of the supplement is high (Campling and Murdoch, 1966). In general, however, supplementation with concentrates will decrease roughage intake, the rate of substitution increasing with increasing quality of the roughage. Substitution may be complete where very high-quality roughages are given, for example spring grass (Broster *et al.*, 1975a).

Concentrate : forage ratio

If high-energy intakes are to be achieved, it is necessary to overcome the physical limitations to intake associated with diets consisting predominantly of roughage. This can be done by adding to the ration a highly digestible source of energy, usually starchy concentrate. However, such modifications can, as discussed elsewhere in this chapter, have repercussions on rumen fermentation and milk fat content, on energy partition between milk and body tissue, and on incidence of digestive disturbances. Furthermore there is the substitution effect of concentrate inclusion in the diet on forage consumption (*see above*). All these must be considered in deciding the optimal concentrate content in the ration. The upper limit, beyond which no further advantage accrues to additional concentrates, turns out to be around 75% of the total ration.

Protein content

A reduced protein content of the total ration will undoubtedly depress intake (Elliott and Topps, 1963a, b; Elliott, 1967). The critical level of protein inclusion will depend on the forms in which nitrogen is supplied. Provided a readily fermentable source of nitrogen is available to meet the needs of the rumen micro-organisms, together with an adequate supply of amino acids in the correct proportions to meet the requirements of the cow herself, it is possible that a protein level as low as 12.5–13.5% will be adequate for cows of good performance potential (Thomas, 1971; Van Horn *et al.*, 1976), and higher levels will not improve intake or performance.

MANAGEMENT FACTORS

Access time

The effect of time of access to food on the amount consumed depends on the composition of the ration. Where intake is regulated predominantly by physical means, the daily maximum voluntary intake can be consumed in about 6 hours (Wilson and Flynn, 1974). Increasing time of access to hay from 5 to 24 hours daily raised intake by only 20% (Freer and Campling, 1963). In contrast, much larger increases in intake of high-concentrate rations can be achieved by a similar change in time of access (Freer and Campling, 1963; Bines and Davey, 1970). It seems likely that intake of diets of intermediate composition will increase with increasing time of access in relation to the proportions of roughage and concentrate present.

When it is desired to achieve high energy intakes, as well as increasing the proportion of concentrate to roughage (*see above*), adequate time must also be allowed for the diet to be consumed. Where concentrates are fed only in the milking parlour, the form in which they are offered will influence the amount the cow will consume during the very short period of access. Thus, over 3 minutes will be required to consume 1 kg of a loose mix, and this will be reduced to about 2 minutes by pelleting and to around 1 minute by slurrying with water (Clough, 1972; Seidenglanz, Golder and Srámek, 1974). If a cow

Table 19.2 RELATIVE IMPORTANCE OF VARIOUS FACTORS INFLUENCING INTAKE IN SOME PUBLISHED EQUATIONS, BASED ON AN EXAMPLE OF A 500-kg COW GIVING 30 kg OF MILK PER DAY, LOSING 0.5 kg LIVEWEIGHT PER DAY AND RECEIVING A RATION OF 75% CONCENTRATES : 25% FORAGE (DM BASIS)

	Intake[c]	Liveweight	Milk yield	LWC	% Conc.
Greenhalgh and McDonald (1978)	17.1	11.1	6.0		
McCullough (1974)	13.8	6.4	10.8	−2.4	−1.0
Bines, Napper and Johnson (1977)[a]	13.5	10.6	4.1	−1.2	
Min. Agric. Fish. Fd (1975)	15.5	12.5	3.0		
Hyppölä and Hasunen (1970)[b]	19.2	17.3	1.9		
Conrad, Pratt and Hibbs (1964)	16.0	12.0	4.3		−0.3
Mean	14.7	10.6	4.9	−0.6	−0.2

LWC = liveweight change

[a]Heifers (values for cows are about 24% higher).

[b]Forage composition adjusted by present authors.

[c]Assumes free access − if access restricted, values must be reduced especially where roughage : concentrates ratio is low.

spends 20 minutes per day in the parlour, it will not be possible for her to consume more than 6–10 kg of loose or pelleted concentrate and if higher intakes are required, further access to concentrates will be needed outside the parlour. This may be in the form of specific feeds between milkings, or of giving selected cows free access to food by means of electronic gates. However, it should be noted that free access to concentrates generally results in very erratic intakes by dairy cows, leading to little or no improvement in performance compared with controlled feeding (Owen, Miller and Bridge, 1969; Wiktorsson, 1973).

Frequency of feeding

This is obviously closely related to access time, the latter being a function of feeding frequency and the time of access at each feeding. Where time of access is to be increased, there is evidence (Kaufmann, 1976) that this can be done most effectively by giving several small meals rather than few large ones. This has the effect, where rations contain high levels of concentrate inclusion, of maximizing total intake and at the same time maintaining a rumen fermentation pattern closer to that required to ensure an acceptable milk fat content and a desirable partition of energy toward milk rather than body tissues (*see below*). Taken to its ultimate conclusion, this means giving the cow continuous access to food throughout the 24-hour period and letting her decide her own feeding frequency − the basis of the concept of complete-diet feeding.

PREDICTION OF INTAKE

Because of the large number of factors influencing the intake of food by the cow, and especially because many of these factors are partly interdependent,

multiple regression analyses may give misleading results. It is particularly difficult to predict the low levels of intake in the critical early lactation period
without the use of complex models (Monteiro, 1972; Forbes, 1977). Equations
derived from an examination of data often include liveweight change as a factor
(McCullough, 1974; Bines, Napper and Johnson, 1977), but the value of this in
predicting intake is very doubtful since it is likely that it is a result of a certain
level of food intake rather than its cause.

At the present time, reasonable predictions by the commercial farmer of
food intake by whole herds or groups of cows are possible, but accurate estimates cannot be made of the intakes of individual cows (Bines, 1976a). The
relative importance of the factors used to predict intake may be gauged from
the equations used by the various authorities whose evidence has been used in
the example in *Table 19.2*.

Food utilization

APPARENT DIGESTIBILITY

The digestibility of a feed is one of the basic measurements contributing to the
determination of its metabolizable-energy (ME) value. It is one of the simplest
ways of evaluating feeds and many thousands of measurements have been made.
It is surprising, therefore, that controversy continues to surround estimates of
digestibility. It is widely recognized that increases in the fibre content of diets,
brought about by increasing either the proportion of roughage in mixed diets
or the fibre content of all-forage diets, cause a decrease in the digestibility of
most components of the diet except the fibre itself, the digestibility of which
usually increases with increasing proportions of roughages in mixed diets.
This relation between ration composition and DM digestibility is clearly illustrated by some results from the Reading experiment which are based on
measurements with 15 barren heifers and 68 lactating cows* of various parities
(*Table 19.3*). The main controversy concerns the effect of level of intake on
digestibility. The difference in digestibility between those values made at
maintenance intake with barren heifers and those made at three times maintenance with milking cows in our experiment, is in agreement with the conclusions of Moe and Tyrrell (1973), who stated that 'there are substantial differences in DE [digestible energy] or ME values of diets as measured with wethers
and steers at maintenance and with lactating cows at high levels of feed intake'.
However, in a more detailed examination of the problem, the same authors
(Tyrrell and Moe, 1975) demonstrated on the basis of American studies by
themselves, Wagner and Loosli (1967), and others, that there was a linear
decline in the total digestible nutrient (TDN) content of a wide range of diets
as intake was increased from maintenance to four or even five times maintenance.
The decline was shown to be greater for low-roughage diets than for high-
roughage diets and, as a corollary, the effect of ration composition was greater
at low levels of intake than at high levels.

---

*Results with 9 and 30 respectively are presented here.

Table 19.3 SOME PRELIMINARY RESULTS ON THE EFFECT OF DIET COM-POSITION AND LEVEL OF INTAKE ON THE DIGESTIBILITY OF DM BY 9 BARREN HEIFERS AND 30 MILKING COWS

Class of stock	Level of intake[a]	Ratio of concentrates to hay		
		60 : 40	75 : 25	90 : 10
		DM digestibility		
Barren heifer	1.0	0.75	0.78	0.78
Milking cows	3.0	0.70	0.71	0.73
Milking cows	3.7	0.69	0.70	0.73
Milking cows	ad lib.[b]	0.68	0.72	0.75

[a] Expressed as multiples of maintenance.
[b] 3.8, 3.9, 4.7 times maintenance respectively for 60 : 40, 75 : 25, 90 : 10 ratios of concentrates : hay.

From Sutton *et al.* (1977). See text for further details.

Table 19.4 SOME PRELIMINARY RESULTS ON THE EFFECT OF FREQUENCY OF FEEDING ON THE DM DIGESTIBILITY OF VARIOUS DIETS OFFERED TO SHEEP AND CATTLE

Animals (No. shown in brackets)	Diet	Intake (approx. multiples of maintenance)	DM digestibility	
			2 meals/day	24 meals/day
Sheep (3)	100% hay	1.0	0.51	0.52
	40% hay, 60% conc.	1.5	0.68	0.68
	10% hay, 90% conc.	1.5	0.81	0.81
Dry cows (4)	25% hay, 75% conc.	2.0	0.78	0.78
Milking cows (3)	33% hay, 67% conc.	3.5	0.72	0.73
	10% hay, 90% conc.	3.0	0.78	0.78

J.D. Sutton (unpublished)

Table 19.5 SOME PRELIMINARY RESULTS ON THE EFFECT OF DIET COMPOSITION AND LEVEL OF INTAKE ON THE RATIO OF THE MOLAR PROPORTION OF ACETIC ACID TO THAT OF PROPIONIC ACID IN THE RUMEN OF MILKING COWS

Level of intake[a]	Ratio of concentrates to hay		
	60 : 40	75 : 25	90 : 10
	Acetic : propionic acid ratios		
3.0	4.2	2.9	2.0
3.7	3.1	2.0	1.8
Ad libitum[b]	3.2	1.9	1.6

[a] As multiples of maintenance.
[b] Approximately 3.8, 3.9 and 4.7 for 60 : 40, 75 : 25 and 90 : 10 respectively.

From Sutton *et al.* (1977)

The small depression in digestibility of the 60 : 40 diet when intake was increased above three times maintenance was of the order predicted by Tyrrell and Moe (1975) but for the higher-concentrate diets no depression at all was detected. Indeed, a small, non-significant increase was measured for the 90 : 10 diet when intake was increased from 3 to 4.7 times maintenance whereas a decrease of about 6% would be expected according to the relationships presented by Tyrrell and Moe (1975). One possible reason for the difference between the two sets of results is that our diets contained a relatively high crude-protein level (17% in the DM). However, other workers have also reported no effect of increased level of intake on digestibility although in at least some of these cases (e.g. Wiktorsson, 1971), this was probably because the increase in DM intake was brought about by increasing the concentrate intake whilst the roughage intake was held constant. Such an explanation does not apply to our CH1 results. Wagner and Loosli (1967) found a depression in apparent digestibility of protein with increase in level of intake. This again was not apparent in our CH1 results.

Clearly the effect of level of feeding on digestibility needs further analysis. The interpretation proposed by Tyrrell and Moe in the USA has been to raise TDN allowances per kilogram of milk in proportion to the observed depression. A further complication is the reduction in urinary and methane energy losses as the level of intake increases, reducing the effect of plane of nutrition on the ME level of the diet (Blaxter, 1962; Van Es, 1975).

In most digestibility studies, diets have been offered in two or three meals daily. Increases in the number of daily meals have failed to influence digestibility of various mixed diets containing between 100% and 10% hay offered to cattle and sheep at between 1 and 3.5 times maintenance at this Institute (*Table 19.4*).

RUMEN FERMENTATION

The contribution of a feed towards the energy required by a cow depends not only on the amount of energy it supplies but also on the chemical form of that energy. Measurement of the amounts of all the major energy-yielding nutrients absorbed from the digestive tract is too complex a procedure to be useful for feed evaluation but determination of the proportions of volatile fatty acid (VFA) in rumen fluid is relatively simple and has been shown to provide a very useful index characterizing the way diets are likely to be used, particularly for milk production (Sutton, 1976).

Many factors are known to affect VFA proportions in the rumen (Ørskov, 1975) and attempts have been made to devise a generalized scheme to incorporate most of them and describe their interrelationships (Sutton, 1976). The most widely recognized response is the fall in the proportion of acetic acid and, to a lesser extent, butyric acid and the increase in the proportion of propionic acid when the roughage content of diet is reduced. The results in *Table 19.5*, which are the means of samples taken at monthly intervals throughout lactation in Expt CH1, well illustrate this effect, but in addition they show that a similar response can be brought about by increasing the level of intake of a particular diet. This effect of level of intake has been reported previously (Bath and Rook, 1963) but it has received relatively little recognition despite its important consequences for milk fat content, which will be considered later.

According to the theory that rumen VFA proportions are related to the maximum fermentation rate (MFR) (Sutton, 1976), a dietary manipulation that results in a lower MFR would be expected to increase the acetate : propionate ratio in the rumen. One such manipulation is to increase the number of daily meals in which the ration is offered. Results reported by Kaufmann (1973) supported this concept but limited studies at this Institute with small numbers of sheep and cattle have shown no consistent effect. A rather different manipulation is to substitute a slowly fermented cereal such as ground maize for a more rapidly fermented one such as rolled barley. Preliminary results from a small group of milking cows with rumen and intestinal cannulas (J.D. Sutton and J.D. Oldham, unpublished) have shown very little effect of such a substitution when the diets contained 60% concentrates but when they contained 90% concentrates there was a marked increase in the acetate : propionate ratio from about 1.4 for the barley diet to about 2.1 for the maize diet. Numerous other factors have been shown to affect VFA proportions in the rumen, oil supplements, the grinding of roughages and the many forms of processing of cereals now available being the most important (Ørskov, 1975; Sutton, 1980).

NUTRIENT UTILIZATION

The efficiency with which dietary energy is used for maintenance (k_m), growth (k_g) fattening (k_f) and lactation (k_l) has been discussed in a number of studies (Agricultural Research Council, 1965; Van Es, 1975, 1976; Moe and Tyrrell, 1973). All the factors are affected to varying degrees by q, the ME content of the diet as a percentage of the gross energy intake (IE). An increase in q generally leads to an increase in the various efficiencies although there is evidence that very high q values are accompanied by a small decrease in k_l. These issues have also been discussed in a recent Feed Manufacturers' Conference (Blaxter, 1974; Alderman *et al.*, 1974; Moe and Flatt, 1974).

Van Es (1976) reported from the analysis of 1150 individual cow energy balances from a wide range of sources that the efficiency of utilization of ME for lactation (k_l) was approximately 60% with a decrease of 0.4% per 1 unit decrease in q. k_l varies in broadly the same manner as k_m with change in q of the ration. Van Es (1976) pointed to the need for measuring separate efficiencies of tissue and milk energy depositions, possibly by regression methods but using, however, some built-in assumptions.

For lactating cows fed large amounts of concentrates, the energetic efficiency with which a particular process is carried out is quantitatively less important than the way the available energy is partitioned between different body processes. In particular, a major effect of increasing the proportion of concentrates in mixed diets of roughages and concentrates is to influence the partition of energy towards body tissue deposition rather than milk production (Blaxter, 1962; Flatt *et al.*, 1969a, b). The form in which this effect manifests itself may be a reduction in the yield of milk but it is more likely to be a serious fall in the fat content with little or no effect on milk yield, resulting in the well known low-milk-fat syndrome (Armstrong and Prescott, 1971).

Van Soest (1963) and Blaxter (1962) concluded that an important consequence of this change in the partition of energy was that the efficiency of milk production does not form a linear function with the hay : grain ratio but exhibits a maximum at some point near the hay : grain ratio at which depression in milk fat content is initiated.

Output by the dairy cow

MILK YIELD AND LIVEWEIGHT CHANGE

The evidence on milk yield and liveweight change as affected by diet composition is by no means extensive and such as is available is conflicting. Reviews are available by Reid (1956), Ekern (1970) and Trimberger *et al.* (1972). It is clear that many of the factors discussed above on food intake and utilization will contribute to the disparity amongst the results obtained, although other factors, too, are involved. Thus one problem is the variation in roughage quality from one experiment to another; a further difficulty is the precision with which observed effects can be attributed to ration composition: they could be due in part to inaccuracies in equalizing energy intakes; variation in units used to describe energy intakes; confounding of level of energy intake and diet composition. Also there is the question of how the food is allocated — for example, according to individual cow needs, or by economic criteria, or limited concentrates plus forage *ad libitum.* All these factors contribute to difficulties in interpretation.

The evidence summarized by Ekern (1970) included experiments by Elliot and Loosli (1959) with 20%, 40% and 60% of estimated ME from grain, in which no differences in milk yield were observed amongst treatments. Whilst an all-forage diet did not support maximum yield, Nelson *et al.* (1968) also found diets of more than 25% grain to have no effect on production. Nordfeldt and Ruudvere (1963) and Nordfeldt and Claesson (1964) performed some excellent

Table 19.6 SOME RESULTS FROM AN EXPERIMENT BY TRIMBERGER *ET AL.* (1972) ON DIFFERENT DIETS FOR HIGH-YIELDING COWS (MEAN VALUES OVER THREE LACTATIONS)

Diet	Liberal forage + restricted grain	Liberal grain + liberal forage	Liberal grain + restricted forage
% DM as grain	27	45	69
DM (kg/d)	18.0	19.2	15.7
TDN (kg/d)	12.3	13.8	11.6
FCM (kg/d)	23.5	25.6	23.9
Peak yield (kg/d)	35.8	39.3	38.5
Fat (g/kg)	38.3	39.7	38.0
SNF (g/kg)	85	86	85
Milk yield (kg/d)	24.2	25.8	24.6
Calving interval (days)	374	411	400
Services/conception	1.6	2.0	1.9
Liveweight change[a]	+58	+38	+38

DM = dry matter; TDN = total digestible nutrient; FCM = 4% fat-corrected milk
SNF = solids-not-fat

[a]From immediately after first calving to immediately after third calving.

experiments with large numbers of animals and involving both hay and silage as forages. Measured as Scandinavian food units, a ratio of 60% from concentrates and 40% from forage is judged to be optimal from their results for cows of moderate milk production capacity. This is estimated to be about 50 : 50 concentrates : forage dry matter. A large-scale experiment by Trimberger *et al.* (1972) covered three lactations by high-yielding cows. Even with good-quality forage fed liberally there was an advantage in raising grain dry-matter intake from 27% to 45% of the intake but not to even higher levels. The differences in dry-matter intake observed amongst the treatments should, however, be noted, as should the high level of performance achieved by these animals (*Table 19.6*).

In Expt CH1 at Reading, for both adult cows and first-calf heifers peak yield was increased both by a greater proportion of concentrates in the diet and by a greater amount of food (*Table 19.7*). Thus 90 : 10 *ab libitum* gave the highest peak yield.

However, persistency in the first half of lactation, measured as the fall in yield per week, was poorest for the 90 : 10 concentrates to hay ad-libitum ration (*Table 19.7*). For heifers (full data for cows not yet available), persistency was not markedly affected by the treatments in the second half of lactation, though the diet 60 : 40 concentrates to hay ratio showed the lowest decline in yield per week (*Table 19.8*).

Thus for heifers and cows there is no major change in pattern of treatment effects over the course of the lactation save for the 90 : 10 ad-libitum ration. This treatment apart, the spread of yields established in the early phase progressed throughout the whole lactation with the outputs in 36 weeks as shown in *Table 19.8*. Higher intakes and higher concentrates proportions increased milk output additively. The 90 : 10 ad-libitum diet produced in heifers a lower total output in 36 weeks than would be anticipated from the peak yield owing to the post-peak fall in yield, apparently associated with a greater incidence of metabolic disturbance on this ration (*see* the 'Health and Fertility' section below). For the adult cows it appears from the data currently to hand that the fall-off in performance in mid- and late lactation for the 90 : 10 ad-libitum diet was less dramatic than for the heifers.

Trimberger *et al.* (1972) found no change in the effect of the treatments when applied over three lactations, nor did Wiktorsson (1970) for treatments applied over two lactations.

Liveweight changes (*Table 19.9* and *19.10*) showed with heifers and with cows a reduction in body loss in early lactation with increasing level of intake but not with increasing proportion of concentrates in the diet; and, in later lactation, greater gains from larger intakes and greater proportions of concentrates in the diet. Thus as the lactation progressed the extra nutrients consumed as a result of diet manipulation did not sustain milk yield to any great extent but induced greater body gains.

MILK FAT CONTENT AND YIELD

Numerous dietary factors have been shown to influence the content and yield of fat in milk (Sutton, 1980); the most important of these is the roughage content of the diet. The serious fall in milk fat content that accompanies a reduction in

Table 19.7 SOME PRELIMINARY RESULTS ON MILK YIELDS OF ADULT COWS AND HEIFERS IN AN EXPERIMENT WITH THREE LEVELS OF INTAKE OF DIGESTIBLE ENERGY DRAWN FROM THREE DIETS

Level of intake	Heifers			Cows		
	Concentrates : hay 60 : 40	Concentrates : hay 75 : 25	Concentrates : hay 90 : 10	Concentrates : hay 60 : 40	Concentrates : hay 75 : 25	Concentrates : hay 90 : 10
	Peak yield[a] (kg/d)					
Moderate	18.4	20.1	23.1	23.7	25.5	29.0
High	20.5	22.7	25.9	26.2	29.9	28.9
Ad lib.	21.5	25.4	26.4	27.1	28.9	34.5
	Persistency[b] (kg fall/wk)					
Moderate	2.2	2.2	3.6	3.9	3.8	4.0
High	3.0	2.2	2.8	5.0	4.7	4.4
Ad lib.	2.2	1.8	3.7	4.7	3.2	5.3

[a]Highest yield sustained for 3 days.

[b]Calculated as: $\dfrac{\text{Peak yield} - \text{week 18 yield}}{\text{No. of weeks from peak to week 18}}$

From Broster et al. (1977). See text for further details

Table 19.8 FURTHER PRELIMINARY RESULTS ON MILK PRODUCTION OF
HEIFERS IN AN EXPERIMENT WITH THREE LEVELS OF DIGESTIBLE-ENERGY
INTAKE DRAWN FROM THREE DIETS

Level of intake	Ratio concentrates : hay		
	60 : 40	*75 : 25*	*90 : 10*
	Persistency in weeks 19–36 (fall in yield, kg/wk)		
Moderate	1.0	1.7	1.6
High	0.8	1.2	1.6
Ad lib.	0.8	1,8	1.3
	Total yield, weeks 1–36 (kg)		
Moderate	3560	3836	4378
High	3996	4593	5202
Ad lib.	4586	5122	4758

From Broster *et al.* (1977). *See text for further details.*

Table 19.9 LIVEWEIGHT CHANGES IN HEIFERS IN EARLY LACTATION:
PRELIMINARY RESULTS OF AN EXPERIMENT WITH THREE LEVELS OF
DIGESTIBLE-ENERGY INTAKE DRAWN FROM THREE DIETS

Level of intake	Ratio concentrates : hay		
	60 : 40	*75 : 25*	*90 : 10*
	Total weight loss (kg)		
Moderate	−63	−64	−58
High	−48	−51	−36
Ad lib.	−20	−40	−28
	Time to maximum weight loss (weeks from calving)		
Moderate	19	16	13
High	11	11	6
Ad lib.	5	7	5

From Broster *et al.* (1977). *See text for further details*

the proportion of roughage in mixed diets is clearly shown in the results of the
Reading CH1 experiment (*Table 19.11*), but these results also show that an
increase in the level of intake of a diet of fixed composition can cause a serious
fall in milk fat content. The reasons for the effect of both these factors on
milk fat content can be traced back to the observations, discussed earlier, that
they also have similar effects on rumen VFA proportions (*Table 19.5*). The
results from Expt CH1 (*Figure 19.3*) clearly show the close relationship between
milk fat content and the acetate : propionate ratio in the rumen, particularly
when the ratio fell below 3 : 1.

The combined influence of level of intake and proportion of roughage on
milk fat content (*Figure 19.4*) has important practical consequences since it
follows that the higher the level of energy intake, the higher the proportion of
roughage needed to maintain a fixed milk fat content. In the CH1 experiment
(*Figure 19.4*) it can be estimated that maintenance of a milk fat content of

Table 19.10 FURTHER PRELIMINARY RESULTS ON LIVEWEIGHT GAIN FROM POINT OF MINIMUM LIVEWEIGHT TO WEEK 36 OF LACTATION AND TOTAL LIVEWEIGHT CHANGE FROM CALVING TO WEEK 36 OF LACTATION IN HEIFERS IN AN EXPERIMENT WITH THREE LEVELS OF INTAKE OF DIGESTED ENERGY DRAWN FROM THREE DIETS

Level of intake	Ratio concentrates : hay		
	60 : 40	*75 : 25*	*90 : 10*
	Liveweight gain (kg)		
Moderate	32	33	54
High	57	57	76
Ad lib.	58	89	129
	Total liveweight change (kg)		
Moderate	−31	−32	−4
High	+9	+6	+40
Ad lib.	+38	+49	+101

From Broster *et al.* (1977). *See text for further details*

Table 19.11 PRELIMINARY RESULTS FOR THE EFFECT ON FAT CONTENT (g/kg) IN MILK OF HEIFERS IN AN EXPERIMENT INCLUDING THREE LEVELS OF INTAKE OF DIGESTIBLE ENERGY DRAWN FROM THREE DIETS

Level of intake	Ratio concentrates : hay		
	60 : 40	*75 : 25*	*90 : 10*
	Milk fat content (g/kg)		
Moderate	42.8	41.0	32.3
High	38.8	35.4	27.1
Ad lib.	40.2	30.6	27.5

From Sutton *et al.* (1977). *See text for further details*

Table 19.12 EFFECT OF THE CONTENT OF LONG ROUGHAGE IN THE DIET ON THE RESPONSE OF MILK FAT CONTENT TO CERTAIN DIETARY VARIABLES

	Milk fat content (g/kg)	
	High roughage	*Low roughage*
Frequency of feeding[a]	*40% hay*	*10% hay*
Two meals per day	39	20
Five meals per day	38	27
Type of cereal[b]	*40% hay*	*10% hay*
Rolled barley	38	25
Ground maize	37	33
Heat treatment[c]	*Long hay*	*Ground hay*
Flaked maize	36	24
Ground maize	36	28

[a]W.H. Broster, J.D. Sutton, J.W. Siviter and T. Smith (unpublished, 1977)
[b]J.D. Sutton and J.D. Oldham (unpublished)
[c]Balch *et al.* (1965)

35 g/kg during weeks 6–18 of lactation required only about 20% hay at the moderate level of intake but about 35% at ad-libitum intakes and that the greater energy intake of the ad-libitum group could be achieved only by adding hay to the diet fed at the moderate level since any addition of concentrates caused milk fat content to fall below 35 g/kg.

These relationships clearly present problems to the farmer wishing to maximize milk production. It is reasonable to ask whether they can be avoided. One possible means is to increase the number of meals in which the daily ration is offered. In a review, Burt and Dunton (1967) concluded that increased

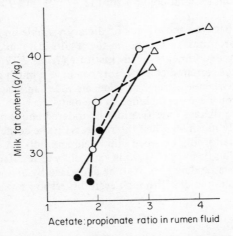

Figure 19.3 Relationships between milk fat content and the ratio of acetic acid to propionic acid in the rumen. (●) Ratio of concentrates : hay 90 : 10; (○) 75 : 25; (△) 60 : 40. Intake ad libitum; (– – –) high intake ; (- - - - -) moderate intake. See text and Figure 19.4 for further details. From Sutton et al. *(1977)*

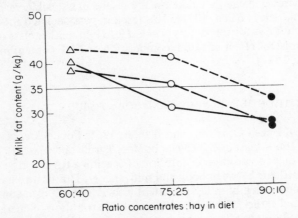

Figure 19.4 Preliminary results on the effect on fat content (g/kg) of milk of heifers in weeks 1–18 of lactation of diet composition and level of intake of digestible energy. (●) Ratio of concentrates : hay 90 : 10; (○) 75 : 25; (△) 60 : 40. (———) Intake ad libitum; (– – –) high intake; (- - - - -) moderate intake. See text for further details. From Sutton et al. *(1977)*

frequency of feeding had little effect on milk composition. However, Kaufmann *et al.* (1975) reported increases in milk fat content of about 5 g/kg when the daily number of meals was increased to six or even 14. In an experiment at this Institute (W.H. Broster and J.D. Sutton, unpublished), in which the concentrates in the diets used in Expt CH1 were offered in either two or five meals daily at the high level of intake, there was no effect on milk fat content for the 60% concentrate diet, but a marked improvement for the 90% concentrate diet when frequency of feeding was increased (*Table 19.12*). It is significant that in Expt CH1 itself the ad-libitum diets included 24-hour access to the food but this failed to maintain milk fat content for the 75 : 25 and 90 : 10 concentrate : hay diets.

The interaction between the effect of a dietary variable on milk fat content and the physical fibrousness of the diet in the results just considered is also apparent from other experiments at this Institute (*Table 19.12*). These results strongly indicate that certain dietary factors can have a much greater influence on milk fat content when low-roughage diets are fed than when more conventional amounts of roughage are included in the diet.

The effects of the dietary modifications considered above on the *yield* of milk fat are normally much less than their effects on the content of fat in the milk because the relationship between milk yield and milk fat content is generally inverse. Thus in Expt CH1, milk fat yield was unaffected by level of intake but there was a tendency for it to be decreased by an increasing proportion of concentrates in the diet although even this response was irregular (Sutton *et al.*, 1977).

SOLIDS-NOT-FAT CONTENT AND YIELD

The solids-not-fat (SNF) content of milk is far less variable than the fat content and the yield of SNF therefore tends closely to reflect the yield of milk. In general, an increase in energy intake usually results in a small increase in SNF content (Rook, 1961; Balch, 1972). This response was detected for the cows in Expt CH1 but not for the heifers (*Table 19.13*). In neither class of stock was there any consistent effect of ration composition on SNF content in the milk (Sutton *et al.*, 1977).

ENERGY PARTITION BETWEEN MILK AND BODY TISSUE

Calorimetric evidence (Armstrong and Blaxter, 1965; Coppock *et al.*, 1964a,b; Ørskov *et al.*, 1969; Flatt *et al.*, 1969a, b; Moe, Tyrrell and Flatt, 1971) indicates that diet composition or infusion of specific VFA can affect the partition of nutrients between body and milk energy. This in turn has been linked to the depression of milk fat content associated with high-concentrate diets as discussed earlier. *Table 19.14* shows the distribution of energy between milk fat and body fat as affected by diet composition in the experiments of Flatt *et al.* (1969a, b). The diet low in lucerne hay favoured body gain more than did the diet high in lucerne hay content.

As noted above, the effect on milk fat content is the dominant feature of the effect of diet on production and as a consequence milk yield *per se* will not

Table 19.13 PRELIMINARY RESULTS FOR THE EFFECT ON SOLIDS-NOT-FAT (SNF) CONTENT OF THE MILK (g/kg) IN WEEKS 1–18 OF LACTATION OF HEIFERS AND COWS IN AN EXPERIMENT INCLUDING THREE LEVELS OF INTAKE OF DIGESTIBLE ENERGY DRAWN FROM THREE DIETS

Level of intake	Ratio of concentrates to hay		
	60 : 40	75 : 25	90 : 10
	SNF content (g/kg)		
Heifers			
Moderate	87.0	88.4	86.4
High	87.0	88.8	87.9
Ad lib.	89.0	89.1	88.1
Cows			
Moderate	88.6	86.7	86.8
High	88.8	88.1	88.4
Ad lib.	87.8	87.6	88.5

From Sutton *et al.* (1977). *See text for further details.*

reflect energy output. Therefore to pursue this issue further it is necessary to consider again milk fat output as affected by level of intake and diet composition. The experiment by Amir (1974) (*Table 19.15*) showed a greater weight loss in early lactation on a 50 : 50 ratio of concentrates : hay than on an 80 : 20 ratio. Bloom *et al.* (1957), however, in a mid-lactation experiment observed the greatest yield of milk and the greatest body loss on the highest (85 : 15) ratio concentrates : hay they employed. Trimberger *et al.* (1972) (*Table 19.6*) did not observe marked differences in body gains amongst their treatment groups. When the contrasting effects on milk fat yield and liveweight change induced by the three diets used in Expt CH1 are plotted (*Figures 19.5* and *19.6*), the effect is in agreement with the above calorimetric evidence that the 90 : 10 diet favoured body reserves at the expense of milk fat yield at each level of intake. The results obtained with adult cows agreed with those obtained with heifers. The 75 : 25 and the 60 : 40 concentrates : hay diets favoured milk fat more strongly than did the 90 : 10 diet.

INDIVIDUAL ANIMAL PERFORMANCE

Attention has been drawn (Strickland and Lessells, 1970; Strickland, 1975; Broster *et al.*, 1975b) to the need to see beyond the mean performance of a group of cows to the performance of the individuals as affected by their genetic potential. This applies equally to response to diet composition as to other factors in the diet. Sutton (1970) has pointed out that cows differ in their response to high-concentrate diets. Thus it is critical in assessment of the feasibility of, for example, complete-diet feeding to consider how individual cows will react to a communal diet both from the nutritional point of view and, indeed, the behavioural point of view (Bryant, 1975).

Table 19.14 MEAN ENERGY BALANCES OF COWS EATING RATIONS OF 60%, 40% AND 20% LUCERNE AND THE REMAINDER CONCENTRATES

Lucerne hay in diet (%)	Total energy retention (kcal/d)	Milk energy (kcal/d)	Body gain (+) or loss (−) (kcal/d)	Yield in milk (kg) of:			Change in body fat (g/24 h)	Net change in fat yield
				Fat[a]	Protein[b]	Lactose[c]		
60	12 250	13 525	−1 275	714	632	853	−138	576[a,d]
40	12 634	13 209	−575	627	669	924	−62	565
20	11 966	10 643	1 323	489	561	750	+144	633

[a]Yield of milk × fat content.
[b]Yield of milk × protein content.

[c] Residual of milk energy − energy in fat and protein   fat, 9.21 kcal/g; casein, 5.66 kcal/g; lactose, 3.95 kcal/g.
          calorific value of lactose

[d]Assuming all body energy to be fat and calorific value 9.21 kcal/g.

From Flatt et al. (1969a, b)

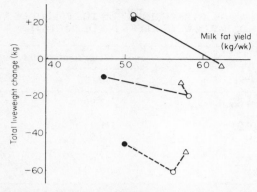

Figure 19.5 Preliminary results on the relationship in weeks 1—18 of lactation between output of milk fat and of liveweight gain by cows in an experiment involving three levels of digestible-energy intake derived from three diets. (●) Ratio of concentrates : hay 90 : 10; (○) 75 : 25; (△) 60 : 40. (———) Intake ad libitum; *(— — —) high intake; (- - - - -) moderate intake. See text for further details. From Broster* et al. *(1977)*

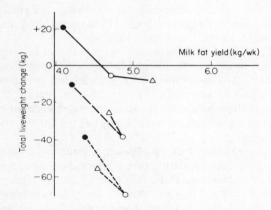

Figure 19.6 Preliminary results on the relationship in weeks 1—18 of lactation between output of milk fat and of liveweight gain by heifers in an experiment involving three levels of digestible-energy intake derived from three diets. (●) Ratio of concentrates : hay 90 : 10; (○) 75 : 25; (△) 60 : 40. (———) Intake ad libitum; *(— — —) high intake; (- - - - -) moderate intake. See text for further details. From Broster* et al. *(1977)*

Health and fertility

Structure, fibre content, food processing, frequency of feeding, food intake and other factors affecting rumen fermentation have been suggested as being involved in the changes in metabolism that are observed in some but not all cows on high-concentrate diets, leading to reduction in the ratio of acetate to propionate in the rumen, changes in endocrinological activity, change in long-chain fatty acid deposition, change in partition of nutrients (*see* reviews quoted by Ekern, 1970; Armstrong, 1968; Jorgensen, Schultz and Barr, 1965; Storry and Sutton, 1969). Huffman (1961) and Miller and O'Dell (1969) (quoted by Ekern, 1970) pointed

Table 19.15 RESULTS OF AN EXPERIMENT ON THE EFFECT OF TWO DIETS ON PERFORMANCE OF DAIRY COWS IN WEEKS 1–8 OF LACTATION

	Ratio concentrates : hay in diet	
	80 : 20	*50 : 50*
Intake of concentrates (kg/d)	18.90	11.30
Intake of hay (kg/d)	4.82	11.23
ME content (MJ/kg DM)	11.2	10.0
Milk yield (kg/d)	30.5	30.4
Fat content (g/kg)	26.1	30.2
FCM (kg/d)	24.0	25.9
Liveweight change (kg)	−17	−50

ME = metabolizable energy   From Amir (1975)
DM = dry matter
FCM = 4% fat-corrected milk

out that cows on diets principally comprising forages maintained good health but those on high-concentrate diets presented problems in maintaining health, which were associated with depressed milk fat percentage and changed proportions of VFA in the rumen. Kesler and Spahr (1964) considered that 13–14% fibre in the dry matter may be a safe lower limit.

Emery *et al.* (1969) reported adverse effects on health of high levels of grain feeding pre-partum, but not so Schmidt and Schultz (1959) or Broster (1971). Trimberger *et al.* (1972) observed that liberal grain feeding plus generous hay had no significant effect on losses of cows over the three years of the experiment. Associated with ad-libitum corn silage it caused increased losses of cows — nine out of ten cows being lost compared with two out of ten for the other treatments.

In Expt CH1 the combination of 90 : 10 concentrates to hay diet with ad-libitum intakes gave some indication of a greater incidence of apparent metabolic disorder and on occasion dramatic falls in yield shortly after peak — observed in the more rapid fall in yield/week for the group for both cows and heifers. Though some recovery occurred, the animals did not achieve the levels to be anticipated from their peak yields (*Table 19.7*) as judged from other treatments in the experiment. Laminitis was a common problem in this experiment but was not associated beyond question with a particular level of diet.

In the experiment by Trimberger *et al.* (1972), the interval from partition to first oestrus and the subsequent oestrus intervals were not affected by liberal concentrates feeding. Even so, liberal concentrates led to significantly longer calving intervals and to the need for more services per conception, associated with more cystic follicles in early lactation. No corresponding evidence is available to date from Expt CH1.

Discussion

LIMITATIONS OF KNOWLEDGE ON CONCENTRATE : FORAGE RATIOS

There is a shortage of evidence on several aspects of concentrate : forage ratios and milk production. These include the effect of silage or dried grass or barn-dried hay, as the main forage; the effect of forages of differing nutritive values and physical forms; the special considerations of the spring-calving herd and the exploitation of grassland; the application of differing concentrates : forage ratios to cows on a group-feeding system with selector feeders, or self-fed silage; and the feasibility of changing the ratio of concentrate : forage according to stage of lactation. Evidence on silage evaluation from the Grassland Research Institute and on hay utilization from the Experimental Husbandry Farms will help to unravel these problems.

LACTATION CYCLE

Whilst it is clear that in early lactation it is desirable to get the cow's energy intake high quickly, there is no advantage in overfeeding her. Frequent feeding and ensuring that she receives a reasonable amount of good-quality hay are time-honoured devices that are effective. Giving vast amounts of concentrates in an effort to redouble lead-feeding advantages are likely to promote digestive upsets. Indeed lead-feeding as recommended merely counters, to some extent, low appetite of the cow shortly after calving.

In mid-lactation the situation changes: it now hinges on the risk of metabolic upset in the cow if she is allowed a diet with a very high energy density at times when her intake capacity is maximal. Judicious revision of the ration composition may avoid this problem, allowing initial development of potential in early lactation and then its exploitation later in the lactation.

Total milk yield, yield of milk solids and health of the cow are reduced by feeding excessive concentrates. The zeal to meet the high-yielding cow's requirements and to raise yield by lead-feeding, that is, by supplementary concentrates, must be restricted by the risks that such practices may run. The need for rations of various M/D values is readily apparent from Technical Bulletin 33 (Min. Agric. Fish. Fd, 1975). Increasing intakes of diets of low M/D does not, according to Expt CH1, compensate for the low energy density in regard to total lactation yield. Wagner and Loosli (1967) however reasoned that the TDN content of a wide range of diets varying in M/D content became approximately equal at a level equal to 4.5 times maintenance. This point needs further study.

OPTIMAL RATIO CONCENTRATE : FORAGE

Kesler and Spahr (1964), McCullough (1974) and Owen (1975, 1976) have arrived at the conclusion that somewhere near 70 : 30 is an optimal concentrates : hay ratio for the dairy cow, as have others (*see* Ekern, 1970). Experiment CH1 would suggest also that the 75 : 25 ratio of concentrates : hay approaches optimal for early lactation — with the possible exception noted above that in very early lactation a higher content of concentrates may be temporarily acceptable. (The concomitant reduction in fat content of the milk reduces the advantage in milk production from giving 75 : 25 concentrates : hay diet *ad libitum*.) Thereafter, least-cost rations and economic criteria may set an upper limit to the acceptable proportion of concentrates in the diet, probably causing it to be reduced rather than to be maintained. This question brings out two issues: the immediate response in terms of milk production and the long-term (multi-lactation response) accruing from liveweight gains amassed in any one lactation.

RESPONSES TO CHANGE OF RATION

The differences in performance amongst the groups of Expt CH1 measure the responses that may be expected on change of ration. The figures amount broadly to some 600 kg of milk per lactation from an additional 1.5 kg of dry matter per day over 36 weeks of lactation, or 500 kg of milk from replacing hay by concentrates for 15% of the dry matter in the ration. The minimum fibre intake, or dry matter as hay, to ensure a particular fat content in the milk has been referred to. These points are subject to immediate economic appraisal. This is the pragmatic outcome of the exercise. The philosophical one is the challenge to the regimented idea of requirements for nutrients. This has been overdone. It has been neither practical nor desirable always to achieve a precise intake by a particular cow. Discretion and economics must play their part, provided the well-being of the cow is ensured. The advance to simplified feeding takes the argument further towards group feeding of a diet approximately appropriate to average needs instead of a precise diet for the individual. The role of studies of energy metabolism, and of ME requirements (Agricultural Research Council, 1965; Min. Agric. Fish. Fd, 1975), in the achievement of these goals is even more apparent than before.

BENEFIT FROM ONE LACTATION TO THE NEXT FROM GENEROUS FEEDING

The second issue raised was the benefit to subsequent lactational performance from further liveweight gains resulting from generous feeding in the current lactation. In Expt CH1 the only massive liveweight gain was 101 kg on treatment 90 : 10 *ad libitum* in 36 weeks of lactation with some 20 weeks still to go to the next calving. It remains to be seen whether such gains are more advantageous than the lesser ones of 50 kg on other treatments. In this regard whilst a small deposition of body reserves during lactation is inadequate to ensure maximum yield in the next lactation (Broster, 1971), excess deposition appears to confer no advantage subsequently (Schmidt and Schultz, 1959; Broster, Broster and Smith, 1969; Broster, 1971; Trimberger *et al.*, 1972). The interesting comparison between cows which were thin or fat at calving by Lodge, Fisher and Lessard (1975) would merit further development. Fat cows eat less than thin ones (Bines, Suzuki and Balch, 1969), a point to bear in mind here. Body reserves can buffer the response of the cow to the current nutritional environment. The mean ad-libitum intakes in experiment CH1 suggest neither that the cow adjusts intake to requirements, nor that a fixed maximum consumption of TDN (Wagner and Loosli, 1967) occurs.

SYSTEM OF FEEDING

It is right that systems of feeding should be evolved to get the food to the cow with minimum effort and expenditure. The requirements of the individual cow at particular times can be catered for by various devices. J.B. Owen expands on these issues in Chapter 18. Various claims, nutritional and managerial, have been made regarding the efficiency of the currently available modifications to the more traditional styles of feeding. Some can be explained in terms of present nutritional knowledge. Factors such as feeding cows in groups, mixing the foods together, frequent feeding, and long-term effects warrant further research such as Owen has instituted. The nutritional understanding we now have should not however be thrown overboard in the light of these new advances, which in themselves are to be applauded. Rather the available knowledge should be used to assist interpretation of what is happening in new systems of food distribution. In this regard the composition of the diet is of paramount importance.

References

AGRICULTURAL RESEARCH COUNCIL (1965). *Nutrient Requirements of Farm Livestock*: No. 2, *Ruminants*. London; Agricultural Research Council

ALDERMAN, G., GRIFFITHS, J.R., MORGAN, D.E., EDWARDS, R.A., RAVEN, A.M., HOLMES, W. and LESSELLS, W.J. (1974). In *University of Nottingham Nutrition Conference for Feed Manufacturers* – 7, p. 37. Eds H. Swan and D. Lewis. London; Butterworths

ALLEN, P., PRESCOTT, J.H.D. and WALKER LOVE, J. (1977). *Complete Diets for Dairy Cows*. Scottish Agricultural Colleges, Technical Note No. 18

AMIR, S. (1974). Paper to Stockman's School, San Antonio, Texas. January 1974

ARMSTRONG, D.G. (1968). *Proc. Nutr. Soc.*, **27**, 57

ARMSTRONG, D.G. and BLAXTER, K.L. (1965). In *Energy Metabolism*, p. 59. (EAAP Publ. No. 11). Ed. K.L. Blaxter. London; Academic Press Eds W. Lenkeit, K. Breirem and E. Crasemann. Hamburg; Paul Parrey

ARMSTRONG, D.G. and PRESCOTT, J.H.D. (1971). In *Lactation*, p. 349. Ed. I.R. Falconer. London; Butterworths

BAILE, C.A. and FORBES, J.M. (1974). *Physiol. Rev.*, **54**, 160

BALCH, C.C. (1972). In *Handbuch der Tierernährung*, Vol. 2, p. 259. Eds W. Lenkeit, K. Breirem and E. Crasemann. Hamburg; Paul Parry

BALCH, C.C., BROSTER, W.H., ROOK, J.A.F. and TUCK, V.J. (1965). *J. Dairy Res.*, **32**, 1

BATH, I.H. and ROOK, J.A.F. (1963). *J. agric. Sci., Camb.*, **61**, 341

BINES, J.A. (1971). *Proc. Nutr. Soc.*, **30**, 116

BINES, J.A. (1976a). In *Principles of Cattle Production*, p. 287. Eds H. Swan and W.H. Broster. London; Butterworths

BINES, J.A. (1976b). *Livestk Prod. Sci.*, **3**, 115

BINES, J.A. and DAVEY, A.W.F. (1970). *Br. J. Nutr.*, **24**, 1013

BINES, J.A., NAPPER, D.J. and JOHNSON, V.W. (1977). *Proc. Nutr. Soc.*, **36**, 146A

BINES, J.A., SUZUKI, S. and BALCH, C.C. (1969). *Br. J. Nutr.*, **23**, 695

BLAXTER, K.L. (1949–50). *Nutr. Abstr. Rev.*, **20**, 1

BLAXTER, K.L. (1956). *Proc. Br. Soc. Anim. Prod.*, 3

BLAXTER, K.L. (1962). *The Energy Metabolism of Ruminants*. London; Hutchinson

BLAXTER, K.L. (1974). In *University of Nottingham Nutrition Conference for Feed Manufacturers* – 7, p. 3. Ed. H. Swan and D. Lewis. London; Butterworths

BLAXTER, K.L., WAINMAN, F.W. and WILSON, R.S. (1961). *Anim. Prod.*, **3**, 51

BLOOM, S., JACOBSON, N.L., McGILLIARD, L.D., HOFMEYER, P.G. and HEADY, E.O. (1957). *J. Dairy Sci.*, **40**, 81

BROSTER, W.H. (1971). *Dairy Sci. Abstr.*, **33**, 253

BROSTER, W.H. and ALDERMAN, G. (1977). *Livestk Prod. Sci.,* **4**, 263

BROSTER, W.H., BROSTER, V.J. and SMITH, T. (1969). *J. agric. Sci., Camb.,* **72**, 229

BROSTER, W.H., CLOUGH, P.A., HODGSON-JONES, L., SMITH, T. and BROSTER, V.J. (1975a). In *Simplified Feeding for Beef and Dairy*, p. 113. Ed. C. Campbell. London; US Feed Grains Council. Leatherhead, UK; Reprint

BROSTER, W.H., SMITH, T., BROSTER, V.J. and SIVITER, J.W. (1975b). *J. agric. Sci., Camb.,* **84**, 173

BROSTER, W.H., SUTTON, J.D., BINES, J.A., CORSE, D.A., JOHNSON, V.W., SMITH, T. and JONES, P.A. (1971–72). *Rep. natn. Inst. Res. Dairy.,* **1971–72**, 74

BROSTER, W.H., SUTTON, J.D., BINES, J.A., SMITH, T., SIVITER, J.W. and BROSTER, V.J. (1977). *Proc. Nutr. Soc.,* **36**, 145A

BRYANT, M.J. (1975). In *Simplified Feeding for Beef and Dairy*, p. 13. Ed. C. Campbell. London; US Feed Grains Council. Leatherhead, UK; Reprint

BURT, A.W.A. and DUNTON, C.R. (1967). *Proc. Nutr. Soc.,* **26**, 181

CAMPLING, R.C. and MURDOCH, J.C. (1966). *J. Dairy Res.,* **33**, 1

CLOUGH, P.A. (1972). *Dairy Fmr, Ipswich,* **19**, 18

CONRAD, H.R., PRATT, A.D. and HIBBS, J.W. (1964). *J. Dairy Sci.,* **47**, 54

COOPER, M. McG. (1955). *Dairy Sci. Abstr.,* **17**, 4

COPPOCK, C.E., FLATT, W.P., MOORE, L.A. and STEWART, W.E. (1964a). *J. Dairy Sci.,* **12**, 1330

COPPOCK, C.E., FLATT, W.P., MOORE, L.A. and STEWART, W.E. (1964b). *J. Dairy Sci.,* **12**, 1359

COPPOCK, C.E., NOLLER, C.H. and WOLFE, S.A. (1974). *J. Dairy Sci.,* **57**, 1371

DENT, J.B. and CASEY, H. (1967). *Linear Programming in Animal Nutrition.* London; Crosby Lockwood

EKERN, A. (1970). In *Dairy Nutrition*, p. 63. Ed. C. Campbell. London; US Feed Grains Council. Mitcham, UK; Vale Press

ELLIOT, J.M. and LOOSLI, J.K. (1959). *J. Dairy Sci.,* **42**, 836

ELLIOTT, R.C. (1967). *J. agric. Sci., Camb.,* **69**, 375

ELLIOTT, R.C. and TOPPS, J.H. (1963a). *Br. J. Nutr.,* **17**, 539

ELLIOTT, R.C. and TOPPS, J.H. (1963b). *Anim. Prod.,* **5**, 269

EMERY, R.S., HAFS, H.D., ARMSTRONG, D. and SNYDER, W.W. (1969). *J. Dairy Sci.,* **52**, 345

FLATT, W.P. and MOE, P.W. (1971). In *Lactation*, p. 341. Ed. I.R. Falconer. London; Butterworths

FLATT, W.P., MOE, P.W., HOOVEN, N.W., LEHMANN, R.P., ØRSKOV, E.R. and HEMKEN, R.W. (1969a). In *Energy Metabolism of Farm Animals*, p. 221. Eds K.L. Blaxter, G. Thorbek and J. Kielanowski. Newcastle upon Tyne; Oriel Press

FLATT, W.P., MOE, P.W., MOORE, L.A., BREIREM, K. and EKERN, A. (1972). In *Handbuch der Tierernährung*, Vol. 2, p. 341. Eds W. Lenkeit, K. Breirem and E. Crasemann. Hamburg; Paul Parrey

FLATT, W.P., MOE, P.W., MUNSON, A.W. and COOPER, T. (1969b). In *Energy Metabolism of Farm Animals*, p. 235. Eds K.L. Blaxter, G. Thorbek and J. Kielanowski. Newcastle upon Tyne; Oriel Press

FORBES, J.M. (1977). *Anim. Prod.,* **24**, 203

FREER, M. and CAMPLING, R.C. (1963). *Br. J. Nutr.,* **17**, 79

GREENHALGH, J.F.D. and McDONALD, I. (1978). *Anim. Prod.,* **26**, 350

HUFFMAN, C.F. (1959). *Feed Utilization of Dairy Cows.* Ames; Iowa State College Press

HUFFMAN, C.F. (1961). *J. Dairy Sci.,* **44**, 2113

HYPPÖLÄ, K. and HASUNEN, O. (1970). *Acta agral. fenn.,* **116**, 1

JORGENSEN, W.A., SCHULTZ, L.H. and BARR, G.R. (1965). *J. Dairy Sci.,* **48**, 1031

KAUFMANN, W. (1973). *Kieler milchw. ForschBer.,* **25**, 245

KAUFMANN, W. (1976). *Livestk Prod. Sci.,* **3**, 103

KAUFMANN, W., ROHR, K., DAENICKE, R. and HAGEMEISTER, H. (1975). *Ber. Landw. Suppl.,* **191**, 269

KAY, M. (1969). In *University of Nottingham Nutrition Conference for Feed Manufacturers – 3,* p. 43. Eds H. Swan and D. Lewis. London; Churchill

KESLER, E.M. and SPAHR, S.L. (1964). *J. Dairy Sci.,* **47**, 1122

LODGE, G.A., FISHER, L.J. and LESSARD, J.R. (1975). *J. Dairy Sci.,* **58**, 696 (abstr. P29)

McCULLOUGH, M.E. (1974). *Optimum Feeding of Dairy Cattle,* 2nd edn. Athens, Georgia: University of Georgia Press

MILLER, W.J. and O'DELL, G.D. (1969). *J. Dairy Sci.,* **52**, 1144

MINISTRY OF AGRICULTURE, FISHERIES AND FOOD (1975). *Tech. Bull. No. 33.* London; HMSO

MOE, P.W. and FLATT, W.P. (1974). In *University of Nottingham Nutrition Conference for Feed Manufacturers – 7,* p. 27. Eds H. Swan and D. Lewis. London; Butterworths

MOE, P.W. and TYRRELL, H.F. (1973). *J. Anim. Sci.,* **37**, 183

MOE, P.W., TYRRELL, H.F. and FLATT, W.P. (1971). *J. Dairy Sci.,* **54**, 548

MONTEIRO, L.S. (1972). *Anim. Prod.,* **14**, 263

NELSON, B.D., ELLZEY, H.D., MORGAN, E.B. and ALLEN, M. (1968). *J. Dairy Sci.,* **51**, 1796

NORDFELDT, S. and CLAESSON, O. (1964). *LantbrHögsk. Annlr,* **30**, 517

NORDFELDT, S. and RUUDVERE, A. (1963). *LantbrHögsk. Annlr,* **29**, 345

ØRSKOV, E.R. (1975). *Wld Rev. Nutr. Diet.,* **22**, 152

ØRSKOV, E.R., FLATT, W.P., MOE, P.W., MUNSON, A.W., HEMKEN, R.W. and KATZ, I. (1969). *Br. J. Nutr.,* **23**, 443

OWEN, J.B. (1975). In *Simplified Feeding for Milk and Beef,* p. 85. Ed. C. Campbell. London; US Feed Grains Council. Leatherhead, UK; Reproprint

OWEN, J.B. (1976). *Wld Anim. Rev.,* **20**, 36

OWEN, J.B., MILLER, E.L. and BRIDGE, P.S. (1969). *J. agric. Sci., Camb.,* **72**, 351

RAKES, A.H. (1969). *J. Dairy Sci.,* **52**, 870

REID, J.T. (1956). *Mem. Cornell Univ. agric. Exp. Stn,* No. 344

RONNING, M. and LABEN, R.C. (1966). *J. Dairy Sci.,* **49**, 1080

ROOK, J.A.F. (1961). *Dairy Sci. Abstr.,* **23**, 251

SCHMIDT, G.H. and SCHULTZ, L.H. (1959). *J. Dairy Sci.,* **42**, 170

SEIDENGLANZ, J., GOLDER, J. and SRÁMEK, J. (1974). *Živočišná Výroba* (Prague), **19**, 243

STORRY, J.E. and SUTTON, J.D. (1969). *Br. J. Nutr.,* **23**, 511

STRICKLAND, M.J. (1975). In *Proceedings of a Symposium on Cattle Experimentation,* p. 34. Ed. P.D.P. Wood. London; British Society of Animal Production

STRICKLAND, M.J. and LESSELLS, W.J. (1970). *Anim. Prod.,* **13**, 379 (abstr.)

SUTTON, J.D. (1970). *Proc. Nutr. Soc.,* **29**, 62A

SUTTON, J.D. (1976). In *Principles of Cattle Production*, p. 121. Eds H. Swan and W.H. Broster. London; Butterworths

SUTTON, J.D. (1980). In *Factors Affecting the Yields and Contents of Milk Constituents of Commercial Importance. Bull. Int. Dairy Fed.* Document No. 125, 126–134

SUTTON, J.D., BROSTER, W.H., SCHULLER, E., SMITH, T. and NAPPER, D.J. (1977). *Proc. Nutr. Soc.,* **36**, 147A

THOMAS, J.W. (1971). *J. Dairy Sci.,* **54**, 1629

TRIMBERGER, G.W., TYRRELL, H.F., MORROW, D.A., REID, J.T., WRIGHT, M.J., SHIPE, W.F., MERRILL, W.G., LOOSLI, J.K., COPPOCK, C.E., MOORE, L.A. and GORDON, C.H. (1972). *New York's Food and Life Sciences Bulletin*: No. 8, *Anim. Science,* Vol. 1, p. 1

TYRRELL, H.F. and MOE, P.W. (1975). *J. Dairy Sci.,* **58**, 1151

VAN ES, A.J.H. (1975). *Livestk Prod. Sci.,* **2**, 95

VAN ES, A.J.H. (1976). In *Principles of Cattle Production*, p. 237. Eds H. Swan and W.H. Broster. London; Butterworths

VAN HORN, H.H., OLALOKU, E.A., FLORES, J.R., MARSHALL, S.P. and BACHMAN, K.C. (1976). *J. Dairy Sci.,* **59**, 902

VAN SOEST, P.J. (1963). *J. Dairy Sci.,* **46**, 204

WAGNER, D.G. and LOOSLI, J.K. (1967). *Mem. Cornell Univ. agric. Exp. Stn,* No. 400

WIKTORSSON, H. (1970). *Swed. J. agric. Res.,* **1**, 83

WIKTORSSON, H. (1971). *J. Dairy Sci.,* **54**, 374

WIKTORSSON, H. (1973). *Swed. J. agric. Res.,* **3**, 153

WILSON, R.K. and FLYNN, A.V. (1974). *Ir. J. agric. Res.,* **13**, 347

WOOD, P.D.P. (1969). *Anim. Prod.,* **11**, 307

WOODMAN, H.E. (1948). *Bull. Minist. Agric. Fish. Fd,* No. 48

20

GROWTH STIMULATION IN RUMINANTS

R.J. HEITZMAN
Institute for Research on Animal Diseases, Berkshire

Introduction

The reason for using growth promoters is to increase the efficiency of meat production without either adversely affecting the safety and quality of the product or the health of the animals. The purpose of this chapter is to discuss

Table 20.1 GROWTH PROMOTERS AVAILABLE FOR CATTLE AND SHEEP

Anabolic agents

Chemical name	Trade name	Preparation	Animal
Trenbolone acetate	Finaplix	I	H, C
Diethylstilboestrol		I, F	S, V
Diethylstilboestrol dipropionate		O	V
Hexoestrol		I	S, L
Zeranol	Ralgro	I	S, H, V, L
Trenbolone acetate + oestradiol	Revalor	I	S, V, L
	Torelor	I	S, B
Trenbolone acetate + hexoestrol		I	S
Trenbolone acetate + zeranol		I	S, V
Testosterone + oestradiol	Implix BF	I	H, V
Progesterone + oestradiol	Implix BM	I	S
Testosterone propionate + oestradiol benzoate	Synovex-H	I	H
Progesterone + oestradiol benzoate	Synovex-S	I	S

Rumen activating anaboles

Monensin-sodium	Romensin	F	S, H, B
	Avoparcin	F	S, H, B

I = implants; O = oil based injection; F = feed additive; H = heifer; C = culled cow; S = steer; V = veal calf; B = bull; L = wether lamb

353

the uses, benefits and mechanisms of action of anabolic agents while at the same time discussing some of the potential hazards to public health and animal health (for other reviews see Barragry, 1974; Heitzman, 1974; Lu and Rendel, 1976; Scott, 1978). Similar aspects of rumen active anaboles are also briefly discussed.

Growth rate and feed conversion efficiency (FCE) in healthy ruminants can be changed by the administration of two types of growth stimulants, the first comprise anabolic agents which have hormonal properties and act on the metabolic processes, and the second consists of rumen active anaboles which modify rumen fermentation. A list of available growth promoters which are used on a world-wide scale to improve meat production from ruminants is given in *Table 20.1*.

In ruminants the gonadal hormones are responsible for the large differences in the rate of growth and fat deposition between males and females. Their decreased levels in castrated males results in the intermediate performance of the steer and is, of course, responsible for the desirable absence of secondary sexual characteristics. The anabolic agents listed in *Table 20.1* are all substances with hormonal activity similar to that of the sex steroids. The use of appropriate exogenous anabolic agents creates a hormonal situation in castrates, females and young stock which is similar to that found in intact adult males and pregnant females. Heitzman (1976) suggested that this induced hormonal situation in which both androgens and oestrogens were present was necessary to achieve a maximum growth rate responses in cattle. In practice implants of oestrogens or combined preparations of oestrogens and androgens are used in young animals and castrates, and androgens alone are administered to females.

Veal calves

Veal production in the United Kingdom is small, but on the continent there is an annual production of 8 million veal calves. Investigations into the use of anabolic agents in veal animals show that growth rates and FCE were greatly improved during the 5–6 week treatment period before slaughter (Van der Wal, Berende and Spritesma, 1975). The results of some of their trials are shown in *Table 20.2*. Optimum improvements were observed in veal calves treated with combined preparations of androgen and oestrogen. There was no explanation why the agents were only effective for about 6 weeks after implantation; and after this period the untreated calves grew faster than treated animals.

Rumen active anaboles cannot be used in veal calves because the animals do not have an established rumen fermentation process.

Beef cattle

The largest use of anabolic agents is in the USA and United Kingdom in beef producing steers and some heifers. On the other hand, rumen active anaboles may be used in all adult cattle because their specific action is on rumen processes which are independent of the sexual status of the animal. In the 1950s and 1960s the synthetic oestrogens diethylstilboestrol (DES) and hexoestrol were widely used in steers. The introduction in the last 5 years of low cost natural

Table 20.2 EFFECTS OF ANABOLIC AGENTS ON THE PERFORMANCE OF VEAL CALVES (DATA FROM VAN DER WAL, BERENDE AND SPRIETSMA, 1975)

Treatment	Dose (mg)	No. of experiments	Time of maximum response after treatment (weeks)	Increase in weight compared to control animals (range in kg)
DES	25	3	4–5	4.9– 9.1
Oestradiol	20	2	3–4	4.1
Zeranol	36	2	6	0.5– 3.4
	200	4	3–4	7.6– 9.7
Testosterone/ oestradiol	20	5	4–5	9.0–15.8
Trenbolone acetate/ oestradiol	140 20		3–5	4.6– 7.6
Progesterone/ oestradiol	200 20	3		

Friesian bull calves were implanted with anabolic agents at 11 weeks of age. The number of animals used in the study was 563.

steroid preparations, such as the synthetic steroid trenbolone acetate and the new oestrogen zeranol, have dramatically changed the pattern of use. The availability of androgens as well as oestrogens has caused a new interest in anabolic agents. Trials have shown that androgens are effective growth promoters in heifers (Best, 1972; Heitzman and Chan, 1974; Galbraith and Miller, 1977) and adult cows prior to slaughter (Beranger and Malterre, 1968), while a combination of androgens (testosterone or trenbolone) with oestrogens (oestradiol, DES, hexoestrol or zeranol) results in a maximum response in growth rate and FCE in steers (Kilkenny and Sutherland, 1970; Koers *et al;.* 1974; Heitzman, Chan and Hart, 1977; Heitzman, Harwood and Mallinson, 1977b; Stollard *et al.,* 1977; Berende, 1978; Galbraith and Watson, 1978; Roche, Davis and Sherrington, 1978). *Table 20.3* compares the results of two trials in steers where the benefits of combining hexoestrol and trenbolone acetate are compared with those derived from implanting either agent alone.

Table 20.3 THE EFFECTS OF HEXOESTROL AND TRENBOLONE ACETATE ON THE PERFORMANCE OF STEERS

Treatment	Average daily liveweight gain (kg)	
	Trial 1	Trial 2
Control	0.84	0.79
Trenbolone	0.91	0.86*
Hexoestrol	0.94	0.99*
Trenbolone acetate + hexoestrol	1.17*	1.05*

Trial 1 was carried out on 60 Friesian steers fed concentrates and maize silage in a feedlot. The dose of hexoestrol was 36 mg (Heitzman, Harwood and Mallinson, 1977b). Trial 2 was carried out with > 1000 steers on 14 farms with different management systems. The dose of hexoestrol was 60 mg in the single implant and 45 mg in the combined treatment (Stollard *et al.,* 1977). The implant of trenbolone acetate was 300 mg in all cases.
*The values were significantly greater than untreated controls ($P < 0.01$).

In contrast to the results in veal calves, the benefits obtained during the initial months after implantation of anabolic steroids were sustained in heifers after one year (Heitzman *et al.,* 1974) and in steers after 6 months (Heitzman, Harwood and Mallinson, 1977b).

Most trials have investigated improvements in growth rate and there is little information on the effects of the newer anabolic agents on FCE and carcase quality. There are reports of increased FCE in heifers treated with trenbolone acetate (Heitzman and Chan, 1974; Galbraith and Miller, 1977) and of improvement in FCE in steers treated with combined implants (Heitzman, Chan and Hart, 1977; Galbraith and Watson, 1978).

Several trials have been performed to investigate if implanting an animal on more than one occasion leads to even better results. Trials using serial implants of hexoestrol in steers (Jones, 1961; Macdearmid and Preston, 1969) produced confusing results, and do not suggest that this practice would be worthwhile. The evidence for zeranol is inconsistent. However, recently some groups have reported benefits from serial implantation in steers (Perry *et al.,* 1970; An Forais Taluntais, 1973), and the manufacturers recommend serial implantation in suckler calves. In other trials no clear benefits were observed in steers implanted

Table 20.4 EFFECTS OF RUMEN ACTIVE ANABOLES ON THE PERFORMANCE OF STEERS

Treatment	Dose/ton (g)	Average daily liveweight gain (kg/d)	Food conversion ratio (kg food/kg gain)	Average daily food intake (kg DM/d)
Control[a]	–	0.92	8.95	8.59
Avoparcin[a]	30	0.94	8.51	8.23
Avoparcin[a]	60	0.99	7.85	8.02
Control[b]	–	1.17	5.88	6.88
Monosenin-sodium[b]	30	1.25	5.37	6.71
Monensin-sodium[b]	40	1.30	5.25	6.81

a Data from Herlugson et al. (1978); b manufacturers trials data (Elanco Products Ltd.).

twice with zeranol (Nichols and Lesperance, 1973; Nicholson *et al.,* 1973). In one small field trial with steers, it was reported that reimplantation of steers 3 months after the first treatment with trenbolone acetate plus hexoestrol produced additional increases in liveweight gain compared with controls and those which had been implanted on only one occasion (Heitzman, Harwood and Mallinson, 1977b).

The evidence on the effect of anabolic agents on carcase size and quality is inconclusive. There is abundant evidence that DES and hexoestrol reduce fat content in treated animals (Alder, Taylor and Rudman, 1964; Everitt and Duganzich, 1965; Macdearmid and Preston, 1969). There is almost no information available on the effect on carcase characteristics of combined implants. A most recent study by Berende (1978) suggested that liveweight gain, FCE and carcase weight were increased and fat content reduced in steers following treatment with trenbolone acetate plus oestradiol, while other studies reported that carcase weight was improved in steers treated with combined implants (Roche and Davis, 1977).

RUMEN ACTIVE ANABOLES FOR BEEF CATTLE

Monensin-sodium and avoparcin, which are antibiotic substances, are rumen active anaboles which act orally. Both compounds reduce the acetate to propionate ratio in the rumen. They also cause a depression of appetite, an improvement in FCE and an increase in daily liveweight gain in cattle. *Table 20.4* shows the performance of steers in two separate trials using monensin-sodium or avoparcin. There is an increasing use of these substances in the United Kingdom and several new trials are investigating if their use can be successfully combined with simultaneous use of anabolic agents. Theoretically it should be possible to obtain the benefits of both anabolic agents and rumen active anaboles in the same animals. The manufacturers estimate that 75—80% of USA feedlot cattle are currently being fed monensin-sodium.

Sheep

The use of growth promoters in sheep has been confined to the small scale use of oestrogens in wether lambs and a few development trials using combined implants in wethers. Hexoestrol and zeranol are licensed for use in the United Kingdom but they have only yielded marginal benefits in trials (Meat and Livestock Commission, 1979) or no benefits (Vipond and Galbraith, 1978). However, in trials with wether lambs implanted with a combination of trenbolone acetate and oestradiol there were reports of increased liveweight gain, carcase weights and FCE (Szumowski and Grandadam, 1976; Coelho, Galbraith and Topps, 1978). This preparation is, however, not yet licensed for use in sheep in the United Kingdom.

The hazards

The potential hazards of growth promoters to the health of stock and the consumer must be fully assessed.

HAZARDS TO RUMINANTS

Hazards in farm animals following administration of anabolic agents are those associated with the hormonal activity of the drug or its metabolites. There is no evidence that at the recommended dose the drugs are toxic or adversely affect the health of the animal. The main hazards observed in meat producing animals are changes in behaviour and interference in reproductive function in breeding animals.

Behaviour changes

In a survey of 1.9 million feedlot steers, Pierson *et al.* (1976) observed that during 1968—70 bulling and riding was responsible for 1.5% of illness and death, and over the next 4 years the incidence of illness and death from bulling and riding rose to 3.7%. The authors suggest that the increases were associated with the increasing use of oestrogens, in particular the changes resulting from feeding 10—20 mg DES daily and the introduction of implants containing other oestrogens.

In Britain bulling has also been a problem in some steers treated with hexoestrol either as a single implant or combined with trenbolone acetate. Normally these problems are only seen for 1—2 weeks immediately after treatment and with careful management the problem is not difficult to overcome.

The use of androgens in steers and heifers tends to produce a more aggressive and active animal.

Changes in reproductive function

The use of hormones to regulate reproductive function has been extensively investigated. Oestrogens and progesterone are used to synchronise oestrus in cattle and sheep without adversely affecting future reproductive performance. The use of hormones to obtain early puberty has, however, met with little success. There appears to be no advantage in using oestrogens and progestins to induce early oestrus in beef heifers (Neville, Williams and Witherspoon, 1974) or young lambs (Cooper, 1979), and there are real disadvantages of using androgens to obtain rapid growth and early puberty in dairy heifers (Heitzman *et al.*, 1979).

Friesian heifer calves were implanted at 4 months and again at 7 months of age with trenbolone acetate or a combined preparation of trenbolone acetate and oestradiol. In comparison with untreated controls there was not only an increased growth rate but also a delay in the onset of puberty, dystocia, poor milk production and virilisation of genitalia.

Trenbolone acetate has also been shown to interfere with the oestrous cycle in mature cows (Heitzman, Harwood and Mallinson, 1977a) and to reduce the number of oestrogen receptors in the uteri of young calves (Kyrein and Hoffmann, 1976). Thus anabolic agents which are potent androgens should not be used as growth promoters in female animals intended for breeding purposes.

PUBLIC HEALTH CONSIDERATIONS

The greatest potential hazard of anabolic agents is that meat products from treated animals may contain amounts of the agent or its derived metabolites (residues*) which are harmful to the consumer. The metabolism of the agent in farm animals can be quite different from its metabolism in laboratory animals and man, and thus it is essential that the residues of the anabolic agent are defined.

The metabolism of oestradiol (Bottoms *et al.* 1977; Dunn *et al.*, 1977; Hendricks and Torrence, 1977) and progesterone (Estergreen *et al.*, 1977) in farm animals has been thoroughly investigated and the residues identified. However, the metabolites of the stilbene derivatives and zeranol have not all been identified.

Determination of residues

Although radiotracer studies provide the methods of choice for studies of absorption, excretion, total residues and metabolites (Aschbacher, Thacker and Rumsey, 1975; Pottier *et al.*, 1975, 1978), radioimmunoassay (RIA) techniques and chromatographic methods are also used (Hoffmann and Karg, 1976; Hoffmann and Oettel, 1976; Heitzman and Harwood, 1977).

Implants of anabolic agents are absorbed over several months and it is therefore likely that there are residues in edible tissues, urine, faeces and blood at slaughter. The concentration of residues in edible tissues is similar to that of the naturally occurring sex steroids in farm animals and is <1 ppb. RIA is the only method sensitive enough to measure these low levels, and methods are being developed for all the anabolic agents.

Monensin-sodium is considered safe if used at the recommended doses. At higher doses there is a greatly reduced voluntary feed intake. In a recent report by the veterinary investigation service (August, 1978) severe scouring and six deaths associated with cardiovascular disorders were recorded in a herd of 40 steers fed monensin-sodium at 10 times the recommended dose. The compound is also much more toxic in equines.

Residues of monensin-sodium have not been found in excess of 50 ppb (the limit of test sensitivity) in cattle receiving up to 750 mg/d of the drug.

Mechanism of action of anabolic agents

The exact mode of action of anabolic agents still remains unclear, and it is difficult to describe a simple single mode of action. The common action of all anabolic agents is to increase nitrogen retention and protein deposition (Van der Wal, 1976). Nitrogen balance studies confirmed that anabolic agents administered parenterally increased nitrogen retention, but they did not alter absorption or metabolism in the alimentary tract (Chan, Heitzman and Kitchenham, 1975).

*Residues are defined as the amount of the anabolic agent (parent compound) and its metabolites remaining in the tissues at any given time.

The most likely action of anabolic agents is through a second hormone which affects general tissue cells. Oestrogens probably affect growth in cattle and sheep by raising the concentration of two protein hormones (insulin and growth hormone), while androgens act indirectly through thyroid hormones and by reducing the effects of the catabolic hormones (the corticosteroids). The possibility that anabolic agents act directly at the muscle should not be ruled out. Further research into the understanding of these mechanisms is necessary.

The main action of the rumen active anabole monensin-sodium is to alter the molar ratios of volatile fatty acids produced in the rumen. There is an increase of 5–15% in the molar concentration of propionate and a reduction of 5–15% in acetate and butyrate concentration. This alteration results in more available energy and substrate for glucose production by the ruminant liver.

Conclusions

Anabolic agents and rumen active anaboles are useful in increasing the efficiency of meat production. If these substances are used at the recommended doses and in the correct manner there is little danger to the health of the animals or the consumer.

References

ALDER, F.E., TAYLOR, J.C. and RUDMAN, J.E. (1964). *Anim. Prod.*, **6**, 47

AN FORAIS TALUNTAIS (1973). *Anim. Prod. Res. Report*, 45

ASCHBACHER, P.W., THACKER, E.J. and RUMSEY, T.S. (1975). *J. Anim. Sci.*, **41**, 962

BARRAGRY, T.B. (1974). *Irish Vet. J.*, **28**, 28

BERANGER, C. and MALTERRE, C. (1968). *C.R. Soc. Biol. de Clemont Ferrand.*, **162**, 1157

BERENDE, P.L. (1978). *III World Congress on Animal Feeding, Madrid 1978.* Paper A–1–12.

BEST, J.M.J. (1972). *Vet. Rec.*, **91**, 264

BOTTOMS, G.D., COPPOC, G.L., MONK, E., MOORE, A.B., ROESEL, O.F. and REGNIER, F.E. (1977). *J. Anim. Sci.*, **45**, 674

CHAN, K.H., HEITZMAN, R.J. and KITCHENHAM, B.A. (1975). *Brit. Vet. J.*, **131**, 170

COELHO, J.F.S., GALBRAITH, H. and TOPPS, J.H. (1978). *Anim. Prod.*, **26**, 360

COOPER, A. (1979). Personal Communication

DUNN, T.G., KALTENBACH, C.C., KORTINIK, D.R., TURNER, D.L. and NISWENDER, G.D. (1977). *J. Anim. Sci.*, **45**, 659

ESTERGREEN, C.V.L., LIN, M.T., MARTIN, E.L., MOSS, G.E., BRANEN, A.L., LUEDECKE, L.O. and SHIMODA, W. (1977). *J. Anim. Sci.*, **45**, 642

EVERITT, G.C. and DUGANZICH, D.M. (1965). *N.Z. J. Agric. Res.*, **5**, 62

GALBRAITH, H. and MILLER, T.B. (1977). *Anim. Prod.*, **24**, 133

GALBRAITH, H. and WATSON, H.B. (1978). *Vet. Rec.*, **103**, 28

HEITZMAN, R.J. (1974). *Vet. Rec.*, **94**, 529

HEITZMAN, R.J. (1976). In *Anabolic Agents in Animal Production,* Suppl. V: *Environmental Quality and Safety,* p. 89. Eds F. C. Lu and J. Rendel.

HEITZMAN, R.J. and CHAN, K.H. (1974). *Brit. Vet. J.*, **130**, 532
HEITZMAN, R.J. and HARWOOD, D.J. (1977). *Brit. Vet. J.*, **133**, 564
HEITZMAN, R.J., CHAN, K.H., RUSSELL, A. and BOUFFAULT, J.C. (1974). *J. Anim. Sci.*, **39**, 210
HEITZMAN, R.J., CHAN, K.H. and HART, I.C. (1977). *Brit. Vet. J.*, **133**, 62
HEITZMAN, R.J., HARWOOD, D.J. and MALLINSON, C.B. (1977a). *Abs. XI Acta Endocrinol. Congress*, p. 462
HEITZMAN, R.J., HARWOOD, D.J. and MALLINSON, C.B. (1977b). *Abs. 69th Ann. Mtg. Am. Soc. Anim. Sci.*, p.44
HEITZMAN, R.J., HARWOOD, D.J., KAY, R.M., LITTLE, W., MALLINSON, C.B. and REYNOLDS, I.P. (1979). *J. Anim. Sci.*, **48**, 859
HENDRICKS, D.M. and TORRENCE, A.K. (1977). *J. Anim. Sci.*, **45**, 652
HERLUGSON, M.L., CORDOVA, G., DYER, A., ZIMMER, P.R. and DELAY, R.L. (1978). *Proc. Am. Soc. Anim. Sci.* ASAS-ADSA Combined Mtg. Paper 520
HOFFMAN, B. and KARG, H. (1976). In *Anabolic Agents in Animal Production, Suppl. V: Environmental Quality and Safety*, p. 181. Eds F.C. Lu and J. Rendel.
HOFFMANN, B. and OETTEL, G. (1976). *Steroids*, **27**, 509
JONES, P.J. (1961). *Experimental Husbandry*, No. 6. p. 62
KILKENNY, J.B. and SUTHERLAND, J.E. (1970). *Vet. Rec.*, **87**, 734
KOERS, W.C., PARROTT, J.C., KLETT, R.H. and SHERROD, L.B. (1974). *J. Anim. Sci.*, **39**, 243
KYREIN, H.F. and HOFFMANN, B. (1976). *Adv. Anim. Phy. Nutr.*, **6**, 91
LU, F.C. and RENDEL, J. (1976). *Anabolic Agents in Animal Production, Suppl. V: Environmental Quality and Safety.*
MACDEARMID, A. and PRESTON, T.R. (1969). *Anim. Prod.*, **11**, 419
MEAT and LIVESTOCK COMMISSION (1979). Unpublished data
NEVILLE, W.E., WILLIAMS, D.J. and WITHERSPOON, D.M. (1974). *Am. J. Vet. Res.*, **35**, 1057
NICHOLS, N.E. and LESPERANCE, A.L. (1973). *Proc. Western Section Am. Soc. Anim. Sci.*, **24**, 304
NICHOLSON, L.E., LESPERANCE, A.L. and MCCORMICK, A.V. (1973). *Proc. Western Section Am. Sco. Anim. Sci.*, **24**, 308
PERRY, T.W., STOB, M., HUBER, D.A. and PETERSON, R.C. (1970). *J. Anim. Sci.*, **31**, 789
PIERSON, R.E., JENSON, R., BRADDY, P.M., HORTON, D.P. and CHRISTIE, R.M. (1976). *J. Am. Vet. Med. Assoc.*, **169**, 521
POTTIER, J., BUSIGNY, M. and GRANDADAM, J.A. (1975). *J. Anim. Sci.*, **41**, 962
POTTIER, J., HEITZMAN, R.J., COUSTY, C. and REYNOLDS, I.P. (1978). *Proc. Am. Soc. Anim. Sci.* ASAS-ADSA Combined Mtg. Paper 418
ROCHE, J.F. and DAVIS, W.D. (1977). *Anim. Prod.*, **24**, 132
ROCHE, J.F., DAVIES, W.D. and SHERRINGTON, J. (1978). *Irish J. Agric. Res.* In press
SCOTT, B. (1978). *ADAS Quarterly Reviews*, **31**, 185—216
STOLLARD, R.J., KILKENNY, J.B., MATTHIESON, A.A., STARK, J.S., TAYLOR, B.R., SUTHERLAND, J.E. and WILLIAMSON, J.T. (1977). *Anim. Prod.*, **24**, 132
SZUMOWSKI, P. and GRANDADAM, J.A. (1976). *Rec. Vet. Med.*, **152**, 311
VAN DER WAL, P. (1976). In *Anabolic Agents in Animal Production, Suppl. V: Environmental Quality and Safety*, p. 60. Eds F.C. Lu and J. Rendel.

VAN DER WAL, P., BERENDE, P. and SPRIETSMA, J.E. (1975). *J. Anim. Sci.*, **41**, 986

VIPOND, J.E. and GALBRAITH, H. (1978). *Anim. Prod.*, **26**, 359

INDEX